THE S. MARK TAPER FOUNDATION

IMPRINT IN JEWISH STUDIES

BY THIS ENDOWMENT

THE S. MARK TAPER FOUNDATION SUPPORTS

THE APPRECIATION AND UNDERSTANDING

OF THE RICHNESS AND DIVERSITY OF

JEWISH LIFE AND CULTURE

The publisher gratefully acknowledges the generous contribution to this book provided by the Jewish Studies Endowment of the University of California Press Associates, which is supported by a major gift from the S. Mark Taper Foundation.

Obstinate Hebrews

STUDIES ON THE HISTORY OF SOCIETY AND CULTURE

Victoria E. Bonnell and Lynn Hunt, Editors

OBSTINATE HEBREWS

Representations of Jews in France, 1715–1815

Ronald Schechter

University of
California Press

Berkeley
Los Angeles
London

Frontispiece: *Napoléon le Grand rétablit le culte des Israélites le 30 mai 1806*, engraving by François-Louis Couché, Paris, 1806. Courtesy of the Library of the Jewish Theological Seminary of America.

University of California Press
Berkeley and Los Angeles, California

University of California Press, Ltd.
London, England

© 2003 by the Regents of the University of California

Library of Congress Cataloging-in-Publication Data

Schechter, Ronald.
    Obstinate Hebrews : representations of Jews in France, 1715–1815 / Ronald Schechter.
        p.   cm.   (Studies on the history of society and culture ; 49)
    Includes bibliographical references and index.
    ISBN 0-520-23557-6 (alk. paper).
    1. Jews—France—Identity.   2. Jews—Public opinion.   3. Public opinion—France.   4. Jews in literature.   5. French literature—19th century—History and criticism.   6. France—Ethnic relations.   7. Jews—France—Social conditions—18th century.   8. Napoleon I, Emperor of the French, 1769–1821—Relations with Jews.   I. Title. II Series.

DS135.F82 S34   2003
305.892'4044'09033—dc21   2002011944

Manufactured in the United States of America
10   09   08   07   06   05   04   03
10   9   8   7   6   5   4   3   2   1

Contents

Acknowledgments

In researching and writing this book I benefited from the generous support of numerous institutions. A Harvard Lurcy Traveling Fellowship and a Harvard Krupp Foundation Fellowship for European Studies enabled me to conduct my initial research in France in 1990–91. A Cultural Exchange Fulbright Fellowship (Institute of International Education) in 1991–92 made it possible for me to continue my research, and I further extended my stay in France in 1992–93 thanks to a Chateaubriand Scholarship Program Research Fellowship in the Social Sciences and a Harvard Whiting Fellowship in the Humanities. In 1996 a postdoctoral fellowship funded by the German Research Foundation gave me the opportunity to share my work in progress with the *Graduiertenkolleg* "Religion and Normativity," at the Ruprecht-Karls-Universität Heidelberg, and three William and Mary Faculty Summer Grants, in 1998, 1999, and 2001 respectively, funded the final stages of writing.

I have also enjoyed the good fortune of wise mentors and generous colleagues. Simon Schama skillfully advised the dissertation out of which this book initially grew, and Patrice Higonnet worked patiently with me as I took my work on representations of Jews in France through subsequent stages. Lynn Hunt, David Bell, and Juliane Brand read the entire manuscript and provided invaluable advice for revisions. Other colleagues, too numerous to name, have read, commented on, and listened to various pieces of the book in the form of conference and symposium papers and drafts of chapters and related articles.

Finally, I would like to thank my spouse, Uta, our son, Arthur, and my parents for their indispensable moral support.

Introduction

SHACHOCH, OR, A DISCOURSE ON THE METHOD

In *Zakhor: Jewish History and Jewish Memory,* Yosef Hayim Yerushalmi
reminds us that the biblical command "Remember!" ("*Zakhor*") and
the Jewish traditions of remembrance paradoxically conflict with the requirements of modern historiography, despite their common attention
to the past. Thus the moral imperative to remember Egyptian bondage,
the destruction of Jerusalem, the martyrs to the faith, and so many other
aspects and events of the Jewish past is at cross-purposes with the critical scrutiny of the historical record that the intellectual progeny of
Ranke, Jewish and otherwise, have adopted as their professional credo.[1]
Similarly, the memory of (often traumatic) events in the relatively recent
Jewish past, particularly from the late nineteenth century, can easily obscure the history that came before. When investigating the relationship
between Jews and Gentiles in France from the death of Louis XIV to the
fall of Napoleon, it is difficult to forget that in the 1880s and 1890s
French politicians would win elections on the sole platform of hating
Jews; that Édouard Drumont's virulent *La France juive* would be a best-
seller; that French citizens were all too ready to presume the guilt of Captain Alfred Dreyfus; that a hero of World War I so famous for his desire
to spare French blood on the battlefield would compete with the Nazis
in enacting anti-Semitic legislation during World War II; that the French
police would round up Jewish children and send them to their death at

Auschwitz; that President Charles de Gaulle would discourse on Jewish arrogance in the midst of the Six-Day War; that in 1980 a prime minister would distinguish between Jews and "innocent Frenchmen" who were killed in an anti-Semitic terrorist attack; that even the dead among the Jews would fail to find rest in the cemetery of Carpentras; that Jean-Marie Le Pen would impatiently dismiss the Holocaust as consisting of historical "details" and openly suspect Jewish officials of dual loyalties.

These images, to borrow the language of memory theorist Maurice Halbwachs, are "gripping abbreviations" that simplify an otherwise complex history.[2] Alternatively, one might say that they constitute a mnemonic prism through which observers of the past, professional or otherwise, typically view the history of preceding periods. Whether informed by a moral imperative to remember or the simple impossibility of forgetting, this prism has long determined the questions that historians have posed about an undeniably important period of Jewish history. It has favored a teleological approach in which the past prefigures the future. Thus those who have valued tolerance of difference and seen postrevolutionary France as conducive to a pluralistic society have tended to highlight the positive elements of Jewish history in the age of enlightenment and revolution.[3] In contrast to this Franco-Jewish variation on the Whig interpretation of history,[4] much of the twentieth-century historiography of French Jewry concentrated on the negative aspects of the Enlightenment and Revolution (including the Napoleonic period). As early as 1928, Robert Anchel emphasized the oppressive side to Napoleon's administration of his Jewish subjects, thus challenging a long tradition of regarding the emperor as a liberator of previously oppressed Jews.[5] If Anchel was before his time in his willingness to criticize a founding father of modern France, in the aftermath of the Holocaust such iconoclastic attacks came with increasing frequency. Initially these revisions of the historical record tended to come from beyond France's borders. In 1968 an American, Arthur Hertzberg, vilified Voltaire as a patriarch of modern anti-Semitism, and in 1979 the Israeli Simon Schwarzfuchs reiterated Anchel's opinion of Napoleon as an oppressor of the Jews.[6] By the time of the bicentennial of the Revolution, however, French writers joined the increasingly monophonic chorus of its detractors by pointing to its perceived offenses against the Jews. The greatest of these was, paradoxically, their admission to legal equality, an act that subsequent generations would call emancipation.[7]

The assault on emancipation was facilitated by at least three factors: a more critical stance among historians toward the very Revolution that enacted the emancipation; the latest outbreak of a "Vichy syndrome" that defined the health of the French polity in terms of its historical attitudes toward and treatment of Jews; and the reassessment of republican assimilationist ideology in light of assertions, from many groups within French society, of a *droit à la différence*.[8] Thus the sociologist Shmuel Trigano was arguing within an increasingly well-established tradition when he called the Jews of postrevolutionary France "hostages of the universal."[9] It was in this context, moreover, that the journalist and historian Patrick Girard could expect to be understood when he professed to have conceived of the idea of writing a book about the emancipation of the Jews while visiting Auschwitz, suggesting that the former was merely a less brutal attempt at eradicating the Jews.[10] These authors did not have a monopoly over the discourse on emancipation. Robert Badinter wrote a celebratory account of the political events leading up to emancipation, and this view corresponded to the official interpretation of the French Jewish community.[11] In all the cases described so far, however, and despite sometimes bitter political differences, the history of the Jews from the Enlightenment through the revolutionary-Napoleonic period has been written with a view to a future that these forces are presumed to have brought into being. As François Furet has observed, however, whenever an event is posited as an advent, its commentators have no choice but to celebrate or execrate it, yet in either case are reduced to commemorating it.[12] Thus the historiography of the Jews of France, particularly in the period surrounding their official entry into the newly conceived *nation*, bears an uncanny resemblance to the historiography of the Revolution. In the Jewish historiography the inaugural event is named "emancipation," which historians have been obligated to argue was either good for the Jews or bad for the Jews, but which they have been dispensed from understanding in its historical context.

This is not to say that the historiography of the Jews in France during the period in question has been without value. On the contrary, the sense of urgency with which writers have fought political battles on the terrain of history has ensured the copious production of monographs, articles, and syntheses that, however teleological, have truly increased our knowledge of the legal, social, and political history of the Jews during the period in question, though in the area of cultural history less has been accomplished. As a consumer of this knowledge, which has facilitated the present study immeasurably, I am grateful for the very historiographical corpus that I am now criticizing. Nor do I pretend to be objective where others were subjective, capable of transcending the concerns and discourses of my age where others have been trapped by one Zeitgeist or another. As a liberal humanist, pluralist, and secular Jew—since we cannot avoid categories, I might as well categorize myself rather than wait to be categorized—I abhor the fulminations of writers and politicians who denounced the Jews as bloodsuckers and natural liars. I approve of those French Gentiles who acknowledged the Jews as equals and called for concomitant recognition of their rights. I applaud the Jews who embraced the values of the Enlightenment and the Revolution without renouncing their Jewish identity, and I sympathize with those who believed that these movements would bring happiness to themselves and all humanity. I believe that the Enlightenment and the Revolution, and even Napoleon, were "good for the Jews," as it were, insofar as they promoted equality before the law, though, as I will make clear later, I do not believe that historical investigation should stop at the question of whether the phenomena in question were good or bad for the Jews.

Despite my subjectivity, I believe that it is possible to treat the topic at hand in such a way that it is not reduced to an origin of phenomena that would manifest their true meaning later, at some future dusk when the Owl of Minerva would spread her historiographical wings. In other words, I propose to follow a methodological path that avoids teleology as much as possible. In a thoughtful meditation on Michel Foucault's famous critique of teleological history, Roger Chartier writes, "History stripped of all temptation to teleology would risk becoming an endless inventory of disconnected facts abandoned to their teeming incoherence for want of a hypothesis to propose a possible order among them."[13] Nevertheless, coherence is possible if we ask what the "facts" of the past meant to contemporaries, how they constructed order, how they fabricated, articulated, contested, and reinvented identities for themselves and others. The conceptual apparatus that informs these goals will be immediately recognizable as issuing from "new cultural history," a subdiscipline that, though no longer very new, has had relatively little impact on Jewish historiography.[14] To subject the Jewish past to the methods of cultural history, however, requires a special effort at avoiding teleology, since perhaps no other history—with the possible exception of German history—is as susceptible to being sucked into the vortex of a twentieth-century telos as is that of the Jews. It is therefore necessary to state that all roads do not lead to Auschwitz, and to resist the perspective of tragic irony that repeatedly treats the Jews of the past, to borrow a phrase from literary historian Michael Bernstein, as "victims-in-waiting."[15] Similarly, I will refrain from constructing a more sanguine or optimistic narrative in which emancipation inaugurates a political-philosophical tradition that postrevolutionary France repeatedly and wrongfully betrayed but which subsists heroically to this day. My aim is to understand what the Jews meant to contemporaries, including themselves, without reference to vindicating or mocking futures.

To achieve this perspective, I would like to reverse the age-old Jewish command *Zakhor* and submit to the opposite imperative: "Forget!" ("*Shachoch*"). I propose to forget what I know about the history of the Jews after 1815, and I ask my readers to do the same, at least temporarily. This proposition might appear flippant, blasphemous, even obscene in light of the moral imperative, among the secular as well as the religious, to remember the suffering of past victims of oppression. Ethical considerations aside, it might also appear impossible, particularly since I have just specified the most salient memory markers to be consigned to oblivion. But if literal forgetting is not a matter of the will, figurative forgetting, or the bracketing of knowledge, is possible. It is possible to imagine that one does not know what will happen in the future of any given age, an easy enough exercise given that we do not know what will happen in *our* future. Indeed, this kind of historical imagination is necessary to the Rankean imperative, no doubt more relevant to historians than the requirement to remember, of *Einfühlung,* "feeling oneself into" a past age. This mental exercise is not only possible; it is worth engaging in because it enables us to ask questions that might not occur to us if we began our investigation by casting our attention toward a known future.

QUESTIONING THE JEWISH QUESTION

The first question to be treated in this book concerns the extent to which Gentiles were interested in the Jews. This might appear to be a pedestrian question, but until now it has not even occurred to most historians to ask it. In their rush to praise or condemn the philosophes and political figures who wrote or spoke about the Jews, historians have failed to ask whether this discourse was significant. They have failed to ask how often French Gentiles wrote and spoke about the Jews, how popular books were in which Jews figured prominently, and how highly regarded the authors of those books were. They have neglected to ask to what extent social reformers were interested in the Jews, how important a subject they were for revolutionaries, and to what extent Napoleon and his non-Jewish subjects were interested in them. It is crucial to pose these questions as a point of departure, for if the Jews were not important to their contemporaries, then their historical significance is in doubt, particularly if one consciously suppresses teleological questions. Eugen Weber has expressed skepticism about the importance of the Jews for French Gentiles, asserting that "the Jewish question was a *Jewish* question," of little or no interest to the French, who "thought about Jews hardly at all."[16] If Weber is correct, then the following study runs the risk of parochialism.

But how does one establish the extent to which "the French" were interested in Jews? With respect to ordinary French people, the peasants who have left frustratingly little record of their mental life, it is difficult to determine when or how often they "thought about Jews." The complaints against Jewish moneylenders in the Alsatian countryside suggest that, in this region of the kingdom at least, Jews were very much on the minds of ordinary people. Moreover, the presence of the Jews in the Bible, the only book most peasants ever encountered and one that significantly determined their worldview is undeniable. Yet the focus of the present book is on representations produced by those who could read, write, and (during the Revolution in particular) speak to large audiences while securing the recording and reproduction of their statements. In other words, it focuses on those who had access to what the French call *la parole.* It was these individuals and groups who had the power to deploy what Stephen Greenblatt succinctly terms *mimetic capital,*[17] and who therefore participated most directly in the production of discourses that assigned cultural meaning to the Jews. How does one work with the sources that these commentators produced? To begin with, it is necessary to do the relatively mundane work of counting and comparing. Thanks to such databases as the ARTFL digital library of French literature,[18] that same group's electronic version of the *Encyclopédie,* and Chadwick-Healey's recently published *Voltaire électronique,* I have been able to quantify references to Jews in enormous corpora, to compare these numbers with references to other subjects of discussion, and to formulate some hypotheses about the relative interest in the Jews. I have also profited from excellent studies in the publishing history of a number of works in which Jews were especially prominent and thereby gathered an impression of how widely read they were. Similarly, I have done the unexciting but necessary work of counting National Assembly sessions during which deputies discussed the status of the Jews and pamphlets addressing the Jewish question during the Revolution. In all these cases, the sheer numbers suggest that historians have vastly underestimated the importance of the Jews to non-Jewish writers, their readers, as well as to political actors and their audiences in eighteenth-century and early nineteenth-century France. They suggest that Jews mattered or, more precisely, that images and perceptions of Jews mattered. For this reason alone they should matter to historians, whether or not their primary area of specialization is the history of the Jews.

Of course, counting is only the beginning of any serious assessment of the degree and nature of interest in any question. Having established that French writers and politicians were paying a disproportionate degree of attention to the Jews, it is necessary to ask what, precisely, they were saying about them. This is all the more crucial in that the content of the texts enables one to answer yet another question to which the quantitative data logically lead, namely: Why was there so much discussion of the Jews in France between 1715 and 1815? As with the question of numbers, this question might also seem obvious, yet historians have repeatedly failed to consider it. Again, the sense of emancipation as an inauguration, the emphasis on the apparent future of the Jewish question in the postrevolutionary age, and the corresponding need to cast retrospective judgments on those who previously addressed the Jewish question have occluded what would otherwise seem surprising: the bizarre preoccupation of French commentators with a tiny and weak minority. The disjunction between the attention to the Jews and their "objective" importance calls for an explanation. In 1789 there were at most forty thousand Jews in the kingdom, roughly one-fifth of 1 percent of the total population. Living literally as well as figuratively on the periphery of France, most were poor, many desperately so, and together they were correspondingly lacking in political power and social prestige. Under these circumstances, the fact that non-Jews spent so much time writing and speaking about them is truly puzzling.

My hypothesis, loosely following Claude Lévi-Strauss's explanation of totems, is that the Jews were "good to think."[19] On the basis of the most recurrent themes in the discourse on the Jews, I shall argue that they facilitated the conceptualization and articulation of a number of ideas that were of special importance to their contemporaries. Among these were the relative merits of "primitive" life and "civilization," agriculture and commerce; the competing forces of fanaticism and tolerance; the role of spirituality in "natural religion"; sincerity and insincerity in human relations; and the possibility of an indivisible "nation" containing public-spirited citizens. To be sure, the Jews were not the only means of thinking about the prevalent ideas of the age. Other groups, other "others," served similar conceptual purposes. As is well known, Europeans of the period used Native Americans, Persians, East Asians, Africans, and a whole host of other "exotic" groups, and men used European as well as non-European women as symbolic variables (or invariables) in philosophical and scientific speculation. In the course of this book and, more systematically, in its conclusion, I shall compare and contrast representations of Jews with those of other outsiders. Yet these very comparisons will show that the Jews were not randomly selected from among the many available examples of alterity and that, although sometimes discursively similar to other marginal groups, their symbolic configuration was unique.

Specifically, centuries of Gentile literature, art, folklore, and (one must not forget) religion had largely determined the qualities contemporaries could plausibly attribute to the Jews, and although iconoclasts occasionally challenged this array of stereotypes, for the vast majority of commentators the Jews were "known" to epitomize commerce, carnality, religious and "national" zeal, hairsplitting casuistry, moral corruption in general, and dissimulation in particular. Indeed, this last feature, I would like to argue, helped to perpetuate discussion of the Jews. The multiplicity of available images by which non-Jews recognized Jews, the list of qualities that made the latter so familiar, contained one that cast doubt on the project of knowing them: their proverbial opacity. Paradoxically, the Jews were both familiar and strange, and indeed their strangeness, their inscrutability, was among the features that made them so eminently recognizable. Thus any assurances of familiarity were immediately undermined by the realization that the Jews were a mystery, and it became necessary to reestablish reliable knowledge about them.

Moreover, the famed obstinacy of the Jews, their alleged hostility to change, their apparently eternal nature made them, more than any other group, ideal figures in the discussion of what was perhaps the greatest question of the day: the possibility of human perfectibility. Precisely because the Jews epitomized the twin features of obstinacy and corruption in the minds of so many contemporaries, they provided an ideal test case for the hypothesis that human nature is perfectible. According to the logic of a repeatedly conducted thought experiment, if the Jews could improve, a fortiori, anyone could improve.

Finally, and this point cannot be entirely separated from the previous one, it is important to consider the impact of an age-old drive to convert the Jews. The famed "dechristianization" that historians have attributed to the eighteenth century, if not earlier times,[20] should have superseded the traditional Christian goal of conversion. As Mona Ozouf has shown in her study of festivals during the French Revolution, however, old habits die hard. Confirming Durkheim's insight into the innate social need for the sacred, Ozouf has shown that even despite the Revolution's assault on orthodox Catholicism, a "transfer of sacrality" characterized revolutionary ritual, and a new civic religion succeeded in performing the integrative function that, under the political circumstances, Catholicism could no longer achieve.[21] I would like to adapt these insights to the relatively *longue durée* of a century and argue that the dream of human perfectibility, which writers of the late Enlightenment, Revolution, and Napoleonic period called *régénération,* was largely the continuation of an older eschatological dream of universal conversion. It is revealing that the term *regeneration* itself was appropriated from Christian theology, where it signified spiritual rebirth. In this context, the otherwise extraordinary French preoccupation with the Jews, and indeed with what contemporaries repeatedly called their moral, physical, and political regeneration, is comprehensible. After all, it was Christian tradition that marked the Jews as eternally obstinate and therefore characterized their conversion as a miracle presaging the millennium. Thus the most available object of a conversionist drive, however secularized, was the proverbially obstinate Hebrew.

Historians have argued over whether Abbé Grégoire, the most prominent advocate of Jewish regeneration, intended to convert the Jews, whether one should take as a programmatic statement his own contention that the acceptance of Jews as equal members of the French community would ultimately make it easier "to convert them."[22] Yet it hardly matters whether the Jews' conversion to Christianity was an important aim for Grégoire, or whether he fought for their rights in the hope of such a conversion. Even if he had remained indifferent to their future confessional identity, Grégoire and others who called for the Jews' regeneration were conversionists insofar as they envisaged and demanded a radical transformation in their moral composition. The continued attempt to transform the Jews in this fundamental way confirms Tocqueville's observation that "though its objectives were political, the French Revolution followed the lines of a religious revolution."[23] This observation is not meant to collapse all differences between Christianity and revolutionary ideology, which themselves must be understood in terms of multiple beliefs, or to claim that the sacred in the experience of all revolutionaries was identical to that of those who thought of themselves above all as Christians. Still, the undeniable similarities between the two ways of thinking, which this study of representations of Jews confirms, emphasize the fundamental role of tradition in the prototypical agent of modernity, and indeed question the sharp dichotomy that historians still draw, implicitly or explicitly, between premodern and modern mentalities.

SELF-REPRESENTATION AND
THE ASSIMILATION OF THE OTHER

The cultural meaning of Jews for French Gentiles, however, is only one part of the story. This book equally seeks to investigate representations of Jews from the perspective of the Jews themselves. In other words, it asks how the Jews described, assessed, and explained themselves, inquires into favored forms and strategies of self-representation, and examines the relationship between self-representation and identity. As with the questions about Gentile representations of Jews, this program also needs to be justified. I have already conceded the numerical, political, and social weakness of the Jews and argued that they were far more important to Gentiles for what they symbolized than for who they were. One is therefore justified in asking why we should inquire into the discursive strategies and mental world of the symbols themselves. My answer is that if the specific features of Jewish self-representation were unique, its forms and strategies raise important questions about the models by which social scientists and theorists of the humanities typically understand the relationship between centers and peripheries; insiders and outsiders; the powerful and the weak; assimilation, resistance, and hybridity; and it calls into question the famously monolithic character of discourse. Precisely how the case of the Jews problematizes these concepts will be spelled out in the course of the book and, more explicitly still, in the conclusion. Here it suffices to say that just as Gentile representations of Jews are relevant to an understanding of the Enlightenment, French Revolution, and Napoleonic period, Jewish self-representation is relevant for the critical assessment of categories of social and cultural analysis that scholars normally take for granted.

In its investigation into Jewish self-representation, this book is informed by three bodies of sources, one of which is relatively familiar to historians of French Jewry and two of which have been almost entirely neglected. The first corpus consists of overtly apologetic literature: books and pamphlets in which writers defended the Jews and their religion from the familiar charges of duplicity, hatred of Gentiles, a penchant for usury, and civic vice more generally. Although historians have cited this literature, they have by and large restricted their analysis to retrospective judgment on the authors, either praising or blaming them for their presumed accuracy or inaccuracy, sincerity or insincerity, pride or subservience, rather than systematically analyzing the relevant texts in the contexts of contemporary discourses about the Jews. The second corpus consists of material that bibliographers tend to group under the rubric of "patriotic liturgy": prayers, songs, poems, sermons, and other sacred texts, usually published but sometimes in manuscript form, in which praise of the kingdom, nation, or empire is the primary subject. Among the occasions for such compositions were royal or imperial pregnancies and births, illnesses, assassination attempts and deaths, entries and coronations, as well as royal, republican, or imperial military victories and peace settlements. The third corpus contains descriptions of royal, revolutionary, and Napoleonic festivals in which Jews formally took part alongside Gentiles in acclaiming France and its leaders. These last two source bases have been almost entirely neglected by historians, who seem to have shared with Zosa Szajkowski the assumption that "Jews always chanted—willingly or forcibly—in honor of all regimes," and that apparent manifestations of patriotism do not give a "true picture of Jewish sentiments."[24]

In response to this skepticism, one could point to the Jewish tradition, dating from Babylonian captivity, of praying for Diaspora rulers and their realms.[25] One could observe that patriotic liturgy was typically composed in Hebrew, a language sacred to the Jews but incomprehensible to any French officials who might have rewarded the Jews' loyalty, and that in some cases the Hebrew originals exceeded their comparatively anodyne vernacular translations—which were indeed sent to the relevant officials—in patriotic zeal and (not surprisingly) sacred allusion. One could point to the fact that the first time a French government required rabbis to lead prayers for the state was in 1808 or 1809, and that by then patriotic liturgy was already a well-established form of Jewish self-representation.[26] Finally, it is worth noting that participation in "dynastic festivals" was a coveted privilege rather than an onerous task. Thus the inclusion of the Jews of Metz in Old Regime festivals was unique to that eastern Ashkenazi community. Even the relatively privileged Jews of Bordeaux do not appear to have obtained a similar right to participate in the dignity of the city and the crown. Like the Protestants of Montpellier, who were slighted by their exclusion from processional self-display,[27] most Jews were barred from formal ceremonies in which French subjects celebrated the monarchy. Finally, the fact that Napoleon excluded Jews from official imperial ceremonies despite their repeated entreaties for admission serves as additional evidence that patriotic acclamation was a sign of distinction rather than humiliation.[28]

Yet the suspicion that the patriotic liturgy and records of Jewish participation in state ceremonies do not give a "true picture of Jewish sentiments" is misplaced not only because of empirical facts. The assumption that Jews praising the state were insincere paradoxically reproduces the ancient discourse that marked them as naturally duplicitous. More seriously still, treating the traces of Jewish self-representation as indicating nothing but truthfulness or deception does an injustice to the complexity of feelings and beliefs, discounts the possibility of ambivalence, and precludes any understanding of the multiple meanings that the texts in question could carry for their creators as well as for their audiences. Indeed, it relies on the same binary conception of human thought and emotion as opaque or transparent that informed the mistrust of and ultimately the inability to perceive Jewish self-expression in the eighteenth century.

By contrast, taking the sources of Jewish self-representation seriously opens up a number of exciting possibilities for the reconceptualization of major categories that until now have determined our view of the relationship between centers and peripheries. The strategies deemed available to marginal groups under pressure to conform to the ideals of the dominant culture have been, by and large, limited to assimilation, resistance, and hybridity. The strategies of Jews examined here, however, raise questions about the explanatory power of these concepts. The ideologies of Enlightenment and republicanism—and, to a lesser extent, Napoleon's version of both—demanded that the Jews relinquish their "particularistic" beliefs and identity in order to achieve regeneration in the midst of a universal community, whether this was defined as an association of enlightened persons, a nation, or an empire. Yet the Jews continued to insist on their Jewishness; they did not assimilate into the surrounding culture. To say that they resisted, however, would be misleading. It would suggest that they rejected the ideology that reforming Gentiles called on them to accept, that they continued to be more Jewish than they were "enlightened" French or Napoleonic citizen-subjects. In fact, Jewish spokesmen continually refused to choose in this manner. Nor did they seek a hybrid solution, a synthesis of the secular European identities on the one hand and Jewishness on the other. What they did, rather, was to appropriate the dominant culture through a combination of sacralization and other familiarizing techniques and to represent it as originally or essentially Jewish. For example, they cast the primitive equality so often praised by contemporaries as already present in biblical antiquity and thus an invention of the Jews that Christians only belatedly discovered. They depicted the courage and zeal necessary for citizenship as an original feature of the people of Israel, the nation par excellence. They likened French leaders to biblical kings and their enemies to enemies of Israel, and thus made themselves French without ceasing to be Jews. Rather than being assimilated into France, then, they assimilated France into themselves.

Jews accomplished these tasks in large measure through the manipulation of language, and their success raises questions about the nature of discourse itself. Often seen as a monolithic and ineluctable aspect of any society, capable of including and excluding by virtue of its formidable definitions, discourse in the case examined here appears more fluid and by no means the exclusive property of the dominant writers and political actors. As we shall see in chapter 6, even Napoleon failed to control the discourse of regeneration, which his Jewish citizen-subjects manipulated by accepting and approving of *him,* of deeming him kosher, as it were, rather than allowing themselves to be regenerated in the manner he envisaged.

Finally, this book will consider the messages that Jews sent to other Jews about their relationship to France and the French and, during the Napoleonic period, to annexed and satellite polities. To reconstruct these communications I shall concentrate on texts written in Hebrew and Judeo-German (German written in Hebrew characters). The texts in Judeo-German, which I shall analyze in chapter 5, confirm my argument that Jews were capable of quickly integrating revolutionary values into their worldview without abandoning or even questioning their identity. The Hebrew texts are even more eloquent in their indication of the kind of assimilation I have already described. Since the Hebrew originals of many patriotic compositions are available, especially for the Napoleonic period, it is possible to compare these to their vernacular translations to determine the extent to which the story the Jews were telling themselves about themselves—to adapt a phrase from Clifford Geertz[29]—was the same as the story they were telling the Gentiles about themselves. On the basis of these texts I shall argue that, if anything, the Hebrew texts, with their unmistakable biblical allusions, went further than the vernacular translations in sacralizing the values with which the Jews were confronted. Thus the practice of self-representation played a

crucial constitutive role in the process by which the Jews came to regard
their adoptive country as their own. It was therefore inseparable from
the formation of new Jewish identities. Some might argue that this was
simply assimilation (into the surrounding Gentile community) in disguise, that it is immaterial whether Jews were able to persuade themselves or others that nothing in their worldview had changed. Yet there
is an enormous difference between relinquishing a sacred identity to
adopt that of a powerful majority and claiming the values of the majority as originally or essentially belonging to one's own marginalized and
maligned community. The difference is in self-esteem, a matter of importance that historians ignore all too often in their rush to understand the
"real" conditions of the people they study.

LACUNAE

Despite the multiple subjects treated in this book, the reader is entitled
to an explanation for certain gaps that it leaves unfilled. In particular, it
contains relatively few references to archival sources. I have consulted
archives in Paris and those provinces in which Jews were concentrated
and have also made use of published document collections to supplement these searches, yet the bulk of the book's evidence comes from
contemporary published material. There are good reasons for this emphasis. Specifically, this book is not, nor does it pretend to be, a comprehensive history covering all aspects of Jewish life in France between
1715 and 1815. If it were, it would have to reconstruct the institutions
of the various Jewish communities and describe the legal status, demo-
graphic conditions, occupational activities, and economic status of its
members, along with other factors in the social life of France's Jews, and
to do this would demand a thorough search of the archives. Fortunately,
much of this labor has already been done by social historians over the
past three to four decades, and the overview of Jewish life attempted in
chapter 1 relies heavily on their work. At the same time, historians have
seriously neglected highly significant published material, especially patriotic liturgy. Thus the source base exploited in this study serves to
some degree as a corrective to past imbalances. More important, one of
this book's central arguments, that is, that Gentiles paid much more attention to the Jews than historians have previously suspected, calls for
analysis of published material. For if an archival document can provide
information on the social, legal, or institutional situation of a particular

group, publications suggest a contemporary interest extending beyond the authorities whose documents were preserved in archives.

Second, it may seem curious that a book about representations of Jews is almost entirely lacking in *visual* representations. I myself found it odd that a culture that was so prolific in verbal representations of Jews produced so few pictures of them. Looking back from the twenty-first century one might expect Gentiles of the eighteenth and early nineteenth centuries to have drawn Jews as frequently as their successors so famously (and infamously) did. Even in comparison to their great willingness to discuss the Jews in writing and in speech, however, the relative absence of visual representations calls for an explanation. I would like to hazard one here: in contrast to later generations, when racism promised its adherents that clues to a person's moral character inhered in his or her physical composition, those who observed (figuratively or literally) the Jews of the eighteenth and early nineteenth centuries believed very nearly the opposite. They saw the Jews' outward appearance as irrelevant to the more pressing matter of their inner condition. As will be shown in subsequent chapters, Jews were typically associated with *opacity,* deception, dissimulation, and by extension with a radical separation between mental activity and physical appearance. Gentiles repeatedly described them as exhibiting a friendly or ingratiating air while simultaneously plotting the doom of their "victims." This is not to say that some elements that would later characterize racism did not already exist in the eighteenth century. After all, this was also the age of the physiognomists, and in at least one case a commentator tried to correlate the Jews' supposed lack of morality with physical evidence of degeneration.[30] Far more frequently, however, Gentiles were impressed by the alleged skill with which Jews could mask their intentions by controlling their appearance. Yet nothing could have been more difficult than to convey the irrelevance of appearance in pictorial fashion.

Third and finally, readers will no doubt notice that when writers and speakers, whether Jewish or Gentile, referred to Jews, they almost always meant Jewish men. As with the problem of pictorial representation, the experience of a subsequent era accentuates the sense of absence, for the Western world in the nineteenth century would see a pronounced interest in the figure of "the Jewess." In the case of France alone one need think only of the wildly successful opera *La Juive* (1835), by the Jewish composer Fromenthal Halévy, or the phenomenal success of the Jewish actress known by the stage name of Rachel, or the comparable attention to Sarah Bernhardt (whose reputed Jewish origins provided a subject of much discussion). Again, as in the matter of visual representation, differing attitudes toward external appearance seem to have played a role, as "the Jewess" of the nineteenth century was almost invariably depicted as beautiful, whereas she was virtually invisible to a period that paid little attention to the physical features of Jews. Moreover, the meanings attached to Jewishness in the earlier period seem to have precluded much attention to Jewish women. Insofar as the "Jewish question" centered on matters of citizenship and nationhood, on whether Jews could be citizens and whether their imagined membership in a *nation juive* permitted or precluded their belonging to a *nation française,* the status of Jewish women could scarcely figure more prominently in the discussion than that of women in general. The political status of women was not entirely ignored, especially toward the end of the period covered in this book, though feminism would not excite much public discussion until later in the nineteenth century. Yet even in the late eighteenth century, the very discursive proximity between Jews and women—their alleged similarities in a culture that saw both as markers of opacity, dissimulation, moral weakness, and private interest—made the matter of Jewish women redundant to the logic of those who considered the rights of Jews. In this respect, women are not entirely absent from this study, as their perceived characteristics appear in the feminization of Jewish men. Moreover, this mental pairing of Jewish and female attributes forestalled a specific discussion of Jewish women in matters other than citizenship, nationhood, and rights. More generally, as Gentiles used Jews to ponder the perfectibility (or lack thereof) of "man," they mobilized the standard imagery of Jewish degradation, which typically crystallized in the figure of the merchant, the usurer, who (at least in the period under discussion) appeared exclusively in the form of a man. With respect to Jewish self-representations, the absence of women was largely a function of the highly patriarchal nature of Jewish society. Excluded as a matter of religious doctrine from positions of power in the Old Regime communities, women could not be expected to share in the fruits of a future *régénération.* The Jewish men who called for equality did not perceive the exclusion of their female coreligionists from the French body politic as a problem in need of a solution.

The following, then, is not an *histoire totale* but a selective history. These very lacunae, some imposed by the past itself, others imposed by an analytical process of selection, can nevertheless yield significant knowledge about the past as well as the present. Both French representations of Jews and Jewish self-representation are not merely important to an understanding of the history of the Jews of France. These twin phenomena are eloquent testimony to the values of the French in the age of enlightenment and revolution, values that we can now confidently say owed more to past ages than their exponents were willing to acknowledge at the time and more than historians have subsequently appreciated. They bear witness to the persistence of tradition into an age that explicitly repudiated tradition and the resacralization of conversionary impulses under the aspect of civic improvement. Finally, and more generally still, they suggest a rethinking of the very categories that have long determined our understanding of how dominant groups produce knowledge of comparatively weak others, and of the choices available to those others in the writing of their own cultural text. In other words, they furnish new perspectives on the inseparable processes by which human beings construct alterities and identities. As such, they are, paradoxically though in quite different ways, what the Jews were to their contemporaries: an occasion for reflection and speculation on matters of universal importance.

A Nation within the Nation?

The Jews of Old Regime France

This book is above all about representations. One might say that it is more concerned with imaginary than with real Jews, though it would be naïve to draw a strict dichotomy between representations and hard facts, myths and realities, discourses and practices, history as it was imagined and *wie es eigentlich gewesen.* The principal subject matter is what people in France thought, wrote, and said about the Jews. In order for these representations to make sense, it is necessary to have a minimum of contextual knowledge about who the Jews were according to the law, how many of them lived in the French kingdom, where they resided, what languages they spoke, what they did for a living, what their religious life consisted of, how they governed their internal affairs, and how they interacted with their Gentile neighbors. This chapter seeks to provide the necessary social-historical context.

One of the most surprising facts about the Jews of Old Regime France, when one considers its history in the *longue durée,* is that they existed at all. Charles VI had expelled the Jews from the kingdom in 1394, and no sovereign ever rescinded this order. In 1615 Marie de Médicis reiterated her predecessor's demand that France be free of Jews, though by then only a handful had managed to obtain special permission to reside there. In 1685 Louis XIV infamously revoked the Edict of Nantes, suggesting something quite other than a tolerance of religious difference, and even Louis XVI, still *rex christianissimus,* swore at his coronation to "extirpate heresy." Despite the official policy of intolerance to non-

Catholics, however, Jews managed as a result of French annexations of foreign territories as well as exceptional arrangements with the crown and local authorities to trickle back into France until they numbered approximately 40,000 on the eve of the Revolution. Of these, between 20,000 and 25,000 inhabited Alsace, 4,000 lived in Lorraine, and 3,500 in and around the city of Metz. Twenty-three hundred lived in Bordeaux and scarcely a thousand in Saint-Esprit, just outside the Basque port of Bayonne. A total of 2,500 lived in the papal city of Avignon and the surrounding Comtat Venaissin. Only a handful, no more than 500, resided in Paris.

The largest concentration of Jews were the Yiddish-speaking Ashkenazim of Alsace, Lorraine, and the neighboring *généralité* of Metz. The Alsatians were a legacy of the Thirty Years' War. Upon obtaining Alsace in 1648 from the Holy Roman Empire, the French state acquired the province's Jews. As part of the settlement at Westphalia, the crown agreed to preserve the laws that entitled lords to settle Jews on their lands and to charge duties of "protection" as well as corvée service. Soon Louis XIV found ways of taxing the Jews himself, charging a *péage corporel* on all who crossed into French territory—a frequent occurrence for peddlers in a region dotted with innumerable imperial enclaves—and adding a *droit de protection* for good measure. Those too poor to pay were expelled, and at least ten times during the eighteenth century intendants ordered the expulsion of indigent Jews. As to those who remained within the province, their utility was measured not only in tax livres but also in terms of their commercial services. Jews traded in livestock and grain and therefore represented an important source of food both for soldiers stationed in the embattled province and for civilians who suffered periodic shortages resulting from war and harvest failures. Moreover, they engaged in moneylending, which despite the taboo associated with that infamous profession proved to be the only source of agricultural credit for cash-poor peasants, and occasionally convenient for military or civilian officials lacking specie.[1]

The Jews' residence privileges in French Alsace, therefore, depended on their ability to appear useful to the state. At the same time, the state was not the only power determining the Jews' fate. The cities of Alsace retained to a great extent the independence they had enjoyed under the Holy Roman Empire. One of their traditional rights was the freedom to determine whether and under what conditions they would accept Jews. Most of the cities were dominated by merchant guilds jealous of their commercial monopolies and therefore remained closed to Jews. Strasbourg explicitly and repeatedly forbade Jews from residing within the city walls. Though it relied on Jewish merchants for meat, grains, and other products, its solution was to permit Jews to enter the city each morning, to charge them (with gratuitously malicious humor) a body tax equivalent to the duty on pigs entering the city, and to force them out each evening. Other cities excluding Jews were Colmar, Munster, and Molsheim.[2]

Throughout the province Jews were almost invariably forbidden to own real estate aside from their own houses, to move from one house to another, and to marry without special permission. Although the terms of their royal *droit de protection* ostensibly entailed commercial freedom, the power of the guilds made this a dead letter. Merchants repeatedly secured ordinances restricting Jewish commerce to the trade in livestock and used goods and to moneylending. Thus Jewish occupations were severely limited. At the top of the ladder were a small number of relatively wealthy bankers and major livestock and grain dealers, with a handful toward the end of the eighteenth century engaging in iron mining and manufacturing. Further down were small-scale livestock and grain merchants. The majority of Jews, however, engaged in the peddling of used clothes and household products or petty moneylending, or some combination thereof, and many were reduced to begging. As a result, poverty was endemic. A census of 1732 reported that only 50 of 1,675 Jewish families subsisted without resorting to moneylending or begging.[3] At midcentury a bailiff commented that the Jews in his district lived "quite badly" and that "a large number" ate no more each day than "a piece of bread or some apples, pears and other seasonal fruits."[4] Though exact statistics are lacking, the repeated expulsions of poor Jews throughout the eighteenth century are themselves revealing.

The restrictions on Jewish liberties were more or less constant until the Revolution. Some changes were made in 1784 when Louis XVI issued letters patent defining the privileges of Jews in Alsace. According to these letters, Jews could engage in mining and large-scale manufacturing, new industries unencumbered by customary guild restrictions, but these liberties, which a handful of entrepreneurs were already enjoying de facto, were useless to all but a tiny minority of rich Jews. They could rent farms, but only if they cultivated the land themselves, an unlikely prospect given their long history of exclusion from agriculture. They could engage in wholesale and retail trade, but the innumerable local restrictions established by merchant corporations remained in effect. Old disabilities, such as the requirement of obtaining special permission to marry, remained in force, the only difference being that now the king, rather than local authorities, enforced them. The humiliating tax on Jewish "bodies" entering Strasbourg was abolished, but the city itself, like most others in Alsace, remained closed to Jews. The most severe measure of the 1784 letters patent stipulated that only Jews who could produce evidence of acceptance by local authorities were permitted to remain in the province. All others were to be expelled. Though the Sovereign Council repeatedly called for the enforcement of this provision, the laxity of royal officials prevented it from being carried out before the Revolution made it irrelevant. Still, until 1789 a considerable number of Alsatian Jews lived under the threat of expulsion.[5]

Apart from the right to reside in Alsace, the only privilege the Jews enjoyed was relative communal autonomy, though even here the word *relative* must be stressed. Louis XIV first authorized an Alsatian rabbinate in 1681, and by the end of the eighteenth century five rabbis officially served as judges to the Jews of Alsace. They had the power to decide civil cases between Jews according to the traditional legal codes, and in 1704 the Council of State ordered all Jews to obey rabbinical decrees or face expulsion. Yet the local tribunals, including the bailiwick courts, magistracies of free cities, and the Sovereign Council itself, repeatedly claimed the right to hear appeals by Jews dissatisfied with the decisions of their rabbis. In addition to the rabbis, the community was administered by lay officials known as *parnassim* or *préposés,* but their principal power was that of enforcing the collection of taxes that seigneurial or royal officials levied.[6]

As outsiders isolated by external and internal factors from Alsatian society, the Jews were especially vulnerable to the prejudices and anger of their neighbors. An undetermined number of Jews were killed in a pogrom in Dachstein in 1657, and though such instances of murder were rare, repeated decrees forbidding the "insulting" or "molesting" of Jews suggest that those offenses were common. An ordinance issued by the intendant in 1765 is particularly revealing: it prohibited Christians from "molesting, mistreating or insulting the Jews," and from "committing any violence or indecency in their cemeteries and synagogues."[7] Between 1777 and 1779 tensions reached a peak when a bailiff named François Hell arranged the forging of receipts alleging repayment of loans to Jewish creditors and defended himself by publishing a pamphlet decrying the "tyranny" of the Jews over the peasants.[8] Despite such outbursts, friendly contact between Jews and Christians does not seem to have been unknown. Indeed, attempts to keep them apart—such as the prohibition by the bishop of Strasbourg on Christian attendance at Jewish weddings and the Sovereign Council's ordinance forbidding Jews and Christians from sleeping under the same roof — indicate that contact between the two groups was frequent enough to trouble officials bent on their separation.[9]

As in Alsace, the Jews living in the province of Lorraine came under French rule as a result of annexation. Initially an independent duchy, Lorraine was occupied by France between 1633 and 1661, and again between 1670 and 1697 before passing definitively to France in 1766. During the first period of occupation military commanders admitted small numbers of Jews, one family at a time, on the basis of their utility in providing grain, meat, and cash to the frontier region. The capital city of Nancy proved inhospitable to those Jews established there, and in 1636 the king expelled them at the request of the municipality. In 1643 the military governor expelled the Jews who had settled there in the meantime when the Counsel General of the Hôtel de Ville denounced them as "completely useless to the city." Other Jews obtained permission to reside in the smaller town of Boulay, only to be expelled during the ducal interregnum in 1664. Under the second occupation they returned to Boulay, and others settled in ten authorized villages throughout the province.[10]

When the dukes regained control of Lorraine in 1697, they tolerated the Jews who had settled there. In 1701 Duke Léopold prohibited Christians from mistreating or insulting Jews and permitted a handful to live in Nancy in order to procure cash for his coffers and luxury goods for the court. In 1715 he appointed a Jew, Samuel Lévy, as his receiver general. Yet Lévy provoked the municipal authorities and the clergy in Nancy, where he defiantly held visible and audible religious services. More seriously, he engaged in *billonage,* the smuggling of coins across borders in order to melt them into less valuable metals for the production of debased coinage, and after numerous complaints from the French government Duke Léopold dismissed Lévy and had him imprisoned. The fall of Lévy provoked restrictive measures against the Jews of Lorraine in general, who in 1720 saw their business activities monitored and regulated. The following year Léopold gave the Jews a quasi-official status by issuing letters of toleration to 73 families in specific locations, but he ordered the expulsion of all Jews who had emigrated to Lorraine since 1680 and soon required Jews to live in restricted quarters of their designated cities and villages. Léopold's widow, Elisabeth-Charlotte, increased the number of tolerated households to 180, but at the cost of

10,000 livres per year. Her successor, the deposed Polish king Stanislas, established a rabbinate in 1737, suggesting the intention of retaining a Jewish population for the long term, though he also raised the protection impost to 14,300 livres. In 1753 he issued an edict of protection for the 180 tolerated families but specified that their residence privileges depended on his "pleasure." [11]

On the death of Stanislas in 1766, the duchy of Lorraine became a French province, as stipulated in a treaty following the War of the Polish Succession. The French crown converted the Jews' fiscal obligations toward the dukes into royal taxes, and by the time of the Revolution was collecting 16,000 livres a year in protection money. It recognized the authority of the rabbinate in civil matters between Jews, charged syndics with the responsibility of collecting taxes, and in 1784 and 1787 authorized the construction of synagogues in Lunéville and Nancy, respectively. The French kings connived at the illegal increase in the Jewish population, and though only 120 families were officially tolerated, 500 resided in the province on the eve of the Revolution.[12]

As in Alsace, guild monopolies prevented the Jews of Lorraine from practicing crafts or keeping retail stores, and prohibitions on their acquisition of real estate prevented them from engaging in agricultural work. Their principal occupations were therefore selling used goods as itinerant peddlers and petty moneylending, and though a few were successful in banking, manufacturing, and military provisioning, the mass of Jews was probably no better off than their coreligionists in Alsace. In Nancy the majority lived off the charity of the wealthy few. Moreover, relations between Jews and Christians in Lorraine were comparable to those in Alsace, as the repeated injunctions against insulting and mistreating Jews indicate. Indeed, as late as 1761 accusations of Jewish sorcery and ritual desecration of hosts were credible to Christian courts, which found the accused guilty, sentenced one to be hanged and burned, and condemned two others to life in the galleys.[13]

Like their coreligionists in Alsace and Lorraine, the Jews of Metz came under French control as a result of annexation. The former imperial city fell to France in 1552, and in 1565 the military governor soon gave permission to three Jews to reside in the city for the purpose of raising money to rebuild the citadel and provision the garrison. In 1574 the lieutenant governor expelled the Jews, probably at the behest of local merchants and the clergy, yet Henri III subsequently issued letters patent allowing eight Jewish families, "as well as their descendants, their families and married or unmarried children," to live in the city under his protection. All of the succeeding Bourbons confirmed these residence privileges, each time admitting a larger number of families, though from 1715 the community had to pay 40,000 livres per year for "protection" that had originally been free.[14]

As elsewhere in the northeast, the Jews of Metz were granted residence rights on the basis of services rendered to the state. In their letters patent of 1603 Henri IV referred to "the faithful conduct of the Jews," and to their "service in the garrison and elsewhere." In his confirmation of the privileges Louis XIII recalled the services of Jews who "lent many of their resources and faculties to the soldiers of . . . [the] garrison during the civil wars when they could not be repaid and when most of them were ruined as a consequence," and Louis XIV would praise them in similar terms.[15] In a memoir on Jewish commerce from 1698, the intendant of Metz claimed that, "by means of their agents" in other countries, the Jews were in a unique position to bring "all sorts of merchandise" into France, despite the prohibitions by foreign princes. He wrote that "by their industry they have all products more quickly and more cheaply than Christians" and advocated a policy of allowing more Jews to settle in France.[16]

Predictably, the established merchant guilds opposed the Jews and, together with the clergy who were scandalized by the presence of infidels in their midst, repeatedly called for their expulsion, though the kings repeatedly declined their petitions.[17] Tensions reached a peak in 1670 when a Jew named Raphaël Lévy was convicted of the "ritual murder" of a Christian child, then tortured and burned alive for his alleged crime. Unsatisfied that the moral pollution had been removed, the *parlement* called for a general expulsion of the Jews from the city. Significantly combining theological and economic arguments, it petitioned the king for "an exemplary punishment avenging the injuries to the sanctity of the religion that Your Majesty professes and stopping the sighs of the people oppressed by the usury and exactions of Jews."[18]

The kings repeatedly protected the Jews from the wrath of their neighbors, but as in Alsace and Lorraine they gave them little more than the right to live in Metz. The Jews' prospects of engaging in agricultural work were blocked by the prohibition against their owning or even renting land. Their opportunities for work in the crafts were limited to those of goldsmith and butcher, other trades being controlled by guilds that would never consider admitting Jews. Even their supposedly "natural" occupation of commerce was limited by local merchant monopolies. As in Alsace and Lorraine, the wealthiest Jews were therefore the military provisioners and bankers: entrepreneurs who supplied the army with cavalry horses, meat, grain, and loans. Yet in 1790 more than 80 percent of the Jews in Metz were classified in the internal register as "poor," and their occupations were the unenviable ones of itinerant peddlers selling used goods, petty moneylenders, and, finally, beggars.[19] These practices did nothing to counter age-old prejudices of Jews as usurers and tricksters.

The Jews of Metz, like their Ashkenazi brethren in Alsace and Lorraine, maintained a significant degree of communal autonomy in civil matters. From the late sixteenth century the community was administered by a council of lay syndics and a chief rabbi. These officers were in turn elected by the richest taxpaying members of the community. Their responsibilities included collecting taxes and dues and representing the community in relations with local and royal authorities. Alongside this executive body was a judiciary, also elected by wealthy members, whose function it was to hear cases between Jews and to judge according to codes based on the Talmud. Headed by the chief rabbi, the tribunal reserved the right to mete out a wide range of penalties, from small fines to the dreaded *herem,* or excommunication. This latter penalty meant not only the removal of an individual from religious practice but also his or her physical banishment from the city; it also required all members of the community to shun the banned person both socially and economically. In other words, it meant social and economic ruin.[20]

The French state repeatedly supported the punitive power of the council and tribunal as efficient means of regulating conduct. Yet the *parlement* of Metz contested the judicial autonomy of the Jewish community and as early as 1634 reserved the right to take on cases between Jews that did not involve matters of "religion or internal police," thus implying its power to adjudicate on a wide range of civil disputes. For a century and a half the rabbis insisted on their rights as final arbiters in matters between Jews and claimed the power to excommunicate members who appealed to the royal courts. The *parlement* consistently opposed the rabbis in this struggle, and the kings, who instinctively recoiled at *parlementaire* claims, typically sided with the rabbis.[21] Only in 1782 did the *parlement* cede the authority to judge civil cases between Jews to the rabbis, perhaps, as one historian has argued, because this gave the magistrates the opportunity to emphasize the legitimacy of historical rights, which they were touting in their own struggles with the absolute monarchy.[22]

Though communal institutions, laws, and religious customs prohib-

iting interreligious fraternization and a climate of economic competition and suspicion kept the Jews of Metz relatively isolated, it would be
wrong to see the community as entirely cut off from the surrounding
world. Local rabbis repeatedly fulminated against the adoption of Gentile practices such as wearing wigs, frequenting coffeehouses, and drinking ritually unclean wine, which suggests that the Jewish community
was not hermetically sealed against outside influences.[23] Moreover, toward the end of the eighteenth century leading members of the community betrayed a sympathy with Enlightenment ideas, which they acquired
through contact with the Jewish *maskilim,* or "reasoning ones," in Berlin, who advocated the study of modern vernacular languages and the
natural and human sciences in addition to the sacred texts of Judaism
and called much of traditional rabbinical scholarship into question.[24]
These *maskilim* would become natural spokesman for their coreligionists when called upon to explain, and usually to defend, Jewish belief
and practice to non-Jews. They were cultural translators and as such
were of vital importance to a community that was never secure in its
rights and, as the record of prohibitions against "insulting" and "mistreating" Jews reveals, repeatedly harassed by hostile neighbors.[25]

In addition to the Ashkenazi populations of the northeast, a smaller
number of Sephardic Jews resided in southwest France. Whereas the
crown had acquired the former through annexations, the latter came to
France officially as "Portuguese merchants" rather than as Jews. In flight
from the Inquisition in Portugal, these "new Christians" found an asylum in Bordeaux in 1550 thanks to Henri II, who saw in the crypto-Jews
a potential stimulus to commercial activity in the Atlantic port city. The
letters patent governing their status entitled them to live in the city (but
not elsewhere), to engage in all types of commerce not regulated by merchant guilds, to purchase real estate, and to bequeath their property.
Succeeding kings would renew these privileges until the Revolution. A
second community of Sephardic Jews emerged in Saint-Esprit, just outside of Bayonne, at the end of the sixteenth century. In 1597, during a
Spanish siege of Bordeaux in which the presence of Iberian immigrants
was feared, the *parlement* expelled those who could not prove at least
ten years' residence in the city, and the majority of refugees settled in
Saint-Esprit.[26] In 1656 Louis XIV gave these refugees the same privileges
as the "Portuguese merchants" in Bordeaux, permitting them to live
and conduct business "with the same freedom and liberty" enjoyed by
the king's "natural subjects," and his Bourbon successors renewed these
rights.[27] In 1723 the pretense of conversion had been dropped, and

the Jews were finally recognized as Jews, though at the cost of 100,000 livres.[28]

Historians have long drawn stark contrasts between the Ashkenazim and the *portugais*. They have characterized the former as poor, pious, isolated, threatened, autonomous, and recognizably different. By contrast, they have depicted the latter as wealthy, secular, well integrated into the surrounding society, secure in their status, governed by French rather than Jewish law, and barely distinguishable from their Gentile neighbors.[29] The sources of this myth are not hard to find. In response to Voltaire's criticisms of Judaism and Jews, the Sephardic writer Isaac de Pinto argued that while the Ashkenazim were poor, uneducated, and embroiled in constant conflict with their Gentile neighbors, the *portugais* were prosperous, enlightened, and on friendly terms with Christians.[30] Thirty years later, when deputies in the revolutionary National Assembly hesitated to recognize Jews as citizens and based their arguments on the alleged separatism of the Jewish communities, Sephardic pamphleteers countered that the Portuguese had always maintained friendly relations with their non-Jewish neighbors and had never constituted a separate nation.[31] Thus the myths of Jewish citizenship *avant la lettre* were defensive postures and say more about the historical circumstances under which they developed than about the conditions they purported to explicate.

To be sure, the corporate wealth of the numerically smaller *portugais* far exceeded that of the Ashkenazi Jews.[32] Yet most of this wealth was concentrated in the hands of a tiny minority. Shortly before the Revolution less than 2 percent of the Portuguese in Bordeaux were designated *négociants,* and at the beginning of the eighteenth century only 10 percent had purchased the right of bourgeois enabling them to own real estate and keep shops.[33] Among the remaining Jews were a large number of paupers. In his inventory of the Portuguese community in 1722, the subintendant wrote that 30 percent of its members lived off of charity.[34] In 1764 a group of Jews protesting against high internal dues claimed that two-thirds of the Portuguese were poor, and more recently a historian of French Jewry has estimated that half the Jews in Bordeaux lived off of charity in the eighteenth century.[35]

Nor were the *portugais* less vulnerable to expulsion than their coreligionists in the northeast. After all, the establishment of the community at Saint-Esprit only came about because of a prior expulsion from Bordeaux. And if the *parlement* was a threat, the crown was not necessarily more protective of the Jews. The original letters patent stipulated, "If

the king or his successors wish to send [the Jews] away, they will have a
delay of one year to collect their goods and move their families and servants." In 1684 Louis XIV expelled ninety-three poor Jewish families
from Bordeaux and other cities in the province of Guienne. The order
was explicit about the reasons for the expulsion: the Jews "are not only
of no utility to commerce, but they are even a burden to the cities in
question by virtue of their poverty."[36] Expulsion orders against the poor
Jews of Bordeaux were issued again in 1722, 1734, 1740, and 1760.[37]

As to the Sephardic Jews' relations with their Gentile neighbors, these
suffered from endemic strains. In 1574 Henri III issued "letters of safe-
guard" making it illegal to "molest" the Jews, a measure that itself reveals the extent to which they were unwelcome in Bordeaux.[38] In 1604
violence against the Jews must have been continuing, since the governor
of Guienne felt compelled to forbid it, but his ordinance did not prevent
the murder of a Portuguese merchant by a mob in 1610, a crime for
which no one was brought to justice.[39] During the revolt of 1675 the
Jews felt so threatened that many emigrated to Holland.[40] The climate
remained tense in the eighteenth century. In 1733 an assistant to the
intendant reported altercations between Jews and Christians outside
churches and claimed that the Jews had to hire "patrol horsemen and
soldiers" to protect them on their visits to the cemetery.[41] Most tellingly
of all, when the news of the National Assembly's 1790 decree recognizing the equality of Sephardic Jews reached Bordeaux, local authorities
had to intervene to prevent demonstrations from turning into a riot.[42]

The notion that the Portuguese were less autonomous than the Ashkenazim is similarly mistaken. From the beginning of the eighteenth century the corporation of Portuguese merchants, significantly designated a
nation, conducted its internal business with considerable autonomy.
Governed by syndics who in turn were elected by a restricted number of
wealthy men, the nation regulated such spheres as education and distribution of charity and also wielded significant punitive power over its
members. It could exact fines from offenders and banish them from the
community. This penalty, called variously baraxa and herem, not only
entailed a kind of spiritual estrangement similar to that of an excommunication. It also involved the physical expulsion of the culprit and
amounted to economic ruin. In this respect, the community's power over
its members was identical to that of the Ashkenazi communities.

A review of the corporation's minutes from 1711 to 1787 reveals its
wide-ranging powers. On numerous occasions it threatened to excommunicate persons officiating or serving as witnesses at clandestine wed-

dings. At least twice it carried out the punishment; on another occasion it fined a witness, and it always annulled the unauthorized marriages. With the help of the local police it imprisoned a man accused of seducing a woman by falsely promising to marry her, and it forced another man to pay alimony and child support to a woman he impregnated but failed to marry. Further regulating domestic relations, the *nation* required marriage contracts to specify the dowry and reserved the right to determine appropriate dowries based on wealth in case of omission. It forced a reluctant bachelor to marry his deceased brother's widow, as recommended by Jewish law, and it excommunicated parents who had abandoned their children. The *nation* even enforced a kind of rent control. When a landlord tried to raise the rent of a widow and her daughter, the syndics ruled that he had violated "divine and human laws" and ordered him to pay damages of 600 livres, plus 100 livres for the poor fund. Until he paid he would be deprived of all community services, including the distribution of meat. Finally the landlord gave in and paid the requisite damages.[43]

The crown formally recognized the self-policing powers of the *nation* in 1760, though it had long accepted such autonomy as a matter of practice. According to the *reglement* defining their powers, the syndics both collected taxes and played an important role in setting rates. They reserved the power to confiscate the property of anyone who fell more than three months behind on their payments. Furthermore, they could expel vagabond Jews, whose conduct was deemed "irregular and reproachable."[44] A comparable corporate organization governed the Portuguese of Saint-Esprit from the mid–seventeenth century and gained the intendant's approval of its constitution in 1753.[45] The Portuguese Jews were even permitted to divorce according to their own laws, and though the proceedings had to take place in the *parlement,* the freedom to divorce, unknown to French Catholics, was in itself a significant concession to Jewish autonomy.[46] The Sephardic institutions were never fully autonomous, since they were dependent on the crown's continued "pleasure," but, as we have seen, the Ashkenazi communal organizations were not truly independent either.

The myth that the Portuguese were principally secular people must also be addressed. Indeed, one of the most striking facts of the history of the Sephardim of France is that they chose, despite the attendant risks, to "come out" as Jews after generations of living outwardly as Christians. By 1686, in a period when the persecution of Calvinists had made the crown's potential for punitive action against non-Catholics painfully obvious, the Jews of Bordeaux had stopped celebrating weddings and having their children baptized in the church,[47] and in 1706 they publicly prayed in Hebrew for the welfare of the kingdom.[48] Compared with the Ashkenazim, they seem to have held their rabbis in relatively low esteem; one disgruntled rabbi even petitioned the intendant of Bordeaux "to make a small reprimand to the heads of the Portuguese nation about the lack of respect and deference that they have for their rabbi."[49] Yet a willingness to challenge religious leaders does not necessarily indicate a lack of religiosity; it may even suggest the opposite, as students of conciliarist movements of all kinds know well. In any event, in 1748 the syndics of the *nation* did not hesitate to fine a member 100 livres and prohibit Jews from speaking to him because he had expressed himself "with an intolerable indiscretion against the most sacred dogmas of the religion" and "scandalously transgress[ed] [the laws concerning] the Sabbath and our festivals." This ruling suggests that irreligious thinking and behavior existed among the Jews of Bordeaux, but it also shows that such deviation was punishable. As late as 1785 the syndics of the Portuguese *nation* viewed a drought as "an effect of God's anger brought on by our sins," and they ordered public prayers, fasting, and charity to remedy the situation.[50]

Indeed, the seriousness with which the Portuguese took their religion appears to have scandalized their Christian neighbors. The 1733 report of the assistant to the intendant complained that the "Jewish people displays an outrageous effrontery in the exercise of its religion." The writer was indignant at the "beautiful ornaments" made of silver and the rich fabrics decorating the Torah scrolls, the "beautiful silver lamps" and chandeliers in the synagogue, which any Christian could see through its open doors. He expressed astonishment at the fact that the Jews "sometimes . . . go to the synagogue barefoot [i.e., on the Day of Atonement] or in untied slippers," that "they sing and pray in their synagogues as loudly as they can" and "use a horn [the shofar, or ram's horn], with which they make an extraordinary noise." He added that "their children publicly use this horn in the streets, and blow it when it is necessary for their great festivals."[51]

Thus the *portugais* were scarcely less separated from their Gentile neighbors than were their brethren in Alsace, Lorraine, and Metz. In addition to the Ashkenazi communities of the northeast and the Sephardic *nations* of Bordeaux and Saint-Esprit, a third Jewish population, which spoke a variant of *provençal,* resided in and around the papal city of Avignon. After the expulsion of 1394 many Jews had fled to Provence, where they lived in relative security until the French conquered the kingdom. After a second expulsion by Louis XII in 1500, most Jews sought refuge in Avignon and the papal cities of Carpentras, Cavaillon, and Isle-sur-Sorgue in the Comtat Venaissin.[52] Although Avignon was technically under the jurisdiction of the pope, from 1732 a diplomatic arrangement between the Vatican and France made the residents of Avignon simultaneously subjects of the pope and the French king. Moreover, for nearly six years following an invasion of June 1768, France governed Avignon and the Comtat Venaissin (renamed Comté Venaissin) as part of the *généralité* of Provence.[53] A dearth of economic opportunities provoked immigration of the *avignonnais,* as they were collectively called, to Bordeaux and Bayonne, where a few hundred were permitted to reside and administer their internal affairs in much the same way as the kingdom's other Jewish communities, though they were seen as a burden when poor and a threat when rich, not least by the *portugais* communities themselves.[54]

Finally, a small number of Jews, never exceeding five hundred, lived in Paris during the eighteenth century. They had no recognized institutions, and the practice of their religion was only tolerated as of 1755. They lived under police surveillance and were subject to imprisonment or expulsion if found without their special short-term passports. Moreover, the Jews of Paris came from all parts of France, to which they frequently returned for religious festivals. The Ashkenazi Jews, for the most part hawkers in old clothes, secondhand goods, and junk, lived primarily in the unsavory quarters of Saint-Martin and Saint-Denis, whereas the Portuguese, often dealers in silk and cloth, tended to inhabit the more fashionable quarters of Saint-Germain and Saint-André. Moreover, the Jewish population was divided between transient hawkers, who risked imprisonment or expulsion at a moment's notice, and the "useful," protected Jews, who provided credit for the army, horses for the cavalry, or jewelry for the queen and dauphine.[55]

This brief overview suggests that despite superficial differences, the various Jewish communities in Old Regime France had a great deal in common. The lack of legal opportunities for livelihood guaranteed the endemic poverty of all the Jewish populations, with a handful of wealthy members only providing the exception that proves the rule. All of the Jewish communities faced religious prejudice and economic resentment, which frequently blended indistinguishably into a general mood of hostility. All faced the prospect of illegal violence at the hands of their neighbors and the legalized violence of expulsion and, on occasion, prosecution for imaginary religious crimes. With the exception of the tiny group of Parisians, all maintained a degree of communal autonomy that contributed to their relative isolation from the surrounding society, though this form of autonomy never provided the security that comes from recognized and uncontested rights.

The isolation of the Jews in closed *corps* governed by internal laws and customs informed the charge, to be discussed in later chapters, that they were a "nation within a nation." That Jews more generally were referred to collectively as *la nation juive,* a name they themselves bore unselfconsciously, did nothing to diminish this reputation, nor did the fact that the Alsatian Jews were officially called *la nation juive d'Alsace,* the Sephardim of Bordeaux *la nation juive portugaise de Bordeaux,* and so forth. Indeed, precisely because the term *nation* served to designate Jews long before nationalism emerged in the eighteenth and nineteenth centuries, one might argue, they were the first identified instance of a general problem—the nation within a nation—that has plagued nationalists for over two centuries.

The expression "nation within a nation" is of course political speech, more a term of abuse designed to exclude (or to deplore self-exclusion) than a sociological description. It is born of a normative political philosophy that posits an ideal polity, that is, the nation, with a single set of laws and values and a single will to which all other group loyalties, identities, customs, rules, and wills must yield. It proudly proclaims its ideal of indivisibility and denounces its anti-value of particularism. As such one is right to question whether there ever was a nation within which other nations could possibly exist. To be sure, there are many possible definitions of *nation.* For Sieyes the nation was (among other things) "a body of associates living under a *common* law," [56] and in this respect the Jews of Old Regime France could scarcely have been a part of the French nation, since they were subject both to internal Jewish law and to laws of exception defining their rights and obligations in the kingdom. Indeed, the varying (though not greatly varying) letters patent under which the various Jewish communities lived would seem to justify calling them nation*s* within the nation.

On the other hand, one could argue that even in the restricted sense of the nation as a body of associates living under a common law, France was not a nation under the Old Regime. It was precisely the abomination of privilege, literally private law, that revolutionaries claimed to be overturning by placing all citizens under a single set of laws, thus giving birth to the nation. In this context the exceptional condition of the Jews might not seem so exceptional after all, and historians have suggested that in the corporate society of the Old Regime the legal position of Jews was no different from that of other people. Gary Kates writes, "The law recognized individuals only insofar as they held membership in a legal group. A tailor needed the protection of his guild, a priest his religious order, a merchant his town corporation, and so on. In this respect, Jews were considered legitimate subjects of the king if they were attached to a legally recognized Jewish community."[57]

Yet it was the question of whether the Jews were "legitimate subjects," indeed of whether they were subjects at all, that was so hotly contested in Old Regime court cases. Whenever Jews sought recognition of rights available to French subjects, they argued that they were *régnicoles,* or royal subjects, but these claims were typically ineffective.[58] The letters patent governing the status of Jewish communities hardly helped. Louis XIV's letters patent for the "Portuguese merchants" of Saint-Esprit permitted them to conduct business "with the same freedom and liberty" enjoyed by the king's "natural subjects,"[59] but this was not at all the same as recognizing the Jews themselves as "natural subjects." Jews repeatedly applied for personal naturalization during the eighteenth century precisely because they knew that the courts were unlikely to regard them as French subjects.[60] In some cases the Jews were held to be neither subjects nor foreigners, which situated them in a kind of legal limbo and placed them in a more precarious position than that of foreigners, who *as* foreigners could occasionally obtain limited privileges.[61] Whatever name one chose (or chooses) to assign to the Jews of Old Regime France, their condition of endemic insecurity nevertheless made them different from other corporate groups. Christian tailors born in France could not be expelled on the king's "pleasure," or for being poor. Nor could priests (with the exception of Jesuits, whose special loyalty to the pope occasionally raised questions about their rights as French subjects), nor could the burghers of the kingdom's cities.

This account is not meant to replace an optimistic assessment of Jewish life with a pessimistic one, to restore what one historian has aptly called the lachrymose history of the Jews,[62] or to gauge the Jews' condition relative to that of other groups on a scale of happiness and misery. The point is to give the legal and social conditions that delineated the possibilities available for the representation of the Jews, both by Gentiles and by the Jews themselves. Given the conditions outlined here, it was nearly impossible for Gentiles to have reliable knowledge about the

Jews—their religion, values, customs, and attitudes toward non-Jews. Paucity of numbers and geographic concentration on France's periphery made meeting a real Jew a highly unlikely occurrence, and the Jews' isolation in relatively closed communities guaranteed that whatever impressions Gentiles had of them would remain informed by age-old prejudices. Indeed, the very marginality of the Jews raises the question—which will be examined in subsequent chapters—of why anyone was interested in them in the first place. As to the Jews themselves, their isolation, their insecurity, and the suspicion that both bred in the minds of non-Jews made effective self-representation crucial. Convincing the non-Jews of France, especially those in positions of power, of their utility to the state and benign intentions toward its inhabitants was not simply a matter of public relations. It was a matter of keeping their homes, their livelihood, in short, their very lives.

CHAPTER 2

Jews and Philosophes

THINKING WITH JEWS

Historians concerned with the relationship between the Enlightenment and the Jews have tended to ask whether the philosophes were anti-Semitic or philo-Semitic, whether their plans for the integration of Jews into Gentile society were a positive or negative development, and whether those Jews who embraced the Enlightenment were liberating themselves or shamefully casting aside their ancient identity. These are all variations on a single question, namely, whether the Enlightenment was good or bad for the Jews.[1] They have been debated since the time of the Enlightenment itself, though some of the terms (such as anti-Semitic and philo-Semitic) are specific to a later age. They will continue to be debated in the future, since they are not susceptible to resolution by means of any historical investigation. The question of whether the Enlightenment was good or bad for the Jews is, more properly speaking, an occasion for the expression of one's feelings about Enlightenment universalism on the one hand and the destiny, character, or obligations of the Jewish "people" on the other. These feelings in turn are necessarily conditioned and justified by one's knowledge of nineteenth- and twentieth-century history, in which the victories and failures of universalism and nationalism appear to confirm, a posteriori, one's chosen or inherited position on the question. By contrast, my principal question will be one that commentators, in their zeal to cast ballots for or against the En-

lightenment, have neglected: namely, why was the Enlightenment interested in the Jews in the first place?

In retrospect the interest that philosophes and their readers showed
in the Jews appears inevitable. The troubled relationship between modernity and the Jews suggests that the Jews had to be prominent in the
thinking of those who, we are continually told, ushered in modernity.
But if one resists the teleological urge to look for origins, the fact that
eighteenth-century French authors wrote so much about the Jews appears puzzling, even bizarre. A search for the word *juif* (and its feminine
and plural variants) on the ARTFL database of French literature yields
2,352 hits for its 474-volume sampling of eighteenth-century books.
This total is 60 percent of the number of references to the English (*an-
glois, anglais,* and inflected forms), France's principal rival, a famous
topic of discussion among philosophes, as well as the name of the English language. (There was no *langue juive.*) Voltaire, the famous Anglo-
phile, in his vast corpus referred to the Jews nearly twice as often (4,394
times) as he did to the English (2,303), as the *Voltaire électronique* indicates.[2] Statistics do not tell the whole story, and it will be necessary to
examine how the Jews functioned in eighteenth-century French writing,
yet the numbers are significant insofar as they suggest an enormous interest in a negligible and relatively powerless population. The Jews were
outnumbered more than two to one by the Basques, another stateless
"nation" that resided on the geographic periphery and spoke a (very)
distinct language, yet there was never a "Basque question" in eighteenth-
century France.[3] Why, then, was there a Jewish question?

The answer, to adapt a celebrated formulation by Claude Lévi-
Strauss, is that the Jews were "good to think."[4] The multiplicity of associations that one could make between the Jews and various concepts
dear to eighteenth-century French thinkers made them an especially
popular object of description, speculation, analysis, imagination, and ultimately reform. Other groups, such as American "savages," Muslims,
blacks, and women, were also rich in symbolic meaning, and indeed the
discursive proximity between the Jews and these other "others" will be
recognized in the following chapters. Yet I would like to argue that the
Jews occupied a special place in the French Enlightenment discourse,
that they were not simply interchangeable with other "marked" figures.
To demonstrate this, it is necessary to move from the question of *why* to
how the Jews were "good to think," and thus to ask what concepts the
Jews helped Gentiles to articulate. A full menu of conceptual possibili-

ties would be impossible to reproduce, but the texts examined in this chapter reveal that Jews were invoked when authors wished to discuss the following ideas: fanaticism and tolerance; carnality and spirituality; the "natural" role of ceremony and dogma in religious belief and practice; the proper relationship between religion and morality; the moral effects of commerce and agriculture; the merits and demerits of "primitive" life and "civilization," antiquity and modernity; uniformity and diversity among human groups; and stasis and malleability in human nature, and the relative desirability of each.

Furthermore, as this brief (and doubtless incomplete) catalogue reveals, the concepts to which Jews were figuratively related typically came in binary pairs. Thus they were most frequently described as primitive or modern, obstinate or malleable (i.e., convertible), essentially agricultural or essentially commercial, but rarely as anything in between. Moreover, these oppositions were highly unstable. Even within a single work the Jews could migrate between poles, signifying one thing in one place and its opposite elsewhere. Still, it would be wrong to assume that any figurative association was as likely as another. Centuries of (admittedly changing) representations in theology, art, literature, and folklore, and the limits imposed by the Jews' actual historical situation, made some associations probable and others less so. Thus Jews were frequently employed to allude to the ideas of fidelity or infidelity but rarely, if ever, used to evoke, say, artisanal skill, or celibacy, or the "fundamental laws" of the French "constitution." The Jews had multiple, but not infinite, meanings.

To give a clearer and more comprehensive account of those meanings, I have chosen for analysis five corpora by French philosophes: Montesquieu's *Lettres persanes* and *De l'Esprit des lois;* the *Lettres juives,* by the marquis d'Argens; the works of Voltaire and Rousseau, respectively; and the *Encyclopédie.* These works were "best-sellers" and therefore tell us something about their readers as well as their authors. This does not mean that readers necessarily agreed with what the authors wrote, but that they were in the same conceptual universe, that they were capable of understanding the reasoning, allusions, and rhetoric of the works in question. Collectively, then, they provide a window onto the image of the Jew in the French imaginary during the age of the Enlightenment.

PERSIANS AND JEWS IN MONTESQUIEU'S WRITINGS

Lettres persanes, the great epistolary novel that in 1721 launched Montesquieu's career as a philosophe, is unequivocally about the possibility of difference. Composed of purportedly real letters written by a Persian traveler named Usbek, his young compatriot Rica, and their correspondents in Ispahan, the *Lettres* coalesce into a narrative treatise that not only examines the diversity of human experience but also muses on the possibility that what is might just as well be otherwise. In a famous passage, Rica writes to Usbek of a bewildered Parisian who responded to the news that he was Persian with the remark, "That's an extraordinary thing. How could one be a Persian?"[5] The humor in this question comes from the recognition of a type of bigotry that does not merely consider others inferior but questions the possibility of their very existence.

The *Lettres persanes* showed that one could be a Persian. It also showed that one could be a Jew, as indicated by the prominent place of Jews in the novel. Jewish characters served numerous functions, as figures of suffering at the hands of religious fanatics, as agents of commerce, and, by implication, as symbols of human greed. Above all, however, the Jews provided an occasion for Montesquieu, in the *Lettres persanes* and elsewhere, to reflect on the *possibility* that human beings might be something other than what they were. This investigation into the possibility of difference, moreover, was inextricably connected to a larger set of questions that continually preoccupied the philosophes, namely, whether human nature was malleable and, if so, whether it was perfectible.

In one respect, the curious presence of Jews in a book about the relationship between Christendom and the Islamic world serves simply to intensify the sense of doubt that Christian readers might have had about their religion's monopoly on truth. That the novel's Jews, like the Muslims, were intelligent, literate, rational thinkers further eroded the sense of Christianity as the only option for civilized persons. When the Muslim Rica receives a letter from Nathanaël Lévi, a "Jewish physician at Leghorn," requesting his opinion on the efficacy of amulets and talismans, he replies, "Why are you asking me? You're a Jew, and I'm a Mohammedan; that is to say, we're both quite credulous." Rica's ironic reference suggested that both Muslims and Jews—in this case a philosophically inclined Muslim and a learned Jewish physician—were aware of prejudices about their intellectual faculties and took them with a grain of salt. Lévi's letter is not included in the novel, but Rica's remark suggests that Lévi got the joke, that he shares Rica's ironic sense of humor and hence his intelligence. Meanwhile, Montesquieu, with a nod and a wink to the increasingly uncertain Christian reader, suggested that Rica and his Jewish correspondent were justified in their mockery, as they themselves were evidence of intellectual prowess among non-Christians. A further blow to the notion of Christianity's superiority came when Usbek reported to his Muslim friend Ibben, without comment, "The Jews regard themselves . . . as the source of all sanctity and the origin of all religion. They regard us [Muslims], on the contrary, as heretics who have changed the law, or even more as rebellious Jews."[6] Implicitly, Christians were heretics as well.

Usbek's comment raises the question of the relative merits of stasis and change in law and belief, and here the Jews played a special role. They were not merely meant to lengthen a menu of religious choices. Throughout Montesquieu's writings the Jews appear in inquiries into the possibility and morality of staying the same and of changing. In most cases they appear in their traditional form as figures of stasis, as Eternal Jews. Usbek writes to his friend Ibben, "You ask me if there are Jews in France? You can be sure that wherever there is money, there are Jews," thus suggesting an unchanging nature. Usbek reinforces this impression by writing, "You ask me what [the Jews] do? Precisely what they do in Persia. Nothing more closely resembles an Asian Jew than a European Jew." Montesquieu elaborated on the image of the Jew as eternal merchant in the story of Apheridon and Astarte, framed in a letter from one of Usbek's Persian correspondents. In that tale Apheridon tries to redeem his sister Astarte from Jews who have bought her as a slave and intend to resell her. Yet the Jews are inflexible to the most desperate entreaties. "My pleas, my tears were in vain," Apheridon recalls, "they continually demanded thirty tomans, and would not take even one less." Only after selling his own daughter is Apheridon able to redeem his sister.[7]

The image of static Jews reappears elsewhere in Montesquieu's oeuvre. In *De l'esprit des lois,* the author juxtaposed mindlessly scrupulous attention to "religious precepts" with a more defensible recourse to "natural law." Although he acknowledged the excessive attachment of some Christians to the letter of the law, he revealingly gave as one example of this defect the alleged refusal of Jews to defend themselves from enemies on the Sabbath, a failure he regarded, without mincing words, as indicative of the "stupidity of this nation."[8] This remark reveals that Montesquieu inherited the long-standing Christian prejudice against the alleged legalism of Jews. Pascal had criticized the "zeal of the Jewish people for their law," and similar accusations came from Bossuet and Fénélon at the turn of the eighteenth century.[9] The Jews' alleged literalism was explained by another traditional complaint against them: their supposed obstinacy. Bossuet in particular expressed indignation against the "voluntary blindness" and "hard-heartedness [l'endurcissement] of the Jewish people," and he denounced them for "their obstinate malice" in rejecting the Savior.[10] Remarkably, the discourse of obstinacy survived intact the Enlightenment assault on Christian orthodoxy. For example, Usbek declares that the Jews "display among the Christians, as among us [Muslims], an invincible obstinacy for their religion, which goes as far as madness." Moreover, in De l'esprit des lois Montesquieu wrote of their "tenacious obstinacy," though here he also attributed this quality to "Mohammedans."[11]

Elsewhere, however, Montesquieu put a positive spin on the Jews' proverbial obstinacy. Thus Usbek, despite his derogatory comments about the Jews' "invincible obstinacy," expresses admiration for the "venerable old age of their religion." He writes, "The Jewish religion is an old trunk that has produced two branches that have covered the entire earth: I mean Mohammedanism and Christianity." He continues, searching for the proper metaphor, "It is a mother who has given birth to two daughters, who have covered her with a thousand plagues."[12]

This sense of noble resistance, the other side of obstinacy, is clearer still in a chapter of De l'esprit des lois comprising a fictional "remonstrance" by an unnamed Jewish writer to the "Inquisitors of Spain and Portugal" on the occasion of the burning of an eighteen-year-old Jewish woman in Lisbon.[13] As with other philosophes, most famously Voltaire, the Jew in Montesquieu's writings was repeatedly a figure of persecuted religious difference. Indeed, the Jew was often identical with the burned Jew.[14] The Inquisition was, of course, the great bête noire of the philosophes, as were the Iberian kingdoms with which they were almost automatically associated. It was nearly impossible for philosophes to discuss Spain or Portugal without mentioning the Inquisition, or the proverbially powerful clergy, or the fanaticism that allegedly characterized both. The Inquisition functioned as a synecdoche for Spain or Portugal or both, which in turn operated as synecdoches for the Catholic Church, intolerance, in short, l'infâme. This relation helps to explain, at least in part, the frequency with which philosophes wrote about the Jews. For if it was practically second nature for Enlightenment thinkers to move from Spain or Portugal to the Inquisition, it was an equally obvious move from any of the above to their victims.

As the "remonstrance" shows, however, Montesquieu's persecuted Jews were not merely victims of fanaticism. They were models of fidelity. The author denounces the Inquisitors by writing, "We follow a religion that you yourselves know God to have cherished once: we think that God still loves it, and you think that he no longer loves it; and since you judge thus, you put to iron and fire those who are in such a pardonable error of believing that God still loves what he loved." Thus Montesquieu's imaginary Jew turned the tables on the Christians, who were now the infidels. The Christians did not merely abandon the Truth originally revealed to the Jews; they abandoned it for faith in a God who himself was fickle. Such a God by definition could not be omnipotent, since omnipotence entailed immutability. A footnote to the "remonstrance" made this explicit. "This is the source of the Jews' blindness," Montesquieu wrote sarcastically, "only to sense that the economy of the divine message is in the order of God's designs, and that it therefore follows as a consequence of his very immutability." This was a theological way of saying that the Inquisitors believed in a mutable, hence imperfect, God, who had proved his imperfection by changing his mind.

The Jews could therefore function as symbols of obstinacy or, alternatively, of the divine attribute of immutability, their own changelessness merely a reflection of divine stasis. At the same time, one sees a different kind of Jew in Montesquieu's writing, a malleable Jew whose characteristics are a function of historical circumstances. Accordingly, Montesquieu qualified Usbek's identification of the Jews as eternal merchants by historicizing their economic situation. In *De l'esprit des lois* he accepted the claim of the first-century Jewish chronicler Flavius Josephus that "his nation" was "uniquely occupied with agriculture" prior to the time of Solomon and that it was "only by chance that the Jews became traders on the Red Sea." In the Middle Ages, Montesquieu argued, the Jews had returned to commerce only because the benighted Christian clergy disdained commercial activity as immoral. Eschewed by all reputable people, "Commerce passed to a nation covered with infamy and soon was distinguished only by the most frightful usury, monopolies, the raising of subsidies and all the dishonest means of acquiring money." Christian leaders, Montesquieu insisted, were no better, and only encouraged the Jews to deal in money so that they could "pillage" them "with the same tyranny" that the Jewish lenders exercised toward their debtors.[15]

Just as he explained the "tyranny" of Jewish merchants in historical terms, Montesquieu envisaged an improved Jew, one who transcended the conditions of persecution and rose to a level of moral and philosophical excellence. In fact, he put the idea of perfectibility into the same remonstrance that praised the proverbial immutability of the Jews:

> You live in a century in which natural enlightenment is brighter than it has ever been, in which philosophy has enlightened the minds, where the morality of your Gospel has been the best known, where the respective rights of men towards each other, the empire which one conscience has upon another, is best established. If you then revert to your ancient prejudices . . . you will have to admit that you are incorrigible, incapable of any enlightenment and any instruction.[16]

In this exhordium Montesquieu has imagined a character who would occupy the imagination of many an eighteenth-century French writer: the Philosophical Jew. This figure appreciates other religions insofar as they are conducive to "morality," and as such propagates the "natural religion" that so many philosophes would embrace. According to natural religion, God endowed all humanity with the faculties necessary for just behavior. His will was therefore simple, available to anyone, rather than mysterious and hidden in arcana. Elaborate theologies and rituals were therefore worse than useless; they were unnecessarily divisive and led believers astray from the truly divine path. One sees elements of natural religion more explicitly articulated when the remonstrant asks the Inquisitors to forget their dogma for a moment and "treat us as you would if, having nothing but the weak rays of justice that nature gives us, you had no religion to conduct you and no revelation to enlighten you." The Jews of Montesquieu's day would have said nothing of the sort. There was no room for natural religion in mid-eighteenth-century Judaism, which rested on the belief that God revealed himself via the Bible and the Talmud. But the Philosophical Jew of Montesquieu's imagination was not based on current circumstances. He was an expression of belief in the perfectibility of humanity. Indeed, the gloomiest perspective the Jewish appellant could envisage was that of an "incorrigible" people.

Did Montesquieu believe in human perfectibility or not? An examination of his writings on the Jews, where the evidence is inconclusive, even contradictory, does not supply an easy answer. His well-known emphasis on such factors as climate, geography, and demography in his explanation of diversity in human laws suggests a kind of determinism that runs against the grain of the more optimistic, humanistic tendencies of the Enlightenment. After all, if despotism was normally found in large countries with hot climates, there was presumably little one could do to avoid it. Yet Montesquieu was obviously dissatisfied with a perspective that reduced human beings to their environment and labeled them "incorrigible." The Philosophical Jew was an imaginative, if imaginary, solution to the dilemma: a figure whose fidelity to an ancient religion suggested the proverbially eternal solidity of the Jewish people, but whose appreciation of Enlightenment principles proved the possibility of improvement, in tradition-bound Jews as well as fanatical Christians. One could be a Persian, one could be a Jew, and, just perhaps, one could be a Philosophical Jew.

THE MARQUIS D'ARGENS'S PHILOSOPHICAL JEWS

If Montesquieu sketched the rough outlines of the Philosophical Jew, the marquis d'Argens filled in the details. Taking his cue from the success of the *Lettres persanes,* d'Argens penned a multivolume epistolary novel entitled *Lettres juives*. Although unknown today except to a few specialists, the prolific d'Argens was enormously popular in his day and was best known for this novel. He began publishing the letters in serial form, two per week, in December 1735. Twenty months, 180 letters, and over 350,000 words later, he had completed his monumental work. Meanwhile, his publisher had begun selling the letters in volumes of 30 and by the end of 1737 had produced six volumes in octavo. By the end of 1739 at least ten editions, most of them pirated, had been published in French, and by 1777 this number had increased to at least seventeen. Numerous translations of the novel also appeared in English, German, and Dutch.[17] According to d'Argens's agent, the authorized publisher printed twenty-one hundred copies of volume 5 in 1737.[18] If that number is accurate and representative of the typical print run, then within forty years more than two hundred thousand volumes of the *Lettres* would have circulated in France alone.

While these numbers are speculative, corroborating evidence attests to the huge popular—if mixed critical—success of the epistolary novel. In February 1737 d'Argens reported that Laurent François Prault, a publisher who had printed works by Voltaire, was trying to lure him away from his current publisher.[19] Voltaire, who repeatedly addressed d'Argens as "my dear Isaac" after the protagonist of the novel and who expressed the most glowing admiration for the *Lettres,* informed d'Argens that the *Lettres* were making a "devil of a noise" in Alsace, Lorraine, and Champagne and that counterfeit editions from Germany were crossing the border in Strasbourg.[20] Abbé Prévost complimented the author by "placing his work at the level of those ingenious productions that perhaps distinguish our century more than do the dense and serious books."[21] According to a courtier to Frederick the Great, it was the *Lettres juives* that sparked the Prussian king's interest in d'Argens, who would indeed live at his court from 1742 until 1768.[22] Not everyone was pleased with the novel. The Jesuit *Journal de Trévoux* unsurprisingly objected to its anticlerical character, and one anonymous author was even moved to write a three-volume refutation of many of its claims.[23] Yet the very controversy excited by the *Lettres* attests to its importance to contemporaries.

As in Montesquieu's anthology, the "Jewish letters" were ostensibly authentic letters merely "translated" from their original language—in this case Hebrew—into French. The correspondents were three *philosophes hébreux:* Aaron Monceca, a Jew from Constantinople traveling in Europe; Jacob Brito, a Genoese Jew; and Isaac Onis, the rabbi of Constantinople. Like Usbek and Rica, these men comment on what they see in their travels, but they also engage in long digressions on every conceivable subject, from religion to political philosophy to the latest Parisian fashions. As in the *Lettres persanes* and other epistolary works involving "exotic" or non-European commentators, the *Lettres juives* afforded an unusual perspective on European values, manners, and customs. It employed what Tzvetan Todorov calls "the device of defamiliarization," thus forcing the reader to reconsider what she or he had previously taken for granted.[24] D'Argens's Jews, like Uzbek and Rica, could therefore look at the Christians, or "Nazareans," as unusual, strange, or bizarre people, and the reader, by identifying with them, could adopt that perspective as well. Moreover, as in *Lettres persanes,* the Jews provided a convenient means of attacking the intolerance of which they are the most easily recognizable victims. Accordingly, the word *Inquisition* and its variants occur sixty-times times in the *Lettres juives,* and though the protagonists escape persecution, the figure of the Jew is accordingly often identical with the *burned* Jew.[25]

The principal theme of the novel, however, is that of human change. Like Montesquieu, d'Argens wondered whether and under what circumstances human beings could or should change. He explicitly questioned the geographic determinism that Montesquieu seemed at times to espouse. As travelers capable of comparing the morals of people in different climates and geographic circumstances, his Jewish characters were able to judge Montesquieu's ideas with authority. Thus Isaac instructs Aaron, "When one examines men in general, one notices many resemblances among them. The difference in climate does not change anything in hearts."[26]

The autonomy of hearts, if not of minds, and their ability to change are arguably the most important themes in the *Lettres juives*. The thematic oppositions between stasis and change, immutability and mutability, stubbornness and flexibility, bigotry and open-mindedness run throughout the novel. As early as the second letter Aaron discusses the ever-changing French fashions, which include both sartorial and religious fads. He writes, "Jansenism reigns today: perhaps tomorrow will be the end of its reign," then asks Isaac rhetorically what he thinks of "a religion subject to change." He answers his own question, using the charged theological language of immutability, "Stability and *immutability* are the marks of truth," and complains that Christians "constantly reproach us our stubbornness [*entêtement*] and our inflexibility" when they should recognize these as religious virtues.[27]

Jacob makes an even stronger and more explicit case in favor of Jewish stubbornness. In a letter to Aaron he asks, "What [other people] could have resisted the persecutions that we have endured without succumbing to the ills that we have suffered?" He proudly declares that "nothing has been able to shake our resolution," and he laments that the "the Nazareans, always accustomed to blame even our most praiseworthy actions, give the name stubbornness [*entêtement*] to our constancy, instead of rendering justice to our patience and our firmness [*fermeté*]." He goes on to ask "why what is known among them as grandeur of the soul and fidelity to Heaven becomes obstinacy [*obstination*] and obduracy [*endurcissement*] among us."[28]

Elsewhere, however, the virtue of religious stasis is called into question. Indeed, the entire narrative of the *Lettres juives* centers around a religious conversion, namely, Isaac's conversion from rabbinical orthodoxy to the Jewish heresy of Karaism. The Karaites were Jews who believed that the divine word inhered in the Bible alone. They consequently rejected the Talmud as a merely human addition to and distortion of an already perfect code. This dissenting sect, on the margins of an already marginal group—there were no Karaites in France—would attract an extraordinary degree of attention from eighteenth-century French writers who were concerned with the Jews and who saw Karaism as a form of natural religion.

Initially the novel betrays no doubts about the perfection of rabbinical Judaism, but after some increasingly bold questions by Aaron about the wisdom of the Talmud and of the rabbis who interpreted it, Isaac begins to reveal his own doubts. Finally he writes of his conviction that the Talmud is a "heap of chimeras and superstitions," a "monstrous work" filled with "absurdities" and "lies," "ridiculous errors," "impostures," "blasphemy," "bizarre *rêveries,*" and prescriptions for "ridiculous ceremonies." He testifies to the superiority of Karaite arguments, which silenced him during an ecumenical council designed to reunite Karaites and "rabbinists." Most convincing was the Karaite argument that the Talmud portrays God as imperfect, as susceptible "to blushing and becoming furious; subject to all the passions, to hatred, despair and repentance." Anyone with such a conception of God "can neither serve nor obey him." The Talmud, Isaac now believes, is filled with "ideas that correspond so little to those we should have of the All Powerful." It "departs in every way from the original simplicity of our religion," which is embodied in "the writings of Moses and the ancient prophets" and conforms to "natural enlightenment" *(lumierre naturelle).*[29]

Ironically, Isaac's Karaism represents both radical change and radical hostility toward innovation. It embodies a dialectical synthesis of stasis and change, stubbornness and flexibility. As a *return* to an imagined original purity, it indicates both a dramatic personal transformation and a stubborn insistence on tradition. Change is only justified insofar as it repudiates and thus corrects a previous, unauthorized change. Still, d'Argens affirmed that moral reform was possible, and the conversion of Isaac proved his point. As with Montesquieu, then, the figure of the Philosophical Jew augured well for the future of humanity.

VOLTAIRE'S OBSESSION

Voltaire was obsessed with the Jews. There is no other way of putting it. He wrote the word *Jew, Jews,* or *Jewish* on average nearly once a week during his very long adult life. It is therefore not surprising that commentators, then and since, should have argued about his opinion of the Jews.[30] It did not help matters that Voltaire sometimes defended Jews passionately and at other times denounced them vehemently. Yet debates about whether Voltaire was an anti-Semite or philo-Semite—or, less anachronistically, a Judeophobe or Judeophile—are beside the point, not only because it is easy to line up apparently friendly or hostile statements to make one case or its opposite but also because any answer to the question would tell us little about Voltaire or the Enlightenment in which he participated. We can applaud Voltaire for his tolerance or condemn him for his intolerance, but applause and condemnation scarcely constitute historical analysis. More interesting, though scarcely considered in the scholarly literature, are the questions of why Voltaire wrote so much about the Jews and how they functioned in his thinking.

Voltaire's obsession with the Jews was frequently inseparable from his obsession with *l'infâme,* the fanaticism that the philosophe saw above all in the Catholic Church. As victims of that fanaticism, the Jews were living (or dead) indictments of the church. Thus Voltaire railed against the Crusaders who, "believing that they were defending Jesus Christ, imagined it necessary to exterminate all the Jews they encountered." He fulminated against the "ridiculous ignorance" of Christians who believed that Jews desecrated hosts, and he denounced the Catholic monarchs for expelling the Jews from Spain.[31] Like Montesquieu and d'Argens, he frequently targeted the Inquisition. The scene of an auto-da-fé in *Candide,* in which Jews as well as Christians suspected of heresy are to be burned, is only the most famous of Voltaire's references to burning Jews.[32] Voltaire even borrowed Montesquieu's conceit of drafting a remonstrance from an imaginary Jew, in this case in the form of a "Sermon of Rabbi Akib," to protest the Inquisition's barbaric persecution of his coreligionists.[33]

If Voltaire associated the Jews with intolerance and fanaticism, however, that association was unstable. He was equally capable of portraying Jews as fanatics themselves as he was of describing them as victims of fanaticism. Thus in the *Dictionnaire philosophique* the biblical Jews were "the most detestable people on earth" who "usurped . . . a little country with the most odious rapine and the most detestable cruelty that history has ever recorded" and who "pitilessly butchered all the inhabitants" of a land "to which they had no more right than they do to Paris or London."[34] This sort of interpretation of the Old Testament, which Christians as well as Jews regarded as sacred, has prompted Peter Gay to argue that "Voltaire struck at the Jews to strike at the Christians." The defamation of biblical figures, whom Christians were obliged to see as their spiritual ancestors, accordingly figured into the rhetorical suggestion that "the paternity of Christianity was only one more argument against it."[35]

This interpretation is persuasive insofar as Voltaire's representations of biblical Jews are concerned, but it does not explain his repeated denunciations of the Talmud and post-Talmudic rabbinical writings, which the church opposed with equal vehemence. Why, for example, was it necessary to attack the "ridiculous fables of the Talmud" or the "rabbinical *rêveries*" of its authors and commentators?[36] One might adapt Gay's claim by suggesting that here, as well, Voltaire was using the Jews to attack Christians. After all, the flawed reasoning he attributed to rabbis was precisely what he deplored in Christian theologians as well. Perhaps he was simply locating "Jesuitical" thinking in the *docteurs juifs* as a way of highlighting the embarrassing similarities between the reasoning patterns of rabbis and priests.

The elaborate dogmatic and ritualistic apparatus of both Jews and Catholics was anathema to Voltaire's stripped-down natural religion. His theology, which permeates his writings, is most succinctly laid out in his "Sermon des cinquante," a fictional account of "fifty educated, pious and reasonable persons" who, without priests, assemble weekly and pray to God to "preserve in our hearts . . . your pure religion" and to "remove from us all superstition." The prayer continues, "If anyone insults you with unworthy sacrifices, abolish those infamous mysteries; if anyone dishonors the Divinity with absurd fables, may those fables perish forever." Finally, the *cinquante* pray, on behalf of "the prince and the magistrate[s]," "may they live and die adoring only one God, who rewards the good and punishes the wicked, a God who could neither be born nor die, nor have associates, but who in this world has too many rebellious children."[37]

It is therefore plausible that in some cases Voltaire assimilated priests to rabbis in order to discredit their theology. Elsewhere, however, he drew affinities between Judaism and Christianity without disparaging the former and in order to emphasize the filial debt owed by Christians to Jews. Here the parentage of Christianity was not an argument against it but a reminder of the need to treat one's parents with respect. Indeed, Voltaire repeatedly used familial language to articulate the sense of a special Christian obligation toward Jews. He had written in his *Notebooks,* "When I see Christians cursing Jews, methinks I see children beating their fathers." This theme recurred in his published works. Thus Rabbi Akib rails at the Inquisitors, "Unnatural children *[Enfants dénaturés],* we are your fathers"; switching gender, he echoes the judgment of Montesquieu's Usbek, "A respectable and unhappy mother has had two daughters, and these daughters have chased her from her house." In *La Bible enfin expliquée* a more complex mother-daughter relationship is established in which Judaism is "an unfortunate mother, respected and oppressed by her two daughters."[38]

Elsewhere Voltaire used family metaphors to assimilate Jews and Christians as children of God and hence "brothers." His "Traité sur la tolérance" contained the rhetorical question, cast in language strikingly similar to that of advocates of legal reform for the Jews toward the end of the century, "Are we not all children of the same father, and creatures of the same God?" and drew a moral imperative from the implied answer, "We must see all men as our brothers."[39] When responding to Abbé Guénée, who had posed as "Six Jews" to protest Voltaire's attack on the Old Testament and the biblical Jews, Voltaire maintained the pretense of a Christian-Jewish *disputatio*. Yet he ended his retort with a call for rapprochement, writing, "The whole world is but a family, men are brothers; brothers sometimes quarrel; but the good-hearted are easily reconciled."[40] That Jews could be both the fathers and brothers of Christians was the message of Rabbi Akib, who wished to see his oppressor "stop . . . persecuting, exterminating those who as men are their brothers, and who as Jews are their fathers."[41]

By insisting that Christians regard Jews as members of their own family, Voltaire was emphasizing the value of fidelity. This virtue, so well known to students of eighteenth-century literature, was not merely useful for stimulating pathos in the sympathetic reader. For Voltaire it was intimately connected to the problem of human change. Again, as for Montesquieu and d'Argens, whether and under what conditions human beings could change, and whether and under what conditions they ought to change were questions that continually preoccupied Voltaire. And again, the proverbially changeless Jews provided ideal material for the relevant thought experiments.

Voltaire did not uniformly oppose what he viewed as the tendency of Jews to remain as they were. In *La Henriade,* the tragedy that made his reputation in 1714, he portrayed the Jewish victims of the Inquisition as heroes for their fidelity to their forebears, and thus for exhibiting precisely the virtue he so often denounced Christians for lacking:

In Madrid, in Lisbon, [the Inquisitor] lights his fires,
The solemn bonfires to which the unhappy Jews
Are sent every year, in pomp, by the priests,
For not having left the law of their ancestors.[42]

Elsewhere he provided solid arguments for the Jews' proverbial obstinacy. He noted in his "Lettres sur Rabelais" that the Jews "claim that
the law of Moses was given to them for eternity; that it is impossible for
God to have changed, to have perjured himself." In his "Questions de
Zapata," a theologian asks his colleagues at the University of Sala-
manca, "How am I supposed to prove that the Jews, whom we burn by
the hundreds, were for four thousand years the favored people of God?"
Again belief in an immutable God—a cornerstone of Voltaire's natural
religion—appears superior to the worship of a fickle Deity. Finally, in
his *Dictionnaire philosophique* he opposed Pascal's indignation at the
Jews' refusal to convert by writing positively of their attempt "to justify . . . their obstinacy [*obstination*]." He suggested that given the
"state of oppression under which the Jewish people suffered, and after
all the promises that the eternal had so often made to them, they could
have hoped for the arrival of a conquering and liberating messiah." Since
Jesus neither conquered the Roman oppressors nor freed the Jews, it was
"understandable" that they did not see him as their Savior.[43]

In other places, Voltaire suggested that the reluctance of Jews to
change their religion was less a matter of virtuous fidelity, or theological
consistency, than a feature they had in common with all other human
beings: a tendency to remain in the religious community into which one
was born. In his poem "On Natural Religion," the reader learns, "It is
by one's nurse that one is a Jew or pagan, faithful [Christian] or Muslim." Using this logic Rabbi Akib could thus ask, in the aftermath of an
auto-da-fé, "What was [the Jews'] crime? Nothing other than having
been born. Their parents begot them in the religion that their forefathers
had professed for 5000 years."[44]

Despite the imaginary rabbi's compelling defense of his coreligionists,
Voltaire was clearly not satisfied with the prospect of the Jews remaining as he believed them to be. The very logic that made religion into a
fact of birth, or a quality imbibed with the milk of one's "nurse," guaranteed that any religion's defects would affect its adherents into the in-
definite future. As for Judaism, Voltaire was thoroughgoing in his critique. He not only denounced the Talmud as a font of superstition but
also rejected the Hebrew Bible as an immoral book, in part because it
praised human beings who engaged in acts of cruelty but above all because it portrayed God as unjust. According to his natural religion, God
had to be just, and any book depicting him otherwise was necessarily
wrong. Thus if d'Argens furnished a solution to Judaism's reputed flaws
in Karaism, Voltaire provided no such option.

Still, Voltaire repeatedly expressed the hope that the Jews would improve. Arthur Hertzberg has asserted that Voltaire saw the Jews as incorrigible due to their "inborn character."[45] If he doubted the ability of Jews to improve, however, this was only because he was never fully convinced of the ability of human beings in general to improve. Witness the famous scene in *Candide* in which the hero asks Martin, a Manichean, whether he believes "that men have always massacred each other as they do today, that they have always been deceitful, fraudulent, treacherous, ungrateful, thieving, weak, fickle, cowardly, envious, self-indulgent, drunk, greedy, ambitious, sanguinary, libelous, debauched, fanatical, hypocritical and stupid." Martin replies, "Do you believe . . . that hawks have always eaten pigeons when they could find them?" and when Candide answers in the affirmative, Martin clinches the argument with the rhetorical question, "If hawks have always had the same character, why do you think men would have changed theirs?"[46]

In his other writings, however, particularly in his historical work, Voltaire displayed the conviction that human beings could and did change according to the circumstances in which they found themselves. With respect to the Jews, he frequently indulged in the stereotypical characterization of them as greedy and dishonest, as all readers of *Candide* know.[47] Elsewhere, however, he explained how Jews had become associated with moneylending. Like Montesquieu, he sought the causes of Jewish moneylending in the historical circumstances of the Middle Ages. In his *Dictionnaire philosophique,* he wrote, "Commerce, a profession long disdained by the majority of the peoples of Europe, was [the Jews'] only resource during those barbaric centuries; and as they necessarily enriched themselves through it, they were called infamous usurers."[48] In his *Histoire générale,* he maintained that the Jews of Spain had become dominant in business prior to their expulsion in 1492 because the Christians disdained commerce and devoted themselves exclusively to the military arts, and because no other means of livelihood was open to them. Similarly, he argued in the same work, Jews had taken over commerce in Poland because the nobles, who lived in "proud idleness," disdained it.[49]

With respect to the other reproaches Voltaire leveled at the Jews—their alleged barbarism, ignorance, fanaticism, and superstition—did he consider these traits to be innate? If so, then his "Chrétien contre six juifs" makes no sense. In that polemic he distinguished dramatically between the barbarity of Jews *and* Christians of past ages and their relatively civilized behavior in modern times. He wrote, "Our fathers were

wild boars, bears, until the sixteenth century; then we combined the gri-
maces of apes with the snouts of wild boars; finally we became men, and
likable men." Similarly, he addressed the "six Jews": You, *messieurs,* you
were once the most detestable and the stupidest lynx that ever sullied the
face of the earth. Today you live peaceably in Rome, Leghorn, London,
Amsterdam." Consequently, he proposed, "Let us forget our past idio-
cies and abominations."[50]

Even in past ages Voltaire identified a number of Jews whom he considered worthy. In his "Lettres sur Rabelais" he praised several medieval rabbis, including Ibn Ezra and Maimonides. He observed that from
the thirteenth to the sixteenth century "the Jews had intelligible, and
consequently dangerous books" (a Voltairean compliment) and that
church leaders burned them precisely because they feared the power
they had to engender doubt in the minds of Christian readers. Closer to
his own day, he praised the seventeenth-century Dutch rabbi Orobio as
"profound without being obscure, well-read, a man with a pleasant personality and an extreme *politesse.*" He extended considerable praise to
Orobio's Dutch contemporary, Spinoza, though he opposed what he
took to be that philosopher's atheism. His favorite Jewish thinker was
Uriel Acosta, who like Spinoza was excommunicated as a heretic by the
Jewish community of Amsterdam, but whose belief in God was never in
doubt. Acosta "professe[d] to be neither Jewish, nor Christian, nor Mohammedan, but an adorer of God,"[51] and in this respect he corresponded to Voltaire's ideal. He was a practitioner of natural religion.

In his own lifetime Voltaire had a celebrated exchange with another
Dutch Jew, Isaac Pinto. In response to Voltaire's attacks on the biblical
Jews, Pinto had published a defense of their beliefs and conduct.[52] Voltaire replied with a letter in which he apologized for the "violent and unjust" passages to which Pinto had objected. Yet he went on to write, "I
will tell you with the same honesty that many people cannot stand your
laws, your books, or your superstitions; they say that your nation has always done much harm to itself, as well as to the human race. If you are
a *philosophe,* as you appear to be, you think as those gentlemen do, but
you do not say so." He added, "Remain a Jew, since you are one," yet
urged Pinto, "but be a *philosophe.*"[53] This is a cryptic imperative, since
Voltaire had already acknowledged that Pinto "appeared" to be a
philosophe. Either Voltaire thought that appearances were deceiving,
and that Pinto was only *potentially* a philosophe, or he was simply urging Pinto to take the brave step that Acosta had taken, that of "coming
out" as a practitioner of natural religion. In either case he seems to have

seen in Pinto living proof that Jews, like other people, could cast off their superstitions and depart radically from the condition of their contemporaries and their forebears. If Montesquieu and d'Argens had described imaginary Philosophical Jews, Voltaire invested a real one, at least potentially, with the qualities he hoped all Jews would adopt.

Ultimately Voltaire gave a contradictory account of the Jews. He praised them for their fidelity to an ancient tradition, at the same time characterized such constancy as merely a feature of human nature, and nevertheless sought a radical change in their beliefs and behavior, which he seems to have considered them capable of achieving. The very inconsistency of this message is revealing, for it exposes a larger inconsistency in Voltaire's thinking, which also helps to explain his continuous return to the Jews. Like Montesquieu, whose belief in the importance of geography and climate in human activity conflicted with his belief in human perfectibility, Voltaire switched nervously between a comforting narrative of progress and a nagging suspicion that human beings were the eternal hawks of Martin's description. Moreover, expressions of pessimism and indeed despair about the prospects of human improvement were more frequent in Voltaire's writing than they were in the work of Montesquieu or, arguably, that of any other philosophe. At the same time and, in my view, not coincidentally, he wrote more about the Jews than any other philosophe, an impressive feat given the popularity of the subject in the age of the Enlightenment. Indeed, the tendency toward extreme pessimism relieved periodically by renewed faith in progress helps to explain Voltaire's extraordinary attraction to the Jews as a matter of philosophical reflection. The Jews provided the best test for the hypothesis of human perfectibility, for if the most notoriously inflexible of people could change, then, a fortiori, anyone could change. The discovery of their flexibility thus heralded the malleability of all humanity. Voltaire therefore surveyed history, his imagination, and his contemporaries for evidence of that eighteenth-century marvel: the improvable Jew. Yet if a few historical figures, the fictional Rabbi Akib, and the real Isaac Pinto were evidence that such a phenomenon existed, Voltaire's pessimism regarding the Jews, along with humanity in general, was sufficiently persistent as to require a repetition, even an obsessive repetition, of the thought experiment. This oscillation between confidence and doubt over the prospects of human perfectibility would fuel the interest in the Jewish question for many French writers and political actors in the succeeding decades, but in Voltaire one sees the phenomenon in its most unalloyed form.

ROUSSEAU'S REFLECTIONS ON JEWS AND OTHER NATIONS

Voltaire's famous rival, Rousseau, also showed an interest in the Jews. Though he did not write nearly as prolifically about them as did Voltaire, he directed his attention to the Jews on numerous occasions and in some of his most prominent works. What is striking about Rousseau's depictions is that they were often in accord with those of Voltaire on the same subject, despite the great theoretical differences that separated the two philosophes. Like Voltaire (and Montesquieu), Rousseau repeatedly depicted the Jews as wealthy, though he also shared Voltaire's belief that much Christian persecution was motivated by envy and greed. He went out of his way to condemn this persecution, which he, like his fellow Enlightenment authors, abbreviated in the image of the Inquisition carrying out an auto-da-fé. For Rousseau the Jews of his day were "unhappy" *(malheureux)* and fearful of Christians, and if the former dissembled before the latter, this was because the intellectual climate made it impossible for Jews to air their true grievances.[54]

Rousseau also resembled Voltaire in depicting the Jews of the Old Testament as intolerant to the point of justifying the destruction of their neighbors and confiscation of their territory, and he saw in their fanaticism the seeds of subsequent wars of religion. At the same time, he justified their "obstinacy," and in his *Social Contract* even used the verb *s'obstiner* to describe their refusal to recognize the gods of their Babylonian and Assyrian conquerors, yet he was careful to note that there was no logical reason for them to abandon their original beliefs. Elsewhere he suggested that their religion was every bit as rational as that of the Christians who sought to convert them, and though Voltaire implied that Judaism was as *irrational* as Christianity, the two philosophes shared the habit of discussing the Jews as a means of thinking about natural religion. Rousseau even compared his own observations about the Jews' natural reasons for embracing their religion with the essential message of Voltaire's "Sermon des cinquante."[55]

Nevertheless, Rousseau clearly departed from Voltaire in his assessment of Moses and the laws he proclaimed to the Israelites. Whereas Voltaire regarded Moses (along with other Old Testament heroes) as morally suspect, Rousseau lavished the biblical legislator with praise. His judgment comes across most vividly in his *Considerations on the Government of Poland,* where he remarked that Moses "executed the astonishing enterprise of instituting into the body of a nation a swarm of miserable refugees, without arts, without arms, without talent, without virtue, without courage, and who, not having a single inch of land, made up a foreign band on the face of the earth." Rousseau added that "Moses dared to make a free people out of this errant and servile gang" and "gave them that durable institution [i.e., the law], which withstood the force of time, of fate and of conquerors, which five thousand years [*sic*] could neither destroy nor even alter, and which survives still today in all its power." The author did not deny, as Jewish apologists would repeatedly do, that this law precluded fraternal relations between Jews and Gentiles. For Rousseau, however, this was precisely the strength of the legislator's gift. Thus, he wrote, "To prevent his people from melting among foreign peoples, [Moses] gave them morals and customs that were incompatible with those of the other nations." Rousseau specified, explaining that Moses "overwhelmed them with specific rituals and ceremonies; he troubled them in a thousand ways . . . to make them eternal strangers among other men." Thus "all the links of fraternity that he placed among the members of his Republic were so many barriers keeping them separated from their neighbors and preventing them from mixing with them." Rousseau concluded, "It is in this way that this singular nation, so often subjugated, so often dispersed, and apparently destroyed, but forever idolizing its law [*toujours idolâtre de sa règle*], has nevertheless preserved itself to our days . . . and that its morals, its laws and its rituals survive and will last as long as the world, despite the hatred and persecution of the rest of the human race."[56]

This, of course, is the most uncompromising image of the Eternal Jew, the legalistic, ritual-bound relic of antiquity weathering the course of human history while remaining excluded from it. Indeed, it is plausible that Rousseau's failure, unusual among the philosophes, to consider the opposite proposition—that is, that the Jews were malleable, like other specimens of humanity—contributed to his relative silence on the Jewish question. In any event, Rousseau's assessment of Moses and the Jews was significant. That he meant it as a compliment both to Moses and to his steadfast descendants matters little when one considers the statement's implications for any attempts to improve the Jews' condition by integrating them into the societies in the midst of which they lived. Thus if other Enlightenment authors invented or discovered Philosophical Jews who heralded the miraculous transformation of an otherwise headstrong people, Rousseau's Philosophical Jew, the great legislator Moses, promised precisely the opposite, namely, the unabated stasis of the Jews and their eternal separation from the human world. More seriously still, Rousseau's postulate conflicted with his more famous proposition, elaborated in his *Social Contract,* that a nation of free people had to be indivisible.[57] In fact, it was precisely these two beliefs, in the indivisibility of sovereignty and the eternal separateness of the Jewish "nation," that would define the "Jewish question" as it emerged later in the century. These opposing propositions constituted the conundrum of the Jews as that republican monstrosity: a "nation within the nation." In retrospect it is ironic that Rousseau, fond as he was of challenging paradoxes, did not attempt to resolve this one. Yet the historically significant fact is that this paradox remained, in print, in speech, and in the minds of those who used the Jews to think about citizenship and nationhood.

THE JEW AND THE QUEST
FOR ENCYCLOPEDIC KNOWLEDGE

An obvious place to look for clues into the Enlightenment's relation to the Jews is the *Encyclopédie,* yet this source has been particularly neglected in the many scholarly treatments of that relationship. No doubt this neglect stems from the very enormity and diversity of the *Encyclopédie,* a work produced by at least 140 contributors from all walks of life and all manner of philosophical inclination.[58] Paradoxically, however, this combination of sheer volume and multiplicity of opinions renders the *Encyclopédie* an ideal source for any investigation into representations of Jews by French writers toward the middle of the eighteenth century. Precisely because it is both so voluminous and so variegated, it enables one to chart the range of possible depictions in a way that the oeuvre of any single author could not.

The words *juif, juifs, juive,* and *juives* occur 2,360 times in the *Encyclopédie,* as its ARTFL computerized version reveals. On the average, some variant of the French word for "Jew" or "Jewish" appears on roughly every seven and a half pages of the 18,000-page work. This is to say nothing of references to the "Hebrews" and their language (1,516), or to "Israelites" (224). By comparison, references to English people and things reach only a slightly higher total (2,598), and instances of the terms *basque* and *basques* number a mere 94. As with French writers more generally, then, the encyclopedists showed an interest in the Jews that far exceeded their numbers and degree of power.

The meaning of all these references is another matter. On first glance it appears arbitrary. The 2,360 hits are spread out among 869 articles. And while one would expect to find references to Jews in articles entitled

"Bible," "Synagogue," "Rabbin," and, of course, "Juif," they also occur in the articles "Puberté," "Verbe," "Costume," and "Menstruel."
Why, in an article on shoes, was it necessary to report that "the Jews [of
antiquity] also had shoes" and that "they were fastened to the feet by a
band"?[59] Similarly, it seems superfluous in an article on cymbals to have
noted that "the Jews also had cymbals."[60] Recourse to the word *aussi*
(also), frequently taken in this context, suggests a purely additive approach to the study of the Jews. I will return to this puzzle later but
would first like to discuss those elements of the encyclopedists' treatment of the Jews that most clearly reveal discernible patterns.

First, as with the other philosophes, Jews frequently signified suffering, and in particular wrongful suffering for one's religious beliefs.
Significantly, the first sentence in the article "Juif," by the Chevalier de
Jaucourt, quotes Usbek's claim in *Les lettres persanes* that the Jewish religion is "a mother of two daughters, who have covered her with a thousand plagues." The author continued with references to "bad treatment" and "opprobrium and vexations" and marveled at the fact that
despite "the horrors that the Jews have suffered," first under the Romans
and later "in all the Christian states," "this people still subsists." In a
passage lifted from Voltaire, Jaucourt presented the tableau that writers
expressing sympathy for the Jews would repeat, in one form or another,
for decades: "Reduced to running from land to land, from sea to sea, to
earn their living, everywhere declared ineligible to possess real estate or
to work at any profession, they found themselves obligated to disperse
from place to place, and never to be able to establish themselves in any
country." Describing France in the "barbarous centuries" of the Middle
Ages, he noted that Jews were "put in prison, pilloried, sold, accused of
magic, of sacrificing children, of poisoning the fountains" and were
"chased from the kingdom," only to be recalled subsequently by greedy
Christian leaders "on account of [their] money" and again subjected to
violent and humiliating treatment. [61]

Jaucourt returned to the persecution of the Jews repeatedly in his
many contributions to the *Encyclopédie*. In his article on the Crusades,
he railed against the "insane and impious" fanatics who "believed that
they were avenging the death of Jesus Christ by slaughtering the descendants of those who had crucified him." His article on the Inquisition
was, not surprisingly, similarly indignant. Yet his descriptions of anti-
Jewish persecution appeared in less obvious places as well. In "Lois" he
gave as examples of barbaric laws those the Visigoths instituted against
the Jews. In an article on the city of Metz he went out of his way to note

that until recently the Jews residing there had been required to "wear yellow hats to distinguish themselves as odious," a practice he saw as evidence "of the barbarity of our forebears." In his 150-word article on the Bohemian city of Egra, he reported that "in 1350 all the Jews there were cruelly exterminated," adding, "Unhappy nation with whom all the countries of Europe have pitilessly played!"[62]

In addition to sharing the tendency of other philosophes to portray the Jews as victims of religious fanaticism, Jaucourt likewise exhibited an aversion to the Talmud and most of the rabbis who interpreted its content. In an article on the Talmud, Jaucourt derided his subject as containing "a thousand *rêveries* to which [the rabbis] attributed a celestial origin." In an article on "oral law," he wrote that the "traditions which the Jews so greatly respect" are "but the product of the fertile inventiveness of the Talmudists, and offer the mind nothing but a heap of trifles, fables and absurdities." Writing on the Targum, the Chaldean paraphrase of the Bible, he deplored its "barbarous style" and "talmudic fables," and in a treatment of the Pharisees he denounced their introduction of "impertinent and ridiculous" traditions into the Jewish religion.[63]

Jaucourt was not alone among the encyclopedists in denouncing the Talmud and the rabbis. Abbé Edme-François Mallet scorned the "fables and *rêveries*" of the oral law and rebuked the "Talmudists, whose belief is nothing but a ridiculous heap of superstitions." Paul-Joseph Barthez mocked the rabbinical claim that fauns and satyrs came into existence when God, in a haste to complete his work before the Sabbath, mixed up the body parts of various creatures; and numerous anonymous articles, including one entitled "Rabbin," reinforced the impression that the "Jewish doctors" had produced little more than "*rêveries,*" "fables," "ridiculous stories," "superstitions," and "extravagance." Denis Diderot, in his massive article (more than thirty thousand words) "Philosophy of the Jews," expressed an equally negative opinion of the "zeal for tradition" that the Pharisees bequeathed to their rabbinical followers. As with Voltaire, the encyclopedists found exceptional rabbis who could be regarded as rational. Jaucourt praised Maimonides precisely because he had produced a summary of Talmudic law that left out "the embellishments, disputes, fables and other impertinences." Mallet praised one medieval rabbi for a digest of Talmudic decisions that did not linger over "useless questions and disputes," and another for an "excellent Jewish book" that defended the Jewish religion against attacks by Christians.[64] These were exceptions, however, that seemed to prove the rule of rabbinical incompetence.

By contrast, the encyclopedists typically depicted the Old Testament as an edifying book, the Jews of antiquity as virtuous and worthy of imitation, and, above all, Moses (and/or God) as a wise legislator. Diderot saw the original religion of the Jews as a natural religion. He lavished praise on the Bible and its "author," Moses: "What a historian! What a legislator! What a philosopher! What a poet! What a man!" The anonymous author of the article "Judaïsme" praised the Bible as a "complete system of Judaism." Jaucourt viewed the Jews' "firm attachment to the law of Moses" as "remarkable" and saw in that law the same "precepts of morality that the natural enlightenment of reason" would reveal to those "deprived of revelation."[65]

Accordingly, the *Encyclopédie* repeatedly lauds the Karaites—there are sixty-nine direct references to the dissenting splinter group—who wisely clung to their perfect Law and rejected the corrupting innovations of the Talmud and its commentaries. As for d'Argens, the Karaites functioned as a foil for the superstitious, hairsplitting, Talmud-bound "rabbinites." Diderot held them in the highest esteem. He praised their withering question, directed always against the rabbis, as to what "would have obliged God to write one part of his laws and hide the other [i.e., the Talmud], or to confide it to the memory of men." Such an inconsistency was incompatible with the Karaites' conception of God, which was "a very simple and very pure idea" of an omniscient, omnipotent, and immutable being. Most important, Diderot, as an advocate of natural religion, approved of the Karaites' belief "that souls, in leaving the world, will be rewarded or punished" for their conduct during life. This belief was evidently effective, for Diderot described the Karaites' morals as "very pure" and attributed to them temperance, a modest and simple diet, and great respect for their teachers, who in turn did not charge for their lessons.[66] In an article devoted to the Karaites, Abbé Mallet praised them in similar terms and regretted the fact that "the works of the Karaites are little known in Europe, though they, more than those of the rabbis, deserve to be."[67]

The perfection of the Old Testament and the worthiness of the Karaites stood in dramatic contrast to the corruption that the encyclopedists believed to have affected both the majority of Jews and Christendom itself since biblical times. The contributors thus confronted the question of progress and its prospects for the future. In contrast to the picture of halting progress from antiquity to the present that one sees (at least periodically) in Voltaire, the *Encyclopédie* often told a story of idyllic beginnings followed by tragic decline. For example, in an article on "Usury," Faiguet de Villeneuve observed that the Jews of biblical times did not lend to each other at interest because God wished to preserve the state of primitive equality in which they lived by preventing the accumulation of wealth that interest payments would have facilitated. He observed that God had "allotted them a delightful country, and he wanted them to live as veritable brothers, sharing their beautiful patrimony without being able to alienate it, forgiving each other's debts every seven years." Under these circumstances, he wished for lending to be a matter of "benevolence and generosity." Comparing the ancient Hebrews to his own contemporaries, Faiguet proposed that "this people of farmers without ostentation and without indolence, almost without commerce and without lawsuits, was not like us in our indispensable habit of borrowing." The Jews did not have estates or fiefs. Their public offices were not for sale. They did not have colonies, nor did they gamble or go to the theater. In what resembled an ideal republic of Montesquieu or Rousseau, Faiguet described ancient Israel as made up of "modest citizens [*médiocres bourgeois*], who all, or almost all, cultivated a piece of land entailed by law in each family," and who "in a happy and constant middling state [*une heureuse & constante médiocrité*] found themselves equally removed from opulence and misery." "Considering the equality that reigned among the Israelites," he continued, driving home the comparison to his decadent contemporaries, "they had . . . neither rank nor honors to maintain," and "with simpler morals, they . . . took charge of their own domestic cares." When a modest loan was necessary, an Israelite capable of granting it thought nothing of helping his neighbor. Thus the Mosaic prescription furthered "the spirit of unity and fraternity that has never been seen among other peoples." [68]

The juxtaposition of primitive equality and modern decadence, which attacked both the "superstition" of the rabbis and the cruelty of Christians that presumably degraded the Jews so badly that they lost their original mental capacities, was nevertheless not as pessimistic as it might appear at first glance. The memory, however imaginary, of an ideal past suggested that humanity was not doomed to its vices. It served as evidence that human beings were not innately bad but had been made so by historical circumstances. Whether they had the power to reverse these circumstances was a troubling question whose very persistence would fuel interest in the Jews for a long time to come. Yet at least the master narrative of decline suggested the possibility of a return to a Golden Age.

For Jaucourt, there were different reasons for optimism. In his article "Juif," he followed the section on Christian persecution of Jews during the Middle Ages with the assessment, "Since that time, the princes have opened their eyes to their own interests and have treated the Jews with greater moderation." In several countries "it has been felt . . . that one could not do without their help." Tuscany, the Dutch Republic, and England in particular had proved themselves "animated with the noblest principles" and given the Jews "all possible kindnesses." Meanwhile, Jaucourt reported, the fate of Europe had become dependent on its decent treatment of the Jews: "Thus scattered in our day with greater security than they have ever had in all the countries in Europe where commerce reigns, they have become instruments by means of which the most distant nations can converse and correspond with each other." Jaucourt elaborated on the metaphor, writing, "They are like the pegs and nails that one uses in a great building, and which are necessary to join all of its parts."[69]

Perhaps, then, commerce and the civilization it engendered were not so bad after all. In many other articles Jaucourt reinforced the impression that these were happy developments and that they were inextricably bound with the presence of Jews. He praised London as a commercial success story in which "the Jews . . . enjoy a beautiful synagogue." He characterized Leghorn as a commercial paradise in which the Jews "possess a beautiful synagogue and public schools" and see the city "as a new promised land." He depicted Frankfurt as a city in which Calvinists, Catholics, "and even the Jews" were "equally well received" and granted extensive liberties, noting that the municipal authorities tolerated religious minorities "with as much wisdom as profit." He painted a similarly sunny picture of Salonica and the cities of Poland, and when writing about Metz, he observed that the admission of Jews "has produced great advantages for the country."[70]

Depending on what part of the *Encyclopédie* one read, civilization was a curse that had erased the natural goodness of humanity or a means of bringing diverse people together for their common interest. This should not be surprising, since these two positions corresponded to the great and never-finished Enlightenment debate over the merits and defects of civilization, which moreover corresponded to two master narratives of human history. For Diderot and most of his fellow encyclope-

dists, the Jews functioned in narratives of decline that criticized benighted rabbis but indicted European civilization even more. For Jaucourt, as for Voltaire, who disdained the nostalgia for a primitive past,
barbarism was barbarism and civilization was the cure, not the problem.
Clearly there was a great deal of middle ground between these positions,
and philosophes were eminently capable of shifting or contradicting
their stances on the matter. Yet as ideal types these narratives and the
ideologies that informed them defined much of what the Enlightenment
was about. In each case, moreover, the Jews provided material for reflection on the trajectory of human history. Whether one adopted the nostalgic or the meliorist narrative, the case of the Jews provided a glimmer
of hope for the future. For nostalgic philosophes, there was always the
hope of return to pastoral Israel. For meliorists there was the sober
promise that the Jews would benefit from the very edifice of civilization
of which they were the "pegs and nails," and that non-Jews would likewise benefit. Since the debate on civilization was never to be resolved,
the Jews, who so often figured in depictions of its bounties as well as its
ills, would continue to constitute a question.

For the encyclopedists, then, as for other philosophes, the Jews were
good for thinking about the prospects of perfectibility, though the paths
to this theme sometimes differed. But why were they discussed in other
contexts, when the issue of perfectibility was remote, if not entirely absent? To answer this question, it is helpful to introduce another pair of
themes that informed the work of the encyclopedists and their contemporaries: opacity and transparency. The Enlightenment's praise of transparency and aversion to opacity are well known. Rousseau regarded
transparency, or the ability of personal thoughts and feelings to be
known by others, as a fundamental precondition of morality in general
and civic virtue in particular. He and other adepts in the cult of *sensibilité* contributed to the popularity of effusive expression of emotion, especially through weeping, as evidence of a person's moral excellence. By
contrast, opacity, the ability to hide one's thoughts and feelings, was the
mark of an immoral person, if not a dangerous conspirator.[71] For the encyclopedists the problem of opacity extended to the hidden character of
much knowledge, which they proposed to make visible. Indeed, Diderot
defined the "encyclopedia" in terms of its goal, which was "to collect all
knowledge that now lies scattered over the face of the earth, to make
known its general structure to the men among whom we live, and to
transmit it to those who will come after us, in order that the labors of
past ages may be useful to the ages to come." This project necessitated

the solving of mysteries, the casting of light on obscurities, and the revelation of secrets. It is not a coincidence that the encyclopedists enlisted the knowledge of craftsmen, whom previous scholars had disdained but who had proverbial access to secret knowledge. The whole point of the *Encyclopédie* was to divulge secrets. Thus Diderot ridiculed those "narrow minds" and "ill-formed souls" who believed that a "well-executed encyclopedia . . . should only take the form of a huge manuscript that would be carefully locked up in the King's library, hidden away from all eyes but his, a state document and not a popular book." He accused such critics of hypocrisy, since they were the same people who "deliver tirades against the impenetrability of the Egyptian sanctuaries," "deplore the loss of the knowledge of the ancients," and "are full of blame for the silence or negligence of ancient authors who have omitted something essential, or who speak so cryptically of many important subjects."[72]

It was not only the Egyptians whom Diderot associated with cryptic knowledge, however. The Jews were similarly mysterious. Indeed, it seems that their proverbial secrecy most attracted Diderot to the study of the Jews, and the drive to unveil their mysteries helps to explain his otherwise puzzling decision to write a twenty-thousand-word article on the Hebrew language, in which he tackled the apparently arid question of whether ancient Hebrew had vowels and punctuation marks. Diderot concluded that the language of the Bible had neither vowels nor punctuation marks, but that both were only added by scholars in the fifth century. He attributed the initial omissions to the "primitive reasoning of those sages of high antiquity, who held as a principle that scholarship was not made for the vulgar, that its avenues had to be closed to the people, the profane, and to foreigners." The sages knew which vowels and punctuation marks were missing from the written text and could supply them orally to their pupils, in the process rendering the otherwise incomprehensible writings intelligible. By making secrecy a feature of the primitive mind, Diderot ran against the grain of the tendency, that he himself had exhibited in his article on Jewish philosophy, to idealize the Jews of the Old Testament. Here he was not blaming the rabbis or the "modern Jews" for the obscurity of their sacred writings. The culprits were the primitives themselves. He wrote, "One cannot ignore that the taste for mystery was that of the savants of earliest ages; it was this that had already partially presided over the invention of sacred hieroglyphics, which forestalled [the development of] writing." He continued, insisting that this "taste for mystery" "has kept the nations for a multitude of centuries in impenetrable darkness and in a profound and universal ignorance, the baneful consequences of which two thousand years of rather continuous work have not yet entirely repaired."[73]

That Diderot was inconsistent in his representation of biblical Jews is less important than the fact that he used them to think about secrecy, that the story of their written culture provided a cautionary tale about the baneful effects of obscurity. Yet if he was not alone among the encyclopedists in his association of the Jews with secrecy, then this common connection also helps to explain why the Jews appear with such frequency in the *Encyclopédie*. It was the Jews' status as the secretive people par excellence that fueled the need for those who investigated them to expose everything about them, all the way down to their cymbals and their shoes.

KNOWING AND CONVERTING

This survey of representations suggests that there was no single way of portraying Jews in the French Enlightenment. On the contrary, the meanings attached to Jews were plural, fluctuating, and often contradictory. Jews could represent antiquity and modernity, or both at the same time. They could signify the primitive simplicity of pastoral life or the sophistication of commercial existence, the separatism of an isolated tribe or the links in a cosmopolitan chain. Depending on the author's moral agenda and theological assumptions, implicit or explicit, the characteristics attributed to them could take on a positive or negative value. Thus the Jews' famed persistence in retaining their religion could indicate fidelity and courage or fanaticism and servility. Old Testament Judaism and its continued practice could appear natural or unnatural, virtuous or vicious, rational or irrational. There were points of agreement among the philosophes, such as the almost universal condemnation of the Talmud and rabbinical commentary. Yet more consistent than the actual qualities attributed to the Jews were the concept pairs with which they were associated. They were unstable poles in the binary logic of the philosophes, but as poles they provided limits and structure to philosophical reflection. The Jews could be natural or unnatural, simple or complex, but in either case they provided a means of thinking about the extent to which one ought to be, or the conditions under which one might become, one or the other.

Indeed, the multiplicity of possible conceptual associations made the Jews a rich symbolic cache on which philosophes could draw when thinking about the issues with which they were concerned. They were sufficiently opaque to serve as a screen onto which Enlightenment writers could project their fantasies. They were sufficiently familiar, however, to inspire confidence in one's ability to known them. It was largely the legacy of centuries of Christian theology that rendered the Jews so evidently knowable. The traces of this legacy can be seen in the fact that anti-Christian philosophes persisted in hurling ancient Christian insults at the Jews, calling them obstinate and literalist. Moreover, with the striking exception of Rousseau, the philosophes inherited another tendency from their Christian rivals, namely, the desire to convert the Jews, or at least the pleasure in imagining their conversion. To be sure, they did not envisage conversion to Christianity. Yet they did imagine a radical transformation in their religious beliefs and practices, and indeed in their whole worldview. Montesquieu's ideal was the Philosophical Jew, the practitioner of natural religion. D'Argens embodied the same ideal in Isaac the Karaite. Diderot and his fellow encyclopedists similarly found their Philosophical Jews among the Karaites. Voltaire raised the stakes by calling on Pinto to abandon the Bible as incompatible with enlightened theology.

Few eighteenth-century French writers or political actors would repeat Voltaire's demand that the Jews give up all their sacred writings in order to become acceptable or "philosophical," since most of the former were themselves unwilling to part with the Bible. Asking the Jews to become Karaites, however, was already demanding enough. In the decades that followed, this request would be repeated, along with calls for other kinds of transformations: social, professional, and, above all, moral. That these radical changes could be demanded is proof that the philosophes did not consider the Jews incapable of improvement. Yet because the Jews were simultaneously symbols in thought experiments about the prospects of human perfectibility *and* real human beings inhabiting the French state—precisely because they were not Persians, or Peruvians, or Banians—this otherwise abstract activity had the potential to result in real, concrete consequences. And in the years surrounding the French Revolution, the potential became actual. Embodied subjects presumed to be convertible would become objects of conversion.

CHAPTER 3

Jews and Citizens

By the time Louis XVI took the throne in 1775, the period of the High Enlightenment was nearly over. Of the writers examined in the last chapter, Montesquieu was twenty years dead, and d'Argens had died in 1771. Voltaire had only three years to live, and Diderot was beginning his last decade of life. Already at the end of Louis XV's reign the attention of readers began to shift from the anticlerical and philosophically speculative works of the philosophes to the protests of judicial magistrates against the despotism of the absolute monarchy. The taboo against discussions of legal or "constitutional" reform was now lifted, and by the time the last Bourbon king of the eighteenth century came to power, writers and readers alike were prepared for more overtly political writing. The prior preoccupation with the Jews changed accordingly, but it did not wane. If anything, attention to the Jewish question grew and became increasingly systematic. The philosophes had considered the Jews in a bewildering variety of aspects, even if the goal of their study was typically a generalized understanding of the merits of civilization, the prospects of future happiness, and the nature of "man." They had integrated the Jews into practically every subject that interested them but rarely devoted more than a few pages to them at a time. By contrast, political writers of the last fifteen years of the Old Regime distinctly identified the Jews as a discrete problem—in both the social scientific and the everyday sense of the term—and sought a solution.

The problem, briefly stated, was that Jews inhabited the same territory as non-Jews, but that rather than forming a single nation, the two
groups maintained an antagonistic relationship with each other. This
chapter examines six of the many solutions offered between 1774 and
1789, five of which were published by writers who would go on to play
prominent roles in the French Revolution. The point of this investigation is not only to show the continuing importance of the Jews to their
French contemporaries but also to examine the ways in which, for a
number of political writers, the Jewish question at the end of the Old Regime was inextricably imbricated with the timely questions of citizenship and nationhood. Jews still conjured associations of religious strife,
of fanaticism and improper worship of the Supreme Being, but they increasingly became "good to think" about what a citizen was, what a
nation was, and under what conditions such entities might come into
existence.

PIETY, SENTIMENT, AND REPUBLICAN POPULISM
IN THE CASE OF THE FALSE RECEIPTS

In 1777 and 1778 thousands of Alsatian debtors refused to repay their
loans to Jewish moneylenders, asserting that their debts had already
been liquidated. As proof they showed receipts signed in Hebrew characters, ostensibly by their Jewish creditors. The Jewish lenders, however,
claimed that the receipts were counterfeits. By the summer of 1779 the
Sovereign Council of Alsace—the province's highest court—had confirmed the forgeries. The magistrates declared most of the debts to be
still outstanding and meted out harsh sentences, ranging from the galleys to hanging, to thirteen men convicted of producing or distributing
the forged receipts. Yet before the case was closed a pamphlet appeared,
entitled *Observations d'un Alsacien sur l'affaire présente des Juifs d'Alsace,* in which the forgeries were justified as a necessity given the rapacity of Jewish moneylenders. Soon thereafter François Hell, an Alsatian
bailiff, confessed to having written the inflammatory pamphlet. On the
basis of his authorship, as well as the discovery of a large quantity of
counterfeit receipts at his home, he became a prime suspect in the forgeries. His authorship of the pamphlet only contributed to his popularity, and after many petitions calling for his release from prison he was
exiled to the Dauphiné in June 1780. Upon his return in 1782 he was
treated as a popular hero, and his reputation as tribune of the peasantry

and scourge of the Jews earned him a seat in the National Assembly in 1789, from which he would attempt to block legislation aimed at recognizing Jews as equal citizens.[1]

Thus Hell wrote his *Observations* not as a piece of detached scholarship or theory but in the heat of a legal and political battle. Like the published legal briefs or *mémoires judiciares* that Sarah Maza has shown to have been so important in the political education of French readers prior to the Revolution,[2] his pamphlet was meant to persuade a "public" that it simultaneously invoked as the highest and most virtuous tribunal. Judging from the author's popularity, the effective petition campaign on his behalf, and his subsequent election to the National Assembly, his pamphlet seems to have succeeded quite well in its rhetorical aims. An examination of his narrative, his arguments, the ideas and authorities he invoked, and the emotions he incited provides a valuable perspective into the mental universe that Hell and his contemporaries inhabited.

Arthur Hertzberg has described Hell as an intellectual heir to Voltaire, but even the most cursory reading of the *Observations* reveals a set of convictions and a narrative style that are entirely at odds with those of the philosophe.[3] The most obviously anti-Voltairean component of Hell's pamphlet is its reverent stance toward Christianity and its pious repetition of Christian clichés. For Hell the suffering of Jews was evidence of their collective and inherited guilt. Thus he wrote, "No one could fail to see in the remnants of Israel the truth of divine prophecy. The blood of the righteous crucified one has fallen back upon them and their children." They are "condemned by the decree of divine justice to wander perpetually," and wherever one finds them, one will see "but the hand of an angry God pursuing them across the centuries and the empires in order to punish them." This prophetic-fatalistic interpretation of Jewish history was nearly identical to that of Saint Augustine and, more recently, Pascal. Yet it was anathema to Voltaire, for whom the refutation of Pascal's sacred historiography was of the highest priority.[4]

Hell's Christian interpretation of the meaning of Jewish suffering, moreover, led him to recount the Jews' history in the Diaspora in a manner diametrically opposed to that of Voltaire. Whereas Voltaire deplored the persecution of Jews by Christian states and peoples and saw it as evidence of ignorance and fanaticism, Hell reported all such persecution, in a circular and self-confirming way, as more evidence of the Jews' inherited guilt. He recorded the repeated expulsions of Jews not as signs of cruelty or intolerance but as "persecutions that the just wrath of

Heaven" used to punish the Jewish people. Moreover, he compounded the sense of the Jews' guilt and justified violence against them by reporting as facts the medieval accusations of ritual desecration of crucifixes and chalices, ritual murder of Christian children at Passover, and the poisoning of wells and public fountains. Voltaire, by contrast, considered such accusations as nothing more than the product of "ridiculous ignorance."[5]

Given Hell's unquestioning adherence to Christian theology, it is not surprising to find him fulminating against the Talmud. Of course, Voltaire derided the Oral Law as well, but for Hell the problem with the Talmud was above all its incompatibility with Christianity. He revealingly called it an "anthology of . . . diabolical inspirations," a "rhapsody of impiety, of blasphemy," and an "infernal code" that inspired "sacrileges." Just as its doctrine was contrary to Christianity, the Talmud of his imagination authorized the mistreatment of Christians. Hell wrote, "Troubling a Christian is, according to this book, a meritorious act, and perhaps that which the Jews practice most scrupulously," adding that "to persecute him is one of their sweetest pleasures." He maintained that bearing false witness against a Christian was "absolutely permitted" by the Talmud and even claimed that the ritual atrocities with which he charged Jews of previous centuries were inspired by it. Yet Hell's Christian orthodoxy prevented him from attacking the Old Testament, and his pamphlet did not contain even a hint of criticism of the patriarchs, of Moses, or even of the Jewish kings, whereas for Voltaire these figures were the object of the most vitriolic attacks. The infamous precept of Deuteronomy 23:19, according to which a Jew could lend at interest to a "stranger" but not to his "brother," remained unmentioned, though usury was the principal complaint of Hell's diatribe. Hell was even willing to give grudging praise to the Karaites, who accepted the Bible but rejected the Talmud. "Though walking in darkness and error," these Jewish heretics "nevertheless perceived some rays reflected in the ancient and true law." Not surprisingly, Hell was quick to point out that there were few Karaites in Europe and none in Alsace, where all Jews were "Rabinites" in the thrall of the Talmud.[6]

At the same time, Hell was not simply a relic from the Middle Ages, and alongside his Christian zeal he betrayed a familiarity with and participation in the culture of eighteenth-century France. What he adopted from his contemporaries in the secular world, however, bore little if any resemblance to Voltaireanism. If a single model had to be identified as best corresponding to Hell's more secular philosophical ideas, political language, and literary style, it would have to be Rousseau. Like Rousseau, and quite unlike Voltaire, Hell idealized the rustic simplicity of the peasants and contrasted their morals with the decadence of the *grands*.

Accordingly, and paradoxically, Hell affected an unaffected manner of writing, assuring his readership that his pamphlet corresponded perfectly to the sentiments of his heart. Indeed, the word *coeur,* so emotionally charged in the era of *sensibilité,* appears repeatedly in the *Observations,* and this transparency was a sign of patriotism. In the very first paragraph, in the guise of an address to posterity, Hell contrasted his "patriotism" with the dominant "egoism" of his day and hoped that a "happy revolution" would "reheat the hearts" of his compatriots. He deplored the "empire of wit and false taste" and urged his descendants to forgive him if his "ideas do not appear . . . sufficiently subtle, or encased in a sufficiently elegant style."[7]

For his contemporaries, however, Hell showed only fear and contempt. "Will I be waylaid?" he asked. "I am certain of it. . . . I will be severely judged by critics." Yet he claimed, "I already know my judges," and in an implicit challenge to the heritage of Voltaire, he identified his hypothetical critic as "the sectarian of tolerance whose eye sees the fanatic in every object, the wit who runs after brilliance, the philosophical mind that knows only how to think." Along with the usurer, such "abettors" would be outraged. They would "mount their tribunal and pronounce a decree of proscription" against the honest citizen. This fear of persecution—which turned out in Hell's case to be a self-fulfilling prophecy—bears an obvious resemblance to that of Rousseau, who famously believed that urbane but superficial wits were plotting against him. His response to this expected martyrdom was also strikingly reminiscent of Rousseau, and Hell used characteristically cardiac language to defend himself: "I will immediately call on my heart, which will absolve me." He confessed (i.e., boasted) that he was "a bit agitated by an excess of patriotism" yet insisted, in quintessentially Rousseauian terms, "my sentiments are pure."[8]

Finally, Hell ended his exordium by promising to accomplish yet another Rousseauian activity: unmasking.[9] Combining that mandate with his claim to patriotic selflessness, he wrote, in language that will be familiar to students of the French Revolution, "I claim to unmask [*démasquer]* crime." He wished to speak out on behalf of "a thousand family fathers who, captive, under the tyranny of usury, languish in silence and obscurity."[10] This conceptual marriage of secrecy and tyranny was not accidental. It was integral to a republican discourse that linked the two practices. For Rousseau, liberty in the civil state required transparency. Secrecy was a sign of cabal, the submission of the general will to private interest.[11] More immediately, the rebellious magistrates of the 1770s linked ministerial secrecy with despotism.[12] This association served to promote the potentially revolutionary ideal of public opinion as a check against tyranny, and indeed to justify the practice of publishing judicial memoirs, the genre to which Hell's *Observations* significantly belonged.

Hell exploited the familiar oppositions of transparency and opacity, publicity and secrecy, liberty and tyranny by casting the Jews in the role of opaque, dissimulating tyrants and their debtors as naïve, selfless citizens. He dramatized the conflict in a lengthy narrative about an honest peasant ruined by malicious Jews. The story begins with a peasant who needs money and "only has recourse to the Jew," whose usurious terms he is forced to accept. He signs an IOU, which the Jew later antedates to augment his profit. When the honest peasant returns to repay his debt, the usurer is prepared to defraud him again: "For . . . the Jews know how to toy with the peasant's good faith, and while pretending to tear up the IOU, by sleight of hand he actually tears up a different piece of paper." It is only a matter of time before the Jew comes to collect from the peasant, who naïvely believes his accounts to have been already settled. Now the usurer threatens the peasant with a lawsuit, and only an additional note attesting to a fictional loan appeases him. The cycle repeats itself, year after year, the peasant's debts, real or fabricated, mounting continuously. Desperate, the debtor borrows from other Jews to pay off the first, but each of these is "a new tyrant" and "another bloodsucker who wants to be sated."[13]

Hell's narrative continues with a sentimental description of a father, his worried wife, and their hungry children, all of whom are inevitably ruined by usury. This story, in turn, is followed by that of a new generation tyrannized by Jewish moneylenders. Hell lingers particularly over a scene in which a usurer successfully tempts a "prodigal son," at an age "susceptible to debauchery," to borrow money repeatedly and at increasingly high rates for the fulfillment of his carnal desires. Again domestic misery is assured, as the son, "altered by the fire of debauchery, drinking from the perfidious cup of usury, swallows in one gulp the patrimony that he does not yet have and the dowry of the woman to whom he is not yet engaged."[14]

Thus Hell combined Christian morality, conveniently embodied in the tale of perennial Christian-Jewish conflict and the story of the prodigal son, with a contemporary melodramatic-sentimental aesthetic in which good-hearted peasants struggled to control their passions. This sentimental moralism, moreover, had unmistakable political implications. It blended seamlessly into the nascent discourse of republicanism, which famously characterized politics as public morality.[15] Hell's political message was clear. The simple, naïve peasants of his pastoral landscape were an implicit reproach against the decadence of city and court and therefore served to further a populist message. Their transparency, moreover, had a political meaning. As in Rousseau, for whom transparent communication of feelings and intentions safeguarded against the subordination of the general will to the selfish ends of particular wills, in Hell's politics such unobstructed communication similarly indicated a healthy body politic. A transparent citizen was a good citizen.[16] By contrast, the Jews as Hell constructed them were thoroughly opaque. They were therefore anticitizens, the objects against which real citizens could be recognized.

Elsewhere Hell continued his contrast between Jews and citizens by denouncing the Jews' status as an autonomous corporation within the body politic. Just as Sieyes would castigate the nobles as *imperium in imperio,* Hell called the Jews a "nation in the nation," using an expression that Jews would hear, in one form or another, for more than two centuries.[17] Furthermore, just as Sieyes marked the nobles as the privileged class par excellence, Hell railed against the Jews as a privileged caste.[18] Indeed, he did not fail to report that the Jews had "*privileges* of which the Protestants of this province, though Christians and good citizens, cannot boast."[19]

Hell used the familiar republican concepts and sentimental rhetoric to persuade his readers that the Jews were national enemies against whom any nominally illegal aggression (such as forgery) was merely just recompense. Just as revolutionaries would call on an exceptional regime to root out alleged enemies of the nation, Hell insisted that only terror kept the Jews from causing more harm. Writing about the ritual atrocities he attributed to the Jews of earlier centuries, he used precisely the sort of language that Marat would employ against "aristocrats," writing, "Thanks to the severity with which the laws have been armed, *thanks to the terror* of the signal executions that these monsters of the human race have been forced to undergo, the atrocious crimes [of the Jews] . . . have become more rare in this century, but all these expiations have not in the least tamed this ferocious heart."[20]

In his battle against the Jews, then, Hell marshaled the combined force of two powerfully emotive discourses: republican and Christian. It was a republican discourse that enabled him to advocate terror against those whose "ferocious heart" prevented their incorporation into the body politic. And it was a Christian discourse that focused Hell's attention on the purely imaginary offenses of an enemy religion. Hell concluded his pamphlet by appealing to the Sovereign Council:

> We adore with you Jesus of Nazareth, whom the wretched children of Israel deny, we offer our devotions with you to him whom they immolated, we bless with you the one they curse every instant of their life; that is to say, we are your brothers in Jesus Christ. We walk the same soil, we breathe the air of the same climate, we pay homage to the same sovereign, that is to say, we are your fellow citizens [concitoyens].[21]

He thus summarized the two kinds of zeal—Christian and republican—that characterized his thinking. Whether his readers hated the Jews with the same ardor as he no doubt differed from individual to individual, yet his popularity and the leniency with which the judges treated him suggest that the discourses of republicanism and Christian zeal were far from contradictory in the 1770s and 1780s. Rather, nourished with the language of sensibilité, they maintained a symbiotic relationship.

A CITIZEN'S "GRAND EFFORT"

Hell was not alone in combining the discourses of Christian zeal and republican patriotism in a sentimental narrative about Jewish depravity. In 1786 Philippe-François de Latour-Foissac, a career officer in the French army who would become a general under the Directory,[22] wrote Le cri du citoyen contre les Juifs de Metz, in which he denounced the Jews as a threat to his city, province, and country. The pamphlet did not focus on a specific court case, but insofar as it dramatized, even melodramatized, the conflict between Jews and "citizens," it resembled Hell's pamphlet and approximated the genre of the mémoire judiciaire. Latour-Foissac even used the trope of the "tribunal" to give a solemn juridical weight to his Cri. Addressing the alleged victims of the Jews, he wrote, "It is your cause that I undertake to plead today at the tribunal of the nation."[23]

Latour-Foissac's pamphlet differed from Hell's in that it did refer to Voltaire, once by name and once, unmistakably, as "the Apostle of tolerance." The author expressed his approval for Voltaire's claim that "you will only find in [the Jews] . . . an ignorant and barbarian people who have long combined the most sordid avarice and the most detestable superstition, and the most invincible hatred for all the people who

tolerate and enrich them." He added that Voltaire was right in concluding that "leprosy as well as fanaticism and usury have been, in all ages,
[the Jews'] distinctive characteristics." Unlike Hell, moreover, Latour-
Foissac dared to cite passages from the Bible in support of the claim that
the Jews were the natural enemies of other peoples. Concentrating on
the Book of Deuteronomy, he cited the precept authorizing Jews to lend
at interest to "strangers" but not to "brothers"; the passage in which
God informs the Jews that he has "chosen you to be his own people,
preferable to all the other people . . . on the earth"; and the divine command, "You shall exterminate all the nations that the Lord your God delivers unto you." He also cited the notorious passage from the Psalms,
"Happy are they who eviscerate the pregnant women [of enemy nations]
and crush their children under the stone."[24]

Nevertheless, these same citations appear to have made Latour-
Foissac nervous, as though he were blaspheming by evidently denouncing their content, and he repeatedly made it clear—or tried to make it
clear—that he had nothing against the Bible. He wrote that the Jews'
conduct was "all the more baneful in that it is based on a badly interpreted law . . . dictated by the Eternal." What the Jews failed to understand, the author claimed, was that they should not take the Old Testament prescriptions "literally."[25] While in some contexts the caution
against taking the Bible literally is an "enlightened" position, Latour-
Foissac's position on the Jews' fabled literalism was identical to that
of Christian theologians such as Fénélon, Bossuet, and (Voltaire's bête
noire) Pascal, all of whom faulted them for taking the law of the Old
Testament so literally that they could not see when the Messiah came
to replace it.[26] Accordingly, Latour-Foissac wrote, "Convinced of the
friendly predilection of the Almighty, and continually envisaging as an
order emanating from his wisdom certain commandments from Deuteronomy, *which a holier law has annulled,* [the Jew] seizes the precept and
executes it literally."[27] Though he freely borrowed from the idiom of the
Enlightenment, he reversed its meaning as understood by the philosophes when he appealed to Christianity as the ultimate truth. Thus in
the very first sentence of the pamphlet he claimed to be living in "a century of reason, *sustained by the sacred dogmas of a holy religion.*"[28]

Even Latour-Foissac's invocation of reason was undermined by his
prolific use of the language of *sensibilité.* The words *sensible, sentiments,*
and even *sensibilité* appear repeatedly throughout the pamphlet, as do
the words *passion* and *coeur.* Like Hell, moreover, Latour-Foissac em-
plotted his narrative as a melodrama in which a domestic catastrophe en-

sues when malicious Jewish usurers defraud naïve Christians. Whereas Hell had employed the *cultivateur* as the virtuous foil for the vice-ridden Jew, Latour-Foissac used the young officer, full of patriotic devotion and utterly unprepared for his inevitable encounter with vice, embodied in the person of the Jew.

Avowedly drawing on his own experience in the infantry, and hinting that he was telling his own story, Latour-Foissac recounted the tragedy of an officer's descent into moral and financial ruin. He described the young man's initial moral and psychological condition: "His open, honest and loyal heart is still in the heedlessness of a profound calm." As soon as the man arrives at his quarters, he becomes "the object of the Synagogue's scrutiny." The Jews recognize the vulnerability of the naïve soldiers and in particular take advantage of the fact that a garrison town such as Metz has taverns and brothels to tempt young men who have just left home for the first time. Such vices require money, and the "Synagogue" is prepared to lend. The Jew's offer to lend is therefore a kind of seduction, an invitation to debauchery, and whereas Hell's story suggested such a seduction, Latour-Foissac quite explicitly referred to the "opportune moments that can make *seductive* and pleasant the ruinous offers they make." The Jew has the quasi-magical ability to read the "heart" of his victim, then puts on the appropriate performance, and inevitably "the transaction is going to be completed, to the certain ruin of the unfortunate borrower." As in Hell's melodrama, furthermore, Latour-Foissac's cautionary tale includes the victim's family, whose suffering is similarly represented in terms of wasted youth and miserable old age: "Oh you sensitive and respectable fathers, you who served [the] fatherland with distinction . . . your final years are condemned to ignominy, your hearts will be broken by just pain." Such fathers have lived to see "these dear children, raised with care in the ways of probity and honor" and "destined to despise the danger of combat" ultimately "fallen victim to Israel at the beginning of a career that they might have filled with honor and the energy of the passions."[29]

The political implications of this tragedy were multiple. At the most obvious level, the author pitted patriotic men against enemies of the nation. He employed the politically charged term *nation* to indicate the community to which he belonged, and in turn characterized the Jews as a separate and hostile nation. He also used the similarly resonant word *citoyen*. In fact, he identified himself in the title of his pamphlet simply as "the citizen." And he reinforced his self-proclaimed attachment to the French "nation" by repeatedly using the term.[30] Like Hell, he seems to have understood the citizen more as a composite of moral characteristics than as a bearer of rights. Among those traits were *sensibilité,* transparency, and devotion to the common good. Again, as for Hell, the figure of the Jew served as an anticitizen. In this respect, the political meaning of the pamphlet was not restricted to the fact that Jews were ostensibly defrauding citizens. Latour-Foissac's depiction of Jews as opaque also had a political significance. Just as Hell had portrayed them as capable of concealing their intentions and desires, Latour-Foissac wrote, "They burn with a consuming thirst to increase their riches, and yet they will feign contempt for the means of augmenting them."[31] Most immediately, this ability to "feign" made Latour-Foissac's Jews adept swindlers. That same skill, however, placed them outside the imagined community of virtuous citizens, who by definition were incapable of feigning.

The same could be said for the political meaning of "pity." Whereas the young officer, though weak in the face of temptation, has chosen a career that places the public safety above his own, the Jew has no such fellow feeling. Latour-Foissac wrote, "Pity, that sweet emanation of sensitive hearts, that generous and consoling sentiment which brings us to lament, to ease the pains and afflictions of the unfortunate . . . pity! the Jews have never known it." This purported difference also defined the boundaries between citizen and anticitizen, Frenchman and Jew.[32]

Quite unexpectedly, however, at the conclusion of his pamphlet the author seemed to temper his wrath and suggested, however vaguely, that the Jews might someday be integrated into the French nation. As if convinced by his own ode to pity, he addressed the Jews, "Oh Israel! Captive under . . . different tyrants, . . . erring . . . without an assured domicile to the four corners of the world, I have not come today to complete your calamities." He assured the Jews that, despite their defects, they would no longer be persecuted. "Under the vigorous government of a wise and all-powerful king," he wrote, "we shall recall you, by way of beneficence, by way of the happy influence of tolerant humanity, to the voice of honor and probity." He further predicted, "Your precarious existence will take on a solid consistency, and you will become, in the State, useful citizens."

What did Latour-Foissac have in mind by making the Jews into useful citizens? His plans were vague, but the author suggested turning the Jews into farmers and in the process improving them morally. He observed that "there is in France a vast, uninhabited country, untilled." He further noted that "the Moors petitioned in vain to live there." Then, remarkably, he wrote, "They were foreigners, perhaps dangerous. You,

I consider you, despite yourselves, to be French; feel the dignity of this name: may it give your debased soul all the energy necessary for the grand effort that I prescribe to you." He therefore urged the Jews, "Obtain these lands; may a new Babylon rise up: may it be the cherished capital of a place of captivity that is sweeter than your ancient fatherland ever was." Giving yet another hint about his conception of citizenship, he exhorted, "Finally become citizens, and may you acquire the precious privilege of paying the state taxes levied on fields that were once arid, but then fertilized by your hands, which have become hardworking."[33]

Thus a pamphlet that began as a libel ended as a program for what others were already calling *régénération*. By encouraging Jewish colonization to "uninhabited" regions of the country, and by alluding to "taxes levied on fields," Latour-Foissac implicitly called for the lifting of the ban on Jewish ownership of land, though evidently he was not prepared to extend such new liberties to northeastern France, where the majority of Jews lived. Yet if his plan promoted the republican ideal of the husbandman-citizen, it undermined the republican goal of indivisibility by suggesting that the Jews could only live among other Jews. Agricultural colonies in remote locations would presumably merely perpetuate the condition of the Jews as a "nation within the nation." On the other hand, one should not be surprised to find contradictions in Latour-Foissac's program, as citizenship itself was a vague category. One knew who was *not* a citizen: the perfidious, selfish Jew. But what a citizen actually was—this was an open and contested question with a long and rancorous future ahead of it. The very vagueness of the concept assured that its formulators would continue to return to the Jews in the hope of an *a contrario* answer.

CITIZENSHIP, FRENCHNESS, AND REGENERATION IN A JEWISH CAUSE CÉLÈBRE

The idea of including Jews in the imagined community of French citizens, either immediately or at some unspecified future date, was not new when Latour-Foissac wrote his *Cri du citoyen* in 1786. As early as 1774 the barrister Pierre-Louis Lacretelle called for Jewish citizenship, though his argument raised more questions than it answered about what such a transformation would mean in practice. Strictly speaking, the question of the Jews' citizenship, present or future, was irrelevant to the specific complaint of Lacretelle's clients, who simply wanted recognition of their right to open shops in a particular city. Indeed, it probably damaged their case, which they duly lost, though it is impossible to know whether a different kind of argument would have led to a favorable judgment. Evidently the brash young lawyer, who would go on, significantly, to become a revolutionary, was more interested in great ideas such as citizenship than in the relatively banal facts of his case. Or perhaps, to put it more cynically, he was more concerned with eliciting attention than in helping his clients. After all, he did succeed in having his dramatic *mémoire judiciare* published in the widely read publication *Causes célèbres,* a coup that did more for his career than simply winning a case would have done.[34] Yet more interesting than assessing Lacretelle's integrity or lack thereof is the question of how the lawyer used the Jews to think about citizenship.

The facts of the case were straightforward. Lacretelle's clients, two Jews from Metz, had recently moved to nearby Thionville in Lorraine to take advantage of a 1767 royal decree permitting merchants who had purchased special licenses *(brevets)* to establish shops without having to pass through the normal process of apprenticeship. The *juge de la police* in Thionville had refused to recognize the licenses, apparently without giving a reason, and his decision was backed by the local merchants' guild and the municipal council. The Jews therefore hired Lacretelle to argue before the Sovereign Court of Nancy that this refusal was illegal and that they should be permitted to open their shops.

Lacretelle noted from the outset that French nationality was not a precondition for buying and utilizing the new licenses. In fact, the 1767 decree was designed to attract foreigners by releasing them from the *droit d'aubaine,* according to which the property of foreigners reverted to the state upon their death. Thus Lacretelle argued, "The intention of these laws is clear and evident. The king wished to increase the number of artisans and merchants, and even to render foreigners participants in this favor." At this point he might have closed his argument, concluding that whether one considered Jews French or foreign, they were equally capable of enjoying the privileges stipulated in their licenses. Yet he did not stop there. He suggested that Jews were capable of being good merchants and artisans, asking, "Has anyone ever doubted their intelligence, their diligence, and their resourcefulness in commerce and industry?" This query came uncomfortably close to raising the question of the Jews' *probity,* which more than a few non-Jews, and perhaps the Nancy magistrates, doubted. Later Lacretelle made it irrelevant by claiming that in distributing the *brevets* "the king wishes to compensate zeal and talent," adding, "It is up to him, without a doubt, to choose [from among the applicants]; but this choice dispenses everything." [35] By this point, however, the question of the Jews' merit had already been raised.

Worse still, Lacretelle asserted, "I dare sustain that they can honor themselves with the title of Frenchmen, of *regnicoles,*" that is, subjects of the French crown. Yet he failed to produce the naturalization papers that would have unequivocally determined whether the barrister was right in what he "dare[d] sustain." As to the appellation of Frenchman, this had more of a moral than a legal meaning. It connoted more than the status of royal subject. Rather, it suggested, among other things, an affective bond with fellow French nationals, a concern for and commitment to their welfare. It was a short step, then, from *français* to *citoyen.* Before he took it, Lacretelle enumerated the traits that characterized the Jews as *français.* One was the possession of "establishments" in the kingdom. Lacretelle declared, "There is not a single one of our provinces in which [the Jews] do not have establishments," which may have been technically true, though it invited the retort that their residence privileges were restricted to a few designated locations. Anticipating this connection, he continued, "In those places where they have been offered exile, they are inhabitants." This was a tautology, and moreover diluted the sense of citizenship in the term *français.* As if to strengthen the empty term *inhabitants,* he added, "[They] are subjects of the king; they live under submission to our laws, protected by them." This claim, however, implicitly raised the question of the Jews' *other* laws, especially the precepts of the Talmud by which rabbis still largely governed and judged. [36]

Other signs of the *français* were "fidelity to the Government" and payment of taxes. Lacretelle added that his clients and their coreligionists were legally permitted to bequeath estates, though this was merely another way of saying that they were not subject to the *droit d'aubaine.* He further observed that "they litigate in our courts," which the magistrates of Nancy must have known was more wishful thinking than reality, since most civil disputes between Jews were settled in rabbinical courts. Lacretelle observed that Jews had lived in the region of Metz for more than two centuries, now suggesting that long-standing residence was a sign of real Frenchness. "Since then," he added, finally using the sacred word, "*ils s'y sont toujours regardé [sic] comme citoyens.*" [37] This phrase had two possible meanings. The reflexive verb *se regarder* could mean "to regard oneself" or "to be regarded." Thus it was unclear— no doubt deliberately so—whether the barrister meant that the Jews regarded themselves as citizens, or were seen as such by others, or both. In the case of self-perception, citizenship would be a matter of will, as in Rousseau's contractual conception. In the case of perception by others, it would be a question of reputation. Either claim was likely to meet with skepticism from the magistrates. Both, moreover, begged the questions of what, morally speaking, a citizen was and to what extent the Jews possessed the requisite attributes.

Lacretelle therefore found himself confronted with the thorny question of the Jews' morality and its relationship to citizenship. He defended the Jews as a group by claiming that "their morals are pure and religious." He added that "they help each other when any of them are suffering" and "punish each other when any of them does wrong," statements that might well have implied uncivic particularism and—contrary to his earlier statement about Jewish use of royal courts—juridical autonomy. As to the popular belief that Jews regularly cheated Gentiles, he tacitly conceded this point, but asked, "Is this the fault of the man [who cheats], or only that of the situation?" He answered his own question by observing that the Jews had been oppressed for centuries. Not only had they been excluded from honest work, "They have been . . . pursued in turn by calumny, hatred and fanaticism." Speculating on the psychological condition of the persecuted and humiliated Jew, he asserted, "Ashamed of himself, and always brought back to himself by need, he concentrates on the love of gold." Regarding the Jew's relationship with his "oppressors," he added, "He cheats them with avidity, for he is pushed to do so by the necessity of living; he cheats them with joy, for this is the only advantage that he can obtain over them."[38] This was hardly a flattering portrait, but Lacretelle implied that ultimately the Jews were not to blame. They were victims of circumstance, and a positive change in their circumstances would lead to an improvement in their morality.

As evidence for this hypothetical claim Lacretelle cited the conditions of Jews in other countries. He compared the Jews of France with those "in Holland, in some parts of Germany, in the English colonies," and in other countries where they lived "closer to the ordinary condition of men," and concluded, "We will find them more honest, more faithful in their agreements, sensitive to honor and sometimes sacrificing their wealth for it." He went on to invoke Moses Mendelssohn, the Jewish philosopher from Berlin. Mendelssohn's very existence was proof of what the Jews could become under the right conditions—in this case the evidently tolerant atmosphere of Prussia under Frederick the Great. He appealed to the patriotism of his audience—both magistrates and readers of the *Causes célèbres*—when he informed them that Good Jews, and even a Philosophical Jew, existed in *other countries,* and that these phenomena were evidence of tolerance and enlightenment. And he appealed to France's self-interest when he noted, barely a decade after the Seven Years' War, that Frederick "finds among the Jews talent that can help him rise up in commerce as well as war."[39]

Lacretelle therefore urged his fellow *français,* "Let us open our cities to [the Jews]; let us allow them to disperse in our countryside." Then, retreating from his suggestion that the Jews were already French citizens, he exhorted, "Let us receive them, if not as compatriots *[compatriots],* at least as men." Elaborating on his appeal to French patriotism, he added, "Let them see that we believe them worthy of loving and serving us. Let . . . their ears hear that sublime and touching word . . . let them know *honor,* that they may become truly French." Again Lacretelle retreated from an earlier position. Not only had acceptance of Jews as compatriots become optional; the Jews whom the attorney had considered *français* were now only *potentially* French. The existing Jews of France were evidently unfit for citizenship insofar as it was understood in moral (rather than strictly legal) terms. They had to change before they could attain the rank of citizens. Lacretelle made this requirement explicit when he insisted, "Let us surround them with the vigilance of our laws; *let us force them to change,* along with their condition; may our rigor in the former matter not cede to our generosity in the latter." He proposed a conditional agreement by which his compatriots would allow the Jews to become citizens. If they should fail to comport themselves accordingly, he threatened, "let them become again forever this degraded people, everywhere proscribed and everywhere miserable; may the states refuse them asylum, and men their pity." He assured his audience, however, that this unhappy scenario would not unfold, and, using a word that would become synonymous with the program for legal reform and moral improvement, he concluded, "Let us not believe that they could thus receive a decree of grace, a decree of *regeneration.* The unfortunate do not have such cold ingratitude."[40]

It is scarcely surprising that a court, perhaps already suspicious of Jews, should have denied their request after their lawyer presented a case such as Lacretelle's. Based initially on the tenuous (and unnecessary) claim that Jews were French citizens, the argument quickly undermined itself in multiple ways and ended by conceding that the Jews were presently characterized by civic vices and would only at some future date

"become truly French." One suspects that the young barrister was playing to the gallery, that is, to the proverbial court of public opinion that
read the *Causes célèbres,* rather than to the magistrates of Nancy. In this
forum he was able to indulge his intellect in questions of morality, citizenship, and human nature, engage in thought experiments about the
future transformation of the Jews, and highlight his own apparent virtue by generously calling for a "decree of regeneration."

If Lacretelle's argument ultimately exhibits a personal intellectual
agenda, it may also reveal something about the "public" to whom the
author appealed and who read his *mémoire judiciaire.* Although it is impossible to know just how his readers responded to his brief, its inclusion in the popular *Causes célèbres* and the future success of its author
in law and politics suggest that Lacretelle had an interested audience,
even if not everyone was convinced by his arguments. They also suggest
that his readers, like the author-barrister himself, found the Jews good
for thinking about citizenship, even if (or precisely because) the content
of this category was questionable. Finally, one suspects that Lacretelle
and his audience found something compelling, if unlikely, about the
prospect of a degraded and corrupt people miraculously brought back
to morality, since this scenario presaged the future perfectibility, or regeneration, of what contemporaries simply called *l'homme.*

MONSIEUR THIÉRY'S PYGMALION FANTASY

Could the Jews improve? The interest in this question was such that
in 1785 the Royal Academy of Sciences and Arts in Metz sponsored a
widely publicized essay contest on the question, "Is there a way of making the Jews more useful and happier in France?"[41] The academicians
received the entries in 1787, determined that none was worthy of a
prize, and repeated the contest, extending the deadline to the following
year. From this new round of essays the academy chose three worthy of
distinction. One of these, by a Jew named Zalkind Hourwitz, will be
considered in the following chapter. The other two essays, one by a barrister and the other by a priest, are worth analyzing here because they
reveal how reform-minded Gentiles used the Jews to articulate, and indeed to conceive of ideas about, the moral constitution of the citizen and
the prospects of a cohesive French *nation.*

For Monsieur Thiéry, barrister at the *parlement* of Nancy, the resolution to the Jewish question was urgent, not so much for the Jews' sake
as for the sake of the Gentiles. He opened his essay with an alarming ac-

count of the social costs of Jewish vice, insisting that the "opprobrium" and "misery" of the Jews "make [them] often dangerous and . . . over-burden us . . . with the weight of their existence." This pronoun, "us," made it clear that for Thiéry the Jewish problem was above all a French problem. Like Hell, he accused the Jews of dealing "cruel . . . blows to that so vital and respectable portion of the citizenry," namely, the peas-antry. He similarly painted a stark contrast between the "husbandman, his hand weighed down upon his plowshare," who "waters with his sweat the soil that he has just traced," and the Jew, who has "spied the instant of his distress" and will take advantage of the situation by "of-fering his cruel favors."[42]

As in the pamphlets of Hell and Latour-Foissac, the Jew was dis-tinguished from the "citizen" not only by his lack of authentic, useful labor—that is, he did not sweat—but also by his nearly magical fore-knowledge of his unwitting victim's distress. Moreover, as in the earlier pamphlets, the author insisted that the Jews did not merely constitute an economic burden as a result of their moneylending activities. They also "contributed greatly to the loss of morality"*(à la perte des moeurs)*. Thus Thiéry used the Jews to articulate and explain a more generalized fear that Maza has identified among French writers in the second half of the eighteenth century, namely, that of luxury *(le luxe)*.[43] Again using the first-person plural to underscore his primary concern with non-Jews, he designated the Jews "the principal artisans of our *luxe*." He made the now-familiar connection between moral corruption and vulnerable youth, attributing to the Jews the ability to identify and profit from the passions of young men: "The attention with which they spy the instant when the *passions* are going to break out, the care they put into fo-menting them, the sinful ease with which they come to satisfy them, are veritable crimes."[44]

At the same time, Thiéry insisted that it was a mistake to view the Jews as "more vicious, more wicked than others" or to attribute to them "a nature that is impossible to correct or to change." For him, as for Lacretelle and the philosophes, the Jews' character was no different from that of other human beings. On the contrary, in a kind of panthe-istic paean, he railed against "insane" authors for "blaspheming against nature" by claiming that "she erred in forming the Jews" and "made them for crime." As to the claim that Jewish law authorized usury and fraud against Christians, Thiéry was similarly indignant, arguing that its "divine Author" could not have written such a code.[45]

Neither inherent, "natural" characteristics nor the divine code of the

Jews, then, explained their current moral condition. For Thiéry, as for Lacretelle, the circumstances of oppression were at fault. He made it clear that Christians, not Jews, were ultimately to blame for the vices of the latter. Again using the first-person plural, and employing the Rousseauian language of unmasking, he wrote, "Let us dare . . . to tear away the imposing mask with which prejudice has constantly covered itself; it is . . . we who must be accused of these crimes." As to "the passion" that the Jews have "for cheating us, for always using guile, cleverness and perfidy against us," he insisted that "it is to the barbaric conduct of our fathers toward them" that these misdeeds must be attributed.[46]

Thiéry proved his case by examining the Jews' history and emphasizing the changes in their character over time. He began with an idealized account of the Jews of biblical times. Like the encyclopedists, he highlighted the pastoral virtue and primitive simplicity of the ancient Hebrews. He explained that the Jews, "born in the first days of nature," were originally characterized by a "simplicity of morals" and "purity of inclinations." This happy isolation did not last, however, as the Greeks, then the Romans persecuted the Jews and corrupted them with their vices. The Jews soon "forgot their primitive simplicity . . . [and] renounced the rustic life . . . for Commerce." In an eclectic mixture of sacred and secular history, Thiéry argued that persecution led to corruption and crime, which in turn provoked the wrath of "a vengeful God" and divine punishment in the form of the destruction of Jerusalem and exile among the "Nations." He then returned to secular historiography, sketching the annals of European Jewry from late antiquity to his own day, lingering over images of streaming blood and Inquisitorial bonfires. Then, reconnecting the historical evidence with the theoretical argument, he observed that it was only natural for the Jews to treat Christians as enemies and to defraud them whenever possible. Such behavior became inevitable when the desire for revenge concurred with the need to survive in an economy that excluded the Jews from all "useful" occupations. Thiéry conceded that his contemporaries did not persecute the Jews in an overtly violent manner, but he denounced the laws that enshrined old prejudices: "These are our Laws which have closed our workshops to the Jews, which have prohibited them from all the Arts and have declared them unfit for even the vilest professions: these are our Laws which have removed from them everything that could soothe and console the heart."[47]

Like Lacretelle, moreover, Thiéry buttressed his argument with examples of virtuous Jews abroad. He pointed to England, where the Jews were "almost naturalized," and to the Netherlands, where they were "elevated to the rank of Citizens"; in both countries, he claimed, they proved themselves worthy of their rights. He asserted, rather misleadingly, that "in Germany, in Prussia, they differ from other Citizens only in their incapacity to attain public offices" and remarked that, as a result of their relative freedom, "It is in Vienna, it is in Berlin that one finds Synagogues full of industrious, enlightened and learned Jews of all kinds." In this context he made the obligatory reference to Moses Mendelssohn, "justly regarded as one of the great Philosophers and best Writers of this century." He appealed to the patriotism of his readers by suggesting that other peoples were further advanced in the application of enlightened laws. After concluding that "wherever the Jews have been made Citizens . . . they have been . . . hardworking and enlightened," he asked, "Will it only be in France, in the bosom of the gentlest and most enlightened Nation, that one will hesitate to follow this rule . . . ?"[48]

Having proved that the Jews were neither innately wicked nor required by their religion to be so, Thiéry proceeded to outline a program for their "happy regeneration." He urged his compatriots: "Assure them . . . the rights of nature and those of humanity; make them Citizens." Yet when he elaborated on his program, it became apparent that he was less interested in rights than in surveillance and coercion. Not all his plans were oppressive. Invoking the pastoral romanticism of so many of his contemporaries, he hoped "to recall [the Jews] to their primitive state" of indifference to money by inducing them to become farmers. Expressing a physiocratic truism in sentimental language, he wrote, "It is only in the bowels of the earth that one finds the generative sap that is the source of all fecundity: it is only by the strength of one's arms that one can turn over and tear out the riches it contains." By settling Jews on uncultivated land, therefore, the state could achieve the dramatic transformation by which "these new citizens, far from being . . . a destructive plague whose ravages desolate our countryside, will contribute . . . to fertilizing it." Thiéry even proposed tax exemptions during an (unspecified) initial period for Jews who were willing to become farmers.[49]

Departing from physiocratic orthodoxy, Thiéry considered manufacture to be productive economic activity as well and praised the artisanal crafts for their moral effect. He therefore proposed encouraging the Jews to take up crafts as a means of "draw[ing] them away from . . . the primary motor of their cupidity," that is, commerce. To solve the problem of customary exclusion of Jews from the crafts, he advocated the establishment of "public workshops." Who would pay for such workshops was left unclear, but Thiéry insisted that they would be necessary in order to "train [the Jews] and survey them" *(les former et les surveiller)*. The call for surveillance (by non-Jews, evidently) betrayed Thiéry's fundamental suspicion that unregenerated Jews would not work of their own volition. Elsewhere the author explicitly deplored the "dangerous idleness in which they . . . languish." Accordingly, he wrote, "It seems to me appropriate to compel *[d'astreindre]* the Jews to devote themselves to some occupation," by which he seems to have meant a "useful" craft, though he neglected to specify how such an occupation was to be recognized. There also remained the problem of how the requirement to work could be enforced. Thiéry did not explicitly call for the expulsion or criminal prosecution of "idle" Jews, though the phrase "to compel" seemed to leave these options open. He did, however, conceive of the ingenious solution of requiring the rabbis to pronounce a solemn anathema against their lazy coreligionists.[50]

Finally, Thiéry modified his proposal for admission of Jews into all professions by advocating their continued exclusion from "the first ranks of society," by which he meant government, administration, and the courts. Again dividing the world into "us" and "them," he asked rhetorically, "How could they govern us while professing principles and sentiments that are foreign to us . . . ? Are we not obligated, above all, to preserve for Christianity the preeminence and the empire that belong to it?" Thiéry continued, "Let us simply leave them the exercise of the precious rights that nature accords to all men," but this meant civil rights, not political rights.[51] Without using the same terminology, Thiéry advocated making the Jews what the Constitution of 1791, following Sieyes, would call "passive citizens," and this was precisely what a number of revolutionary deputies would envisage for the Jews.[52]

In addition to regenerating the Jews through morally edifying work, Thiéry proposed to transform them through education. In a suggestion that revealed both an affinity for sensationalist pedagogy and a tendency toward Pygmalion fantasy, he urged his compatriots, "Let us make ourselves the masters of their first impressions, let us make them as we wish them to become, and they will always be as we ourselves have formed them." His first choice was to "admit the Jews to our public schools," but since he anticipated their opposition to such integration, he was willing to allow them "to choose their own teachers," though he added the telling proviso "that we reserve for ourselves the task of surveying them." Whether "they" sent their children to school with non-Jews or employed state-authorized teachers in their own schools, Thiéry insisted that "the Government must pay . . . the most scrupulous attention" to their education. It must "make itself master of the mind and heart of these children, to succeed in managing them, then to master the sentiments that animate the whole Jewish Nation and to direct them toward its will."[53]

The management of sentiments, however, was not to end with formal education. Thiéry called for the effacement of all outward signs of difference between Jews and non-Jews. Needless to say, it was the Jews' own signs that were to disappear, as Thiéry wrote, "Let us begin by destroying all the humiliating signs that designate the Jews." He hoped to persuade Jewish men to shave their beards, as well as relinquish their characteristic outfits—including, presumably, their religiously obligatory head coverings—and to induce women to stop covering their hair as well. The desire for this sort of unveiling, both literal and figurative, conformed perfectly to the Rousseauian logic of transparency and also endorsed its hostility toward difference. Along the same lines was the author's insistence that the Jews reside among non-Jews. He opposed not only the forced confinement of Jews to special quarters but also the *voluntary* residence of Jews among their coreligionists. Although he did not call for government force in dispersing the Jews, he suggested that the latter would never improve if they had no examples to follow but those of other Jews.[54]

Thiéry's plan to make the Jews citizens began by recognizing their rights and proceeded to restrict them. Ultimately, his conception of citizenship was less a matter of freedom than of conformity, less a question of rights than of duties. The regeneration of the corrupt evidently required emergency action, and the state was the organ of that intervention. Still, Thiéry's scheme appears laissez-faire when juxtaposed to that of his cowinner in the Metz essay contest: Abbé Henri Grégoire.

A DIFFERENT KIND OF CONVERSION:
ABBÉ GRÉGOIRE AND THE REGENERATION OF THE JEWS

It is not the least of the ironies surrounding the Jewish question in late eighteenth-century France that the person whose name is so intimately connected with the defense of the Jews simultaneously denounced them in such violent language that the casual reader might have mistaken his pamphlet for yet another libel à la François Hell. In his *Essai sur la régénération physique, morale et politique des Juifs,* Abbé Grégoire referred to the Jews as "contemptible" and "pitiless." He called them "thieves" and "frauds" and dehumanized them as "parasitcs," "vulture[s]," "vipers," and "the scum of the earth." He wrote, "No one has taken the art of deceit further than the Jews, and of lying in wait for misfortune, in order to fall basely upon their victims." Employing the now-familiar language of unveiling, he complained, "Just when you flatter yourself to have *unveiled* all the resources of their brigandage, they throw you into new traps." [55]

Like Hell and Latour-Foissac, Grégoire illustrated his claims with a story about a Jewish moneylender who, "under the *mask* of an infernal generosity," tells his debtor that he can wait for repayment in order to collect more interest; he went on to enumerate other typical forms of trickery, such as forgery and the burning of false IOUs. Similarly, he denounced the Jews' "malignant influence" on public morality, calling it "a contagious illness that alters the purity of the national morality." He accused Jews of preying on young men in particular, of "encouraging *libertinage* through usurious loans." Like Latour-Foissac, he asked rhetorically what would become of a young officer "whose passions are about to bloom" and of his comrade-in-arms "whose affairs are disturbed by gambling or debauchery." He answered his own question, "The Israelite will introduce himself then [and] jingle his coins." [56]

Grégoire's depiction of the harm Jews allegedly caused the peasantry was clearly informed by Hell's diatribe. Like the Alsatian bailiff, Grégoire presented a melodramatic scene in which Jewish usury has led to domestic misery, the tragic corruption of an otherwise virtuous farmer and his family, both in the present and for future generations. In an allusion to the false receipts case, he recounted the fall of the "honest Husbandman," who, "ruined by the Jews" and "debased by indigence," took the crucial "step to make himself a scoundrel." Again, as in Hell, a family is present to augment the pathos. The peasant's wife, if she has not yet died of grief, will join her husband in a new life of fraud, "and their ill-raised children will prepare a race of perverse citizens for the following generation." [57]

The abbé directly connected the Jews' alleged immorality to their religious beliefs. He was particularly incensed against the Talmud, "this sewer in which the deliriums of the human mind are accumulated," and which, in his opinion, taught antisocial behavior, especially lying, hypocrisy, and the fraudulent treatment of Christians. [58] He believed that the regeneration of the Jews "could be reconciled with their religious laws," but by "religious laws" he meant only the Old Testament, in which he, like many philosophes, saw the precepts of natural religion. He therefore praised the Karaites, the "declared enemies of the oral traditions . . . and of the Rabbanists," as "the most honest people among the Jews" and "the most intelligent," and regretted that they were so few in number.[59] In effect, Grégoire was asking the Jews to convert not to Christianity but to Karaism, the idealized Jewish version of natural religion and the choice of Isaac Onis, the hero of the *Lettres juives* and the prototypical Philosophical Jew.[60]

At the same time, Grégoire did not blame the Talmud alone for the moral baseness he attributed to the Jews. He also blamed the Christians whose oppression of the Jews had supposedly led to their ethical decline. Even the infernal Talmudic logic that supposedly sanctioned their "crimes" was, in Grégoire's formulation, "our work," insofar as persecution induced the rabbis to think as they did. Thus, he wrote, "Their fear is the fruit of slavery, misery has withered their heart, despair has provoked their aversion and led them toward vengeance. Such is the incontestable genealogy of many crimes and *the unfailing march of human nature* in similar cases."[61] Like so many other commentators on the Jews in eighteenth-century France, Grégoire's interest in the Jews appears to have stemmed from an interest in human nature.

Grégoire's hypothesis that human nature was uniform, and that the Jews were no different than other human beings, rested on empirical evidence culled from history and the observation of behavior by Jews and non-Jews in other countries. Like so many other writers of the century, he posited a golden age of Jewish antiquity. In biblical times, he claimed, Palestine was a "flourishing" land whose inhabitants disdained commerce and were more "occupied with agronomy" than any other people at the time or since then. As a moral critic of commerce, Grégoire reported with satisfaction that there had been "among the Hebrews little circulation, little exchange." This was because their laws were "almost opposed to the spirit of commerce," as one could easily see in the institution of the jubilee, which "brought them closer to . . . primitive equality."[62]

It was only with the destruction of Jerusalem and dispersal among the nations, Grégoire wrote, that the Jews "degenerated from their ancient Israelite probity." Accordingly, he provided a detailed account of the Jews' history in the Diaspora. Like Montesquieu, Voltaire, and the encyclopedists, he denounced the fanaticism of medieval Christians who preached hatred and provoked massacres against Jews. Similarly, he recounted the cynical machinations of medieval princes, who exploited the Jews for their money, expelled them in order to confiscate their property, then recalled them when they again needed specie. When discussing the centuries closer to his own age, he railed against the Inquisition and accused the French state of persecuting Jews, though with less violent means. He asked, "What could become of the Jew, crushed by despotism, proscribed by the laws, showered with ignominy, tormented by hatred?" The answer: "He was viewed with contempt, he became contemptible."[63]

More evidence for the merely circumstantial nature of Jewish vice came from "striking exceptions" to the rule of Jewish vice. Wherever Jews were permitted to take up "honest work," he claimed, they "were not at all degraded by usury"; he went as far in his quest for examples as the virtuous Jewish farmers of Lithuania, the Ukraine, and Persia and the honest artisans of Morocco, Ethiopia, and "the Orient." Regarding the exceptions among Jewish thinkers, Grégoire mentioned Isaac Pinto, the Dutch Jew with whom Voltaire had polemicized, and invoked the case of Mendelssohn, writing that "a nation that can honor itself with having possessed Mendelsohn [sic] is at least at the dawn of reason." He took comfort in the fact that the sage of Berlin had left behind disciples who, in his view, were "disgusted with all the rabbinic rubbish" and had "prune[d] down the human additions to the [divine] law without affecting the truth of its principles." He even counted some of these Philosophical Jews among his friends.[64]

Having demonstrated that the historical circumstances of persecution were responsible for the vices he attributed to the Jews, Grégoire outlined his plan for regenerating them. Like Lacretelle and Thiéry, he claimed citizenship as his goal for the Jews. Invoking that republican monstrosity to which Lacretelle and Hell alike had referred, he asserted that the Jews collectively constituted "a state within the state" and attributed this condition to the fact that "the Jew" was "never treated as a son of the fatherland." He predicted, "Once he has become a member of the nation, attached to the State by bonds of pleasure, security, liberty and comfort, . . . one will see his *esprit du corps* diminish . . . he will cherish his mother, that is to say his fatherland, whose interest will be mixed with his."[65]

Despite the accretion of sentimental language and family imagery, when he elaborated on his plan Grégoire proposed discriminatory surveillance and coercion as the preferred means of integrating the Jews into the French *nation*. Though he insisted that the Jews "are men like us . . . before they are Jews," he resolved to treat them first and foremost as Jews, that is, as guilty until proved innocent. Specifically, he proposed banning Jews from selling anything on credit. Evidently defensive about the implications of such restrictive police measures for the rights of individuals, he wrote, "This law only appears to contradict the principles of civil liberty, whose advantages we wish to extend to *the whole nation.*" He added Beccarian utilitarianism to his invocation of the public good, writing, "The Jews only constitute a small portion of any nation that has the greatest interest in preventing brigandage; thus the government . . . will still reach its goal, which is the happiness of the greatest number." Apparently the same goal justified Grégoire's proposal to cancel all outstanding debts by "Christians" to Jews—thus resolving the "affair of the false receipts" by accomplishing legally and with the stroke of a pen what Hell and the Alsatian forgers had endeavored to achieve illegally and at the cost of exile, the galleys, or their own lives—and to prohibit *all* "Jewish" loans to "Christians" in the future, whatever the rate of interest charged.[66]

These measures were designed not only to protect the non-Jewish citizenry from what Grégoire called "judaic rapacity" but also to constitute the Jewish portion of the citizenry by transforming uncivic Jews into citizens, who according to the author's implicit logic were by definition useful and honest. This is the only interpretation that explains the otherwise curious reasoning behind the following if-then proposition: "If one wishes to create a people, if one desires that the Jews become citizens, the proscription of . . . promissory notes must enter . . . into the plan." Moreover, Grégoire linked the prohibition on all Jewish loans to "Christians" to the radical transformation of the former by using the language of conversion. Suggesting that someday trustworthy Jews could be allowed to lend money, he wrote, "While waiting for *the heart to be converted,* we shall stop the ravages of usury."[67]

In the meantime, the "political" and hence "moral" regeneration of the Jews required a strict control of their occupational practices. Accordingly, Grégoire proposed diverting them from moneylending toward occupations that instilled civic virtue. Even honest, transparent exchange of fairly priced products for money was to be discouraged, since "the spirit of commerce" was opposed to that of patriotism. In addition to prohibiting moneylending, Grégoire wished to forbid Jews to purchase mortgages, "without which usury would re-enter by this door." He also proposed limiting the amount of real estate they could purchase to prevent them from becoming landlords to non-Jews. Insofar as Jews

acquired farmland, they should be required to cultivate it, though Grégoire would permit them to solicit the assistance and agricultural skills
of non-Jewish workers. Finally, the abbé called for the Jews' exclusion
from inn-keeping, an occupation that would apparently tempt them
to engage in "the adulteration of food products," which might "present
travelers with . . . health hazards."[68]

In his plan to divert the Jews from baneful occupations to useful
work, Grégoire expressed high hopes of turning them into artisans. He
was aware that the guilds would certainly oppose the admission of Jews
into their ranks. Therefore, like Thiéry, he advocated the establishment
of "free workshops," which he hoped would be financed by "ardent and
sensitive souls" and "philanthropical societies." If he was reluctant to
coerce non-Jewish guild members, he had no such qualms about coerc-
ing Jews, who, he proposed, "might even be obliged in certain places
only to inhabit houses that they have built, and only to wear fabrics that
they have produced."[69]

Grégoire also hoped to see Jews become farmers and thus return to
their imagined state of primitive virtue. In a rhapsody that bears a striking resemblance to Latour-Foissac's "grand effort," he wrote of a regenerated Jew: "The rustic tasks will then call the Hebrew to our fields,
once watered by the blood of his forefathers, and which at that time will
be watered by his sweat; he will leave his manor to breathe the pure air
of the hills." Yet unlike Thiéry, who had proposed tax incentives for
Jews wishing to take up farming, Grégoire merely wrote of "some of our
colonies, and many of our provinces," that "are asking for hands," and
he vaguely advocated "that the voice of the government call [the Jews]
to these countries."[70] Was such a "call" to be an invitation or a sum-
mons? Given the author's penchant for coercive measures, the latter
could not be ruled out.

Finally, Grégoire's project for the transformation of the Jews' occupations involved their admission to state service, in both the military
and civilian sectors. Seemingly intoxicated by his imagined ability to
form and transform the Jews at will, Grégoire asked, "If I can make a
husbandman of a Jew, why could I not make him a soldier?" He claimed
that the Jews, once "such a bellicose nation," still possessed "the germ
of valor" and would be good soldiers if properly trained. Similarly, he
called for the opening of state offices to the Jews. At the same time, however, he made a long list of offices that Jews were *not* to fill. He proposed
forbidding them from serving as tax collectors, treasurers, customs
officials, bursars, and in other occupations that provided easy opportu-

nities for embezzlement, since "one must never lose sight of the character of the people that one proposes to rectify."[71]

In his zeal to correct the Jews, Grégoire also sought to transform their education. He called for the opening of all educational institutions to qualified applicants of all religions. Yet liberty turned to coercion when Grégoire claimed that, for an indeterminate number of years, "one can *force* [Jewish] children to attend our schools and submit them annually to exercises and public examinations." This mandatory integration would expose young Jews to the arts and sciences, and they would "acquire, even without wishing to, healthy ideas which will be the antidote to the absurdities" that they would otherwise learn from their families.[72]

Grégoire's proposed pedagogical jurisdiction extended as far as the proverbially dark interiors of the synagogue. Aiming directly at the rabbis, he proposed abolishing their office altogether. In addition to divesting the rabbis of all civil or police power, he also wished to take away their *spiritual* authority, their mandate to educate their congregations on matters of religion. In their place, at the head of the synagogues, would be instructors specially trained in French schools and chosen in national competitions. Grégoire even called for the Jews' obligatory attendance at sermons by Christian clergymen, protesting that "obliging the Jews to learn is not forcing them to convert." He suggested that "the government could usefully employ this path to instill in the spirits and hearts [of Jews] reasoned principles regarding all the branches of the duties of the citizen." As to the rights of the citizen, Grégoire was impatient with the idea, claiming simply that "submitting [the Jews] to the hearing of addresses is not contrary to the rights of humanity."[73] What these rights were Grégoire left unclear, but in any event they were beside the point from his perspective. Clearly Grégoire, like so many of his contemporaries, believed that a citizen was more of a moral person with particular features—such as selflessness, utility, transparency, *sensibilité*, courage, physical strength, and a desire to work—in other words, imperatives or duties, than an individual bearing rights.

In addition to controlling Jews' occupations and education, Grégoire argued for controlling their residency. He reviled the confinement of Jews to special quarters, which in his view both damaged their health and perpetuated their "hatred of Christians," and insisted that it was necessary to "isolate" the Jews from one another, "to break, insofar as it is possible, all communication between them." Did Grégoire intend for them to be dispersed by force? This was not clear, though he was explicit in recommending that villages fix the number of Jews allowed, and that they admit only Jews who could prove that they were artisans, artists, farmers, or proprietors (presumably of their own homes only), for without this precaution "the Israelite . . . would soon be the usurer . . . the vulture of the canton."[74] Grégoire therefore had two conflicting goals: the dispersion of the Jews among non-Jews and the limitation of their population among non-Jews, whom they would evidently harm in larger numbers. To achieve a balance would presumably require careful population management.

Regarding those Jews who might resist regeneration, Grégoire proclaimed, "It is necessary . . . to constrain the bad ones." The coercive tone of this imperative only corroborated the message sent by the repeated use throughout the *Essai* of verbs such as "oblige" *(obliger)*, "demand" *(exiger)*, "constrain" *(contraindre)*, and "force" *(forcer)*.[75] The desire to transform the Jews so fundamentally and the readiness to employ the full coercive power of the state toward this end betray the assumption that, of all "nations," they were the least susceptible to change. That the Jews were stubborn, inflexible, or "timeless" were clichés that Grégoire shared with clerics and philosophes alike. The appearance of these assumptions alongside a case for the Jews' malleability only confirms their persistence (and ironically points more to the stubbornness of the prejudice than to its object). Thus Grégoire, who wanted to convince his reader that Jews became virtuous in countries where they enjoyed esteem and performed useful work, and who deplored the fact that "all the laws passed against the Jews always suspect them of a native and indelible wickedness,"[76] could seemingly not avoid portraying them as inflexible, and even justified further laws against them by invoking the same assumption. He wrote that "this nation has preserved an almost invariable character" and contradicted his own argument about the role of historical circumstances in the Jews' character by claiming that "the difference of centuries and of countries has often reinforced [the Jew's] character, far from changing his native traits."[77] These representations utterly undermined the humanism exemplified in the claim that the Jews "are men like us . . . before they are Jews" and suggested that they were phenomenal exceptions to human nature, more Jews than "men."

This impression of exceptional stasis or invariability was reinforced by the author's repeated assertions that the Jews were abnormally attached to their beliefs. He wrote, à la Voltaire, "The fervor of the Jews inclines singularly toward fanaticism."[78] At the same time he was capable of citing Bossuet, for whom the Jews' "pride" was "an inveterate malady," and in several places characterized the Jews as "obstinate," a term of abuse that both theologians and philosophes had made into a cliché.[79] This proverbial stubbornness explained the author's repeated portrayals of the regeneration process as arduous and long, just as it justified the numerous calls for surveillance and coercion. Again using the charged language of obstinacy, he wrote, "One will see Jews persist [s'obstiner] in continuing their odious practices, their usurious maneuvers." Happily, he added, their "swindles" would be "easier to recognize" and would "bring on more severe punishments." Similarly, he predicted, "their depravation will have a limit, when they ceaselessly see the public eye behind them surveying them, and punishment next to crime."[80]

In retrospect one already sees Grégoire the apologist of the Terror in these words. Yet if the nascent *terroriste* is discernible, so is the *convertisseur*. By exceptionalizing and essentializing "the Jew" as peculiarly rebarbative, Grégoire made Jews' ultimate conversion into virtuous citizens and pious practitioners of natural religion all the more spectacular and also promoted his own prodigious skills as a Pygmalion who could mold human beings into their most desirable form. Grégoire indulged his conversionist fantasies by taking on the challenge of a people who were almost by definition inconvertible, who seemingly dared him to try to convert them. He was therefore ready to employ all possible means, from gentle persuasion to the public eye, and finally to coercion and punishment, in the heroic project of regeneration.

MIRABEAU, MENDELSSOHN, AND THE PLURALIST MODEL OF REGENERATION

There was another way of conceptualizing the regeneration of the Jews in the years just prior to the French Revolution, one in which surveillance, coercion, and punishment were not the main principles. Witness the book by the comte de Mirabeau, *Sur Moses Mendelssohn, sur la réforme politique des juifs: Et en particulier sur la révolution tentée en leur faveur en 1753 dans la grande Bretagne* (1787). There the future revolutionary made a case for "political reform," that is, legal changes permitting the Jews to exercise the rights that Mirabeau deemed universal. Far more optimistic about the prospects of moral improvement, among Jews as among human beings more generally, Mirabeau simply argued that if the Jews had the liberty to exercise "honest" professions and enjoyed the esteem of their neighbors, they would be good citizens.

Mirabeau devoted the first fifty-eight pages, nearly half the book, to a eulogy for Mendelssohn, who had died the previous year. Beginning with an account of the "indigent Jew" who as a child already pondered the works of Maimonides, Mirabeau went on to laud the "modern Plato" for his prodigious intellect, prolific scholarship, and moral excellence. For Mirabeau the Jewish philosopher epitomized *sagesse,* a quality that combines both intellect and virtue. Thus he praised *Phaedon,* which like its Platonic namesake attempted to prove the existence of God, primarily because it confirmed "the harmony of moral truths and . . . the system of our rights and duties." Like his fellow practitioners of natural religion, Mirabeau believed that immortality was a precondition of justice, which was not always served in this world and therefore required posthumous rewards and punishments. Similarly, Mirabeau praised *Jerusalem,* Mendelssohn's plea for confessional tolerance and the separation of religion and the state, not only for its "rare logic," "sustained force," and "graceful style" but also for its moral message, summarized in Mendelssohn's words from the book: "'The Almighty having created the free spirit of man, all the enterprises formed to constrain him [in matters of religion] through the fear of torture, the weight of tribute, the exclusion from public employment only produce habits of hypocrisy and baseness.'"[81]

Intellect and virtue combined as well in the economic theory that Mirabeau attributed to Mendelssohn. The son of one of the founders of physiocracy, Mirabeau was happy to report that, according to Mendelssohn, the enactment of physiocratic policies would lead to nothing less than "the regeneration of the human race." In particular, the physiocrats' demotion of commerce and finance to "sterile" economic activities fused perfectly with Mendelssohn's highly moralistic condemnation of those same activities. Thus Mirabeau had the Jewish philosopher opine that viewing money as "the unique goal of every enterprise" was "the principal cause of the corruption of the cities, in which each person . . . thinks only of profiting from the delirium of avid and unregulated passions." Consequently, Mirabeau's Mendelssohn reviled the apologists of such lucrative activity, that is, the mercantilists. He could not share with these "superficial thinkers" and "mercenary panegyrists" the conviction that the "pestilential fermentation" of commerce was a "productive activity." On the contrary, he saw in the "horrible plague of commerce and finance . . . the most fertile source of every type of misery and corruption."[82]

The connection between this apparently physiocratic denigration of mercantile activity and the perceived need for moral improvement among the Jews would have been obvious to any contemporary reader. Thus if the "regeneration of the human race" was what Mendelssohn sought when warning against the evils of trade and money, it was clear that he was beginning with the regeneration of his own "nation," apparently long steeped in the corrupting pursuit of lucre. To make this point unmistakable, Mirabeau wrote that Mendelssohn sought for the Jews "admission to the *innocent professions*" and that "it was above all from a great latitude accorded to their industriousness that he expected their *regeneration*."[83]

In an age of *sensibilité* an effective means of praising a person was to emphasize his or her fidelity to family and friends. Mirabeau wrote of the "pure, sensitive and penetrating morality that [Mendelssohn] indefatigably practiced throughout the entire course of his life" and was especially appreciative of Mendelssohn's "sweetness of friendship, domestic union, [and] care for his family." Similarly, he esteemed Mendelssohn's fidelity to his God and his religion. Describing the philosopher's response to an attempt to convert him, Mirabeau cited Mendelssohn's published letter to the proselytizer, "'I attest before God that I shall remain inviolably attached to my law as long as my soul does not take on another nature.'"[84] Like the fictional Jews in the writings of Montesquieu, Voltaire and the marquis d'Argens, the real Moses Mendelssohn served to reverse the spin on the proverbial "obstinate" Jew by representing the refusal to convert as a virtue.

Mendelssohn was, in short, the prototypical Good Jew. His existence signaled the potential of all Jews to *sagesse*. Mirabeau wasted no time making it clear that his aim in writing the life of Mendelssohn was to disabuse his readers "of the prejudice that allows us to excuse the iniquitous abuse of social force against the Jews by representing them to ourselves as incapable of ever becoming either morally estimable or politically useful." He reiterated this message in the conclusion of his eulogy, asking rhetorically, "Can it not be said that his example . . . must reduce to silence those who insist with a quite ungenerous tenacity on painting the Jews as too debased ever to produce a race of estimable men?"[85]

A skeptical reader might have retorted that Mendelssohn was the exception that proved the rule, and Mirabeau was obliged to persuade his readers that there would be more Mendelssohns in the future. Indeed, the very first lines of his biography suggested a miracle of nature rather than a predictable occurrence: "A man thrown by nature into the midst of a debased horde, born without any kind of fortune, . . . has risen up into the ranks of the greatest writers that this century has seen born in Germany."[86] At the same time, however, Mirabeau suggested that if a Mendelssohn could emerge in such lamentable conditions, one could expect even more Jews like him under favorable circumstances. Just what these circumstances would be was the subject of his *Sur la réforme politique des juifs,* which immediately followed the biography. In this section Mirabeau laid out a systematic treatment of the causes of and cures for the Jews' moral and legal ills.

He began with an account of the laws that oppressed the Jews "in the majority of countries in Europe." He noted that in many places Jews were permitted only a brief asylum, in some cases no longer than a night, and that in other countries they had been "received only under the most onerous and humiliating conditions." As such they were "not citizens" but "barely tolerated inhabitants." Mirabeau showed particular indignation at the restrictions governing Jews' domestic existence, such as the special permission required for marriage and additional taxes to be paid for each newborn child. The Jews were therefore "robbed of domestic happiness," and the implication was that they could not be expected to be virtuous under such circumstances. Mirabeau went on to record the vocational restrictions that prevented Jews from earning an honest living and "rendering services to the state." Excluded from the military, agriculture, and the capacity to own land, and barred from nearly all the crafts, arts, and sciences, they had little recourse but to petty commerce, which in turn produced such a paltry income that they had to supplement it with the "dishonest profession" of money-lending.[87]

According to Mirabeau, the mistaken belief that the Jewish religion prevented its practitioners from performing their civic obligations rationalized the oppressive laws against them. The author therefore railed against the "intolerant priests who have collected calumnious stories," as well as the recent accusations by Hell, who had "heap[ed] together all the fabulous absurdities scattered in all the anthologies of lies" in order to deceive the public.[88] He replied with a spirited defense of "the law of Moses," arguing that "its commandments are not at all in contradiction with those of justice and humanity." On the contrary, he claimed, betraying his rustic romanticism and aversion to commerce, this law was "particularly founded on agriculture, and even specifically contrary to trade, which of all the professions could most naturally lead to [fraud]." He was less generous when it came to the Talmud and the "sophisms of the Rabbis," but he insisted that the main cause of deficient morality among the Jews was persecution.[89]

Like other reformers, Mirabeau supplied a history of the Jews to show that they had once been virtuous. He noted that "the Jews were useful subjects of the Roman Empire," where they enjoyed "considerable privileges," such as eligibility for civil and military positions and, in a passage that betrayed the author's federalist sympathies, observed with approval that the Jews had obtained "permission to live conforming to their own laws." He added, changing "subjects" to "citizens," "They preserved for more than four centuries the unlimited enjoyment of all the rights of citizens; it suffices to say that they fulfilled the duties thereof." Unfortunately, under the decadent empire the Jews "were oppressed, deprived of their laws and their patriarchs, subject to Roman magistrates, excluded from civil employment and from the honor of serving the *patrie,* surcharged with burdens without compensation, reduced to the vilest class of beings." The rise of Christianity only made matters worse, as the church fathers, "dedicated to fanaticism," bullied weak leaders into "destroying the wise laws of their predecessors."[90]

Mirabeau's account of Jewish history during the Middle Ages much resembled the accounts of Montesquieu and Voltaire. "Never has any people suffered such cruel, sustained and lengthy persecution," he wrote, and went on to list the outrageous crimes of which they were accused, including ritual murder, poisoning of fountains, and treason. Under such conditions, he argued, it was understandable that they would have "occasionally avenged themselves on individuals of the Christian religion [by defrauding them] for the cruelties that they had suffered." In such behavior he saw "nothing that does not conform to the nature of man."[91]

Regarding the history of the Jews in more recent years, Mirabeau conceded that notable improvements had been made. Though "Spain and Portugal have remained in all the barbarity of their prejudices," the Dutch Republic and Great Britain, in his view, treated Jews almost as equals. The latter countries provided even more evidence for Mirabeau's argument, for there "the Jews are the closest to enjoying the rights of citizens, and it is also there that they are very useful members of the state." Summarizing his reasoning, he asked, "What else can one conclude from the current situation of the Jews in Europe, if not that they are worth more where they are better treated and that an infallible way of making them better is making them happier?"[92]

Yet in France they were still oppressed, still reduced to morally degrading commerce and moneylending, and this was "the veritable . . . cause of the corruption of the Jews." Asking his readers, "Do you want the Jews to become better men, useful citizens?" he went on to lay out his program for regeneration. Most important, he argued that it was necessary to "banish from society all degrading distinctions" between Jews and Gentiles and to "open for [the Jews] all the paths to sustenance and acquisition." This meant allowing and "encouraging" the Jews to take up farming and the crafts, but Mirabeau envisaged no discriminatory restrictions on Jewish business practice. Like other reformers, he was concerned about education and wished to "take care that" the Jews, "without neglecting the sacred doctrine of their fathers, . . . learn to know better nature and its author, morality and reason, the principles of order, the interests of the human race, [and] of the great society of which they are a part." But he did not call for coercion, surveillance of instructors, or the replacement of rabbis with state-licensed preceptors.[93]

Mirabeau was even prepared to retain the civil power of the rabbis and to recognize the Jews' right "to live and be judged according to their own laws." Evidently he so admired the Roman arrangement of leaving each people its own laws that he was willing to apply it to the Jews of his day. In contrast to Rousseau's doctrine—later furthered by Sieyes and other republican revolutionaries—that corporate bodies were cancers on the body politic, Mirabeau maintained that "every society is composed of little private societies which each have their own particular principles" and "inspire in their members separate sentiments and prejudices." He added, "The world survives nonetheless; and the nations that are well, that is to say freely, governed, prosper." He insisted that "the great and noble task of the government consists in making each of these divisions turn to the profit of the greater society" and observed that "the greatest enjoyment of liberty" would produce in each group a "greater degree of attachment" to the larger society.[94]

Ultimately, Mirabeau's plan conformed precisely to what Jewish leaders themselves would request when the National Assembly deliberated on their status in 1789: corporate autonomy *and* civil equality. The revolutionaries made it clear that for them citizenship was not compatible with "particularism." Mirabeau's synthesis of corporatism and human rights, however, suggests that this outcome was not preordained. There were other ways of imagining a nation besides the model of a centralized, uniform, and "indivisible" community of like-minded citizens.

CHANGE AND CONTINUITY IN
THE HISTORY OF A PREOCCUPATION

As chapter 2 and this chapter have shown, between the Regency and the Revolution Jews appeared in French writing on a multiplicity of topics. They were the subject of discussions on religious tolerance and fanaticism, standing alternatively for victims and perpetrators of fanaticism. They populated discussions of natural religion, which was sometimes identified with an idealized Mosaic period and nearly always contrasted with the apparently irrational and unnatural legal, ceremonial, and spiritual aspects of Talmudic Judaism. They appeared in expositions of economic ideas, sometimes signifying modern commercial practices, and at other times representing an antique agricultural economy. Accordingly, they could and did stand for antiquity and modernity, primitive social configurations and civilization. Implicitly or explicitly, by virtue of these mental associations, Jews entered discussions of political ideas about pluralism and the possibility of integrating different types of people into a polity, the relationship between self-regarding, "particularistic" groups and a potentially indivisible *nation*.

The Jews therefore provided a means of thinking about what a citizen was. Significantly, whereas historians and political scientists have tended to think of eighteenth-century notions of citizenship in terms of rights, the Jewish question suggests that in fact political thinkers were more interested in the moral attributes of citizens. That is, they thought of the citizen less in terms of a rights-bearing person and more in terms of a set of moral qualities. Thus they defined the citizen as displaying selflessness over egotism, courage over cowardice, productive utility over sterile idleness, transparency over opacity, and in constructing these oppositions depicted the Jews in terms of the negative poles, thus conceiving of them as anticitizens. Moreover, speculation on the future transformation of Jews from anticitizens to citizens revealed the continuing preoccupation of eighteenth-century French writers with the problem of human perfectibility. The fact that citizenship, Jewish and otherwise, was thought of in terms of perfectibility only underscores the extent to which contemporaries viewed it as a set of moral qualities rather than a set of rights.

French interest in this marginal group was therefore not a marginal matter. By demonstrating the frequency with which philosophes and their successors discussed Jews, ancient and modern, fictional and real, and by mapping the ideas and concerns about which the Jews were "good to think," these two chapters, I believe, constitute a significant revision of our understanding of eighteenth-century French thought. Yet the very multivalency of "the Jew" in the contemporary imaginary, its apparently overdetermined character as a symbol, suggests a need for greater precision about the relationship between the meanings attached to representations of Jews and the historical experience of the educated French elite in the eighteenth century. Toward this end it is instructive to ask whether certain of the mental associations listed earlier were more prevalent in the period of the philosophes (roughly corresponding to the reign of Louis XV) or in the decade and a half prior to the outbreak of the Revolution.

A juxtaposition of the writings analyzed in chapter 2 with those discussed in this chapter reveals some important changes over time. The philosophes tended to invoke Jews in polemics denouncing fanaticism, urging tolerance of (certain kinds of) religious difference, and promoting a "natural religion" supposedly common to the three Western monotheistic faiths when stripped of their unnecessary dogma. By the 1770s, however, more explicitly political or constitutional concerns took the place of the struggle against *l'infâme*—despite the fact that religious conflicts had helped to engender the new preoccupation with issues of government and sovereignty[95]—and Jews figured in the ensuing questions about the meaning of such charged and imprecise terms as *citoyen* and *nation*. Accordingly, if the ideal Jew of Montesquieu, Voltaire, and the marquis d'Argens was a Philosophical Jew who reconciled natural reason with religious faith, writers advocating the regeneration of the Jews in the 1770s and 1780s tended to envisage a Jewish citizen equipped with patriotic feeling and the ability to be immediately useful to the *patrie*.[96]

This new preoccupation with civic questions marked another transformation revealed in the writings on the Jews. Specifically, the philosophes frequently envisaged a cosmopolitan ideal. Accordingly, Voltaire could vilify Jews past and present as overly nationalistic. Although he did not have access to the word *nationalistic* he (along with many contemporaries) saw the Jews as the *nation* par excellence. Other philosophes depicted them as essentially cosmopolitan—without necessarily abandoning the contradictory belief in their status as nation—and saw this presumed cosmopolitanism in a positive light. D'Argens made the international (and traveling) character of his fictional Jews a fundamental source of their wisdom, and Jaucourt could portray real Jews as a means of facilitating communication between countries, the "pegs and nails" of European civilization. By contrast, the commentators on the Jewish question in the 1770s and 1780s were highly nationalistic. They represented themselves as patriotic citizens whose first loyalty was to the French *nation*. Like their predecessors, they had no trouble maintaining the contradiction that Jews were cosmopolitans on the one hand and a nation on the other. Yet both designations were now typically negative. There was very little ideological space for a positive cosmopolitanism, as in d'Argens and Jaucourt. At the same time, the persistent association of Jews with a discrete nation made it difficult to envisage their integration into a French nation. Mirabeau is a revealing exception, since he could permit a degree of Jewish autonomy on the strength of his pluralistic federalism. Still, the dominant view was that a "nation within the nation" was a monstrosity.

Finally, a diachronic examination of the written statements on the Jews reveals changes in attitudes toward commerce and its apparently attendant phenomenon of civilization. The philosophes were far from unambiguously happy about commerce. Montesquieu, through the character of Usbek, disparaged it as essentially "Jewish" by remarking with apparently jaded resignation, "Wherever there is money, there are Jews," and if the same author could criticize the medieval church for disdaining commerce altogether, his historical explanation of the circumstances that led Jews to practice it suggested that their association with trade called for an excuse.[97] Voltaire could suggest the improving character of trade by situating the enlightened deists of the "Sermon des cinquante" in "a populous commercial city."[98] Yet any reading of *Candide* vitiates the impression that commerce and the European civilization to which it was attached entailed the "best of all possible worlds," and the recurrent appearance of swindlers, Jews as well as non-Jews, in the novel reinforces this pessimistic assessment. Finally, the *Encyclopédie*, in its pronouncements about the Jews, sent a mixed message about the benefits of commerce and civilization. Jaucourt's affirmative statement about commerce and civilization was undermined by fellow encyclopedists who imagined ancient Israel as a precivilized and consequently morally superior society.

If the philosophes expressed ambivalence about commerce and civilization, however, those who wrote on the Jewish question in the 1770s and 1780s were almost uniformly negative. Hell contrasted the ideal citizen, the peasant, with its anti-image, the Jewish moneylender, and imagined a coalition between Jews and rich non-Jews corrupted equally by novel philosophical ideas (such as tolerance) and greed. He represented the danger of the Jews as consisting precisely in their ability to encourage the consumption of the most conspicuous and immoral fruits of trade: luxury. Latour-Foissac's schema is nearly identical in this respect. His gullible but virtuous citizen is a young officer, not a peasant, but the implicit moral contrast between a traditional and virtuous occupation and the immoral character of commerce is similarly decisive in marking the Jew as seductive and dangerous, and for him the principle weapon available to the Jew is the proximity to *luxe*. His solution to the Jewish question was agricultural, and if he offered it as an afterthought, Thiéry, Grégoire, and other regenerationists would make it central to their program. Mirabeau shared his father's disdain for the "horrible plague of commerce and finance" not only on the physiocratic grounds that such activities did not produce real wealth but also on moral grounds, since they constituted the "source of every type of misery and corruption."

The tendency of the writers considered in this chapter to equate the danger of the Jews with their ability to encourage luxury and thus corrupt the morality of otherwise decent citizens confirms Maza's argument that *luxe* and *moeurs* were among the most prevalent preoccupations of French writers in the last third of the eighteenth century. By contrast, it casts some doubt on Colin Jones's more sanguine depiction of attitudes toward capitalism on the eve of the Revolution.[99] Nevertheless, even if prevalent attitudes toward trade, money, and consumption in the 1770s and 1780s were more ambivalent than either of these historians suggests, the fact that these economic realities were issues for thought, discussion, and debate guaranteed that the Jews, so intimately associated in the popular imaginary with money, would remain a favorite topic of writers despite their lack of actual economic importance.

This last statement suggests the presence of continuities as well as breaks, and indeed it is important not to let the ruptures conceal the continuities in French representations of Jews in the eighteenth century. After all, despite their differences, the writers of the 1770s and 1780s considered in this chapter shared with the philosophes some fundamental concerns, which moreover informed their choice of the Jews as objects of interest. Political economy was one such concern, and whether they defended or disparaged commerce or agriculture, eighteenth-century French writers repeatedly invoked the Jews in the process of articulating economic ideas. Insofar as they moralized economic activity, praising some forms of labor, production, exchange, and consumption as furthering virtue and deploring others as leading to vice, writers betrayed a related preoccupation with morality. This preoccupation, furthermore, directly informed writings on the Jews, who had long been represented in strictly moral terms. Whether a Jewish patriot was more virtuous than a Jewish cosmopolitan depended largely on the period in which a particular author was writing, but the tendency to use Jews in discussions of morality remained continuous. Finally, economics and morality were subfields of a larger investigation, prototypical of the eighteenth century, into the nature of "man."

That Jews provided a way of talking about "man" is suggested in Lacretelle's declaration, otherwise a non sequitur in a legal dispute regarding a very specific set of privileges claimed by two Jews, "The real question of this case is . . . whether Jews are men." Mirabeau's claim, "The Jew is more a man than he is a Jew," which Grégoire repeated almost verbatim, further indicates that when eighteenth-century French writers discussed the Jews, what they really wished to discuss was human nature.[100] Nearly all the writers examined in the past two chapters referred implicitly or explicitly to some ideal Jew or Jews whose existence proved that the "nation" as a whole was not incorrigible, that is, that they were just as perfectible as all "men." Montesquieu invoked a hypothetical writer protesting the cruelties of the Inquisition. D'Argens created the Karaite Isaac Onis. Voltaire idealized the fictional Rabbi Akib and the real Rabbi Orobio and suggested that Isaac Pinto could similarly achieve the status of a *juif philosophe*. The *Encyclopédie* contained its exemplary Jews as well. For Lacretelle, Mirabeau, Thiéry, and Grégoire, it was the sage of Berlin, Moses Mendelssohn, who proved that Jews were "men" with the same potential for greatness inherent in all members of the human race. Exemplary Jews proved that circumstances rather than innate characteristics made "men," and that by transforming those circumstances for the better, one could change all types of humanity. As a limiting case in the range of human types, they operated in thought experiments demonstrating that if the most recalcitrant, *obstinate* people could improve, then all peoples could improve.

This characterization makes the writers on the Jewish question appear quite scientific, even mathematical; they assigned an apparently precise algebraic function to the Jews—namely, the quality of obstinacy—then plugged them into equations to derive logical conclusions about human nature. Yet Max Horkheimer and Theodor Adorno have noted the paradoxical proximity of rationality and myth in the "dialectic of Enlightenment." I have argued elsewhere that these philosophers are wrong in attributing the "anti-Semitism" of eighteenth-century thinkers to the perceived irrationality of Jews, who were in fact typically seen as all too rational possessors of an *esprit calculateur*.[101] Yet the fundamental observation that the Enlightenment contained mythic elements is confirmed by other aspects of the Jewish question. Here the mythic and the rational can be seen as merging insofar as the Jews were imagined as at once eternally refractory and changeable. It was upon this latter assumption of tractability that the whole regeneration hypothesis rested. And if this assumption could be proved through empirical reasoning—that is, by pointing to evidence of virtuous Jews in different places and at different times—the ancient, unexamined, and unconscious memory of obstinacy, confirmed myriad times by the New Testament, centuries of Christian theologians, folklore, and even the philosophes themselves, made Jewish regeneration into a kind of miracle.

The phenomenon of the Good Jew, as epitomized in Mirabeau's eulogy to Mendelssohn, was a prodigy on the order of the *homines feri,* the beast-reared "wild men" (and women) whose dramatic emergence from the woods into civilization fascinated eighteenth-century readers.[102] Moreover, if the two types of phenomena—the beast-turned-human and the self-made Jewish philosopher—served the scientific study of "man," they also betrayed a sense of wonder on behalf of contemporaries who repeatedly referred to them. They were both miraculous in the sense that beasts and Jews were considered equally unchanging, but both rose wondrously in the eternally fixed Great Chain of Being. One might add these miracles to the "two great mythical experiences in the eighteenth century" identified by Foucault: "the person blind from birth who regains his sight and the foreign spectator who is thrown into an unfamiliar world."[103]

Mona Ozouf adds to Foucault's short list "the individual who is rebaptized as citizen in the [revolutionary] festival," and though numerous candidates could be cited for "great mythical experiences," her suggestion can help to explain further the contemporary preoccupation with Jewish regeneration. In her study of revolutionary festivals, Ozouf argues that in the wake of official dechristianization, revolutionaries replaced the old forms of the religious life with civic festivals that sacralized the values of the *nation* and represented the citizen as a new kind of person, perfectly integrated into society as well as the natural world *tout court*. By describing this transcendent being as "rebaptized," she underscores the religious implications of what in the years surrounding the Revolution was called *regeneration*.[104] What does the conceptual and symbolic proximity between regeneration and baptism reveal about the impulse to regenerate the Jews? Is it a coincidence that the term *regeneration* had as its original meaning spiritual rebirth, typically through baptism? Before answering these questions, it is worth considering the narratives of Jewish regeneration more closely.

Writer after writer told a variant of the following story. In the beginning the Jews were a great people. They exhibited the primitive virtues of equality, simplicity, transparency, and courage. Then a great catastrophe occurred, and they were dispersed throughout the world. Suffering persecution and contempt from Christian leaders and neighbors, they declined morally as well as physically. The understandable need for subsistence and the equally comprehensible desire for revenge induced them to cheat. This lamentable condition would change, however, and the Jews would be regenerated. Those writers who envisaged this transformation disagreed about the best means of achieving it, as the works examined in this chapter show. For Mirabeau, civic and political equality coupled with the esteem of non-Jews promised to regenerate the Jews. For Grégoire, Thiéry, and indeed Latour-Foissac, some combination of coercion and surveillance would be necessary. Still, the narrative structure of their writings was identical in that it included an idyllic beginning, an unhappy middle, and a comic denouement characterized by a return to the Golden Age. The family resemblances between this story and others in eighteenth-century France are striking. *Parlementaires* invoked a distant past when France was free, contrasted that age with a succeeding period of absolutism, and hoped to recover their ancient liberties in the immediate future. Philosophes repeatedly invoked a happy, virtuous, and wise antiquity prior to a long period of ignorance, cruelty, and misery and saw themselves as inaugurating a new age, as good as or superior to the classical past. Revolutionaries idealized classical antiquity, reviled the age of "feudalism," and saw themselves as returning to, if not surpassing, the greatness of the Golden Age.

If these stories resemble one another, it is because they all took as their model (no doubt unconsciously) the three-act biblical drama of Paradise, Paradise Lost, and Paradise Regained. Jean-François Lyotard has argued that modern "metanarratives" of liberation take their cue from the ancient Judeo-Christian story.[105] At this point Ozouf's observation about the "mythic" experience of the "rebaptized" citizen takes on additional meaning. Ozouf similarly argues for a secularization of religious experience, though she restricts her analysis to the period between 1789 and 1799. I shall have more to say in chapter 5 about the "transfer of sacrality" effected in the French Revolution and the relationship between this phenomenon and the continuing interest in the Jews. For now it is sufficient to note that this concept helps to explain the fact that otherwise "modern" thinkers (including Grégoire, whose calling as priest did not prevent him from espousing the most modern revolutionary opinions) sought what they revealingly called the regeneration of the Jews.

Rita Hermon-Belot has shown a possible affinity in Grégoire for the Jansenist variant of "figurism," which viewed events occurring in the history of the Jews as prefiguring similar events in the history of Christianity.[106] Whether this is a literally accurate account of the eschatological origins of Grégoire's interest in the Jews is questionable, but in a certain sense it is permissible to say that Grégoire and *all* advocates of Jewish regeneration were figuratists. Not that they consciously saw the salvation of the Jews as necessary to that of Christians. But the story of the Jews' emancipation, however secularly cast, could not fail to remind educated non-Jews in France of the dramatic metanarrative of Eden, the Fall, and Redemption, a story that was in turn, at least in its best-known version, unthinkable without the Jews. The "lachrymose history" with a happy ending was a comforting story to all who believed or wished to believe in their own regeneration, and in this respect it is not accidental that the revolutionaries applied the goal of "regeneration" (using that very word) to the French *nation* as a whole.

Whether considered as a story or a set of claims, mythology or science or some dialectical combination thereof, the textual corpus of the Jewish question in eighteenth-century France was confused, self-contradictory, and undeniably troubling to its authors. The Jews were eternally the same yet capable of radical change. They were harbingers of (often fearful) modernity and relics of the most distant past. They were cosmopolitans in the form of a nation. They were prototypically specific, peculiar, yet they enabled one to identify the universal principles of human nature. They were fundamentally strange, inscrutable, opaque, and yet eminently familiar. Moreover, the ideas about which they were "good to think" were notoriously difficult to fix: the citizen, the nation, "man," all these were proverbially nebulous. Finally, the redemption narrative that they illustrated could not be fulfilled in this world. Yet these very contradictions, ill-defined concepts, and utopian dreams of redemption guaranteed that the Jewish question would be repeatedly rehearsed, as though repetition would resolve these irresolvable antinomies.

CHAPTER 4

Contrapuntal Readings

Jewish Self-Representation in
Prerevolutionary France

The previous two chapters demonstrated that Jews played a disproportionately important role in the writings of philosophers, reformers, and
social commentators in eighteenth-century France. This chapter aims
to show how Jews responded to this mountain of literature in which
French authors claimed to describe them. It examines Jewish strategies
of self-representation as revealed in three types of texts. The first consists
of standard apologies for the Jews and their religion; the second comprises "patriotic liturgy," or the religious devotions performed on occasions of state importance; and the third is made up of symbolic actions
with which Jews attempted to convey messages about their relation to
France and the French. More will be said about these sources, their advantages and disadvantages for historical analysis and interpretation,
but first it is necessary to justify the project of investigating Jewish self-
representation in the first place. One might question the relevance of
such an endeavor, particularly since the Jews constituted such a small
minority in prerevolutionary French society. If the Jews were primarily
of *symbolic* importance to discussions of other issues, then why inquire
into the responses of the "symbols" in question to the manner in which
they were used?

First, the contrapuntal responses of Jews to the discourses that
defined them shed additional light on those very discourses.[1] Specifically,
the tensions and contradictions in the Jewish texts highlight some of the

principal tensions and contradictions in the Enlightenment itself: between individualism and communitarianism, the arguments for historical and universal rights, the value of freedom and equality, respectively, and the relative claims of tradition and reform. Furthermore, we know little about how groups marked as inferior have responded to the discourses marking them as such, particularly in the early modern period. Insofar as historians have been interested in self-representation, they have tended to focus on political leaders or socially elevated groups. Even for the modern and contemporary periods, where marginal groups are a more important focus of research, scholars have tended to assume that the choices these people faced were between complicity and resistance. The case of the Jews of prerevolutionary France, however, reveals other possibilities than this binary rendering of the available choices suggests.

APOLOGETIC LITERATURE

The most direct way of responding to books and pamphlets that criticized the Jews and their religion was to write books and pamphlets in their defense. Of necessity the Jews had to speak the language of those they hoped to persuade, which in this case was the language of the Enlightenment. Thus the examples of apologetic literature discussed here appealed to the ideals that so many of their contemporaries, including their adversaries, claimed to cherish: tolerance, nature, sentiment, justice, equality, rights, and patriotism, to name only a few. Yet these concepts were never fixed. They were variables whose meaning changed according to the agenda of the person or persons who invoked them. Even insofar as they pointed to a relatively predictable set of referents, the key concepts of the Enlightenment clashed with each other. The values of individualism and communitarianism, freedom and equality, science and folk wisdom, civilized complexity and savage simplicity were so mutually inimical that the greatest minds of the century failed to resolve these contradictions. Predictably, the Jews who chose to defend themselves in the idiom of the Enlightenment were similarly prone to contradict themselves. Rather than assigning them high or low marks for consistency, however, it is more fruitful to treat their attempts as a means of highlighting the fissures of an Enlightenment discourse that is all too frequently seen as monolithic and, moreover, of showing how the Jews

were able to appeal to their readers precisely by invoking these contradictory values.

One of the most widely read apologies for the Jews in the eighteenth
century was literally titled *Apologie pour la nation juive* (1762) by the
Dutch economist Isaac Pinto. Commissioned by Jacob-Rodrigues Péreire, the official spokesman of the "Portuguese" Jews of Bordeaux, the
Apologie set out to refute the charges that Voltaire had leveled against
Judaism and its practitioners. That it was widely read is proved by the
fact that it sparked a debate in France and elsewhere about the relative
merits of Voltaire's and Pinto's claims. Reviews of the *Apologie* appeared
in the *Monthly Review* and the *Bibliothèque des sciences et des beaux
arts,* and Pinto in turn replied to his critics in both journals. Louis Petit
de Bachaumont, barometer of intellectual fashions, recorded the controversy in his famous *Mémoires secrètes.* Finally, as discussed in chapter 2, Voltaire replied publicly to Pinto, praising him as an unusually
philosophical Jew but nevertheless insisting on his prior criticisms of
the Jewish religion.[2] It is therefore worth looking more closely into the
Apologie.

Pinto's pamphlet directly addressed the themes that Voltaire in particular and the French Enlightenment in general had designated to constitute the Jewish question: the validity of Judaism, in its biblical and
Talmudic forms; the national and/or international character of the Jewish people and their relationship to the Gentiles; the moral character of
the Jews and their susceptibility (or lack thereof) to change. What is
most striking about the *Apologie,* however, is not any single message it
sent but the self-contradictory impression it gives. Yet these contradictions are eloquent testimony to the conflicting demands that were placed
on the Jews in mid-eighteenth-century France, and in turn to the conflicting values of the French Enlightenment.

The most glaring contradiction in the *Apologie* concerns the claims it
views as permissible on behalf of individuals and nations, respectively.
The pamphlet begins by criticizing Voltaire for presuming to cast judgment on "an entire nation." Pinto argued that all generalizations call
for extreme caution, but that "circumspection must be even greater
still when a whole people is in question." Pinto asked rhetorically,
"Could one justly condemn the entire English nation for the execution
of Charles I or all the French from the time of Charles IX for the Saint
Bartholomew's Day massacre?"[3] By choosing historical examples such

as the execution of the English king in 1649 and the massacre of Protestants in 1572, he implicitly accused Voltaire of assuming the plausibility not only of collective guilt but of inherited guilt as well, thus placing him in the same category as his worst enemies, namely, the fanatical Christians who continued to blame Jews for the alleged crimes of their ancestors toward Jesus.

In his opposition to generalizations about whole "peoples" or "nations," Pinto appeared to espouse a radical individualism. He asked, "If in the whole world there are not two perfectly uniform faces, nor two men whose ideas are the same; how can one claim to draw with one stroke the moral portrait of a people[?]" At the same time, however, he undermined this individualism with repeated claims on behalf of "nations." The very title of his pamphlet betrayed his belief in discrete nations. Pinto did not clarify matters when he suggested that the one thing the Jews had in common was a tendency to become like the people among whom they lived. "Dispersed among so many *nations*," he wrote, "they have adopted . . . in each country, after a certain time, the character of the inhabitants." He continued, "A Jew from London resembles a Jew from Constantinople as little as the latter resembles a Mandarin from China." Pinto epitomized this capacity to acquire the character of the host people by writing, "The Jew is a chameleon, who everywhere takes the colors of the different climates that he inhabits, the different peoples he frequents, and the different forms of government under which he lives."[4]

The image of the chameleon was the very opposite of that of the eternal Jew, obstinately refusing to acquire the values of the host country, but Pinto attacked this prejudice at the cost of any sense of Jewish specificity or nationhood. Matters became even more confused when he sharply distinguished between Sephardic and Ashkenazi Jews. He urged Voltaire and his readers more generally not to confuse the former with "the mass of the other Children of Jacob." He observed that the Sephardic Jews "do not wear beards, do not affect any singularity in their dress," and that "the wealthy among them push refinement, elegance and pomp . . . as far as the other nations of Europe." The separation between the two groups of Jews was so vast, Pinto reported, that a Sephardic man who married an Ashkenazi woman "would no longer be recognized as a member of [the] synagogue" and "would not even be allowed to be buried among his Portuguese brethren." On the basis of these differences Pinto claimed that "a Portuguese Jew from Bordeaux and a German Jew from Metz appear to be two absolutely different be-ings."[5] But Metz and Bordeaux were in the same country. What, then, accounted for the great differences between the Jews of the two cities?

In part, Pinto suggested, circumstances played a role. "Is it surpris-ing," he asked, "that, deprived of all the advantages of society, . . . de-spised and humiliated from all sides, often persecuted, always insulted, the debased and degraded nature in [the Ashkenazi Jews] would appear to deal only with necessity?" This euphemistic way of saying that the Ashkenazi Jews cheated gave way to the more explicit claim that "the contempt with which they are covered stifles the germ of virtue and honor in them." Like other apologists, Pinto took great pains to defend the Jewish religion and consequently argued, "It is not to this ancient, divine and sacred [Jewish] religion that one must attribute the baseness of sentiment of certain German or Polish [Jews]. It is necessity, it is per-secution, it is accidents that make them as they would those who, pro-fessing another religion, found themselves in the same circumstances." The implication was that the Sephardic Jews had more extensive privi-leges and were held in higher esteem than the Jews of northeastern France. Elaborating on his description of Sephardic specificity (i.e., su-periority), Pinto boasted that since the end of the fifteenth century the "Portuguese" had "brought great wealth" to the Netherlands, "greatly increased the trade of the [Dutch] republic," and "facilitated the indus-try" of their non-Jewish compatriots. The Sephardic Jews also possessed "irreproachable morals," proved by their unusually low crime rate.[6]

In addition to the argument from circumstance, Pinto had recourse to another explanation for the perceived differences between the two groups. He claimed that the Sephardic Jews traced their ancestry directly to the tribe of Judah and believed their ancestors to have lived in the Iberian Peninsula as of the sixth century B.C. This claim might well have provoked the question of whether the famous persecutions in Spain and Portugal had not led to moral decline among the Sephardim. Yet it con-tained the advantage of suggesting that they did not descend from the Jews who had condemned Jesus. That Pinto felt defensive about any possible association with the Jews of the time of Jesus is further indi-cated by his extended refutation of the charge that they were collectively guilty of the Crucifixion, though Voltaire never suggested that they were and even condemned as fanatics those who made this connection.[7] At the same time, Pinto wished to benefit from a constructed heritage of more than two millennia to distinguish his "nation" from others, includ-ing the Ashkenazi Jews.

This imagined ancestry suggests another contradiction in the *Apologie*. In addition to the simultaneous evocation of a Jewish nation, Jewish nations in the plural, and individuals to be judged on their merits rather than their affiliations, Pinto depicted the Jews at once as infinitely malleable and eternally the same. On the one hand, circumstances accounted for their virtues or vices, and as chameleons they blended into the colors of their surroundings. On the other hand, they maintained an identity based on the collective memory of a remote tribal past. Indeed, in his conclusion Pinto invoked Voltaire's own plea "that the Christians stop persecuting and despising *those who, as men, are their brothers, and who, as Jews, are their fathers,*" thus combining universal humanism with a plea for special familial respect.[8] This was an odd way of ending an essay that began with a challenge to the moral significance of ancestry, and it only underscored the irresolvable contradiction of an ethos that could not choose between respect of the "man" for himself and the special preference for kin and nation.

This contradictory ethos, however, was not the invention of Isaac Pinto, and its summation in a quotation from Voltaire only underscores its immanent presence in the French Enlightenment itself. It was this bricolage of imperatives that valorized humanity in general yet sentimentalized family attachments in particular, valued fidelity—otherwise known as stasis—while urging change. As figures of the proverbial past and the quintessentially modern, the national, and the cosmopolitan, Jews like Pinto were caught in a web of contradictions. Representing themselves in this discursive environment carried the risk of reproducing that very same web. This did not mean that their representation was doomed to fail to persuade, only that it would more than likely fail to be consistent.

Five years after the appearance of Pinto's *Apologie*, another Jewish writer came to the defense of his coreligionists. The occasion was a bitter dispute over the legality of Jewish participation in the new royal program, established in 1767, allowing foreign as well as French merchants to purchase master's licenses without having gone through the traditional stages of apprenticeship and training as journeymen. As noted in the previous chapter, Lacretelle turned this issue into a cause célèbre by (haltingly) arguing for Jewish citizenship in 1774. Yet conflict over the new legislation erupted as soon as it was announced, since five "Avignonese" Jews immediately took advantage of the opportunity to purchase licenses and set up shop in Paris, provoking the heated response of the Six Corps, the federation of Parisian merchant guilds. The Six Corps challenged this threat to their monopoly in the *parlement* of Paris and published their brief, which denounced the Jews as the eternal enemies of Christians and, owing to religious beliefs that purportedly justified fraud and usury against Gentiles, inherently untrustworthy as merchants.[9]

The defamatory accusations of the Six Corps provoked a number of Jewish responses, the most comprehensive of which was a seventy-one-page pamphlet by Israel Bernard de Valabrègue, bibliographer for Hebrew and "Oriental" languages at the Bibliothèque du Roi and lay leader of the Avignonese Jews in Paris. He posed as an anonymous English "milord" writing to his correspondent in Paris about the legal battle between Jews and the merchants' guilds, though he gave readers a clue to his identity by signing the pamphlet with the initials J.B.D.V.S.J.D.R., which stood for Israel Bernard de Valabrègue, Secrétaire-Interprète du Roi. In his *Réflexions d'un milord,* the fictional lord spent little time on the question of the legality of Jews' entry into the Parisian market. Instead, he produced a general apology for the Jews and their religion to counteract the slanderous pamphlet of the Six Corps, which he summarized as "the recapitulation of a multitude of ridiculous fables, invented during centuries of ignorance," and which "should never reappear during an enlightened century."[10] Yet this invocation of the Enlightenment made Valabrègue no less immune to self-contradiction than Pinto had been five years earlier.

Like Pinto's *Apologie,* the *Réflexions d'un milord* expressed great confidence in commerce. It began with the English observer praising this "branch of human industry." "The more [it] occupies Citizens," he wrote, the more commerce "become[s] useful to society." Owing to this mercantilist-utilitarian ideology, the author did not have to excuse the Jews for engaging in commerce. Apparently untouched by the nostalgia that many of his contemporaries felt for a precivilized state, he had no need to invoke the historical circumstances of Jewish commercial practice. Later making the connection explicit between the Jews and trade, the author cited Jaucourt's article in the *Encyclopédie,* calling the Jews "the instruments" of commerce and comparable to "the pegs and nails that one uses in a great building." Yet the author transformed Jaucourt's cosmopolitan picture by making commerce the proper activity of "Citizens," thereby suggesting that it was a civic virtue and of primary benefit to the state in which it was practiced. It was not simply the utility of commerce that Valabrègue's correspondent stressed. Rather, it was its utility to the *state*. Thus the writer claimed that since admitting the Jews, England's trade had increased by half, and that Holland's had increased by two-thirds. He reported similar gains for the cities of Hamburg and Leghorn. He held orthodox, Colbertian assumptions about the importance of trade, which he made explicit by writing, "A country that has neither gold nor silver mines can only attract [gold and silver] to it through commerce." The implications for France were clear enough. The Englishman suggested that the French would reap even greater rewards from Jewish trade than would other countries, since in France the moneyed classes had only "the ambition to place their children in the church, [nobility of] the robe or sword," and "each time a merchant or trader buys an office for his son . . . commerce loses a man and his capital." In their place came novices who "only add weakness of knowledge to an even greater weakness of means." Of all peoples, the Jews could most successfully "unite the knowledge and the means" necessary for trade, and the author predicted that France's trade would "be tripled or quadrupled" if Jews were given unrestricted trading privileges.[11]

Accordingly, the "milord" praised those French kings who had seen the utility of the Jews for the kingdom's commerce. He observed that "Henri II knew how essential it was for him to increase the springs of commerce in his states." Thus when "the Portuguese-Jewish merchants appeared," this wise king "welcomed them." The letters patent that he accorded the merchants proved "extremely useful" to the state in their stimulation of trade, following Valabrègue's account, and Henri III renewed them accordingly in 1574. Louis XIV, instructed by Colbert in the importance of trade, confirmed the privileges of the Portuguese in 1658, and Louis XV prudently followed suit in 1723. Valabrègue not only catalogued the privileges of the Portuguese in France—neglecting to mention the less privileged Ashkenazim in the northeast—but also culled European history for precedents to the policy he advocated. He noted that Emperor Honorius had protected the Jews, that Pope Gregory the Great treated the Jews of Italy well, and that Louis the Pious gave many privileges to those under his rule. Elsewhere he catalogued the countries in which Jews were well treated, dated the origins of their privileges, and praised the relevant sovereigns for their wisdom in recognizing the utility of a Jewish population. The fictional English observer added his own experience to the evidence provided by history and assured his correspondent, "I have traveled, and I have hardly seen any country in Europe, Asia or Africa where the Jews are not received."[12]

Precisely what it meant to "receive" the Jews, however, remained unclear. The implication was that this custom was universal and, by extension, natural. The wisdom culled from history further supported the idea that tolerance toward the Jews was prudent policy. Yet this historical approach clashed with the author's initial dismissal of past "centuries of ignorance" and special praise for his "enlightened century." Moreover, by emphasizing the wise policies of past rulers, Valabrègue departed from the typical portrayal of Jewish history as a tearful narrative of persecution. He even managed to relate the "appearance" of the Sephardic Jews in France without mentioning their recent expulsion from Spain and Portugal. Consequently, the *Réflexions d'un milord* lacked both the sense of urgency in improving the Jews' condition and the key argument typically used to explain their reputed vices.

The author of the *Réflexions* insisted that the Jewish religion itself was perfect, that it contained nothing immoral or antisocial. He defended the precept in Deuteronomy allowing Jews to lend at interest to the "stranger" by citing the Catholic commentator Don Calmet, who argued that the word *stranger* referred only to the Canaanites, a proscribed people to be treated as enemies, and not to foreigners in general. He also quoted the gloss of Saint Ambrose, who maintained that usury in biblical times was "a way of making war against" people whom one could "kill without crime," and that the early rabbis already forbade the exercise of this right. To prove that the Jews were not predisposed to treat Christians as their adversaries, he referred to the historian Basnage, who had argued that the Jews regarded Christians as Idumeans, or descendants of Jacob's brother Esau, and as such deserving of affection. He also cited Don Calmet's commentary on the prescription, "You shall not hate the Idumean, because he is your brother, nor the Egyptian, because you were strangers in his land" (Deut. 23:8, 9) as evidence of the "generosity" and "appreciation" that Jews were required to feel toward their non-Jewish neighbors.[13]

Nevertheless, this exposition of Jewish law, guaranteed by the authority of Christian theologians, only begged the question of why the Jews had a reputation for fraud and usury. Having dispensed with the lachrymose narrative in order to emphasize the precedents for tolerating the Jews, Valabrègue jumped ahead to a happy but hypothetical future in which they would repay the kindness of their host nation by treating them fairly. He thus tacitly conceded to the prejudice that the Jews of his day were dishonest and implicitly ascribed this vice to historical conditions. Responding to the Parisian merchants' claim that the Jews had no *patrie,* Valabrègue's lord promised that "the land that nourishes them

will become a new *patrie* for them" and asserted, always the mercantilist, "They *will not be tempted* to carry the riches away from [the land]
to which they owe them." To the objection that the Jews had "neither
sovereign nor leaders," he answered, a fortiori, "They *will only be* all
the more attached and more obedient to the Sovereign who protects
them." Unlike other foreigners, moreover, they would be "exempt from
that secret prejudice that every man who emigrates preserves despite
himself in favor of the government under which he was born." Finally,
the "milord" implored, "Let [the Jews] enjoy all the rights of citizens,
[and] they *will certainly have* the soul of a citizen."[14]

Valabrègue's recourse to a future in which the alleged shortcomings
of the Jews would be resolved suggested that they were happily malleable, while his sanitized history of their relations with Gentiles gave
the impression of benign stasis, and thus undermined the sense of a need
for change. This contradiction expressed the insecurity of the apologist
who feels compelled to say that everything is fine and that, besides, it
will get better. It also reveals the bifurcated leanings of the very Enlightenment it invoked. At once practically and empirically respectful of the
lessons of history—a tendency no doubt augmented by the reverential
citation of ancient custom so prevalent among the *parlementaires*—and
idealistically impatient with the status quo, Valabrègue's "enlightened
century" lurched unpredictably from one direction to the other. Unwilling or unable to detach himself from any of its favored principles, the
"milord" went along for the ride.

Two decades later Isaïah Berr Bing of Metz took up the pen on behalf of
his maligned people. The occasion for his apology was the publication
of Latour-Foissac's *Cri du citoyen contre les Juifs* (1786), though Bing
also acknowledged the relevance of his work at a time when the Metz
Academy was soliciting essays on the possibility of "making the Jews
more useful and happier in France."[15] His *Lettre du Sr I. B. B. Juif de
Metz, à l'auteur anonyme d'un écrit intitulé: Le cri du citoyen contre
les Juifs* employed very different strategies of persuasion and ultimately
a radically different ideology from those of Pinto and Valabrègue.
Whereas his apologetic predecessors praised commerce and civilization,
Bing idealized the primitive equality of his biblical ancestors. While
Pinto and Valabrègue made no distinction between rights and privileges,
Bing saw rights as natural and universal. Finally, he repudiated the cool
rationality of the Dutch economist and the fictional English lord and
adopted the impassioned language of the heart. His apology was no less

contradictory than previous ones had been, as it appealed simultaneously to antiquity and modernity, the dictates of God and those of the
Enlightenment. Bing was able to use these ambiguities, however, to
make a compelling case for reform in the legal status of the Jews.

One of Bing's most formidable rhetorical weapons was his use of the
language of *sensibilité*. Latour-Foissac had used this idiom, repeatedly
referring to hearts, souls, tears, and sentiments, as a means of eliciting
the reader's sympathy and establishing his credentials as a sensitive,
therefore virtuous, citizen. Bing had no difficulty appropriating this
same language in his refutation of the officer's accusations. At the very
beginning of his *Lettre*, Bing insisted that he wrote his response to the
Cri du citoyen "without having any other design at first but to comfort
myself by throwing my thoughts outside of myself and giving full vent
to my sensitivity *[sensibilité]*." Only later did he realize the value of his
thoughts toward elucidating the principles of his religion to "honest
men" who did not share Latour-Foissac's "sentiments with regard to us"
but held prejudices that could be refuted only through a reading of the
sacred texts, themselves written in an opaque "foreign language." By
contrast, Bing portrayed his adversary as an insincere person whose mo-
tives "are not pure," who was "inspired by some private animosity."[16]

Having taken the moral high ground in this manner, Bing went to
great lengths to correct Latour-Foissac's depiction of the Jews as "nour-
ishing the most invincible hatred for the nations" among whom they
lived and, worse still, obeying religious laws designed for "authorizing
that hatred and legitimizing usury." On the contrary, he insisted, both
the Bible and the Talmud required Jews to respect, deal honestly with,
and show compassion for non-Jews. He cited, among other biblical passages, God's reminder that the Jews had been strangers in Egypt and
should therefore "love the stranger, give him bread, furnish him with
clothing in his need." Bing even suggested that Judaism was more generous and tolerant than Christianity, since the latter required acceptance
of a specific faith as a precondition for salvation, whereas in Judaism
"reason and religion concur to teach that we all have a common right
to the eternal bounty of our Creator." He elaborated on this position
by discussing the work of the medieval Jewish philosopher Moses
Maimonides, who laid out the rules for Jewish behavior vis-à-vis Gentiles. According to Maimonides, all peoples who observed seven commandments, known collectively as the Noahides, would attain, in Bing's
words, "eternal felicity." The Noahides required Gentiles to forbid idol-
atry, blasphemy, incestuous or adulterous relations, murder and assault,

theft and fraud, and the consumption of flesh from unslaughtered animals, and demanded that they "maintain justice." Consequently, Jews were required to "love [them] as brothers, visit their sick, bury their dead with ours, [and] assist their poor as those of Israel."[17] Since Christians conformed to the Noahides, Jews were obligated to treat them accordingly.

Thus Bing assimilated Judaism to the natural religion of the philosophes by characterizing it above all as a religion of justice in which the righteous of all faiths attain posthumous rewards. If the Jews truly held such benign beliefs, why did they have a reputation for fraud and usury? Whereas Pinto had attributed such bad habits to the Ashkenazim alone and Valabrègue had only hinted at their existence among Jews more generally, Bing made an explicit case for Jewish vice as the result of persecution. Rather than denying the accusations, he claimed that Jews did engage in usury and fraud, but he insisted that "circumstance" and "necessity" explained this unfortunate propensity. He asked, "What do you want them to do? Cultivate the sciences? You do not allow it. The earth? They may not do so. Enter the corporations and trades? Not that either. Exercise civil functions? Even less. Nevertheless, nature has submitted them to the same needs as you, and after all they have to live!"[18]

To emphasize the force of historical circumstances in the moral constitution of the Jews, Bing offered an extended account of Jewish history. Like the majority of philosophes who examined that history, Bing idealized biblical Israel. He emphasized the role of the law in fostering morality and equality. It was in this context that he praised the statute forbidding the charging of interest on loans to "brothers." The "Divine Legislator" had instituted this law, according to Bing, because he wished "to maintain in the nation that spirit of family which was to bring together and tie all the Orders, all the Members of the State more closely together." God wished to make the Jews into "a religious and agricultural people who adored their God by cultivating the land that he gave them," not a commercial people who accumulated capital through the collection of interest. There were other "fundamental articles in our constitution," Bing continued, that encouraged the pastoral life. Among these was the Jubilee, which stipulated that every seven years all pecuniary debts be canceled and that every fifty years all debts, whether monetary or material, be forgiven and all slaves freed. The effect of the Jubilee years was "to maintain among us the most equal reparation of wealth, liberty and happiness, and to prevent the powerful from eventually drawing to himself all the advantages of society while the weak carried the burdens." Bing wrote that God "proposed to make us citizens by attaching us to the land that nourished us," thus implying that the qualities of the merchant were incompatible with the virtues of citizenship. The "Legislator" knew that "wealth is inseparable from luxury, and that luxury in turn engenders the vices that sap the foundations of the strongest states."[19]

It was only because the Jews rebelled against this wise constitution and chose luxury over simplicity, Bing informed his readers, that they fell from the ideal society that God had encouraged with his laws. Bing interpreted the destruction of the First Temple and the Babylonian Captivity as punishment for the accumulation of luxury and consequent decline in morality under Solomon. In an exegesis that combines the indignant anger of the prophets with the Rousseauian critique of urbane decadence, he launched into a sentimental cautionary tale about the dangers of mercantile wealth. "Even we, alas!" he confessed, "we had a cruel experience of this truth." At the time of Solomon, the king's ships brought "merchandise as precious as it was useless" to Judea, and the craftsmen of Tyre provided opulent products for the rich of Jerusalem. Soon "the pure pleasures that nature gives for a small fee" no longer sufficed, and ostentatious display became the norm. The wealthy grew indolent, allowing themselves to be driven in "elegant carriages, surrounded by a troop of attentive slaves to fulfill their least desire," and "ancient simplicity disappeared completely." The mercantile spirit triumphed as everything could be bought. "The man put his honesty up for sale, the woman her charms," and "sincerity was banned from all hearts." Religion itself succumbed, as the Jews fell into a "gross epicureanism" and ridiculed the dogma of the afterlife and the Last Judgment. Finally, crimes of all kinds "inundated our unhappy country, and we drew a just and terrible punishment."[20]

Ironically, the story Bing told of the Jews' fall from primitive happiness greatly resembled the Christian explanation of their sufferings in the Diaspora. Though the Christian variation blamed the postexilic misery on the Jews' "obstinate" refusal to accept Jesus, in both versions the Jews brought their punishment upon themselves by defying God's will. Nevertheless, from the moment the Jews lost their independence, Bing emphasized the behavior of Christians in determining the Jews' fate. Significantly, he did not locate the most crucial moment of Jewish decline at the time of Roman domination. Since the Romans retained Judea in its laws and did not infringe on the rights of its inhabitants, the Jews could flourish even under foreign tutelage. It was with the Middle Ages, in Bing's conception of Jewish history, that decline really set in. Bing wrote of "the strange mania" that provoked the Crusaders to conquer the Holy Land and resulted in the deaths of thousands of Jews in Europe. Whereas Pinto and Valabrègue had either avoided this grim period or focused on the tolerance of those who condemned excesses, Bing lingered over the dreadful scene of helpless but faithful Jews in the face of Christian fanaticism. He recalled the fate of Jews trapped in their synagogues while Crusaders "assailed them, made them endure the most horrible torments to force them to convert." Emphasizing the virtuous nature of the Jews' mythic stubbornness, he praised their "indestructible constancy," a trait that only "irritated the Crusaders" and further provoked their wrath. Domesticating the tableau with a collective portrait of "old men, women, children, spouses, lovers," Bing continued, "No one was sacred to them, no one was spared by those whose fury could not be satiated by the flowing of blood and piles of corpses."[21]

For four hundred years, Bing wrote, the Jews lived in a climate of "fanaticism" in which "horrible fables" and "incendiary declamations" placed them in continual danger. Given this history of persecution, he argued, it was not surprising that the Jews as a people should have declined both intellectually and morally. "Their members, individually subject to massacres on the slightest pretext, must have become enervated and cowardly, must have feared everything, been suspicious of everything, regarded life as a horrible journey, only occupied themselves with matters of survival." In recent centuries the condition of the Jews had hardly improved. No longer accused of using the blood of Christian children in religious festivals, desecrating holy objects, or working for Satan, Jews were "in the more enlightened centuries" considered innately immoral and fraudulent, incapable of engaging in the arts and sciences, and unfit for civic equality. The only modern exceptions were Vienna and Berlin, where "the Jews are less repulsed from society and find more encouragement" and consequently "provide many savants in all fields." In Berlin especially the favorable condition for Jews could be seen in the "sublime genius" Moses Mendelssohn, as well as a few publicly esteemed natural scientists. Still these exceptions merely proved the rule that the Jews in general were persecuted and therefore morally and intellectually weak.[22]

Regarding the situation in present-day Metz, the author described the plight of "around four hundred families, who have neither the liberty to cultivate the earth nor to practice the arts and trades." Under the circumstances they could only engage in commerce, an activity for which

Bing had already expressed the utmost distaste. Even the conditions for this enterprise were miserable, he observed. Wholesale trade was impossible, since local ordinances restricted Jews to a tiny quarter and forbade them from owning stores in the city. Retail trade was also severely restricted, in part because local trade guilds held monopolies in the sale of many products, and in part because Jews were restricted in their freedom to display even those goods they were permitted to sell. On top of these obstacles was the crushing burden of special taxes that the Jews had to pay in return for their protection. The result was not merely the degradation of Jewish dignity but the prospect of starvation. Bing claimed that 40 percent of his brethren in Metz "languish[ed]" in poverty, and the other 60 percent "experience[d] all the horrors of indigence." The "pyres of the Inquisition" were gone, but the Jews were now condemned to "a more horrible punishment, that of death by hunger." Again domesticating the tragedy of the Jews by focusing on the effects of suffering on families, he invoked the "tyranny of need, the horror of experiencing it oneself, and . . . the even greater horror of seeing one's wife, one's children, all those whom one holds most dearly in the world, feel its cruel blows." Under these circumstances it was natural that some Jews would find a justification for fraud and usury "in *the law of nature,* which imperiously commands all beings to provide for their subsistence."[23]

Bing's conception of rights was therefore markedly different from that of Pinto and Valabrègue. Whereas these earlier apologists thought of rights primarily as privileges established by custom and confirmed by the rational self-interest of governments, Bing dispensed entirely with this view. For him rights were natural and universal, prior to any approval by princes and superseding any contractual arrangements that violated them. Moreover, they were the precondition for morality rather than a reward for usefulness to the state. Bing wrote of a "cruel logic" that "deprives us of the natural rights common to all men" and results in misdeeds that Christians interpret as disqualifying Jews from those very rights. In his call for improvement in the Jews' condition, therefore, he asked "neither for grace, nor favor, nor privilege," but for a "law which will restore to force . . . the natural rights common to all men." He specified:

> We plea that this cruel barrier separating us from other citizens be lifted; that the humiliating distinctions keeping us removed from their occupations be abolished; that each person be permitted to live where he chooses; that no means of acquisition [of property] be closed to us; that the exercise of

no art be closed to us; that arms destined to the service of society not be condemned to inaction; that we be placed in range of cultivating the faculties of the mind; . . . that the state establishments in favor of the sciences be open to us along with all the other members of society; that finally we, who can and wish to fulfill the duties of citizens, have the same rights.[24]

To defend his brethren from Latour-Foissac, Bing appropriated his adversary's ideas and language. Fashioning himself as a sensitive soul whose transparency guaranteed the truth of his message and established him as a virtuous citizen deserving equal treatment from his French compatriots, Bing railed against luxury and commerce as the bane of any society, whether biblical or modern, and as such repudiated the mercantile utilitarianism of Pinto and Valabrègue. He appealed to nature both as a moral quality and as a scientific principle applicable to humanity and capable of explaining psychological conditions, but he went further by explicitly deriving, from both senses of the term, a theory of natural rights. According to this conception, citizenship demanded Spartan morality, equality of rights if not of condition, intense affection for other citizens, and unadulterated concern for the common good.

If these notions are familiar as staples of the radical Enlightenment, however, Bing was far from maintaining an uncritical admiration of the ideas of his century. In response to Latour-Foissac's charge that the Jews were "superstitious," he answered that if this meant showing "the most inviolable attachment" to the Jewish religion, he was happy to confess to this characteristic and hoped "quite sincerely that we [Jews] shall always be [superstitious], in spite of the progress of fashionable philosophy, in spite of its aversion for the ceremonial, and for everything that it cannot, as it were, touch with its finger."[25] The superiority that Bing attributed to his moral and civic values over the "fashionable philosophy" of his day consisted precisely in the fact that they were ancient rather than modern, sacred rather than earthly, and of divine rather than human origin. His republicanism was a biblical republicanism, stamped with the highest imprimatur, and if it constituted the best solution to the long-standing dilemma of how human beings should live, this was only because its author was the Creator himself. Of course, the Enlightenment itself was not a monolithic movement. It contained its own self-critique, articulated most famously by Rousseau, and consequently "fashionable philosophy" was quite often the prime target of fashionable philosophy. There was plenty of room within the intellectual culture of the day to denounce skepticism and justify philosophical principles on theological grounds, and in fact this was the method of choice among practitioners of natural religion. Certainly Gentiles writing about Jews freely mixed religion and *philosophie*. They rarely failed to express their belief in God and typically limited themselves to denouncing the Talmud, the rabbis, and their evidently false interpretation of the divine law. Yet it was precisely within the interstices of a multilayered Enlightenment that Bing was able to insert his most rhetorically powerful argument: that the Jews should possess equal rights not because their religion merely conformed to the moral requirements of citizenship but because it invented citizenship. As such their fabled obstinacy itself was the key to their regeneration, since it was their faithful stewardship of the ultimate Legislator's revelation that prepared them for membership in the French nation.

In 1788 Zalkind Hourwitz, self-styled *juif polonois,* published the last of the prerevolutionary Jewish apologies. One of the three essays "crowned" by the Royal Academy of Arts and Sciences of Metz for its treatment of the question, "Is there a way of making the Jews more useful and happier in France?" Hourwitz's *Apologie des Juifs* was the only entry by a Jew.[26] Although exceptional in a number of respects—for example, this *Apologie* was the only one written by a Jew to criticize the Talmud and the rabbis—its exceptional status is in itself interesting. In particular, it underscores the limited extent to which Jewish apologists were willing to depart from the strictest orthodoxy or to blame the reputed failings of their fellow Jews on poor interpretation of Jewish law. More important, precisely because this essay received the official praise of a reform-minded academy, it reveals the compromises necessary for anyone who aspired to the status of Philosophical Jew.

Hourwitz fashioned himself as a Philosophical Jew unique in his ability to explain the Jewish people and their religion to non-Jews, claiming that he was the only Jew to be both learned in the relevant religious texts and capable of "explaining them in French." He confessed to limited skills in French, owing to his Polish origins and late exposure to his readers' language. Yet he turned this apparent handicap to his advantage by arguing that one who has not mastered a language is incapable of dissimulating. When he "deplore[d] . . . the absolute negligence of [his] education" and apologized for his "incapacity . . . in the French language," he was not merely following the classical rhetorical device of pleading incompetence. He was also reversing the popular image of the Jew as skilled in trickery. His very deficiencies forced him to resort to "a few simple reflections drawn from common sense," which he apparently feared were "very weak arms against the seductive eloquence" of those who might malign the Jews, but which nevertheless guaranteed his honesty. Like Bing, then, Hourwitz utilized the discourse of transparency, so important in prerevolutionary and revolutionary culture and all the more so in matters relating to the Jews, to place himself in the position of the artless speaker of self-evident truths. Ironically, Hourwitz was able to profess his artless transparency while filling his work with learned allusions to Greek and Roman mythology, philosophy, and history, as well as Renaissance literature and works of "enlightened" contemporaries, in the process proving that the education he "deplored" was in fact quite extensive. Similarly, he could boast of his ability to acquire a foreign language by apologizing for his poor French, which he paradoxically dubbed, in a self-conscious conceit, "*sarmatico-français.*"[27] He thus portrayed himself as the ultimate autodidact, a Jew who mastered the canon of his people and went on to acquire European culture at an astonishing rate. The phenomenon that he presented to his reading public was that of a French Mendelssohn, a living example of the possibility of Jewish regeneration.

Still, in his defense against accusations of immorality, Hourwitz took the highly assertive and potentially antagonizing step of claiming that the Jews were *already* the most virtuous of all nations. They were "the most sober, the most industrious, the most peaceful and the most submissive [to state authority] of all peoples." Moreover, he claimed, they were frugal, faithful in marriage, and charitable, refrained from the bad Gentile habit of dueling, and in general maintained a disproportionately low rate of criminality. In addition to their virtue, Hourwitz argued, the Jews were useful to the states that tolerated them. Like Pinto and Valabrègue and unlike Bing, Hourwitz boasted of the Jews' commercial skills, which in his view contributed to the wealth and power of the state and provided an example for less capable Christian merchants.[28]

Still, Hourwitz undertook to explain the popular image of Jews as morally inferior and eternally antagonistic to Gentiles. He took special care to defend the Old Testament from the charge that it encouraged the Jews to hate other peoples. On the contrary, he contended, Moses was "the most tolerant and the most charitable of all legislators." Hourwitz claimed that "no precept in [the Old Testament] is repeated as often as that of tolerance and love of the *Guer,*" or stranger, and counted twenty-two instances of this commandment. He noted that God repeatedly reminded the Jews that they had been strangers in Egypt and must therefore sympathize with the plight of strangers in their own land. Mosaic law even permitted "full liberty of conscience" to those foreigners who were idolaters but observed the rest of the Noahides, which Hourwitz designated "natural law." And if Moses required Jews to love foreign idolaters in Israel, then their descendants must all the more love "the Christians, who adore the Supreme Being, and give them asylum."[29]

With respect to the Talmud, Hourwitz gave an ambiguous impression of its influence on the Jews' moral and intellectual faculties. He departed from orthodoxy by condemning the allegorical portions of the Talmud known as the Agada, which he called "absurd and reprehensible," yet he did not see anything in these stories that promoted Jewish antipathy or dishonesty toward Gentiles. In general, he approved of the legislative portions of the Talmud, writing that "the good qualities of the Jews are the perfect submission to the Sovereign, industry, sobriety, charity and conjugal fidelity," and that "all these virtues are the effect of the severity of the Talmud." Elsewhere, however, he held that "not all the Rabbis [discussed in the Talmud] were equally enlightened," and that "one finds in the Talmud some opinions that are not very moral." One such opinion was that in business transactions Jews were permitted to profit from the error of the *nacri,* or foreign idolater. Though Hourwitz claimed that those Jews who categorized Christians under the rubric of *nacri* were in error, he did not consider the original precept "scrupulous."[30]

At the same time, Hourwitz cautioned against explaining the Jews' behavior by citing their religious books. He wrote, "It is absurd to attribute to all Jews the sentiments of a few obscure rabbis unknown to the majority of them." He claimed that "the majority of Jews do not understand the Talmud . . . or do not esteem it enough to take it as a rule for their conduct." More generally, he wrote, *"Religion has no influence on nearly all the actions of the Jews,"* and maintained that religious books were "little read and even less followed, so that custom and prejudices always prevail over religion."[31] This startling claim no doubt left much of his audience wondering why Hourwitz had bothered to explain the Jewish religion if it had no influence on their actions, though it must have pleased many readers to see a Philosophical Jew maintain a less than reverential attitude toward his religion, which he described alternately as imperfect and irrelevant. Still, the question of the Jews' bad reputation remained.

Like other apologists, Hourwitz admitted that the Jews were not perfect, though he insisted that their most serious vices were a tendency to petty swindling and usury. Furthermore, he considered these vices nothing more than the effect of persecution: "The barbarism and fanaticism of past centuries, the biases, negligence and the private interests of ours; these are the only causes for the beginning and the duration of [the Jews'] oppression, which is in turn the cause of their real vices, which hatred and interest exaggerate."[32] Like Bing, Hourwitz went into great detail about the miserable conditions of the Jews of his day, citing their exclusion from most trades and professions, the restrictions on the business activities that were left to them, and the crushing burden of extraordinary taxation. He even expressed his surprise that "there are still honest people in [the Jewish] nation, and that vengeance and desperation have not driven three-fourths to revolt or to become highway robbers." He doubted whether "all the stoics in the world, in the place of these Jews," would be "more patient and more honest than they are."[33]

By contrast, Hourwitz maintained that Jews were honest, "happy," and "useful" wherever their circumstances were favorable. It is striking that Hourwitz, an Ashkenazi Jew, reiterated Pinto's claim that the Sephardic Jews of Bordeaux and Bayonne were both "more enlightened" and "more honest" than "their brethren in Metz" and made similar claims on behalf of the Sephardim of England and the Netherlands. Yet he made it clear that far from possessing any innate superiority, the Sephardic Jews simply enjoyed legal advantages that led naturally to an increase in virtue. Thus the Ashkenazi Jews of Poland and Sweden also boasted a higher level of morality in consequence of their relative freedom, and even in Austria, where Joseph II had only recently instituted reforms in the form of a *Toleranzpatent,* its improving effects were already beginning to show.[34]

Having determined the legal factors involved in the level of morality among the Jews, Hourwitz proposed to improve the situation in France. His solution consisted simply in recognizing the Jews' equality. He stated that "the means of making the Jews happy and useful" is "returning to them the right of citizen of which you have deprived them against all divine and human laws." What he meant by "human" laws he did not explain, but he made it quite clear that he did not mean historical precedent. He impatiently dismissed the suggestion that research into the legal history of the Jews' status was necessary or even relevant to the project of reform, writing that "witches would still be burned, [trial] by duel and ordeal would still be ordained if, before abolishing them, it had been necessary to return to their obscure sources."[35]

Thus Hourwitz appears, like Bing, to have endorsed a conception of rights as natural and God-given rather than historical. When it came to specific measures, however, Hourwitz's reasoning bore a significant resemblance to that of Thiéry and Grégoire in that often the goal was less equality itself than the specific effect of a specific law on the morality of Jews in particular. For example, Hourwitz demanded on behalf of the Jews the freedom to trade in all products, yet when he argued that they should be allowed to keep open shops with full displays and to live "among the other citizens," he reasoned that this would increase publicity and scrutiny so that "they will have . . . less of an inclination, less of a necessity and less facility in cheating and buying stolen goods." When arguing for the admission of Jews into all the crafts and professions, including agriculture, he did not invoke the natural equality of all human beings but cited the predicted social consequence of these measures, which would "diminish . . . the number of merchants, and consequently of swindlers." Hourwitz demanded the opening of French schools to Jewish children not because every child had the right to an equal education but because this reform would, among other things, "facilitate instruction in [the Jews'] conduct." Hourwitz's plan even included discriminatory measures against the Jews, laws of exception that the author claimed would prevent abuses in their business conduct. Thus, in order to increase transparency and accountability, he called for a prohibition on the use of Hebrew characters in all account books and contracts, whether between Jew and Christian or between Jews. More discriminatory still was his proposal that the state require all loans *from Jews* to soldiers or "any other person who is not a merchant" to be notarized, and all sales *by Jews* to be verified by exact bills indicating "the quantity, quality, price and time of delivery of each article." Presumably non-Jews would be allowed to lend to soldiers without having their contracts notarized and to sell goods without providing detailed bills.[36]

Ultimately Hourwitz's ideological proximity to Thiéry and Grégoire explains his success in the Metz Academy's essay contest. Apparently the jury was pleased that a Jew not only was willing to part ways with the rabbis but also could advocate a program of regeneration including exceptional measures that, in Rousseauian language, would force the Jews to be free. The jury was happy to see such a policy advocated by Gentiles as well, but the fact that a Jew could endorse this vision appeared as the most palpable proof that the desired transformation was possible. Evidently it persuaded the royal censor Camus, who praised the second edition of the *Apologie* as containing "very sensible reflections and a more extensive and more cultivated erudition than one might believe to exist among the Jews." The Parisian revolutionary Jacques Godard held a similar view of the "famous Hourwitz," whom he cited in a pamphlet in favor of Jewish rights as an example of the intellectual potential among the Jews. Hourwitz's favor went as high as Malesherbes, Keeper of the Seals, who consulted the *Apologie* for his project of legal reform for non-Catholics, and who also helped the author to succeed Valabrègue at the Royal Library.[37] Evidently Hourwitz had played his role well, and if he alienated himself from the rabbis and their followers, he provided Gentile reformers with another example of the Philosophical Jew.

Self-contradiction was endemic to Jewish apologetic literature. Pinto's individualism contradicted his communitarianism, and his implicit promise of perfectibility was hard to square with his claims for the virtue of fidelity to an ancient heritage. Valabrègue also invoked the past and the future simultaneously, though his past was the precedent of "receiving" Jews rather than the imagined genealogy of descendants of Judah. Bing was less sanguine about the past and constructed a lachrymose narrative of Jewish history to underscore the need for reforms, but if he was more consistent in this respect, his critique of "fashionable philosophy" sounded shrill after his harmonious hymns to tolerance and equality. Hourwitz wished to defend the ancient faith of the Hebrews, and even his attack on the rabbis resembled the Karaites' call for a return to a pure, original Judaism. Yet at the same time the *juif polonois* was sufficiently modern to be skeptical about the moral effect of *any* religion on its members, and his conception of rights pointed in opposite directions, toward equality and discrimination, toward treating the Jews as though they were the same as other citizens and considering them fundamentally different. Still, the contradictions of the Jews were the contradictions of the place and time in which they lived, and it was their appeals to opposing principles that made them interesting to Gentile readers, who were grappling with the same problems. And if the imaginary Jews discussed in the previous two chapters enabled non-Jews to articulate and address these same issues, then the introduction of real Jews into the discussion could not fail to attract attention.

PATRIOTIC LITURGY, PATRIOTIC PERFORMANCE

The apologetic literature suffered from one contradiction that could not be overlooked. At its most basic level, the apology was meant to refute accusations leveled against the Jews. The most common of these accusations, however, was that Jews were untrustworthy. How could *any* pamphlet be credible if written by a Jew? The almost inherent unreliability of the standard Jewish apology induced the Jews to supplement this form of self-representation with others. Jewish communities throughout France indicated their loyalty to the state by celebrating royal marriages, praying for "happy deliveries" of successors to the throne, holding thanksgiving services when their prayers for a dauphin were answered, praying for divine intervention when a king, queen, prince, or princess was ill, celebrating royal recoveries, and mourning royal deaths. Furthermore, they celebrated the coronation of Louis XVI, prayed for French victories in war, and celebrated the agreements that ended hostilities. Such occasions generated texts—prayers, poems, songs, sermons—that were either ostensibly addressed to or at least delivered in the presence of an omniscient God. As such they were less susceptible to the charge of insincerity, for if many Gentiles expected Jews to lie to them as a matter of course, no one suspected that they would lie to God. Thus the genre of patriotic liturgy itself helped to create the sense of transparency that was already at a high premium in a culture of *sensibilité* and was all the more desperately needed by the proverbially dissimulating Jews. Other groups prayed for the king, his family, and his causes, but when the Jews engaged in this activity, it had a special significance. On the one hand, it was striking that the mythically distinct *nation* was praying for a nation to which, by so many accounts, it did not belong. On the other hand, it was hard to deny the sincerity of people when they addressed God. Yet the Almighty was not the only audience of the Jewish devotions, and though they were typically composed in Hebrew, they were normally translated into French and published, sometimes in bilingual editions but more often simply in the vernacular, to accommodate the Gentiles—royal officials and other prominent non-Jews—for whom copies were designated.

Less frequently but no less eloquently, Jews took part alongside Gentiles in local festivities marking important state occasions, and the chroniclers who recorded the most minuscule details of these celebrations have left behind invaluable records of Jewish participation. These performances, like the published texts of patriotic liturgy, also had an advantage over the apology. Unlike the standard apology, carefully constructed and therefore subject to suspicion, especially when produced by Jews, the actions of groups involved in a celebration gave the impression of heartfelt spontaneity, however scripted they were in reality. These performances nevertheless sent messages. What messages did Jews send as they filed through the city, rabbis and lay leaders, adults and children, on foot and on horseback, wearing their Saturday best, praying, singing, carrying regimental-style banners, playing musical instruments and offering other forms of entertainment, greeting officials and on one occasion even Louis XV himself? Anthropologically inclined historians have demonstrated how one might profitably "read" processions of this sort as though they were written texts, though historians have been slow to apply this method to the history of the Jews.[38]

Accordingly, Jewish historians have been reluctant to take seriously either the evidence provided by patriotic liturgy or the accounts of Jewish participation in dynastic festivals. Even after compiling extensive bibliographies of Jewish patriotic liturgy under successive French regimes, one specialist in the history of French Jewry cautioned that "Jews always chanted—willingly or forcibly—in honor of all regimes," and suggested that apparent manifestations of patriotism may not give a "true picture of Jewish sentiments." Commenting on Jewish participation in a festival celebrating the reestablishment of the *parlement* of Metz in 1775, he wrote that "Jews were always forced to participate in festivities for every event."[39] Other historians, by virtue of their neglect of the sources in question, have implicitly doubted their reliability.

The claim that Jews were forced to "chant" or to participate in dynastic festivities is simply wrong. Christians were required to pray whenever bishops issued pastoral letters to that effect, but Jews were outside ecclesiastical jurisdiction.[40] Inclusion in processions, moreover, was a privilege rather than a burden. The Catholics of Montpellier snubbed their Protestant neighbors by excluding them from parades, and whereas the Jews of Metz were allowed to participate in royal festivities, their coreligionists elsewhere in the northeast appear never to have been invited.[41] Regarding the "true picture of Jewish sentiments" more generally, obviously the Jews wanted to portray themselves to the authorities as loyal to the crown, but this in itself is no reason to suspect them of insincerity. Prayer for the sovereign was a religious obligation stipulated by the Bible and the Talmud and part of the regular Hebrew liturgy, and there is no reason to suppose that Jews took such prayers any less seriously than they did others in their liturgy.[42] On the contrary, prayers written in Hebrew, such as that of the Provençal rabbi Jacob de Lunel on the occasion of Damiens's attempt to assassinate Louis XV in 1757, suggest a heartfelt devotion to the king.[43] Nevertheless, the sources in question are not simply the raw data by which the historian can gauge the Jews' level of affection for the monarchy. Even where Jews sent an ambivalent or polyvalent message in their published services and other records of their devotions—where the fulfillment of a religious obligation was coupled with signs of dissatisfaction and where defensiveness and pride shared the page with submissive obedience—indeed precisely points such as these, where the message was complex, provide the best window onto the legal questions and social tensions with which the Jews had to contend and their strategies for addressing them.

The most urgent impression to be made in any patriotic performance was that of loyalty to the sovereign, and Jews worked toward creating this impression in a number of ways. Specifically, composers of occasional prayers on behalf of the king repeatedly described him as a sacred being. When Louis XV fell dangerously ill in 1744, the Portuguese community of Bordeaux asked God to "scatter far from his Sacred Person all the ailments that converge to overcome him." When Damiens attacked the king in 1757, the Avignonese and Portuguese communities of Bordeaux and the Jews of Metz independently expressed outrage at the attempt on the "sacred person" of the king. The occasional liturgy made it clear, moreover, that the king's sacredness derived from his status as chosen by God. In an appendix to a prayer for the dauphin's health in 1765, Valabrègue (the author of the *Réflexions d'un milord*) translated the daily (!) prayer for the royal family in which the Avignonese Jews invoked God as "You, who alone dispense sovereign power." The service in which the Jews of Lorraine concluded their mourning over Louis XV included thanks for the "sweet consolation" that God had given "in placing upon the same throne [as Louis XV] a scion of this illustrious and mighty Bourbon race." The Jews of Metz celebrated the succession of Louis XVI by praying, "Behold the wonderful scion whom the hand of God has placed upon the throne," and in other published prayers one learns that God "crowns," "elects," and shares his "glory" with the king.[44]

One of the most common images used to designate the king's status as chosen was that of anointing. In a personal address to Louis XV upon his visit to Metz in 1744, Rabbi Jonathan Eibeschütz proclaimed, "It is toward the Lord God of Israel, who by his omnipotence gives victory to kings, that we fix our gaze and raise our hands to secure from him the exaltation, grandeur and power of his Anointed." On the occasion of the king's final illness thirty years later, another rabbi of Metz publicly promised God, in return for the monarch's recovery, "Our children will sing with the joy of their hearts: *now that we know that our God has re-established the health of his Anointed.*" This allusion to the Psalms of David (Ps. 20:7) implicitly likened the French king to David, the anointed king of Israel. Elsewhere this comparison was explicit. Jews from Carpentras (during a period of French rule) recalled Psalm 89 when they urged God to "preserve the King, assure Louis the Well-Loved (as [you] once [assured] David your Servant) that his race will last eternally and that his throne will subsist as long as the Heavens," and in a prayer on the occasion of Louis XVI's coronation Valabrègue and his Parisian congregation addressed God, "You defended from his proud enemies, / David of old, our King, our Father; / Preserve as well our young Louis, / And make his reign long and prosperous."[45]

Elsewhere the Bourbon king received the name of David's successor, Solomon, who was similarly anointed. In a personal address to Queen Marie-Leczinska upon her arrival in France in 1725, the rabbi of Metz praised her husband, Louis XV, as "the Solomon of our days." More often, the comparison between the French king and the wise, powerful, and prosperous Solomon was implicit, as in the many citations of Psalm 72, originally composed for Solomon's coronation. Thus the Jews of Lorraine alluded to Solomon's empire when they asked God, on behalf of Louis XVI, "May he reign over a thousand Nations," and the Avignonese of Bordeaux and Paris celebrated the birth of the dauphin by praying for Louis XVI, "May his posterity be eternal and innumerable as the sands of the shore! May the kings of the earth and the islands seek his alliance and give him rich gifts! May he be obeyed from one sea to the other, and from the source of the rivers to the ends of the earth!"[46] In a coronation ode for Louis XVI, Valabrègue was more prolific still:

The banks of two seas will border his States,
One Hundred unknown Peoples will pay him homage;
Despite their pride and their rage,
His Rivals will kiss the trace of his steps.

His Vessels, returning at the accustomed time,
Will be charged with gold from faraway lands;
And the Arab, sending his Princes,
Will pay him perfumed tribute.

Nothing will stop his victorious days;
One Hundred Nations will come to acknowledge him.
Each will want to have him as master.
All will bless his glorious reign.

His name will have as much splendor in the world,
As the sun, in its long course,
Spreads out its vivid light,
And the years will not lessen his glory.

All the nations will sing his exploits,
All will celebrate his infinite grace,
All will be blessed in him,
All will seek the gentle yoke of his laws.[47]

Just as they assimilated French kings to the anointed biblical kings, Jews frequently indicated their patriotism by comparing France's enemies to the foes of Israel. As early as 1706 the "Portuguese merchants" of Bordeaux, still officially considered "new Christians," prayed for the success of Louis XIV's arms against Spain. Choosing Psalm 3 as the basis of their supplication, they recited, "Lord, how my enemies and adversaries have multiplied! Many have risen up against me; But you, O Lord, are my protector, my glory, and He who raises up my chief; thus I shall not fear the thousands of peoples who surround me." In 1744 Eibeschütz of Metz compared the Austrian enemy to the villainous peoples of the Bible, imploring God, "who made a terrible noise when he accompanied King David in battle against the Philistines," to accomplish a modern version of that miracle and "cast a lightning bolt onto the heads of all [the king's] enemies." More militant still was his prayer that "this God, who, by an angel sent to King Hezekias, exterminated one hundred eighty-five thousand Assyrians in a single night," likewise "spare not one of those who have dared to raise their arms against our king."[48]

Similarly, the Franco-English conflict was the subject of much patriotic liturgy. The Jews of Metz portrayed the rivalry in terms of the ancient struggle between Israel and the island kingdom of Tarshish. They used the occasion of the queen's pregnancy in 1778 to castigate the English, asking, *"Why has a nation assembled in tumult? Why has it formed vain projects?"* They celebrated an unnamed victory, claiming that God's *"mighty hand has smashed the vessels of proud Tarshish,"* and interpreted this intervention as prophesying the birth of a dauphin. Three years later the queen's second pregnancy resulted in the birth of a dauphin, and again the Jews of Metz saw an occasion to militate against England. Isaïah Berr Bing (the author of the response to Latour-Foissac) composed a special thanksgiving hymn and, noting that the happy event coincided with the naval victory by the comte de Grasse over Admiral Graves at the Battle of the Capes, he and the congregation thanked God for this "double sign" of his "goodness and omnipotence." Repeating the reference to the wicked island kingdom, they sang, *"The Kings of Tarshish and their Islands trembled,"* and further thanking God for his intervention, they continued: "On the surface of the seas, which they dared to arrogate [as their] Empire, your divine breath dispersed their Vessels." The Jews of Lorraine similarly celebrated the dauphin's birth with an ode that referred to the conflict between France and England. Comparing England to "swelling waves" that attempt "to exceed their limits," and the French king to a divinely empowered Moses, they ordered their sovereign, "Present yourself, Louis: extend your mighty hand, and strike them, that they recede." The rabbi of Carpentras also showed his disdain for the English enemy, and in a published letter of congratulations to the duc de Crillon on the taking of Minorca in 1782, he compared the "proud" English to the Amalekites, the wicked biblical enemies of Israel.[49]

In addition to denouncing foreign enemies, Jews were prolific in cursing the internal threat posed by Damiens in 1757. The case of Rabbi Lunel has already been mentioned. Similarly, the Jews of Metz displayed their disgust for the "wicked man" who had shown "the patricidal temerity to raise his hand" against the king. The Portuguese of Bordeaux called Damiens a "black soul," a "bloody monster," a "Child of Belial," an "execrable assassin" and "parricide," and uttered an anathema against Louis XV's actual and potential enemies: "May all who would rise up against [the king] be destroyed. . . . May their lips rest mute, that they cannot propose their evil designs; may their eyes go dark, that they cannot conduct their steps . . . may their sword pierce their own hearts, and may their weapons be smashed." On the news that the king was out of danger, the same congregation thanked God for his intervention and issued another curse against the enemies of the crown: "May those who could hate [the king] be confounded; . . . may fire devour them; may they perish and their memory with them." The Avignonese congregation in Bordeaux similarly responded to the Damiens crisis by cursing all the king's foes: "May his enemies be vanquished; . . . may all who dare attack him be annihilated . . . may their tongues be melted in their mouths, and their entrails undone in their bodies." For good measure, following the king's recovery, the rabbi led the congregation in pronouncing yet another curse, this time hoping that the king's enemies would "be buried in the abysses" and "sink to the bottom of the waters like a mass of lead."[50]

The violence of the language used to curse the king's enemies suggested that the Jews' attachment to the monarchy was not simply a matter of obedience but of affection. This impression was all the more necessary in a culture that simultaneously valorized *sensibilité* and regarded the Jews as opaque and skilled at dissimulation. Responding to both ten-

dencies, Jewish composers of patriotic liturgy undertook to guarantee
the authenticity of their emotions, to emphasize the pain and suffering
that *they* experienced when the royal family underwent an ordeal, or
conversely *their* joy on occasions of royal happiness or success. To indicate their empathy, they made full use of the easily recognizable imagery
of hearts and tears. To be sure, there were liturgical precedents for this
imagery, especially the Psalms. Yet in a culture that valued such emotional outpourings, it had a particularly poignant meaning. Accordingly,
when Louis XV fell ill in 1744, the Jews of Metz published a prayer in
which they asked God to "have compassion for our misery, and receive
in the plenitude of your mercy the torrent of our tears"; the Portuguese
of Bordeaux similarly urged God to be "sensitive to the bitter tears" that
his worshipers shed. During the king's final illness, the Jews of Lorraine
publicly asked God to "receive the fervent prayers of your faithful Servants, Children of Israel, prostrated before you with a broken heart and
humbled in pain." The same community publicized its pain upon the
king's death, "Let us raise our voices, let us all pour out the bitterness
with which our hearts are filled." The Jews of Metz mourned by praying, "God of truth! You see the depths of our hearts; it is there that true
grief and pain have established their seat," and the rabbi of Carpentras
commanded his congregation, "Children of Israel, tear your clothes [in
mourning] . . . lie down in the ashes, cry bitterly, like a mother crying
over her only son, who has just been taken from her."[51]

Emergencies involving other members of the royal family also required outpourings of tears. The dauphin's illness in 1752 moved the
Portuguese community of Bordeaux to urge God to "be sensitive to our
tears," and Valabrègue's Parisian congregation made an identical plea
when the dauphin fell ill again in 1765. The Jews of the Comté Venaissin
supplicated God on hearing of the illness of the king's son: "Our eyes
drowned with tears, we pour out our souls before you." The Portuguese
of Bordeaux went further still, imagining the suffering of the dauphin
and the royal family and apparently feeling the pain that these reflections provoked: "Look in pity on the disquiet, the pain and the deso-
lation into which the cruel illness of our Dauphin throws the King and
the Queen, his tender father and mother, our august Dauphine his
dear wife, the precious Princes his children, and the virtuous Princesses
his sisters! What pain these distressing reflections add to our own an-
guish, piercing our hearts with new arrows!" Similarly, the queen's illness in 1768 incited the Portuguese congregation of Bordeaux to pray,
in a tableau of *sensibilité,* "Deign . . . to cast your eyes upon your people,

plunged in grief: see our pale, disheartened faces: our women and children bathed in tears: lend an ear to our trembling; sighs, cries and sobbing fill our homes."[52]

Empathy for royal pain also meant sensitivity to the queen's suffering in childbirth. All Jewish prayers for the "happy delivery" of the queen showed a concern for labor pains. The Jews of Alsace asked God to exempt Marie Antoinette from "the sentence that you pronounced against Eve," and the community of Metz prayed, "Make her forget her pain, and may she shed only delightful tears of tenderness, in tasting the ineffable joy of giving her royal Husband a scion worthy of his virtuous Father." In an even more explicit assertion of empathy with the queen's labor pains, the Jews of Lorraine proclaimed, "When you [Marie Antoinette] were still carrying this precious token of the royal union, we felt the pain: you are delivered from [the pain], and we are happy."[53]

It was only a short step from expressing empathy with the royal family to imagining one's own inclusion in that family. The most common way of expressing such a relationship was to portray the king as father to the Jews. When the dauphin fell ill in 1765, the Jews of Bordeaux asked God to show "the paternal goodness with which our good King treats us." Jewish leaders in Alsace referred to "the continual kindness that [the king's] paternal hand sheds upon the nation," not specifying which nation was meant, and on more than one occasion the Jews of Bordeaux invoked the "filial love" that prompted them to pray for the royal family. During Louis XV's final illness the Jews of Metz asked God not to recall "the father of his nation and ours," and their counterparts in Alsace, not distinguishing between the king's two progenies, simply prayed, "Great God! Give us back our Father."[54]

The language of the Jewish patriotic liturgy cannot fail to strike the twenty-first-century reader as obsequious. Yet language that seems excessively flattering today was considered appropriate in the eighteenth century, especially where royalty was the object of description. Moreover, in the contemporary idiom of *sensibilité,* highly emotional language was the only way to indicate one's sincerity, and Jews more than anyone else had to secure an air of truthfulness. These cautions against anachronism, however, are by themselves insufficient to convey an understanding of the meanings conveyed by the Jewish performances considered here. For the messages were more than simply formulaic expressions of loyalty conforming to the rules of the day. Rather, they constituted a set of highly self-assertive claims regarding the Jews' moral and legal status in the French kingdom.

Regarding the many assertions of kinship between the Jews and their "father," the king, these were more than confirmations of obedience to the sovereign. By invoking the well-known image of the king as father to his people, Jews were also alluding to the equally well-known royal responsibilities to his "children." In other words, they were suggesting that he owed them protection at the very least. By casting themselves as his children, a relationship that was by no means self-evident to everyone in the kingdom, they were engaging in a sort of election. They were *choosing* their sovereign. This sense of election was simultaneously reinforced and justified by references to the process by which God, who famously selected his Chosen People and subsequently chose their kings, later still elected the king of France. Furthermore, the temporal gap between these divine choices emphasized the precedence of the Jews and their ancient kingship over the relative newcomers to God's favor. The configuration of a Gentile king and his Jewish children was accordingly reversed. Figuratively speaking, the Jews were now the fathers, and the French kings were their children, an image that corresponded to many contemporary descriptions of the Jews as fathers or mothers to the Christians in general.

The sense of Jewish priority through antiquity was especially resonant in a neohumanist culture that valued the distant past and in which claimants to power, most famously the *parlementaires,* regularly invoked history as the basis of their rights. It is in this context that one sees the multiple meanings of the Jews' repeated references to the king's anointing. These were not merely indications of the Jews' loyalty to a king on the strength of his divine right. They were also reminders of the origins in ancient Jewish history of the very ceremony by which French monarchs, beginning in the Middle Ages, secured the obedience of their subjects. It was in this way that Jews appropriated, or *reappropriated,* the very symbols of the king's legitimacy. As representatives of God's Chosen People, they authorized themselves to deem the king worthy of his charge. Their references to David, new or reincarnated, as God's *servant* only augmented the impression of the king's responsibilities toward God's oldest worshipers, and convenient reminders of divine wrath against those who persecuted them further effaced any notion of the king as rightfully holding the fate of the Jews in his hands.

Simultaneously, Jewish spokesmen invoked another tradition, namely, that of royal toleration for the various communities. Often this precedent was merely implied, as in the depictions of France as an "asylum of the unfortunate," led by a monarch who "protects those who take refuge in his midst." Elsewhere the connection to the Jews was explicit. The Portuguese of Bordeaux declared themselves "content and happy under the protection of the greatest of Kings." Similarly, the Jews of Metz implored God on behalf of an ailing Louis XV in 1774, "Preserve for us the Sovereign . . . who does not cease to protect the Worshippers of your holy Name," and the Jews of Lorraine prayed, "From the depths of dejection [resulting from] a dispersion that has cast us among all the Nations of the earth, you have remembered us . . . by establishing us under the Empire of the Bourbons and the Scepter of Louis XVI."[55]

To emphasize the precedents for toleration, authors of acclamatory liturgy frequently referred to the prior kings who had protected the Jews. When Eibeschütz of Metz addressed Louis XV on behalf of "the Hebrews, your faithful Subjects reposing in the kingdom in the shadow of your Protection and Tolerance," and thanked him for the "special grace that the Kings your Predecessors and Your Majesty" had granted to the Jews, he alluded to the letters patent that permitted Jewish residence in the city. The community was more explicit still when praying for a successor to Louis XVI, "this just and beneficent Prince, who . . . wished to take pity on our dispersion; and to confirm recently with his august seal the asylum that their beneficence procured us." The Sephardim of Bordeaux went even further in their use of royal occasions to refer to their privileges in the kingdom. In 1766 Jacob-Rodrigues Péreire, the "agent" of the Portuguese community who had commissioned Isaac Pinto's *Apologie* four years earlier, included a footnote in the prayer for the dauphin's health, published in the highly visible *Mercure de France*. The note claimed, "The Portuguese Jews in France enjoy the same privileges as native Frenchmen, by virtue of the *lettres patentes* of Henry II, renewed and ratified from reign to reign." In a prayer for the queen's health in 1768, Péreire reprinted the note, revising "privileges" to read "rights," and in a prayer for the "happy delivery" of the queen in 1779 he revised the note again, now adding that his community's charter had been registered by the *parlement* of Paris in 1550.[56]

In addition to the published texts of patriotic worship, accounts of dynastic festivals further contribute to an understanding of Jewish self-representation. The same occasions that inspired patriotic liturgy—especially those honoring royal births and entries by members of the royal family—might call for participation in organized public festivities. When invited to participate in these ceremonies, Jews took the opportunity not only to represent themselves as patriotic and loyal to the crown but also, as in the occasional liturgy, to underscore their rights in the kingdom. Since their "audience" included adversarial and even hostile elements in French society, these performances operated as a defensive response to persons or groups that might call Jewish rights into question. In this respect they therefore served a quasi-legal purpose. By praising the king and thanking him for his "favor," the Jews publicly defended their precarious status and reaffirmed the king's obligations toward them. Furthermore, certain features in their self-representation—especially the (often exaggerated) display of wealth and references to services rendered to the crown—suggested that any royal favor offered to the Jews was prudent policy.

The most numerous and detailed accounts of Jewish participation in dynastic festivals come from Metz, where Jews engaged in patriotic performance on repeated occasions. Their audiences with Marie-Leczinska and Louis XV, in 1725 and 1744, respectively, and their participation in festivities for the reestablishment of the *parlement* in 1775 have already been mentioned. They also took part in celebrations surrounding the birth of the dauphin in 1729, the birth of the duc de Bourgogne in 1751, Louis XVI's accession to the throne in 1775, the birth of the dauphin in 1781, and an entry by the comte de Provence in 1783. Although documentation is richest for the Metz festivities, this community was not alone among the Jews of France in celebrating royal occasions alongside non-Jews. Jews in the Alsatian town of Bischheim-au-Saum greeted the dauphin's birth in 1781 with a fête to which Gentiles were invited, and in Bordeaux the Portuguese community showed similar hospitality in celebrating both this royal birth and that of the duc de Normandie in 1785.[57]

As with the printed acclamatory texts, the Jews' symbolic actions conveyed a message of devotion to the monarchy. The arms of the king, queen, and other members of the royal family were ubiquitous. Fleurs-de-lys and dolphins (symbolizing the dauphin) decorated the synagogue, the houses of the Jewish quarter, and the triumphal arches erected on the *rue des juifs* in Metz. They adorned processional banners, nocturnal illuminations, and a "triumphal chariot" that appeared repeatedly in the Metz festivals and featured a mechanical dolphin capable of devouring the fish surrounding it. Royal portraits and monograms, bejeweled crowns, cockades of royal blue and bourbon white, and similarly colored decorations all reinforced the message of Jewish loyalty, which was literally expressed in plentiful inscriptions reading, "Vive le roi!" "Vive la reine!" "Vive monseigneur le dauphin!" and so forth.[58]

Use of the symbols of royalty, however, indicated more than obedience or affection. It suggested that the Jews belonged to the French kingdom, that they were subjects (a claim their adversaries repeatedly disputed), and that they had a consequent right to state protection. That the monarchy—in the form of the king, a member of the royal family, or an agent of the crown—permitted the Jews to make this symbolic statement was still more evidence of the right they were claiming. Indeed, the primary object in such patriotic performances was to publicize the Jews' reputed status as subjects or, at the very least, inhabitants with the right to the crown's protection. Thus when the Jews of Metz paraded through the streets, the rabbi, syndics, and deputies followed by forty elders, all in solemn Sabbath dress, and successive "companies" of community members led by notables, they were giving visible expression to their constitution. In case anyone failed to notice, they sang the praises of the monarchy and had trumpet players and other musicians supplement their visibility with audibility. They took care to repeat their performance at key points around the city, stopping at the bishopric (and appearing on the balcony with the bishop himself), the *parlement,* the residence of the military governor, the citadel, and the office of the *intendant.* In Bischheim and Bordeaux similar processions were accompanied by cannon fire, a sound that was appropriately militant and hence patriotic, as well as conveniently audible to anyone who might have missed the start of the spectacle. In all three locations the synagogue was open to non-Jewish visitors, creating a transparent impression of the mythically opaque people, and this type of cultural translation was accompanied in Metz by literal translation, as the Hebrew canticles composed and performed for the specific occasions were translated into French and distributed among Gentile observers.[59]

The publication of the Jews' legal status was accompanied by signs justifying their residence in France as useful to the kingdom. Thus the Metz processions always included horses, a reminder of the utility the Jews of that city exhibited as purveyors of cavalry horses. In the 1729 celebration of the dauphin's birth, according to an admiring Jewish chronicler, the men in the "company" headed by a certain Abraham Lévy were mounted on "magnificent horses," and this made sense, since Lévy was a horse dealer who would sell nearly three thousand horses to the army in the coming years.[60] The role of Jews in the provisioning of the army also explains the otherwise curious fact that, in the Metz festivals at least, some of them carried swords, a privilege otherwise limited to the nobility.

More generally, Jews signified their utility to the state by displaying their corporate wealth, even to the point of exaggerating it. According to observers of the Metz festivals, participants wore clothing of the richest materials: satin, silk, velvet, damask, and silver as well as gold brocade. Even the "magnificent horses" were dressed for the occasion, their heads and torsos covered with scarlet cloth and golden bands, and their hair plaited with blue ribbons. The triumphal chariot, drawn by four horses and driven by a postilian with plumed hat and white gloves with golden fringe, was covered with a royal blue tapestry and "a kind of filigreed arch formed by grains of coral and crystal," on top of which sat a crimson velvet cushion supporting a "well-gilded royal crown." One can only guess at the cost of the predatory dolphin. Expenses, moreover, were not confined to processional displays. In Bordeaux the royal births prompted the illumination of the Jewish quarter, and whenever festivals took place in Metz, the Jewish quarter was illuminated for three consecutive nights. In Metz the Jews' houses were given a new coat of white paint, trimmed with lamps, and decorated with copper and brass plaques, candelabras, and mirrors. On display inside the synagogue were tapestries hanging from the walls, as well as "all the ornaments of the tabernacle." The official account of the Bischheim celebration reported a sanctuary illuminated with candles and "decorated with the richest ornaments."[61]

Of course, with the display of wealth came the risk of confirming stereotypes about Jewish greed. Therefore, it was necessary to combine the appearance of wealth with that of generosity, and the most obvious method of achieving this goal was to give gifts. According to the chronicler of the festivities on the occasion of Marie-Leczinska's entry into Metz in 1725, the city's Jews presented the queen with a gift of "three cups, one of which was made out of rock-crystal, trimmed and enriched with precious stones, and the others of which were gilded silver." Although the cups were edifyingly decorated with representations of "two remarkable actions of King Solomon and the Queen of Saba," to whom the royal couple were compared, their monetary value could not have gone unnoticed. Jews also spent considerable sums entertaining Christians, and all records of their participation in royal celebrations mention their hospitality. A Jewish chronicler boasted that upon the birth of the dauphin in 1729, his brethren in Metz lined the *rue des juifs* with casks of wine, and that guests could have their glasses "filled to the brim" as many times as they pleased. He noted the presence of an all-night "open table" at which "anyone who wanted ate and drank, regardless of their rank or religion," and that in addition to this a "splendid dinner" was given for "the syndics and chiefs of the community, the cantors, the authorities and some Christian notables." Gifts of money were distributed to poor Christians and Jews alike, and a bonfire kept them warm. At Bischheim Cerf Berr, the richest Jew in Alsace, distributed bread, wine, and money to poor Christians of the town and neighboring villages. Following the distribution of charity was a lunch for 120 Jewish notables and Christian guests, and later Berr hosted a public ball at which "the people" danced to the music of a large orchestra, consumed large quantities of food and drink, and warmed themselves with a bonfire. Meanwhile, according to the official account, in his own house he hosted a dance and dinner for "lords and ladies," to whom he served "refreshments of every sort, with as much choice as profusion." Finally, the minutes of the Portuguese community in Bordeaux record the distribution of food and money "to all the poor of the city, Catholics as well as Jews" on the occasion of the dauphin's birth; they mention that upon the birth of the duc de Normandie, alms were again given to the poor, "both of the city and of our Nation." Such acts of generosity served to challenge stereotypes about Jews as greedy or, in the case that they were generous, that they directed their generosity only toward other Jews. But gift giving is typically a self-assertive act, as anthropologists studying the potlatch phenomenon have long known. It calls attention to the wealth of the person who is presenting the gifts and conveys a corresponding status to the giver. Considering the claims to rights with which Jews accompanied their performances of munificence, one wonders how their audiences responded.[62]

All acts of Jewish self-representation had multiple audiences. Insofar as they featured prayer, their primary audience was God, since there is no reason to imagine that any of the Jews in question doubted his existence. But there were other audiences as well. One must not forget the Jews themselves, who read each other's apologies and patriotic liturgy and were coparticipants in the dynastic festivals. At the risk of raising the thorny question of sincerity and thus giving the impression that the choice for the Jews was between lying and telling the truth, it is nevertheless reasonable to imagine that they were highly pleased with themselves and their performances. After all, they managed to present their religion and their people in a positive light, not only defending both against charges of immorality and hostility to the Christians who made up what was increasingly known as the French nation but, better still,

affirming the priority of their religion in the very creation of the principles and rites of kingship and the values appropriate to a common-
wealth. With the telling exception of Hourwitz, who compromised the
integrity of the oral law and rabbinical tradition—though only to
reaffirm what he regarded as the fundamental values of Judaism—none
of the Jews charged with the task of defending the *nation juive* gave up
an iota of the heritage that Gentiles so often questioned or attacked. Indeed, they represented themselves as bearers of multiple gifts to their
French neighbors. At the most basic level, these gifts were utility to the
state and the wealth by which such utility was guaranteed, even if this
wealth was more hypothetical, dependent as it was on good laws and
sound policies, than real. More important still, from the standpoint of
the Jews' religious identity, they consisted of the values that contemporaries increasingly associated with citizenship.

The responses of non-Jewish audiences in France are easier to document, though it is important to distinguish between representatives of
the crown and other groups within the kingdom. Royal officials tended
to welcome expressions of devotion to the *patrie,* despite the Jews' uncertain legal status. Thus after receiving a French translation of the
prayer that the Portuguese community had recited on the occasion of
Louis XV's illness in 1744, the Marquis de Tourny, *intendant* of Bordeaux, sent it on to the king. Subsequently, the comte de Saint-Florentin,
a minister at Versailles, informed Tourny that he considered the prayer
"very good, and of an appropriate style, although unusual," and reported that the king was "very happy with the proof that [the Jews] have
given of their zeal." Similarly, when the dauphin fell ill in 1752, the same
community published its devotions and sent exemplars to Tourny, who
in turn forwarded copies to Saint-Florentin, as well as another minister,
D'Argenson. Tourny reminded the ministers of the prayer that the Jews
had composed for the king's health in 1744 and signaled their attention
to this new sign of loyalty. D'Argenson thanked the *intendant* for the
"two copies" of the service; he added that the rabbi "will doubtless have
composed a canticle on the recovery of this Prince," and requested a
copy. Tourny in turn sent D'Argenson "the canticle that the rabbi of the
Jews of this city composed on the recovery of Monseigneur the Dauphin."[63] It is also significant that the controller-general, Loménie de Bri-
enne, owned a copy of the prayer recited by the Jews of Metz for Louis
XV's health in 1744, and that Marie Antoinette kept a bound volume of
Jewish prayers in honor of her husband's coronation in her private li-

brary. Whether they were fully persuaded by these devotions is an open question, but they kept them, indicating that they took them seriously. Finally, the fact that two of the Jewish services were published in the officially authorized *Mercure de France* suggests a positive reception on behalf of the monarchy.[64]

The monarchy was not all of France, however, and if it promoted toleration, limited though it was, of the Jews on the strength of their perceived utility to the state, there were many elements within French society that were hostile to any Jewish presence. In such a climate, manifestations of Jewish patriotism may have exacerbated tensions rather than reducing them. In this respect a detail in the account of the festivities for the dauphin's birth in 1729 is telling. According to the chronicler, after leaving the confines of the city to greet the governor of the citadel, the Jews of Metz returned to find the gates locked. The situation was rectified, and "on the order of the authorities the gates were opened." One suspects that the "authorities" in question were the royal agents, representatives of state rather than local interests. But there remains the question of why the Jews had been locked out in the first place. At nightfall it was normal to close city gates, yet one wonders whether an exception might have been made for another corporate group processing to demonstrate its patriotism. Was this the case of an overly scrupulous gatekeeper? A charivari-style prank? Perhaps resentment played a role in the temporary lockout. A more clear-cut case of local opposition to Jewish festivities can be seen in Saint-Esprit when the Portuguese community proposed to celebrate the end of the Seven Years' War outside their quarter. The municipal council prevented them from doing so, which earned it a rebuke from the governor of the province of Guienne, significantly an agent of the French state. Finally, Zalkind Hourwitz reported that the "magnificent illumination that [the Jews of Metz] made . . . on the occasion of the birth of the Dauphin" provoked such resentment that local Christians planned to set fire to the Jewish quarter, a plan that was only thwarted by the discovery of "a large quantity of combustible materials" at "numerous places on the *rue des Juifs.*"[65] Perhaps Hourwitz's accusation was fanciful, but at the very least it revealed the suspicion that Christians might retaliate against the symbolic claim that there was a place in French society for the Jews.

In their many responses to Gentile attempts to describe, categorize, and reform them, the Jews did not send a single, unambiguous message.

Their self-representation did not consist simply in denying prejudices about them and asserting their moral excellence, and though they did have recourse to these strategies, they more frequently mobilized stereotypes to their advantage. Thus Jewish apologists admitted, implicitly or explicitly, that their coreligionists had moral failings, chief among them a penchant for usury and fraud, but they blamed these failings on the Christians, who had persecuted them in the past and failed to treat them as equals in the present. They admitted to their fabled obstinacy but gave this quality a positive spin by depicting it as fidelity, the mark of a sensitive soul and a good citizen. In some of the apologetic literature and, more regularly, in patriotic festivities, Jews seized upon the mistaken belief that they were in general wealthy and argued, explicitly or in the rhetoric of symbolic action, that they were consequently useful to the state and its inhabitants. Elsewhere they gave the opposite impression, that they were poor but indifferent to money, with which baneful circumstances had forced them to occupy themselves. But here as well they pointed to legendary features of their constitutional history, namely, the pastoral simplicity of their ancestors and the primitive equality that their religious laws encouraged. Indeed, even these methods of turning the tables on the Gentiles drew on truisms that non-Jews themselves had developed in their own Enlightenment critique of Christendom. Thus despite the conflicting messages conveyed by Jews, a remarkably coherent strategy is nevertheless discernible, namely, that of appropriation.

The strategy of appropriation manifested itself elsewhere as well. One sees it in the Jews' likening of Bourbon monarchs to the anointed kings of Israel, and it is evident in the suggestion that values known by contemporaries as modern and "enlightened"—equality, a respect for "nature," and civic virtue—were originally Jewish. The Jews could therefore take credit for having given the world in general and France in particular both kingship *and* values that would soon be recognized as republican. Thus conceived, they were not only good subjects and citizens but also the original, primordial subject-citizens, and their value to the nascent French *nation* was precisely in their mythically long-standing experience as a nation. If they were a nation within the nation, then, this was a good thing for the French, who could learn from their Jewish neighbors how to be a nation. These forms of appropriation, taken together, enabled the Jews to accept the demands of their Gentile contemporaries—who required their devotion to France and promised in return some form of integration into the polity together with extended, though not necessarily equal, rights—without compromising their self-image as a people faithful to an ancient, divine, and therefore change-less Law. If they were obstinate, then, they had good reason, according to their own standards and, paradoxically, according to the logic of the very people who claimed the right to change them.

CHAPTER 5

Constituting Differences

The French Revolution and the Jews

EMANCIPATION AS A HISTORICAL PROBLEM

As with historical writing on the Enlightenment and the Jews, commentary on the Jews and the Revolution has tended to derive from the question of whether the "emancipation" that the Revolution enacted was good or bad for the Jews. Historians have repeatedly asked, implicitly or explicitly, whether the National Assembly's famous decree of September 27, 1791, was the origin of a long tradition, tragically interrupted by the Dreyfus Affair and the Vichy regime, of hospitality toward the Jews, whom the French thenceforth regarded as compatriots; or rather the prelude to assimilation, the death sentence for a traditional Jewish identity and therefore merely a bloodless means of eliminating the Jews.[1] These questions are methodologically objectionable not only because they set up a false dichotomy but also because they are teleological. In other words, they view the historical phenomena in question in terms of their presumed outcomes and thus prevent an understanding of the time and culture that produced these phenomena in the first place. This chapter, by contrast, inquires into why revolutionaries spent so much time and energy thinking about the Jews, discussing and debating their status and proposing and passing laws directed at them specifically; and it asks what contemporary representations, by Gentiles as well as Jews, of the relationship between the Jews and the mythically emerging French nation can tell us about the Revolution itself: its values, its discourses, its contradictions.

First, however, it is worth being precise about what, legally speaking, the fabled emancipation of the Jews actually amounted to. The decree of September 27, 1791, reputedly emancipated the Jews, but what did it actually stipulate? Given the historical weight attributed to this piece of legislation in Jewish history, the wording of the bill (subsequently signed into law by the captive king Louis XVI) makes for disappointing reading:

> The National Assembly, considering that the conditions necessary to be a French citizen, and to become an active citizen, are fixed by the Constitution, and that any man who, combining the said conditions, takes the civic oath and undertakes to fulfill all the duties that the Constitution imposes has the right to all the advantages that it assures:
>   Revokes all adjournments, reservations and exceptions inserted in the preceding decrees regarding individual Jews who shall take the civic oath.[2]

The second paragraph of this bill reveals that it was merely a revocation of restrictions, the "adjournments, reservations and exceptions" that the Assembly itself had passed in decrees that it now evidently regretted. For example, on December 24, 1789, the Assembly had ruled that "non-Catholics who have otherwise fulfilled all of the prescribed conditions . . . for being electors and eligible [for public office], shall be able to be elected to all decrees of administration," and that they "are capable of all the civil and military posts." Yet it explicitly excluded "the Jews, on whose status the National Assembly reserves the right to pronounce." On January 28, 1790, the deputies added the Portuguese and Avignonese Jews to the list of those potentially eligible for public office, but this decree did not apply to the Ashkenazi majority. In September 1790 the deputies ruled that religion was not a bar to eligibility for the newly created judicial assemblies, except in the case of the Jews, on whose status the Assembly once again "reserve[d] the right to pronounce."[3]

Moreover, since it was precisely the question of the eligibility of Jews for public office that had fueled so many debates and ended in so many "adjournments, reservations and exceptions," the decree of September 27 changed the status of only a handful of Jews, namely, those who fulfilled the stringent conditions (monetary and otherwise) for what the Constitution of 1791 designated "active" citizenship, or citizenship with political rights such as the franchise and eligibility for public office.

The prospect of Jews becoming "passive citizens," that is, citizens protected by the state but not enjoying political rights, was uncontroversial, and many of those who opposed active citizenship expressed a willingness to recognize the Jews as passive citizens, alongside women, minors, and indeed the majority of the French population, who were too poor to qualify for active citizenship.[4]

How many Jews were eligible for active citizenship? It is impossible to say with certainty, but the Constitutional Committee responsible for the distinction between active and passive citizens had made it clear as early as September 1789 that by restricting active citizenship to men aged twenty-five and above who paid annual direct taxes worth three days' labor they would exclude five-sixths of the French population.[5] If the median income of Jews was comparable to that of Gentiles in France, the number of potential active Jewish citizens would have been no more than twenty-five hundred. Yet the grinding poverty of the Alsatian Jews, the itinerant status of many (who could not have met the requirement of stable residency), and the scarcity of well-off Jews in any part of France would suggest a much lower number. One can derive a more realistic, though probably still inflated, estimate by extrapolating from the list of Jews admitted to take the civic oath in Nancy. Less wealthy than the *portugais* of Bordeaux, the Jews of Nancy were nevertheless better off than the majority of their coreligionists in France. Still, with a population of about five hundred at the time of the Revolution, the Nancy community produced only sixteen active citizens.[6] Even if one took the case of Nancy as representative of the proportion of eligible active Jewish citizens throughout France—a move that would no doubt inflate the number of such citizens substantially—one could scarcely derive a number higher than one hundred. And many, if not most, of this number would have been composed of the Portuguese and Avignonese Jews who had been "emancipated" by the decree of January 28, 1790, thus attenuating even further the practical significance of the 1791 law.

Moreover, even the minuscule number of active Jewish citizens would only have designated the simple *votants,* men who were entitled to vote for electors who in turn chose the actual officials. Indeed, the political rights of the *votants* were so circumscribed that they were scarcely recognized as such, and one self-described opponent of active citizenship for the Jews nevertheless proposed they be permitted to exercise their "civil right" of "voting in the primary assemblies of the nation."[7] As to the higher grades of active citizenship deemed out of reach for the Jews, electors had to prove that they paid direct taxes amounting to ten days' worth of labor per year, and there were hardly any Jews in the kingdom who could fulfill this requirement. Fewer still could pay the notoriously burdensome *marc d'argent,* roughly fifty days' worth of labor, required for eligibility to the national legislature, and the possibility that any Jew qualified at this level would actually be elected remained purely hypothetical. Even after the lifting of all property qualifications in the fall of 1792, not a single Jewish deputy was elected to the Convention.

One might suppose that the decree of September 27, though it accorded significant political rights to only a negligible, if not hypothetical, number of people, nevertheless made it more difficult to deprive the Jews of their *civic* equality. After all, if Jews could no longer suffer discrimination in the sacred exercise of national sovereignty, how could one single them out in matters of ordinary civil rights, which the deputies supposedly regarded as universal? This makes intuitive sense and seems to conform to the reasoning of those Jews who fought hard for the long-awaited law. Of course, the degree to which Jews would have suffered from civil discrimination without the decree of September 27 is a matter of counterfactual speculation. Yet it is striking that the very next day the Assembly did not flinch from issuing a law of exception. The decree of September 28, less well known than that of the previous day, required the Jews of Alsace to submit to the departmental authorities lists of any Gentiles to whom they had lent money.[8] Non-Jewish moneylenders were not covered by the decree, nor did it apply to loans between Jews. Like many of the laws passed by the revolutionary assemblies, this one was not enforced, but the fact that it was passed indicates something less than a full commitment to the principle of universalism for which the revolutionaries were famous. When seen in the context of other discriminatory measures, such as the ruling by successive assemblies that the Jews, unlike other *ci-devant* corporations, could not have their collective debts nationalized, one wonders not whether emancipation was good or bad for the Jews but whether anything deserving of the name in fact occurred during the French Revolution.[9]

Nevertheless, it would be insufficient simply to conclude that the revolutionaries failed to treat the Jews as equals, an observation that, though quite true, would tell us scarcely more about the period under investigation than the claim that emancipation was bad for the Jews. The point of highlighting the limits to the revolutionary policies vis-à-vis the Jews is rather to underscore the incongruity between the considerable energy devoted to the debates defining the famed Jewish question and the negligible legal impact of any possible outcome. This incongru-

ity constitutes the real historical problem at hand. During the two-year
tenure of the National Assembly, issues relating to the Jews were discussed at no less than thirty-two sessions, twenty-five in the first year
alone. At least forty deputies spoke at these discussions, among them the
most celebrated revolutionaries: Mirabeau, Talleyrand, La Rochefoucauld, Dupont de Nemours, Noailles, Le Chapelier, Duport, Barnave,
and Robespierre. Debates were impassioned, on occasion lasted for
hours, and more than once degenerated into shouting matches. This is
to say nothing of the quiet attention of the Constitutional Committee,
to which matters of Jewish citizenship were repeatedly adjourned, or the
Finance Committee, which addressed the question of Jewish corporate
debt. One must add to this set of data the petitions of the Paris municipality in favor of Jewish citizenship, contrary petitions published by the
municipalities of Strasbourg and Colmar, the pamphlets of various Jacobin clubs (in favor of Jewish equality), scores of pamphlets by writers
offering opinions and proposals on the Jews' status in France, and the
extensive coverage of relevant National Assembly debates in the period-
ical press.[10]

All this attention was directed toward the Jews at a time when the
revolutionaries had to confront such pressing matters as the abolition of
privilege, rural unrest, an increasingly militant popular movement, the
highly controversial reorganization of the church and nationalization of
its lands (the Civil Constitution of the Clergy), the intransigence (and
eventual flight) of the king, the problem of the émigrés and the menace
of war, and the breakdown of judicial, legislative, and administrative institutions at the local, provincial, and national levels, not to mention the
immense task with which the National Assembly had originally charged
itself: the drafting of a constitution. Under these circumstances, why did
the revolutionaries return again and again to the Jews, or, more precisely, to the tiny fraction of the already minuscule population of Jews
whom the outcome of the debates might actually affect? On February 26, 1790, after more than a dozen sessions in which deputies discussed the Jews, the duc de La Rochefoucauld-Liancourt asked the
Assembly to set a date for yet another discussion. Guy-Jean-Baptiste
Target, president of the Assembly and member of the Constitutional
Committee, conceded that "the question regarding the Jews is very important" but added that "we have more important matters to treat." He
observed that "what we pronounce in regard to the Jews only interests
a portion of men; yet fixing the order of the judiciary power, determining the number and mode of the French army, establishing regulations

on finances, these are three objects that interest the whole kingdom and demand all of your attention." He therefore called for "an adjournment to the question of the Jews."[11] Between this Rousseauian belief that legislation must affect the entire body politic, not "a portion of men," and the obstacles set by a few deputies from the northeast—who expressed the fantastic belief that any extension of political rights to Jews would be the first step toward a Jewish takeover of their provinces and threatened peasant uprisings in the event of such measures—advocates of continued discussion of the Jews' status had a difficult time making themselves heard. (This difficulty explains the two-year delay between the first mention of the Jews and the decree of September 1791.) But why did they wish to be heard in the first place?

SEPARATING THE WHEAT FROM THE CHAFF:
EQUALITY AND DISTINCTION IN THE
REVOLUTIONARY CONCEPTION OF CITIZENSHIP

To my knowledge, the only historian to pose the question of why the National Assembly took time out of its busy schedule to address Jewish matters is Gary Kates. In a review article on Arthur Hertzberg's *French Enlightenment and the Jews,* Kates argues, "Since there were so few Jews in France, and since they played little role in the Revolution, they were easily turned into symbols of something else." This is quite true. More problematic, however, is Kates's claim that the revolutionaries "used the issue [of the Jews] to test what was then perhaps the most fundamental political question: Would the promises inherent in the Declaration of the Rights of Man and Citizen translate into equal political power for all Frenchmen, regardless of status, or would those leading the Revolution stop short of democracy by limiting the political power of certain kinds of people?"[12] This is an elegant hypothesis, which the historical evidence nevertheless belies.

Although it would be misleading to divide the revolutionaries, as historians have typically done, into friends and foes of the Jews, it is possible to identify proposals that advocated some improvement in the Jews' legal status. I have identified twenty-six deputies who made such proposals, and only four of them could be accurately described as democrats: Grégoire, Robespierre, Duport, and Dominique Garat. These men all actively opposed the Constitutional Committee's *régime censitaire* that relegated the poor to the status of passive citizens and excluded all but the very rich from lawmaking. Yet the remaining twenty-two showed no such reservations about "limiting the power of certain kinds of people," and many among them professed explicitly antidemocratic beliefs. Among these deputies were Talleyrand, Rabaut Saint-Étienne, Thouret, and Le Chapelier, who were on the very Constitutional Committee that proposed the restrictive Constitution of 1791. Le Chapelier was famous for the law bearing his name that prohibited workers' associations, and both he and Thouret had split from the Jacobin club when it began to admit nondeputies as voting members. La Rochefoucauld, who also spoke in favor of Jewish rights, was a prominent member of the same faction; at one point he expressed interest in allying with the ultraconservative deputy Malouet (who advocated making Catholicism the state religion) to keep the Assembly from moving to the left, and the duc de La Rochefoucauld-Liancourt, who also pleaded the Jewish cause, considered a similar strategy. The comte de Clermont-Tonnerre, who famously defined the arrangement by which the French nation would "refuse the Jews everything as a nation and give them everything as individuals," was also the leader of the *monarchien* party that favored a bicameral legislature (to temper the influence of the urban masses) and an unlimited royal veto. He allied himself with Malouet, with whom he founded the "Impartials," a club that advocated a powerful monarchy equipped to repress all civil disturbances. Other strong monarchists who spoke on behalf of the Jews were Bouche, Briois de Beaumetz, the comte de Sèze (who defended the king at his trial), and Mirabeau, who also advocated property qualifications for active citizenship. Meanwhile, Dupont de Nemours had no trouble believing simultaneously that the Jews should have equal rights and that only property owners should be allowed to vote.[13] As to Barnave, who similarly supported Jewish rights, his rapid conversion from a Jacobin to a monarchist who advocated even greater restrictions on political rights than were stipulated by the Constitution of 1791 reveals a very thin commitment to democracy.

Indeed, one suspects that for most of these men proclaiming the equality of Jews and non-Jews was a way of drawing attention away from their antidemocratic agenda. It was relatively costless, since it resulted only in the enfranchisement of a negligible portion of the population, whereas a real commitment to democracy entailed the empowerment of the "dangerous classes," the poor in the cities and the countryside, the masses of people clamoring for bread at affordable prices and menacing the *"riches égoïstes"* with continued revolutionary violence. The Jews provided a convenient occasion for proclaiming one's commitment to equality *without* taking any steps toward democracy. More convenient still, the Jews enabled deputies to declare their belief in equality even as they refused to consider the abolition of slavery or even the enfranchisement of free blacks in the colonies. Although Grégoire and Robespierre were simultaneously abolitionists and advocates of Jewish rights, among deputies they were the exception that proved the rule. Robert Badinter has noted the poignant contrast between the "emancipation" of the Jews on September 27, 1791, and the Assembly's decision, just three days earlier, to make the colonial assemblies—which had consistently and bitterly attacked even the mildest proposals for greater racial equality—responsible for "'the state of non-free persons and the political state of men of color and free blacks.'" He suggests that the legislation on the Jews was "a kind of moral compensation" for deputies who had just permitted the "absolute negation of the Rights of Man."[14]

How the deputies felt about abandoning their principles and retaining colonial slavery is difficult to know, and whether their consciences were assuaged by passing the decree of September 27 is a matter of speculation. Yet the intimate coexistence of proposals suggesting a commitment to inclusiveness and a policy of deliberate exclusiveness sheds light on the culture of the National Assembly. The very fact that the deputies compensated for acts of exclusion with symbolic acts of inclusion suggests a generalized premium, at the very least, on the appearance of largesse. Most of the deputies, at least initially, were reluctant to "liberate" the Jews, or even the richest among them, and when Duport moved on December 23 that "no cause for exclusion may be opposed to any Frenchman, either for being an active citizen or for being eligible for public functions, that has not been pronounced by the decrees of the Assembly," his proposal was defeated by a vote of 408 to 403.[15] Nevertheless, what is striking about this opposition was that a disproportionately small number of deputies actually spoke out against improving the Jews' status. Whereas at least twenty-six voiced their opinions in favor of Jewish rights, I have found evidence of only eleven representatives speaking against these proposals.

Any effort to place this group on the right-left political spectrum is doomed to failure. Just as the twenty-six deputies examined earlier were far from a block of democrats, their eleven outspoken opponents were hardly a bastion of right-wing politics. Abbé Maury, who repeatedly defied attempts at proclaiming the equality of the Jews, literally defined the right wing in terms of the deputies who sat near him and voted with him on a number of issues, including the royal veto (which he supported) and the Civil Constitution of the Clergy (which he opposed). François de Bonal, the bishop of Clermont-Ferrand, was similarly conservative, and in addition to opposing active citizenship for Jews, he opposed the nationalization of church lands and the laicization of church organization. His fellow ecclesiastic and opponent of Jewish rights, the bishop of Nancy, was a *monarchien* who supported a strong executive and law and order. Yet other opponents of efforts at recognizing Jewish equality had left-wing credentials. Thiebault, the curé from Metz, opposed equal rights for Jews but at the same time spoke out against property qualifications for active citizenship. François Hell, whose opposition to Jewish equality was not surprising after his infamous diatribe of 1779, also wrote a primer designed to "instruct the people of Alsace in revolutionary principles." The prince de Broglie, who envisaged a future integration of Jews into political life but opposed legislation that would define their equality in the present, was a member of the Jacobins of Colmar and had fought for American independence. He was a staunch supporter of the Civil Constitution of the Clergy and took measures to enforce it in Alsace. Perhaps the furthest to the left among the eleven was Jean-François Rewbell, who opposed active citizenship for the Jews but also opposed attempts at strengthening the crown, supported the sale of church lands, and held membership in his local Jacobin club. Before becoming a member of the Directory government, he would distinguish himself by denouncing royalists and voting for the execution of the king.[16]

Thus opposition to Jewish rights was no more reliable an indicator of one's place on the political spectrum than was support of those same rights. More significant for an understanding of the political culture in which the debate on the Jews was situated is the fact that a disproportionately small number of deputies spoke against the amelioration of the Jews' status. This imbalance suggests that it was politically easier to hold such a position than to proclaim it, which in turn implies that the revolutionary political culture required the appearance of inclusiveness even as exclusions were being enacted. A comparison between François Hell's December 1789 speech against active citizenship for Jews and his 1779 diatribe constitutes further support for this hypothesis. In 1779 Hell had excoriated the "wretched children of Israel" and depicted the historical persecution of the Jews as "the just wrath of Heaven" for their crime of having "immolated" Jesus. In 1789 he proclaimed, "I would think myself blaspheming against the Supreme Being if I said that divine justice pursued all the descendants of an entire people because, according to his immutable decrees, the inhabitants of a city or of a very small country of the same people had been the necessary instruments for the achievement of the mystery of our salvation." In 1779 he represented the Jews as innately corrupt, writing, "Everyone knows how to analyze the Jewish character. One knows his perverse dogmas, his crooked mind, his fraudulent character, his barbaric heart." In 1789 he represented the vice of Jews as the product of persecution, insisting, "To refuse [the Jews] almost all the legal means of subsistence is to force them into crime . . . to reduce them to the harshest slavery." He even proposed a decree stipulating: "All Jews born or domiciled in France, and those who will be born in the future, shall enjoy all the rights that *the other French citizens* enjoy, fulfilling all of the duties." Elsewhere he undermined this general claim with particular exceptions. He opposed declaring the Jews "eligible for all positions" in legislation and administration because Jewish usurers would, in his view, force their debtors to vote for them. In addition to infringing on Jews' political rights, he advocated restrictions on their civil rights. Although he proposed permitting them to "exercise all the trades," he advocated forcing Jews who bought land to cultivate it themselves and restricting them from taking collateral for noncommercial loans to "Christians." He also sought to require Jews to obtain permission before moving to a new town or city (which would only admit those with a verifiable trade and up to one-sixth of the population) or marrying. These restrictions, however, were justified by the assumption that "you will force the Jews to become better and happy if you force them to become hard-working, useful and honest."[17] This logic and the proposed restrictions were remarkably similar to those elaborated by Grégoire two years earlier. Yet Hell clearly felt compelled to conceal his discriminatory proposals in a package marked "inclusion."

Significantly, Grégoire himself had undergone a political makeover since writing the prerevolutionary essay that made him famous. In the fall of 1789 he published *Motion en faveur des Juifs,* in which he recapitulated many of the claims of his previous *Essai sur la régénération physique, morale et politique des Juifs,* arguing essentially that the Jews' faults were the product of persecution, not an innate propensity or the fundamental precepts (as he understood them) of the Jewish religion. He concluded with a proposed decree abolishing special taxes levied on Jews, confirming their right to acquire property (landed and otherwise) and to exercise all trades and professions, and recognizing that "assimilated to citizens, they share the advantages thereof, provided that they sustain the costs." Yet conspicuously absent from this *Motion* were the scathing attacks on the Jews that had made his *Essai* look so much like Hell's diatribe of 1779. Also missing were the many restrictions on Jewish liberties that had marked Grégoire's earlier work, though the author managed to insist that the Jews pay off the debts that their communities, now to be abolished, had contracted under the Old Regime.[18]

These transformations of political language reveal the extent of the pressure on deputies to appear generous, hospitable, and inclusive. The process of defining a *nation* necessitated exclusion as well as inclusion. Patriots quickly excoriated émigrés, aristocrats, and vaguely defined enemies of liberty. The production of a constitution that guaranteed the power, wealth, and status of the men who had initiated the Revolution entailed further exclusions: the poor, men of color, and women. Yet the very length of the list of people to be excluded from sovereignty only increased the pressure on revolutionaries to make grand gestures of inclusiveness. In the moral economy of the Revolution, it was evidently prudent to be discreet about excluding and to make grand inclusive gestures. Thus even those who took the political risk of appearing ungenerous by opposing active citizenship for the Jews tended to present themselves as generous. Both Rewbell and Maury were careful to insist that it was the Jews themselves who did not wish to be members of the French nation, therefore making their exclusionary proposals appear to be no more than the granting of requests. Moreover, only the need to appear inclusive explains the otherwise bizarre conclusion to Hell's December 1789 speech with a proposal for a decree "that all Mahometans, notably the subjects of the Turkish emperor, in Europe and in other parts of the world, shall enjoy, through the empire of the French, all the rights, honors and advantages that the French citizens enjoy."[19] There was no "Turkish question" to be resolved in France, but Hell needed to display his generosity as a member of the French nation, all the more so since he had just effectively proposed excluding a group already inhabiting French soil from full citizenship.

In this context, the "emancipation" of the Jews and the prior statements of support for them can be seen as analogous to other famous gestures of hospitality and largesse. One is reminded, for example, of the Assembly's conspicuous generosity on the Night of August 4, when those with privileges (and even those without them) dramatically repudiated them. In both cases the proclaimed sympathy with mythically suffering humanity and the call for a single, inclusive legal community provided the opportunity for exhibiting the noble traits of the generous citizen. The word *noble* is not entirely figurative because thirteen of the twenty-six deputies who spoke in favor of ameliorating the Jews' conditions were noble, and ten of them had been elected for the Second Estate. It is not fanciful to suppose that the conspicuous generosity in both the abolition of privilege and the reform of the Jews' status derived at least in part from a noble valorization of gift giving and hospitality. Whatever the roots of this impulse to theatrical generosity, certain moments in the history of the National Assembly suggest that potlatch-like ceremonies were central to its operation.[20] Similarly, the loudly proclaimed willingness to improve the lot of the Jews and the comparatively muted opposition to such a program are reminiscent of other symbolic gestures of inclusion, such as the conferral of honorary French citizenship upon foreigners deemed friends of liberty and of the spectacular "delegation of foreigners" led by Anacharsis Cloots (and significantly including the *juif polonois* Zalkind Hourwitz) before the National Assembly on June 19, 1790. In all three cases the French nation was able to proclaim its openness to outsiders, though these outsiders remained safely small in number.[21]

Indeed, one of the most striking aspects of the debates over what kinds of people could be citizens is the evident pressure to welcome, enfranchise, display hospitality toward, or otherwise include some excluded group. It is worth recalling that the debates of late December 1789 were not solely about possible degrees of citizenship for Jews but also about the political status of Protestants, actors, and executioners, all groups that were both traditionally maligned and small, if not negligible, in number. Yet each group found at least one champion in the Assembly. Clermont-Tonnerre spoke out on behalf of the rights of Jews, actors, and executioners. Pierre-Louis Roederer, the deputy from Metz who had organized the essay contest on the "means of making the Jews more useful and happier in France," was now silent on the Jews but defended the actors. The bishop of Clermont-Ferrand wished to adjourn on the Jews and actors but was willing to make otherwise qualified Protestants eligible for all grades of active citizenship. Briois de Beaumetz similarly called for a decree in favor of Protestants while bracketing the question of Jews and actors, though he later spoke in favor of the Jews of Bordeaux.[22] It would be pointless to attempt to account for all of these positions. Yet just as with the Jewish question alone, one must ask why the deputies spent their time and energy arguing over the precise status of Protestants, Jews, actors, and executioners, especially since they were simultaneously establishing general rubrics (e.g., on the basis of wealth, age, and gender) that otherwise determined political rights.

Why Protestants, Jews, actors, and executioners? One thing these groups had in common was their negligible size. One might say they were "good to emancipate" precisely because they were all too small to constitute a real danger to the power of the men who had begun the Revolution and quickly saw themselves threatened by potential rivals among the masses. But why these tiny groups and not others? Why not Quakers, atheists, violinists, and coachmen?

Protestants and Jews were not merely practitioners of a religion differing from the kingdom's official faith. Both had historically included within their ranks apparent but feigned believers in Catholicism (crypto-Protestants or crypto-Jews). Furthermore, they were suspected of harboring theological justifications for treason (in the case of Protestants) and financial trickery (in the case of the Jews). They were therefore viewed as opaque and skilled at dissimulation, whereas revolutionary political culture demanded precisely the transparency of a Rousseauian "sensitive soul" whose beliefs and intentions appeared unambiguously through sincere words and unequivocal gestures.[23] In this context one can see the symbolic proximity between Protestants and Jews, on the one hand, and actors and executioners. Quite apart from their reputation for immorality, actors may well have been feared for their professional capacity to dissimulate. And the executioner, beyond his apparent cruelty in choosing a profession of killing, was literally masked. Thus all four groups were masked, literally or figuratively, and arguing about their status in the new nation was a symptom of the revolutionaries' preoccupation with transparency.

If the substitutive principle worked insofar as revolutionaries had to find at least one outside group to welcome, then the process of constructing candidates for inclusion was not arbitrary. It obeyed a certain symbolic logic, a semiotics of perceived moral qualities with which the revolutionaries were otherwise preoccupied. That the Jews attracted more attention than Protestants, actors, and executioners (who were all "emancipated" on December 25, 1789) suggests the extent of their multivalency. As seen in the previous chapters, the Jews in eighteenth-century France could stand for many qualities, which often stood in binary opposition to one another. They were simultaneously credulous and clever, irrationally attached to superstitious beliefs and in possession of a hyperrational *esprit calculateur*. They were traveling cosmopolitans, yet their attachment to the Jewish "nation" was proverbial. They represented antiquity and modernity, capitalism (with its attendant dangers of greed and luxury) and a morally superior political economy based on simplicity and equality. These moral qualities—and economics was thoroughly imbricated with morality in the eighteenth century as in the following two centuries—were of the greatest political importance in a revolutionary culture that viewed politics as public morality. They enabled revolutionaries to define the objects that were so often invoked but so ill-defined: the citizen and the nation.

The Jews therefore facilitated the discussion of matters that, despite the apparently particularistic nature of the Jewish question, were deemed of universal importance. As Kates has recognized, "The debate over Jewish emancipation was thus a debate over what it meant to be a French citizen."[24] Yet precisely because the Jews represented moral qualities, they facilitated a moralization of citizenship, a consideration of its moral attributes (and, by implication, its duties) rather than a definition in terms of rights, and they enabled the deputies to sidestep the thorny issue of whether the "promises inherent in the Declaration of the Rights of Man and Citizen" would lead to democracy. Furthermore, since the Jews' perceived traits were so numerous, and indeed contradictory, they provided an ideal cache of symbols with which to articulate civic ideals. One could denounce their esprit de corps or praise their familial devotion according to one's beliefs (or claimed beliefs) about the priorities a citizen ought to set. One could denounce their attachment to traditions as a means of expressing the idea that a citizen should be rational and modern, or one could praise the moral precepts of Judaism as a way of valorizing traditional *moeurs,* which many contemporaries considered the guarantor of civic virtue and public happiness.[25] The Jews therefore constituted a problem, or, more precisely, revolutionaries constituted them as problems, which they then undertook to solve. The very difficulty of resolving such notorious problems as the conflict between religion and the state, individual liberty and the common good, and particularism and universalism assured that the Jews, who as symbols assisted in the articulation of, and apparent solutions to, such dilemmas, would remain a subject of repeated discussion. Moreover, however revolutionaries manipulated the symbols adhering to the Jews in the contemporary imaginary, they were sure to find a wealth of meanings out of which they could make their claims. The sacred texts of Christianity, the more recent voluminous literature on the Jews, and centuries of folklore had combined to produce a rich menu of symbolic choices. Paradoxically, then, it was as much the Jews' familiarity as their alterity that made them objects of revolutionary scrutiny and speculation.

Lest the revolutionary preoccupation with the Jews appear too cerebral, rational, mathematical, or scientific, it is necessary to emphasize its
emotional and sacral aspects. Following Émile Durkheim's insight into
the defining role of the sacred in all societies, Mona Ozouf has shown
how the French revolutionaries, despite their famous efforts at rational-
ization and secularization, quickly reconstituted the sacrality formerly
provided by Catholicism with festivals designed to sanctify the new values of the Revolution.[26] One sees a similar dynamic in the treatment of
the Jews between 1789 and 1791, though it is already perceptible earlier in the century. The traditional, pre-Enlightenment, and Christian
conception of Jews—and indeed the "problem" that they had posed for
centuries—was that they obstinately refused to convert. Their obstinacy
was so great that for many millenarians, including the Jansenists, their
conversion signaled the Second Coming. Despite the distinctly modern
and secular features of the French Revolution, its adherents inherited the
Christian metanarrative of Paradise, Fall, and Redemption. They repeatedly told the story of degraded humanity restored to the innocence of its
mythical beginning. Among the linguistic clues they left to their debt to
traditional religion was their repeated use of the word *regeneration* to
describe the radical transformation of those affected by the Revolution.
As a technical theological term regeneration signified the rebirth, often
through baptism, of the soul. Even in its secularized guise, the concept
maintained the implication of conversion. The "new man"[27] of the revolutionaries was like a religious convert in the sense that both underwent a radical change in identity and a purgation of ancient moral pollution. It is understandable that in such a chiliastic atmosphere the Jews
would appear. Revealingly, among some of the most outspoken advocates of the "regeneration of the Jews"—a term ostensibly meaning only
their moral improvement and inclusion in French society—were the
Jansenists Martineau, Bouche, and, most famously, Grégoire. Yet one
did not have to be a Jansenist to fall under the millenarian spell of a
Revolution characterized by the belief in the imminent regeneration of
humanity. With the support of the Enlightenment tenet of human perfectibility, many revolutionaries could express their belief in this optimistic philosophy by envisioning the regeneration of the Jews, reputedly
the most degraded and corrupt of peoples. Of course, there were some
who wished to deny Jews the "title" of French citizen. But even this ironically obstinate position is suggestive of a process of selection, a separation of the wheat from the chaff, defined in ancient religious terms.

The significance of this last point cannot be overstated. For if the Revolution has been remembered as the triumph of universalism, with historians and other commentators drawing correspondingly positive or negative judgments about its worth, the Jewish question shows that this was only one part of revolutionary ideology. Universalism shared the stage with distinction, and if citizenship was often conceived as a natural outgrowth of one's humanity—or, more precisely, of one's being a man—it was just as frequently characterized as the function of extraordinary qualities belonging only to a distinguished few. If the drive for universal citizenship led some to extend the offer of inclusion as far as the proverbially excluded Jews, the very particularism with which the latter were associated provided a caveat against trying to integrate a famously intractable nation into one that was meant to be indivisible.

APPLYING FOR CITIZENSHIP: THE JEWS PRESENT THEIR QUALIFICATIONS

The Jewish responses to the attention of the revolutionaries further the impression that the Revolution itself suffered from a split personality, that it valued uniformity while demanding exceptional virtue and strove for indivisibility while rewarding distinction. Not surprisingly, the pamphlets and speeches through which Jews represented themselves before the simultaneously welcoming and suspicious French people reproduced the very contradictions of the Revolution. This was not simply because they wished to please their judges and therefore invoked, sometimes indiscriminately, the values of the latter but because the Jews who were most qualified for the hazardous job of cultural translation cherished at once the universalism that justified their equality and their own specifically Jewish identity. They carefully negotiated the ideological ambiguities of the day in order to make the paradoxical case for their inclusion *as Jews* in the otherwise indivisible French nation. Ironically, their case for a revolutionary transformation of their condition depended on the traditional absolutist argument that they were useful to the state, not as Frenchmen but as Jews, and it implied that they were willing to pay, literally as well as figuratively, for their rights in much the same way as they had done under the Old Regime. These contradictions, however, merely point to the persistence of traditional ways of thinking—about Jews but also about the composition of political communities—in an avowedly revolutionary culture.

The very first petition that Jews presented to the National Assembly eloquently, though no doubt unconsciously, expressed the dilemma that they faced. On August 26, 1789, fittingly the day on which the Declaration of the Rights of Man and Citizen was issued, a "deputation" of Parisian Jews congratulated the deputies for having "restored man to his original dignity" but went on to observe that "the people" continued to view the Jews "as strangers to the French Nation." They therefore asked the deputies "to make . . . particular mention of the Jewish Nation and thus to consecrate our title and rights of Citizens."[28] The contrast between universal terms such as "man" and "the people" on the one hand and the "particular" case of "the Jewish Nation" on the other speaks volumes about the competing agendas that the Jews had to negotiate. It is all the more striking in that the Jews of Paris, unlike their coreligionists elsewhere in France, were not organized as a corporate body. The political climate of the Revolution militated against the condition of *imperium in imperio* that Abbé Sieyes had so recently denounced in his celebrated attack on the privileged nobility.[29] Yet the Jews' identity as a discrete nation was sufficiently important to them that they wished to maintain it despite an avowed desire to be regarded as something other than "strangers to the French Nation."

The impression of indivisibility could only have been further attenuated when the six Jewish "deputies" chosen to represent their coreligionists in Alsace, Lorraine, and Metz published an open letter to the National Assembly less than a week later. In that publication the spokesmen echoed the Parisian Jews' request for "the title and rights of Citizens" but explicitly asked to retain their historical right to autonomy in civil matters between Jews. Later that fall Isaïah Berr Bing published a pamphlet that also called for equality, as well as the continuation of Jewish self-governance. More striking still, he gave it a title that suggested a persistent sense of Jewish particularism: *Mémoire particulier pour la communauté des Juifs établis à Metz.*[30]

At the same time, a "particular" memoir for the Jews of Metz suggested that their interests were not identical with those of other Jews, and quickly it became apparent that there was no single Jewish nation in France but rather a plurality of Jewish groups, each with its own interests. Specifically, though the Ashkenazim were pleased to see deputies in the National Assembly plead their case, the Portuguese communities of the southwest had a different agenda. Already enjoying relatively broad civil liberties as a result of royal letters patent and hoping that the Revolution would quietly preserve these advantages, the Sephardic Jews were actually alarmed to see the Jewish question raised. As early as August 14, 1789, the "deputies of the *Nation juive portugaise*" published an open letter to Abbé Grégoire, thanking him for his concern about the Jews but urging him not to support any legislation on their behalf. Distinguishing themselves from their coreligionists in the east, they wrote, "If the unfortunate conduct or fate of some Jews of Alsace and the Three Bishoprics induced the National Assembly to pass any Regulation that should be common to all the Jews in the Kingdom, those of Bordeaux, as well as all their Compatriots, would rightly regard this as an injustice equally gratuitous and cruel." Ironically, they were able to make this claim while designating themselves the *Nation juive portugaise*. Legally speaking, this was their title, but the Revolution had given the word *nation* a completely new meaning. In any event, the Portuguese were clearly afraid that any discussion of Jewish rights in general would place those of the *portugais* in particular at risk. They expressed these fears more explicitly still after the Assembly's December 24 decision to suspend judgment on the political rights of the kingdom's Jews, when they promised that they, unlike their misguided brethren, would never "constitute a class of Citizens separate from all others."[31]

The impression of fragmentation must have been all the more vivid when the Ashkenazi communities of Lunéville and Sarguemines in Lorraine broke ranks with their officially designated representatives based in Nancy. In response to the August 31 request by the Ashkenazi deputies to "preserve our Synagogues, our Rabbis and our Syndics in the same manner that all exist today," dissenters wrote in a published *Mémoire* that this was "diametrically opposed to the interests of the Jews of these two cities." They appeared to oppose corporate autonomy altogether, writing of their wish to "cease forming a private corporation." Yet later they contradicted themselves by asking the National Assembly's permission "to choose a Rabbi and Syndics residing in Lunéville and Sarguemines." Evidently they only opposed their subservience to a community based in Nancy and indeed complained that they had long suffered under the "yoke" of "arbitrary taxes" levied by the "so-called Rabbis" and syndics in that city.[32]

The cohabitation of universalism and particularism manifested itself not merely in the pairing of vows of dedication to the common good with a *sauve qui peut* style of advocacy. It characterized the Jewish pamphlets in other ways as well. Specifically, discussions of rights frequently combined claims about the universal rights of "man" with references to specific historical rights. Thus the prototypical Ashkenazi *Adresse* of

August 31, 1789, suggested that the Jews' claims rested upon the "essential and imprescriptible rights of Man," then went on to point out that "our existence is so legal that the deposit of our laws exists juridically in the archives of the Parlement of Metz, of Nancy, and of the Sovereign Council of Alsace." Similarly, in their open letter to Grégoire the *portugais* of Bordeaux observed that the Declaration of the Rights of Man and Citizen "repulses all particular measures," yet on the next page they alluded to specific historical rights, the royal letters patent that had enabled their *nation* to participate in the election of deputies to the Estates General. When the Jews of Bordeaux petitioned the National Assembly at the end of December, they invoked "the honorable rights attached to the quality of French Citizen" but then enumerated in detail the historical rights of the *portugais* and *avignonnais* for the last 240 years. A "deputy" for the Jewish community of Saint-Esprit similarly exulted, "The decrees of the august Assembly . . . call all men to the right of citizen," but he also listed the specific liberties of the local Jews as a result of letters patent, including the "faculty . . . of possessing real estate, of selling and acquiring, of making contracts, and of inheritance."[33]

Why did Jews repeatedly point to their particular historical rights? Why were they not content to invoke the natural and universal rights of "man"? Strictly speaking, the latter should have trumped the former. More problematically still, historical rights were *privileges,* literally the "private laws" that adhered only to particular individuals and groups and served as the most obvious means of distinguishing them from others in the eyes of the prerevolutionary state and its inhabitants. The reign of privilege, however, was precisely what the revolutionaries had so repeatedly and vehemently declared themselves against, apparently abolishing it with the greatest ceremony on the Night of August 4. Sieyes defined the *nation* as a group of people living under the same laws,[34] and the statements of countless revolutionaries appear to have reflected unanimity on this principle. Moreover, this was precisely the principle behind the movement to abrogate all legal distinctions between Jews and others. How, then, could advocates of equality between Jews and non-Jews invoke precisely the precedents that had distinguished the Jews from their Gentile neighbors? Invoking any precedent at all was hazardous in a Revolution that otherwise loudly proclaimed its contempt of precedent. Invoking historical privileges would appear to have been even more hazardous. It suggested that the Jews indeed saw themselves as a "nation within a nation."

Of course, Jews were not the only corporate group that wavered between arguments for universal rights and pleas for special privileges. The nobility most famously appealed to both types of rights, especially early in the Revolution, and it is reasonable to attribute the Jews' contradictory pleas to the simple fact that petitioners tend to produce long series of reasons for their claims, a habit that increases the risk of contradiction. Clearly this was at play in the Jewish petitions, yet what is historically significant is the fact that the contradiction in Jewish self-representation reflects a contradiction within revolutionary discourse itself. The fabled universalism of the Revolution always accompanied a valorization of special qualities that distinguished individuals and groups from others. Joan Scott has shown how the feminist writings of Olympe de Gouges exposed the pretense of revolutionary universalism by revealing the fact that citizenship was actually embodied in the form of a white man.[35] Similarly, the petitions of Jews reveal the extent to which revolutionaries saw citizenship as a particular set of qualities inhering in an elite subset of the population. They suggest that, statements about universal equality notwithstanding, a citizen according to revolutionary ideology was typically a person who distinguished himself from the masses in certain ways. The well-known debate over property qualifications for political rights tends to obscure the shared assumption of all the participants that a citizen was a special kind of person with specific virtues, namely, honesty, a selfless concern for the general welfare, and the ability to discern its best interests. The antidemocratic majority merely expressed the conviction that a minimum degree of prosperity guaranteed those virtues, while the democratic minority saw them as independent of wealth. In this respect, citizenship was far from universal, and the rights of citizen were in a sense privileges obtainable exclusively by those who deserved them.

Only this paradox can explain the otherwise inexplicable frequency with which the words *citoyen* and *françois* were combined with the word *titre* (title), so long associated with titles of nobility and similar privileges. In August 1789 the Jews of Paris petitioned the National Assembly to "consecrate . . . our title and our rights of Citizens." Their coreligionists from eastern France likewise called for "the title and the rights of Citizens." The dissidents of Lunéville and Sarguemines expressed themselves identically, and other Jewish pamphleteers from throughout France similarly associated citizenship rights with "titles." Accordingly, it was necessary to be *digne* (worthy), and Jewish petitioners repeatedly promised that they would prove themselves, or had already proved themselves, "worthy" of the titles they requested.[36] The Jews, however, did not invent the sense of citizenship as a distinguishing privilege earned only by the worthy. This definition was part and parcel of revolutionary discourse, coexisting uneasily with declarations of allegiance to the opposite principle of universalism.

Under the circumstances, the standard regenerationist argument that the Jews would acquire the virtues of citizens upon obtaining the corresponding rights was of limited use, since a strong current of republican ideology suggested that those very rights should be granted only to men who had already proved their merit. To be sure, the former argument was made. After all, the promise that Jews would improve when granted rights was the logical corollary to the claim that their vices were the product of oppression. Thus the syndics of the Lorraine community baldly stated, "We wallow in the same inertia, and we preserve all the vices with which we are reproached," predicting only that moral regeneration would be evident "in our children." Their counterparts in Alsace addressed their non-Jewish neighbors, "Citizens, we shall strive to be what you are when we have the same title and the same rights as you!" The combined address of the Ashkenazi deputies similarly used the future tense to describe their regeneration, promising that upon acquiring the "title" of French citizen, they "will not delay in giving proof of their patriotism and devotion."[37]

In addition to these hypothetical claims, however, representatives of the Jews were compelled to demonstrate that they already possessed the elevated moral qualities of citizens. Reference to letters patent was one way of creating this impression, since they appeared to mark the Jews' merit in the past, or at least their utility to the state. Even more effective, since it did not bear traces of privilege, was the standard apology for the Jewish religion, the presentation of Judaism as a religion that promoted civic virtue. This apologetic strategy, as described in the previous chapter, had served to refute typical eighteenth-century accusations against Judaism: that it authorized usury and fraud, that it endorsed religious separatism and contempt for Gentiles, and so on. It was all the more useful in the revolutionary context. The values that apologists had shown to be inherent to Judaism now constituted the official morality of the revolutionary French *nation*. In this environment what distinguished the Jews as citizens with all the requisite virtues was precisely their adherence to a religion with severe standards of morality.

At a minimum, apologists had to refute the charge that Judaism authorized usury in loans to non-Jews. Isaïah Berr Bing's 1787 defense had argued that the notorious passage in Deuteronomy permitting Jews to lend at interest to non-Jews but forbidding them to take interest from "brothers" was justified because God wanted to preserve the "primitive equality" of the Jews. In the fall of 1789 Bing's *Mémoire particulier* offered an abbreviated version of this argument and referred the reader to the 1787 pamphlet. At the end of January 1790 the *Pétition des Juifs* on behalf of the still disenfranchised Ashkenazim justified the controversial precept by arguing that preferred treatment of one's own nation over foreigners was only natural, in antiquity as in modern times, though they assured their readers that they regarded France as their nation.[38]

Of course, demonstrating that the Jews were not authorized by their religion to commit usury only proved that they were no worse than others, and the notion of citizenship as a form of distinction pressured them to show that Judaism induced its adherents to exhibit positive virtues. Thus the *Pétition des Juifs* represented Judaism as the sort of natural religion that the philosophes had considered conducive to moral behavior. Its "three principal dogmas" were "the unity of God," "the immortality of the soul," and "future punishments and rewards." These were precisely the doctrines that Voltaire had deemed necessary to justify God's actions and, by extension, to promote a sense of justice in his worshipers. More specifically, the petitioners noted that Jews "never fail to pay to the poor the tithe that the Christians pay to the Clergy," a remark that subtly suggested corruption in the Church and a more just distribution of alms in Judaism. They added that the Jews "have a religious respect for the authors of their days," that "they do not die without receiving the benediction of their fathers or giving it to their children," that "their teacher is respected by them as a father," and that they have a "profound veneration" for "the elderly."[39]

Accordingly, Bing lamented that "the public does not sufficiently know how this Religion is austere in its principles, demanding in its asceticism, and how it is scrupulously observed." He highlighted the "extreme frugality" that had "preserved [the Jews] from the depredations of luxury," thus addressing the fear of *luxe* so frequently expressed by eighteenth-century moralists. Polemics against the Jews had often accused them of promoting luxury by providing money to young men with apparently uncontrollable desires. Now Bing took the opportunity to modify the common association of Jews with luxury. Like the petitioners mentioned earlier, he also foregrounded the familial virtues of the Jews, which Grégoire and others had publicized in the prerevolutionary literature on regeneration. He wrote, "The conjugal union is still inviolably respected by [the Jews]; the authority of heads of family is still not disdained, and the elderly do not languish among us from a contempt that reveals a neglect for the most sacred duties."[40] The repeated use of the word *still (encore)* suggested a contrast with the more modern Gentiles who had evidently forgotten the simple morality of their predecessors. It played upon prevalent assumptions about the purity of antiquity and decadence of modern civilization and suggested that the Jews, far from being incapable of morality, were perhaps after all the guardians of an ancient but otherwise neglected purity.

The implication in much of the Jewish pamphlet literature during the Revolution was that Judaism was not only compatible with citizenship but actually the fount of civic virtue. When the syndics of the Ashkenazi communities observed, "It is on the diligence or indifference with which one practices the duties of Religion that the diligence or indifference with which one practices social duties depends," they politely made room for Christianity but implicitly reminded their audience of Judaism's role in the origins of "social duties." Similarly, the syndics of the Lorraine community commented on the Golden Rule, "*love your neighbor as yourself* [is the] sublime precept which includes all of the duties of man in society." Of course, Christians knew this command from the Gospels, but here Jewish spokesmen took the opportunity to recall its Old Testament origins. Finally, the petitioners of January 1790 emphasized the place of the Golden Rule in the Jewish tradition by recalling the Talmudic story of the pagan who asked Rabbi Hillel to teach him the "law of Moses," to which the latter responded (in the version of the petitioners): "*My son, love your neighbor as you love yourself, that is the law of Moses; the rest is but commentary and explication.*"[41]

Membership in a religion that demanded a high ethical standard, and indeed seemed to have invented morality altogether, could therefore be portrayed as a sign of distinction, and precisely the sort of distinction that the "title" of citizen, with all its moral implications, demanded. More persuasive, however, would have been any signs that the Jews had actually taken part in public life. This of course was difficult, especially for the Ashkenazi Jews, since precisely the restrictions they sought to abolish prevented them from proving their public-spiritedness. The Jews of Bordeaux could boast that some of their wealthier members had participated in the primary elections for the Estates General—with David Gradis chosen by the city as an elector. They could also point to their participation in the "patriotic regiments," to which they had been "elected up to the grade of Captain." Both Sephardic and Ashkenazi

Jews living in Paris similarly vaunted their service in the National Guard, their readiness "to shed their blood for the glory of the nation and the support of liberty," as evidence of their patriotism. The Jews of the east remained excluded from local elections, as well as the National Guard, though the Nancy community attempted (unsuccessfully) to gain admission to the local militia.[42]

What all Jews were permitted to do for the *patrie* was to contribute money and valuable objects. On September 15, 1789, a Jewish member of the National Guard in Paris appeared before the National Assembly in his guardsman's uniform to make a patriotic donation of twenty-five *louis,* thus symbolically demonstrating two forms of service to the nation. The Bordelais Jews proudly recorded a "patriotic gift of 161 pairs of silver shoe buckles," no doubt in response to the trend of shoe buckle donation that had begun at the Café Procope in Paris. In eastern France as well, the revolutionary authorities did not repudiate Jewish gifts to the state. For the Jews of Lunéville and Sarguemines such presents were the only way to prove their merit as patriots. Challenging the National Assembly to "judge . . . whether we are unworthy of the title of Citizens," they reported that as early as August 3, 1789, "we offered . . . to furnish a Patriotic Contribution for the needs of the State." In response, the municipality of Lunéville ordered "that a List of zealous Citizens shall be made, AT THE HEAD OF WHICH SHALL BE PLACED THE COMMUNITY OF JEWS . . . followed by the other Citizens and Communities animated with the same spirit, who have declared that they wish to contribute to the Public good."[43]

Ironically, the Jews of Lunéville and Sarguemines achieved the level of moral distinction implied in the revolutionary conception of citizenship by playing the role that otherwise earned them the mark of vice. They served the *patrie* as providers of specie. To be sure, they were giving, not lending. Moreover, the revolutionaries generally represented monetary sacrifice as a mark of patriotic devotion and hence a suitable substitute for government or military service. Simon Schama has described this "cult of self-dispossession" in which "giving something of one's own to the Nation became a demonstration of patriotic probity." Such potlatch-style gift giving no doubt mirrored the conspicuous generosity that has been shown to have been a characteristic mode of the National Assembly and was all the more appropriate for Jews precisely because other avenues of patriotic service were closed to them. In this respect, as in others, the Jews resembled another group that was barred from military and government service: the kingdom's women, who performed their civic duties by encouraging patriotic gifts.[44] Even at the level of active citizenship the National Assembly had come very close to portraying the capacity to serve the commonweal as a function of money. By limiting political rights to those men who paid a predetermined amount in taxes, the deputies sent the message that civic virtue was fungible and that payment in cash would be accepted in lieu of service.

Still, *dons patriotiques* by Jews necessarily had a different cultural meaning from comparable gifts by Gentiles. In addition to alluding to the general image of the Jew as essentially a provider of cash, in the midst of debates over rights the "gifts" must have conjured up the historical image of Jews paying for their privileges. Under absolutism in France as elsewhere, whatever rights the Jews obtained depended primarily on their perceived utility to the state. That utility, moreover, was typically calculated in monetary terms. The crudest expression of this arrangement could be seen in the "protection" and "tolerance" duties levied on the Ashkenazi Jews in Alsace and elsewhere in eastern France. Ironically, then, at just the moment when spokesmen for these Jews denounced the infamous Brancas tax and comparable duties and earned the support of deputies such as Dupont de Nemour, who insisted that "protection is owed and is not for sale," Jews risked giving the impression that, once again, they were purchasing their rights.[45]

Yet so strong was the need for the Jews to distinguish themselves, to prove that their particular subset of the population merited the coveted title of citizen, that their spokesmen reverted to the style of self-representation characteristic of the reign of Louis XV, when their perceived utility to the state was based on their proverbial ability to produce money. A decline in the prestige of physiocracy, with its valorization of agriculture and literal discounting of commerce as well as industry, probably made it easier for the Jews to portray themselves as liquid, hence useful. More immediately significant in this respect was no doubt the state's acute financial crisis. Jewish representatives therefore repeatedly pointed to their reputed prowess with money. If patriotic gift giving was a symbolic means of sending this message, the pamphlet literature explicitly reinforced the point. Thus Bing, after characterizing the Jews in terms of primitive virtue, went on to insist that the Jews were especially skilled entrepreneurs, writing, "The habit of calculating probabilities gives the Jews a rare intrepidity that enables them to undertake any business venture." Grégoire had attributed a *génie calculateur* to the Jews. Now Bing was manipulating these prejudices by affirming that the Jews were truly adept at calculating but insisting that the effects of this habit were positive. Rather than making them dishonest, he claimed, calculating made them intrepid. In case one worried that an intrepid Jew was all the more dangerous, Bing wrote, "we [!] are more the agents of circulation than the owners of gold," and assured his audience that the money handled by Jews would, as he put it, "all . . . return to the mass of effective riches of the [French] Nation."[46]

The *Pétition des Juifs* made the same point but more directly. "Frenchmen," the petitioners wrote, "Do not forget that every time . . . the Jews were chased out of France, your interest soon forced you to have them return." Expounding on this historical lesson and, like Bing, appealing to the image of circulation, they stated that Philip the Bold, "in his Letters Patent concerning the recall of the Jews, said in his own words, *that he found no other means of reestablishing the exhausted finances but by recalling the people who are fitted to make commerce flourish and circulate money.*" If the French wanted to know what their country would be without the Jews, they needed only "look . . . at Spain, where agriculture is languishing, and where agriculture would be flourishing, if *three hundred thousand Jews* who had been chased out still existed there." The petitioners added sternly, "And let the sad example of this Kingdom be a useful lesson for your own."[47] These historical examples were well known to readers of Montesquieu, Voltaire, and authors of the *Encyclopédie*, all of whom had represented the medieval expulsion of Jews as emblematic of the greed and stupidity of the Dark Ages and who had portrayed the Spanish expulsion of Jews as a major cause of its subsequent economic decline.[48]

Of course, the Jews of revolutionary France were not threatened with expulsion. On the contrary, their residency in France was more secure than it had ever been. Even the strongest opponents of Jewish rights were not proposing expulsion. Rather, it was the petitioners themselves who were threatening a Jewish exodus should the Revolution fail to provide them with the rights they sought. It was well known, thanks in large measure to Mirabeau's writings, that Joseph II had taken steps in the 1780s to lift some of the most burdensome restrictions on the Jews of the Austrian empire. Although the Habsburg emperor had by no means placed them on an equal footing with his Catholic subjects, his act of enlightened absolutism was a potential embarrassment in France, particularly during the Revolution, when so many saw in their political activity the culmination of a "century of philosophy." The Jewish petitioners played upon this insecurity when they wrote, "Austria is at your doorstep; and it is to be feared that Austria should soon receive in its bosom some of these men who would continue to be treated as slaves among you, and whom she treats as free men." They added, in a prophetic tone, "It is then that you will complain all the more of the weakness of trade, and of the scarcity of currency, and of the mendicity that will besiege you from all directions." Finally, they rephrased their argument, writing bluntly, "Some of these Jews are rich. Almost all of them are devoted to commerce. . . . Is France truly in the condition to give as a present to her neighbors their activity and their wealth?"[49]

Austria was hardly a paradise for the Jews, most of whom were quite far indeed from the status of "free men," and to emphasize the fact that "some" Jews were rich obscured the fact that the majority were not and that many lived in grinding poverty. But the pressure to make such claims must have been strong in the midst of a culture that repeatedly treated citizenship as a mark of extraordinary virtue, repeatedly reduced the Jews to their reputed function of cash providers, and was experiencing a real financial crisis. The cultural and financial climate was such that the petitioners could even vaunt the Jews' reputed ability to reproduce and thus add useful citizens to the *patrie*. Grégoire had done much to popularize the myth of Jewish fecundity, which for him and others was a source of worry. The petitioners spun this prejudice to their advantage and even predicted the further augmentation of their population from new immigrants should France welcome the Jews as equals. These grateful new citizens would presumably nurse the country back to financial health.[50]

In a sense, then, Jewish leaders suggested a willingness to purchase their emancipation, just as they had purchased their privileges under the Old Regime. And in the end the revolutionary state effectively charged the Jews for their "equality" by declining to nationalize the debts of the former Jewish *nations,* though it assumed the debts of other former corporations. While it would be mistaken to assume that exaggerated claims to special financial prowess were the *cause* of the exceptional bill with which the Jews were presented upon their official entry into the French nation, the correlation between these claims and the terms of admission to the rights of citizens suggests a tacit assumption by all parties that when Jewish rights were at issue, payment was forthcoming.

Hannah Arendt recognized the ironic sense in which Jewish citizenship was treated as a privilege at the time of the Revolution, though she fell victim to the myth—perpetuated in some measure by the Jews themselves—that the state truly needed Jewish cash to function.[51] Nor did she fully appreciate the significance of the paradox she perceptively discerned. If the revolutionaries treated the Jews simultaneously as participants in universal citizenship and a special case requiring exceptional attention, and if the Jews could embrace their identity as a particular *nation* within the otherwise indivisible French *nation,* these paradoxes only reveal the contradictions under which revolutionary ideology labored. They point to a concept of citizenship as simultaneously universal and particular, a natural outgrowth of one's humanity and the function of extraordinary qualities belonging only to a distinguished few. François Furet called attention to the contradiction between revolutionary ideology (in its egalitarian form) and the apparent "reality" of political conflict, in which some people and parties simply have more power than others.[52] Less well appreciated, however, is the extent to which, even at the level of ideology, the revolutionaries sent (and followed) mixed signals.[53] Their failure to achieve democracy is well known, but it has typically been seen as a sellout, an ignominious retreat in the face of material "interests." Yet this was less a failure to live up to their principles than an indication that the principles were contradictory from the beginning. Democracy was a problem for the same reasons the Jews were a problem. Citizenship was both a natural right and a reward for distinction, and citizens had to be ordinary and extraordinary at the same time. This mixed message, furthermore, accounts at least in part for the failure of the revolutionaries to stop what they started. Once they proclaimed the Declaration of the Rights of Man and Citizen, the title of which itself indicated the dual nature of the new civic personage, it was possible for all groups and individuals to demand their share of power and prestige, on the strength of their humanity, or on the strength of attributes that distinguished them from the crowd—or, in the strange case of the sansculottes, on the strength of an ordinariness that made them special.

It is insufficient, however, simply to point to the Revolution's shortcomings, as though the historian's task were only that of retrospective judgment. One must try to place the contradictions that plagued the Revolution in their proper historical contexts, to determine what roles the values and conditions of the Old Regime played in the splitting, as it were, of the revolutionary personality. Again the Jewish question is instructive. In the representations of Jews produced by Gentiles, as well as in Jewish self-representations, one can discern a reluctance to part with certain habits of the Old Regime. The statements and actions of National Assembly deputies, with regard to the Jews and elsewhere, have revealed the persistence, or perhaps the atavistic return, of a conversionary impulse, a desire to correct the recalcitrant that was no less messianic for its articulation in the Enlightenment language of human perfectibility. At the same time, as both the statements of deputies and the Jewish pamphlet literature have shown, the intolerance of difference, epitomized by the refusal to accept the Jews as they were, coexisted with an equally long-held stake in the principles of distinction and hierarchy. The habit of assigning rank and corresponding prestige to a bewildering degree of individuals, corporations, and estates did not die easily. In fact, it did not die at all, despite the language of and belief in the contradictory ideal of human equality, but rather reemerged in the guise of moral distinction. That the Jews were long associated with morality, as carriers of either vice or virtue but never morally neutral, only added to the long list of preconditions for their persistence well into the postrevolutionary era as idées fixes in the minds of their neighbors.

THE STORY THE JEWS TOLD
THEMSELVES ABOUT THEMSELVES

In addition to the Jewish question as articulated by revolutionaries and the Jews' efforts at convincing their Gentile neighbors of their civic qualities, messages sent by Jews to their coreligionists afford us yet another perspective on the Revolution. The documents revealing Jewish self-representation before the French in general are far more numerous than those that show the Jews representing themselves and their historical situation to other Jews. This is not surprising, since the need to prove themselves worthy of the citizenship they sought forced Jews to appeal to those with the authority to change their situation, and these addressees were obviously not Jews themselves. Moreover, the interest that Gentiles showed in the Jewish question provoked repeated responses by the object of inquiry, as it were, and the reluctance of the former to acknowledge the full equality of the latter guaranteed renewed petitions, apologies, and self-descriptions on their behalf. Despite this imbalance, there are a few documents that allow us to glimpse Jews in the process of explaining their historical situation to their coreligionists.

A comparison between the story the Jews told themselves about themselves—to borrow a phrase from Clifford Geertz[54]—and the story they told non-Jews about themselves reveals that their proclaimed attachment to the French *patrie* corresponded to a passionately held self-image. Since the texts in question were written in Judeo-German (i.e., German in Hebrew characters) and Hebrew, respectively, there is no question about their intended audiences. Here Jews were communicating with their coreligionists. It would be rash to conclude from this that there was a single, uniform manner in which Jews perceived themselves and their relationship to revolutionary France. Nor would it be sufficient to conclude simply that the Jews were sincere when they assured the French of their devotion. The communication between Jews tells us much more than that. It reveals the astonishing rapidity and ease with which members of a reputedly traditional culture were able to assimilate ideas that by most accounts were quintessentially modern. Yet the image of assimilation must not be misunderstood. The Jews were not assimilated by the dominant culture, despite the proclaimed intentions of most Gentile regenerationists. They assimilated that culture into their own. That is to say, they recognized its values as their own without undergoing a fundamental transformation of identity. To those Jews who might have worried that they faced a choice between nations, they affirmed that no such choice was necessary. The Jews could have it all: membership in a new community of equal citizens and an ancient *nation juive*.

Two invaluable sources of Jewish self-representation directed at a Jewish audience are the work of Abraham Spire, a printer from Metz. The first of these is a 110-page book, written in Judeo-German and entitled *Beschreibung von der Veränderung, oder Aufruhr in Frankreich, was man nennt Revolution* (Description of the change, or uprising in France, which is called Revolution). This account of political events in Versailles and Paris (with some information about the provinces) between early May and early November 1789 preceded a weekly newspaper by the same author, entitled simply *Zeitung* (Newspaper), which appeared twenty times between early November 1789 and late March 1790.[55] In the first issue of the *Zeitung*, Spire boasted of one hundred subscribers, and if this is accurate, one can assume that about as many readers had bought his *Beschreibung*, which served in large measure as an introduction to and advertisement for the subsequent journal. Simon Schwarzfuchs estimates that for every subscriber, fifteen to twenty people read the journal. But even if this figure is too high, the appearance of the *Zeitung* as well as the *Beschreibung* point to a significant presence of Jewish readers who saw the events of the Revolution as sufficiently important to read about. The journal was short-lived, but this was the fate of most newspapers, and given the relative isolation of the Ashkenazi Jews from French society and culture, what is remarkable about the weekly newspaper is that it existed at all. It bears witness to a sense among a significant number of French Jews that what was hap-

pening in the capital mattered to them. If, as Benedict Anderson has argued, newspaper reading contributes to a sense of "imagined communities," then Spire's publication suggests that as early as the fall of 1789
Jews were imagining themselves as part of a community that went well
beyond the *rue des Juifs*.[56]

Instilling the notion that the Jews belonged to the French nation was
evidently one of Spire's first priorities. In the *Beschreibung* the author
took great pains to explain all terms that related to French geography,
history, and administration. Thus, when referring to the bishop of Bordeaux, he added in a footnote, "Bordeaux is the capital of the province
Guyenne; a pretty city 195 hours from Paris"; he wrote similar notes
explaining the locations of Toulouse, Chartres, Poitou, Aix, and other
provincial capitals. In other footnotes he described landmarks in Paris,
such as the Palais Royal ("the *hôtel* and garden of the Duc d'Orléans"),
the Tuileries ("the garden of the royal palace"), and the Invalides ("a
beautiful *hôtel* that Louis XIV had built as a rest home for old soldiers").[57] These descriptions gave the distinct impression of a civics lesson, and elsewhere Spire reinforced his political message.

Spire's feelings about the Revolution were evident in his account of
the parade that opened the Estates General, which he revealingly defined
as "a religious procession." The sense of sacredness pervades his description of the Estates General, both in the emphasis on harmony between the three orders and in the special attention to the clergy. Spire
spent a great deal of time recounting the words and actions of clergymen—he himself was a rabbi—and even defined the crucial word *constitution* for his readers as "the rights of the kingdom in worldly and
spiritual matters," thus giving equal weight to religious concerns. His
account of the decision by some of the clergy to join with the Third Estate in the establishment of the National Assembly suggests the importance of religious men to the completion of the Revolution: "As soon as
the clergy took their places, a joy so great was produced that tears ran
from [the deputies'] eyes."[58]

Spire showed equal gratitude toward the king, to whom he gave much
of the credit for the joining of the three estates. De-emphasizing the
conflict between the king and his subjects, as well as the tensions between the orders, Spire described a spontaneous coming together of the
French nation. His account of the scene on June 24, following the king's
order to the first two estates to join with the third, echoes the enthusiasm of his fellow revolutionary journalists:

As the people learned of this complete union they ran in great joy to the palace and called in their loudest voices to the king and the queen. It was as though commoners, deputies and clergymen were all mixed. No difference was seen, as though all were simply patriots. The king and the queen appeared on a balcony. Then came a cry of "Long live the king and the queen!" All hearts were softened.

He added, now noting the existence of an opposition to the Revolution, "Who could ever think to report . . . lies to the king about a nation that shows such sincere and free devotion to its king?"[59]

Like other revolutionary enthusiasts, Spire projected a vivid image of the Revolution's enemies. These were the "aristocrats," defined simply as "those who force with violence" *(Gewaltzwinger),* and were opposed by "patriots," the "nation," and the "people." Spire held the aristocrats responsible for all the Revolution's misfortunes, as well as the miseries of the Old Regime. Thus, after describing the horrors of the Bastille, "which for many hundreds of years swallowed innocent people," he reported, "And this was all because of the aristocrats, without the knowledge of the king." The annihilation of the aristocrats was as justified as the destruction of the Bastille that embodied their wickedness, according to Spire, who lingered for nine pages over the events of July 14. Especially striking in this account is the matter-of-fact ease with which the author portrayed the killing of "aristocrats." The reader learns of Delaunay, the governor of the Bastille, that "the people trampled on [him]," that "he was stabbed many times," and that "his head was cut off and stuck on a pike." All this was justified because of the governor's "treason." Spire similarly noted the "treason" of the mayor, whose murder he also coolly recounted: "One took a dagger, the other a pistol, and with a shot [the mayor] lay on the ground. His head was cut off, his body given to the people who, full of angry rage avenged themselves on him, and his head was carried around on a pike." Elsewhere he justified the pillaging of the Saint-Lazare monastery—monks were excluded from his otherwise respectful attitude toward the clergy and were repeatedly depicted as greedy—on the grounds that "the people were needy." And he defended the grisly assassination of Foulon on the assumption that he had shown himself indifferent to the hunger of the people, having reportedly said, "Let them eat hay."[60]

Spire appears therefore to have absorbed the most extreme version of revolutionary ideology according to which what the people did was by definition right, their anger was always justified, and those they killed were ipso facto enemies of the nation. His conception of "the people" was so idealized that he incorporated the French word into his German description, writing consistently of "das Peuple" rather than using the otherwise available word, "das Volk," as though the sacredness of the people could only be rendered in the language of the revolutionaries. But how did Spire conceive of the relationship between the Jews and "das Peuple"? Neither his *Beschreibung* nor his *Zeitung* dealt exclusively with Jewish matters, and though these were discussed, the greater part of Spire's work focused on the Revolution *tout court*. This is in itself significant, since it suggests an identification with the French nation. Elsewhere, however, the connection between Jews and Gentiles in revolutionary France was made explicit. When discussing the National Guard, for example, an evidently egalitarian institution that "comprises rich [and] poor, as though there were no difference," Spire proudly reported that among the members were Jews, some of whom had been named officers, and he elsewhere affirmed the principle of equality by asserting that the guardsmen "made no distinction [between Jews] and Catholics."[61]

Spire also connected the Jews and their non-Jewish compatriots by reporting the charitable contributions of the former. He proudly noted that his coreligionist Moshe Treni presented 600 livres to the National Assembly on September 14, adding that the deputies cheered when they learned that Treni was a Jew. He informed his readers that throughout the month of July the Jews of Paris had made contributions to the poor; that the Jews of Metz had sold flour "to the common people" for two and a half sous a pound, well under the current price of four sous, thus incurring a loss of thousands of livres; that for three months during the previous winter the same community had given free bread to the poor; and that the Jews of Nancy had engaged in similar acts of charity. Clearly Spire considered such acts crucial to the success of the Revolution, and accordingly much of the news he reported in his *Zeitung* related to "patriotic gifts." He enthusiastically described the contributions of silver shoe buckles by the city of Bordeaux, the National Assembly, and the habitués of the Café Procope and encouraged his readers to donate theirs as well, since, in his estimation, if everyone followed the example of these generous citizens, the public treasury would grow by 40 to 50 million livres. He called attention to the National Assembly's incentive to charity: the deputies would publish the name of anyone who offered one-quarter of one's income to the state. He happily reported that the French merchants of Constantinople had made a patriotic donation of 24,000 livres and that they had bought all French slaves from the Turks so that they could be sent back to France "to enjoy freedom"; and he claimed that the French merchants of Tunis had engaged in similar acts of charity and redemption.[62]

This fantasy of redemption suggests an association in Spire's thinking between generosity and liberation. The connection was not always as simple as the idea that a generous person could redeem a slave. It alternatively conjured a conception of self-emancipation through charity, as though the Jews could make themselves citizens, that is, liberate themselves, by demonstrating their generosity in acts of charity. Yet even as Spire lauded the civic generosity of Jews and Gentiles alike and exulted in the apparent fact that citizens no longer distinguished between Jews and Gentiles, he had to confront the painful fact that precisely the equality of the Jews was in question, despite the increasing evidence of their patriotism. Indeed, glaringly absent from his *Zeitung* are the debates on Jewish citizenship in late December 1789. The *Beschreibung* mentioned Grégoire's and Clermont-Tonnerre's attempts to discuss the matter in September and reported Berr Isaac Berr's appearance before the National Assembly in October.[63] Yet the five *Zeitung* issues following the debates that ended December 24 with the de facto exclusion of Jews from the rights of active citizenship were entirely silent on this decision, as though it were simply too horrible to mention. It was only in the context of the Assembly's debate on the legal condition of the Sephardic Jews that Spire discussed the adjournment of December. He then wrote:

> With the decision of December 24 recognizing the Lutherans [i.e., Protestants] as citizens *[Citoyens]*, the judgment on the Jews of Metz, Alsace and Lorraine was adjourned, since opposing thoughts were seen and a portion of the inhabitants of the latter two provinces have tried every means against the holy people, in order to banish them mercilessly, so our hope is to wait for the time when reason will destroy this disgraceful prejudice that corrupts humanity.[64]

Spire continued with an account of the debate over the status of the Portuguese and Avignonese Jews. He cited a speech by Talleyrand denouncing those who would exclude them from the status of citizens:

> Why should true justice and common sense *[die menschliche Vernunft]* still have thoughts of disgust and prejudice against the divine faith? The Jews have so long been seen as created only to be excluded from the divine plan. It has so often been said that they must be lost and errant, without protection and without a fatherland *[sonder Vaterland]*, which is believed like the illusion that people who have a different color have an inferior nature. Is this not a divine insult to believe that all people are not [God's] children?[65]

It is highly unlikely that Talleyrand said anything of the sort, especially on January 28, when he in fact cautiously based the argument in favor of the *portugais* and *avignonnais* on their historical rights (i.e., privileges), as confirmed in royal letters patent.[66] The speech Spire put into the mouth of the bishop of Autun is based on the idea of natural equality, confirmed by natural religion, and is much more characteristic of Grégoire than of Talleyrand. Whether Spire confused Talleyrand's words with another statement in favor of Jewish rights, or was misinformed, or simply fabricated the speech is impossible to determine. In any case these words reveal more about Spire's own beliefs and hopes than about Talleyrand. They confirm his faith in human equality and attest to his hope that "true justice and common sense" might soon permeate the thinking of his would-be compatriots. Accordingly, no result of the January 28 debate could have satisfied Spire. Excluding the Portuguese and Avignonese from the possibility of active citizenship would have been a grave injustice from his perspective. Yet when they were, paradoxically, singled out for equality, Spire could not be jubilant. He wrote, "This decision was an insult to the Jews of the other provinces," and further, "An obstacle is to be feared from these people who do not have the feelings necessary to leave for our posterity the inheritance of this happy time. Our hope is in God's care."[67]

The National Assembly's decision therefore left Spire thinking, rather uncharacteristically, of the Jews in the first person and viewing the French, whom he seems to have regarded as truly living in a "happy time," as a separate people, if only for the moment. Significantly, however, he published an erratum in the following issue, noting that the words "an obstacle from these people" should have read "[an obstacle from] certain persons." Clearly he did not want his readers to have the impression that he regarded all of his non-Jewish neighbors as adversaries. The proof of his conviction in the unity of the French nation and of the place of the Jews in that unity, however, came not from this retraction but from the fact that Spire continued to publish his newspaper. He mentioned the agitation for citizenship on behalf of the Ashkenazi Jews of Paris in February and March, but his primary goal remained relating events of relevance to the whole French nation. He even devoted a special issue to the events of February 4, when the king promised to accept the Constitution and to raise the dauphin as a constitutional monarch. This "patriotic speech," according to Spire, made the day "an eternal monument."[68] Of course, the Jews' place in the Constitution that Spire was already praising remained to be determined. Yet Spire was already a French citizen, in thought and sentiment if not in law, and sought to teach his coreligionists a similar attitude toward the *patrie*.

A very different kind of source, but no less valuable to the historian, is a pair of related poems on the Revolution, written in Hebrew in 1790 and 1792, respectively. The author was Moïse Ensheim, who like Abraham Spire lived in Metz, but whose intended audience extended beyond the local and regional Jewish communities. He published the first of the two poems, a nineteen-stanza ode to the National Assembly entitled *Shirim al va'ad ha-gadol asher be-medinat tsarfat* (Songs on the great meeting in the State of France), in the Hebrew journal *Ha-Meassef* (The Collector). Based in Berlin, *Ha-Meassef* was the organ of Jewish intellectuals known as the *maskilim,* or "understanding ones," who were sympathetic to the European Enlightenment and who, like Moses Mendelssohn, sought a synthesis between secular and divine knowledge. *Ha-Meassef* and its readers were a natural venue for the *Shirim,* as Ensheim himself had close ties to the *maskilim* of Berlin. He had worked in Berlin as preceptor to Mendelssohn's children between 1782 and 1787, and in a number of ways his life mirrored that of the prototypical Enlightened Jew. Like Mendelssohn, Ensheim was born to a poor family, received a traditional Jewish education, found his teachers lacking, and turned to an intensive autodidacticism, teaching himself French, German, Latin, Greek, and Arabic. Ensheim even became a mathematician of some renown, whose work was appreciated by Lagrange and Laplace. But his interests were not strictly academic. He sought to improve the legal condition of his coreligionists, aided Abbé Grégoire in the preparation of his *Essai sur la régénération,* and consulted with the radical priest at the time of the debates in the National Assembly on the legal status of the Jews.[69]

Yet Ensheim's poem was directed at Jews, especially the learned Jews who read *Ha-meassef*—among whom were Jews from Metz—and who could be expected to understand his many biblical allusions.[70] It begins with the lines, "The husbandman plants a vine. / He shall be patient and await his grapes," a couplet adapted from Isaiah's "Song of the Vineyard," in which the prophet describes a farmer who planted a vine and "looked that it should bring forth grapes." In Isaiah's parable the cultivator yielded inedible grapes, since God was angry at the "vineyard," which symbolized the house of Israel turned unjust. Yet Ensheim applied this fertility image to the work of the French electorate, writing, "Likewise nations begin by appointing / Wise counselors with understanding hearts." He suggested a more auspicious outcome for their work than for the work of the sinful "vineyard" and praised the "leaders of the nation" *(pinot am)* in language culled from Proverbs, "In justice shall they give stability to the land, / Support to the throne [and] shall do righteousness."[71]

Did Ensheim see himself as part of the "nation" *(am)* or the "land" *(aretz)* for which the wise counselors provided "stability"? His next stanza left the question open:

> Happy are you, oh land! Your king is enlightened *[maskil]*.
> Surely with you shall righteousness and truth meet.[72]
> In the word of his mouth he returns from exile
> So many of your dispossessed sons.

The use of the vocative "oh land!" was ambiguous, since it could have included the Jews but might just as easily have indicated wistful congratulations to a foreign people. Yet the exclamation in the first line was taken verbatim from Ecclesiastes 10:17, in which the prophet exulted, "Happy are you, Oh land, when your king is the son of free men." If Enlightenment was the modern version of a free birth, the biblical provenance of the line hinted at Jewish inclusion in the well-governed country. This impression was augmented by the even more familiar allusion, in the second line of the stanza, to Psalm 85:11, which promised, "In our land shall righteousness and truth meet." Was France the New Israel, and were the Jews parties to the millennial transformation at hand? If not, then why did Ensheim refer to the "exile" from which "your dispossessed sons" would return at the king's word? Clearly the notion of "exile" was more applicable to the Jews than to French Gentiles, no matter how oppressed by the Old Regime. Moreover, filial metaphors had long been a standard means of recalling the common heritage of Jews and Gentiles, and Voltaire had referred to the Jews as dispossessed sons to remind Christians of their responsibilities toward them.[73] Ensheim reinforced his familial imagery by referring to the Old Regime as a time "when enmity between brothers spread," thus suggesting that these brothers included the Jews, and he symbolically located the Jews at the center of this unhappy history by exulting, "Behold, the altar of Ba'al has been broken!" thus comparing the overthrow of despotism to Gideon's destruction of the Canaanite altar.[74]

In the tenth stanza Ensheim finally addressed the Jews explicitly, summarizing the now familiar story of the Jews' decline from ancient greatness in a poignant couplet: "House of Jacob, you have suffered abundant grief. / You fell through no fault of your own." Yet he quickly balanced this grim account with a proclamation of hope: "May your heart be strengthened, for there is a future. / Justice has come near to you, and the year of salvation." Readers familiar with Isaiah would have recognized this reference to the prophet's promise of a future when the inhabitants of restored Zion would proclaim, "And the year of my redemption has come." Later Ensheim reinforced the sense that the Revolution in France was affecting the Jews. Switching from the second to the first person and addressing God, he offered thanksgiving on behalf of himself and his brethren, writing, "Oh awesome God, the Most High, God of all Creation! / You have done wonders unto us." He further likened the Revolution to the miracle of Creation itself by paraphrasing Job's prayer, "To the wind you give weight, to the sea its limits," and continued, emphasizing God's miraculous power to create ex nihilo, "Your hand has given form to everything. / Out of darkness you have called forth processions of light / And order out of emptiness."[75]

Ensheim went on to praise the legislators in the National Assembly:

Happy are you who distribute justice.
The last generation will praise you.
Behold you have established a monument for yourselves.
Your name will be eternal like the moon.

Although the subject here was the Gentile lawmakers, Jewish readers would have recognized the comparison between the Constitution on which the Assembly was currently working and a prior great agreement, namely, the covenant between God and the Davidic dynasty, thus described in Psalm 89: "Like the moon it shall be established forever." Finally, in the last stanza, Ensheim exulted, "A people is born. It shall bless itself in you. / For you have risen to stand in the breach," and he promised the deputies, "Until the end shall you be great in praise / As long as the heavens are above the earth." Thus he ended his song with an allusion to a still earlier covenant, that between God and Abraham. According to that archetypal agreement, in return for obedience to the Law, God had promised Israel, "Your days and the days of your children will be multiplied in the land which the Lord swore to give to your fathers for as long as the heavens are above the earth."[76]

Ensheim therefore sent the message that the Revolution in France concerned the Jews not only insofar as those living under the authority of the National Assembly were obligated to obey the laws it enacted but also insofar as the revolutionary values of equality and justice were Jewish values, revealed by God and enshrined in the highest of all laws: the Torah. By likening France's history to that of the ancient Israelites, portraying the events of the present day as though they were the fulfillment of prophecy and moreover creating these impressions in the language of the Bible, Ensheim effectively represented the Revolution as a sacred event. At the same time, this sort of sacralization was also a form of appropriation, which together with the assimilation of contemporary civic values to the ancient Jewish tradition created the impression that no one deserved the title of French citizen more than the Jews themselves, the original bearers of principles that Gentiles were only just discovering.

In the fall of 1792 Ensheim published a second Hebrew poem on the Revolution, entitled "A Song to the Precentor by Moïse Ensheim, Sung on the Day When the Hand of the Inhabitants of Our Fatherland Prevailed over All the Surrounding Enemies."[77] The occasion for this composition was a republican festival in Metz celebrating the recent French victory over the Austrians in nearby Thionville. As under the Old Regime, and in a telling contradiction from the principle of indivisibility, the Jews of the city were allowed to participate in the festivities as a discrete group, though officially their status as a *corps* had been abrogated. To show their patriotism and solidarity with their Gentile compatriots, the Jews invited the soldiers who had fought at Thionville into the synagogue, where special Thanksgiving services took place. As part of the service a chorus of Jews sang Ensheim's Hebrew song, to the tune of the "Marseillaise," according to one subsequent account, and indeed at least some of the stanzas scan with the revolutionary anthem.[78] Of course, the Gentile guests could not have understood the Hebrew song, so a translation was prepared. This translation was very loose, and its implications will be considered further. The Hebrew original, however, is crucial for an understanding of how Ensheim interpreted the Revolution for himself and his coreligionists and, in particular, how his stance had changed since nearly three years earlier.

An obvious clue to the change in the author's attitude can be seen in the very title of the newer text, in which Ensheim referred to "Our Fatherland." Since the Roman concept of *patria* evident in the French *patrie* had no exact equivalent in Hebrew, Ensheim supplied the word *moledetenu*. Deriving from the root *yalad,* which in its infinitive form means "to be born," *moledet* literally refers to the place where one was born and suggests a kind of *jus soli,* a right of citizenship based on birth, and the suffix *-enu* indicates the first-person plural in the genitive case. Thus *moledetenu* is roughly "the place where we were born." It indicates

an almost literal naturalization, which corresponds to the legal naturalization that the National Assembly enacted approximately one year
prior to the composition, and thus approximates "Our Fatherland" insofar as both suggest status via birth.

Moreover, the Song to the Precentor indicates a dramatic radicalization in Ensheim's commitment to the Revolution and a corresponding
rage against its enemies. In this respect it corresponds to the Manichean
picture that Spire had presented of a struggle between patriots and aristocrats. Yet Ensheim's second song was performed in the shadow of
events that had marked a further radicalization of the Revolution: the
fall of the monarchy in August, the outbreak of war shortly thereafter,
and the domestic bloodbath of the September massacres. It accordingly
reflects the mood of the Revolution at its most vengeful, beginning:

> Fallen, fallen is the wicked kingdom.
> The abomination has been banned.
> Our fetters have been cut off. They have burst.
> The oppression has ceased.

This stanza, like many in both of Ensheim's poems, is rich in biblical
symbolism. The first line recalls Isaiah's exclamation, "Fallen, fallen is
Babylon," and suggests, with the second line, that the monarchy was a
wicked institution, as hateful in God's eyes as Babylon.[79] It has therefore
been "banned," and here Ensheim used the word *herem*, alluding to the
fearful decree of banishment with which rabbis had punished recalcitrant Jews until very recently. The line "The oppression has ceased" further babylonized the Old Regime by alluding to Isaiah's prediction of Israel's return from Babylonian exile, at which time the Jews would taunt
the king with the exclamation, "How the taskmaster has ceased, the oppression has ceased."[80] Again, then, Ensheim appropriated the history
of France by characterizing it as sacred history and describing contemporary events in apocalyptic terms.

The song continued with binary divisions, typical of the Old Testament as well as much revolutionary thinking, between good and evil,
freedom and slavery. Thus Ensheim and the chorus warned that "the
kings of the earth have come together to make us slaves" and urged their
compatriots of all religions:

> Arise, volunteers of the people!
> Take courage and be as men.
> Your sword is a sword of vengeance,
> A sword of the equal and the free.

Again a biblical reference was present, as Deborah in the Book of Judges had praised those "volunteers of the people" who had fought against the Canaanites. Voluntary zeal was necessary, as the Song of the Precentor later revealed, because of both the threat of foreign enemies and the presence of traitors in France's own midst. In order to create the image of the "aristocrat," which Spire had merely rendered *Aristokrats* but which lacked a precise Hebrew equivalent, Ensheim railed against "those who wear fur cloaks." This image alluded to the connection between luxury and deceitfulness that was already quite common at the time of the Revolution and all the more poignant at a time of scarcity. It also recalled the false prophets against whom Zechariah had fulminated for wearing fur cloaks "in order to deceive." Ensheim embellished the theme of deception by likening the nation's enemies to the hypocritical courtiers in the Book of Proverbs, who "with a flattering mouth make ruin."[81]

Despite the frightful prospect of external and internal enemies, Ensheim's republican song ended on an affirmative, triumphant note, which moreover embodies the combination of vengeful zeal and identification with the *patrie* that marks the entire composition:

> Happy are you, Oh Land of France! Happy are you!
> Your [would-be] destroyers have fallen to the dust.
> In the house of your justice is quiet security,
> Powerful confidence in the might of your sons.

Again, as in Ensheim's earlier poem, the use of the vocative "Oh Land of France!" did not in and of itself verify the Jews' membership in the *nation,* though in the 1792 composition the nation was metaphorically consecrated through the image of Erets Tsarfat, a neologism that conjured images of the Holy Land, Erets Yisrael. The reference to "your sons" did not guarantee Jewish parentage of the French citizens whose deeds the composer and his brethren were praising. Yet the use of the term *moledetenu* in the song's title cleared up the ambiguity by metaphorically consecrating the ground that the volunteers of Thionville had defended and confirming the adoption of those sons by the proud Jewish parents.

Or did it? Certainly the Song to the Precentor indicated a greater identification with and commitment to France than had the *Shirim.* Nevertheless, this process of symbolic naturalization was not complete in either of Ensheim's texts. Both bore the marks of Jewish specificity. After all, Ensheim not only had recourse to biblical allusions that referred

specifically to the sacred history of the Jews. He articulated his praise of
the French people in a language they could not understand. This was especially problematic in a political culture that demanded absolute transparency and in light of a popular belief in the special propensity of Jews
toward duplicity. It is no doubt for this reason that Isaïah Berr Bing
"translated" the text into French and eliminated references and images
that might be obscure to non-Jewish readers, thus purging Ensheim's
very Jewish text of its specificity and transforming it into a recognizably
universal statement of revolutionary affirmation.[82] He succeeded in his
work, and the biblical images that fill Ensheim's original text are either
entirely absent or changed beyond recognition in Bing's French version.
The "wicked reign" that conjured images of idolatrous Babylon was
rendered as "tyranny." Aristocrats were no longer likened to false
prophets "who wear cloaks of fur." Rather, Bing chose to depict them
as those who live "under gilded panels." In his praise of the legislators
of France, he removed the psalmodic formula, "Your name will be eternal like the moon," which was present in both the *Shirim* and the Song
to the Precentor, and replaced it with the classical reference, "You have
erected a monument more durable than bronze."[83] And Bing simply dis-
posed of all obvious biblical references, such as Ensheim's metaphor (in
both compositions) for the fall of the Old Regime, "Behold, the altar of
Ba'al has been broken down!"

In a sense, what happened to Ensheim's words is analogous to what
the discourse of transparency and indivisibility seemed to mandate for
the Jews themselves. The pressure that Bing appears to have undergone
to purge Ensheim's text of its obscurities corresponds to the pressure on
the Jews in general to rid themselves of their proverbial particularism.
On the other hand, Ensheim and Bing published the Hebrew song and
its rendering in French in a single, bilingual edition. This was not the
first time that Jews had published their devotions to the state in dual-
language editions, nor would it be the last. The use of the Hebrew language served as a kind of guarantee of authenticity, a promise that what
the Jews were saying was not merely a show of flattery, but that it corresponded to their most deeply held feelings to which, moreover, God was
literally the witness. What is most significant for an understanding of the
French Revolution, however, is that even in the fall of 1792, at the height
of the cult of indivisibility, it was nevertheless possible for the Jews, so
long assigned the role of the self-regarding group, to praise the *patrie*
not only as citizens but also as Jews. In this regard the Hebrew text constituted both a message to the Jews—those who attended the festival

and those who read the edition subsequently—that the Revolution was cause for celebration and a message to Gentiles (who could not read the words but recognized their Jewish provenance) that the Jews were not ready to disappear as Jews. If it urged Jews to embrace the revolutionary nation, it simultaneously eluded the Revolution's famous universalism. The festival at Metz was undoubtedly extraordinary, perhaps unique, but when read in the context of the pamphlet literature in which Jews boasted of their extraordinary qualities and argued for their inclusion in the *patrie* on the basis of these features, it confirms the tendency of even those Jews who were most enthusiastic about the Revolution to maintain and even to celebrate the old habits that had so long justified their exclusion. In a sense, then, they seem to have defied the order of *régénération* by suggesting that any fundamental change in their character would diminish rather than augment their level of morality and hence value to the fatherland.

How can one explain this apparent transgression of the rules of the Revolution? Hannah Arendt has argued that postrevolutionary Jewry was extraordinarily naïve about the political situation in which it found itself. Yet the texts surrounding the Jewish question during the Revolution, whether directed at Gentiles or Jews, support a very different interpretation, though perhaps one that is more in keeping with Arendt's more important observation that the Jews were neither exceptional specimens of humanity nor mere spectators in history but, on the contrary, participants in that history.[84] The Jews were neither extraordinarily naïve nor extraordinarily clever, but rather products of their time, despite their marginal status, and as such their behavior can tell us a great deal about revolutionary culture. They were able to represent themselves as an exceptional people because the Revolution, in spite of its proclaimed universalism, simultaneously valued extraordinary qualities in its citizens, whom it distinguished from noncitizens by comparing their relative levels of wealth or virtue. Even after the overthrow of the constitutional monarchy and the proclamation of universal male suffrage, the citizen was still imagined as a special kind of person: a selfless, stoic, and irreproachably honest man. Ironically, if the Jews served as this ideal's "other," as the duplicitous purveyors of effeminate luxuries and corrupting values, their famously rigorous Old Testament, evidently miraculous longevity as a distinct nation, and apparent usefulness to the *patrie* as coparticipants in the revolutionary potlatch enabled them to serve as positive figures of civic distinction. This was because their self-image, perhaps forged in the furnace of Gentile surveillance but nevertheless persisting in communications between Jews, corresponded strikingly to the revolutionary self-image and because their understanding of the historical moment was very much like that of the revolutionaries themselves. Both Jews and revolutionaries saw themselves as heirs to a heroic, ancient tradition of extraordinary virtue. Both saw themselves as possessing the greatest laws, whether these derived from nature or the will of the sovereign on the one hand or divine revelation on the other. And both habitually employed the master narrative of Paradise, Paradise Lost, and Paradise Regained to explain their past and present historical circumstances. Yet these very similarities reveal an otherwise forgotten feature of the Revolution. If later generations would take the discourse of regeneration literally and qualify the revolutionaries as progenitors of modernity, the manner in which the Jewish question was discussed, debated, and imagined by all concerned casts a bright light on another aspect of revolutionary culture: its dependence on old habits, old images, in a word, tradition.

CHAPTER 6

Familiar Strangers

Napoleon and the Jews

Between 1792 and Napoleon's rise to power at the very end of the decade, public discussion of the Jews waned significantly. The September 1791 legislation removing all legal distinctions between Jews and non-Jews, combined with the prior decree of religious freedom in the Declaration of the Rights of Man and Citizen, made it difficult to speak of "the Jews" as a discrete group. At the same time, the abolition of the former Jewish corporations made it difficult for the Jews to register any collective grievances, or indeed to make any collective statements about themselves whatsoever. No officially recognized rabbis or syndics could speak on their behalf, and any attempt to articulate specifically Jewish concerns risked provoking the accusation that the Jews were still a "nation within the nation."

With Napoleon's accession to power, however, new conditions stimulated renewed attention to the Jews. The First Consul's concordat of 1801 regulating the state's relationship with the Catholic Church, together with his decision from 1802 to establish officially recognized Calvinist and Lutheran churches, represented a dramatic departure from the Revolution's claim that religion was a private matter. Meanwhile, unofficial spokesmen for the *ci-devant* Jewish communities complained that the revolutionary settlement had led to disrespect for rabbis and widespread refusal to pay synagogue dues that had once been obligatory and were now merely optional, and they repeatedly petitioned government officials for a solution comparable to that of Catholics and Protestants.[1] Most important in a state that rapidly took on the characteristics of a dictatorship, the leader's particular interest in the Jews prompted their return to prominence in the public imagination. As this chapter will show, Napoleon and his supporters used the Jews as symbols in a discourse designed to glorify and justify a regime whose roots in a coup d'état desperately needed legitimacy. At the same time, however, the message the Jews themselves sent about their relationship to the new ruler reveals the limited control that even a proverbial master of propaganda ultimately had over the discourse that supported his right to rule.

On May 30, 1806, Napoleon issued a decree in which he complained that "certain Jews, exercising no other profession besides that of usury, have placed many cultivators . . . in a state of great distress." He therefore proposed "to come to the rescue of those of our subjects whom unjust greed has reduced to such miserable extremes." His solution included a one-year suspension in the execution of all court judgments in favor of Jews whose noncommercial loans to farmers in Alsace and the recently annexed Rhineland had been disputed. Yet the emperor did not stop with this discriminatory act. His decree went on to order the convocation of an "assembly of individuals professing the Jewish religion and inhabiting French territory." This group, which historians have come to identify simply as the Assembly of Notables, was to be selected by prefects and to include "rabbis, proprietors and other Jews most distinguished by their probity and enlightenment." The notables' task was to suggest ways of "recalling their brethren to the exercise of useful arts and professions in order to replace, through honest industry, the shameful practices to which many of them have resorted from father to son over many centuries." As a result of their counsel it would be possible, Napoleon claimed, "to revive among those who profess the Jewish religion . . . the sentiments of civil morality *[morale civile]* that unfortunately have been deadened among a large number of them by the state of abasement in which they have long languished."[2]

When the notables convened on July 23 in Paris, imperial commissioners presented them with a list of twelve questions about Jewish law and its relation to both the recently promulgated *Code civil* and the unwritten rules of civic virtue. The questionnaire began with three queries concerning Jewish marriage practices and, in particular, laws relating to polygamy, divorce, and intermarriage. The next three questions asked whether Jews considered "the French" to be their "brothers" or "foreigners," what Jewish law stipulated about their relationship to one another, and what duties it mandated regarding defense of the *patrie* and obedience to the Civil Code. Next the notables were to report on the rabbis: how they were chosen, what powers they had over the Jews, and whether these "forms of election" and "police jurisdiction" were a matter of law "or only consecrated by custom." Finally, the emperor wished to learn whether Jewish law forbade the exercise of any trade or profession, whether it authorized usury on loans between Jews, and whether it permitted it between Jews and "foreigners" *(étrangers)*.[3]

Within three weeks the deputies produced a lengthy report showing that there were no conflicts between their religion and their civil obligations and that, on the contrary, their religion positively demanded obedience to the law of the land and concern for its inhabitants' welfare regardless of their religion. They observed that although bigamy had once been permitted in the case of the levirate marriage—in which a man took his deceased brother's widow as his wife even if he was already married—this practice had been abolished during the Middle Ages. They noted that Judaism permitted divorce in certain circumstances but insisted that any divorce was valid only when concluded in accordance with the laws of the land. They claimed that intermarriage was not prohibited but was frowned upon. The notables went on to assure the emperor that they regarded the French as their brothers and that they were prepared to fight and die for the *patrie*, that their rabbis no longer claimed any "police jurisdiction" over their flocks, and that Jewish law both encouraged all honest work and prohibited usury, regardless of the religion of the borrower.

At some point, however, Napoleon appears to have doubted the authority that the Assembly of Notables would carry with the Jews under his rule, and on September 18 he ordered the deputies to convoke "an even more imposing, more religious assembly" charged with converting the answers to the twelve questions into points of doctrine that "could be placed next to the Talmud and thus acquire, in the eyes of all Jews in all countries for every century, the greatest possible authority." He named this new assembly the Grand Sanhedrin, after the rabbinical court of ancient Jerusalem, and stipulated, "according to ancient usage," that seventy-one men be called to compose this august body, though he departed from the old form by requiring twenty-five of its members to be laymen.[4] After electing the Sanhedrin participants, the initial Assembly of Notables would continue to meet during the next six months to establish a centralized system of Jewish consistories whose tasks would include the enforcement of civic virtue as defined by the Sanhedrin. Yet public attention would shift toward the meetings of the Grand Sanhedrin in February 1807 as this extraordinary synod solemnly confirmed the Jews' duties vis-à-vis the emperor, his laws, and the Gentiles over whom he reigned.

The Sanhedrin's principal accomplishment was the elaboration of a religious doctrine that emphasized the duties of Jews toward the state and its inhabitants. This mandate entailed the repetition of many of the arguments that apologists for Judaism, both Jewish and non-Jewish, had made for decades, if not for centuries. For example, the Sanhedrin affirmed the Jews' obligation to regard "the French" as their brothers by invoking biblical and Talmudic precepts requiring the ethical treatment of all human beings, regardless of their religion. Similarly, it affirmed the importance of "useful professions" by invoking passages from Jewish law. The synod's most novel ruling concerned the distinction between "religious and political dispositions," judging the former "absolute and independent of circumstances and times" and the latter dependent upon historical conditions.[5] This distinction both explained the fact that rules governing sacrifices in ancient Jerusalem no longer applied and justified the rabbis' more recent relinquishment of juridical power for a more strictly spiritual role. Since the French laws recognizing the political power of rabbis had long since been abolished, the Sanhedrin had little choice but to recognize the legal status quo. Yet even this affirmation of the status quo would be crucial in creating the moral foundations for a specific type of Jewish life known to later generations as *franco-judaïsme*.

While the doctrinal innovations and limitations of the Sanhedrin have been a matter of much discussion among French Jews to the present day, more significant for an understanding of the Napoleonic period is the symbolic use to which the emperor attempted to put both assemblies and their response to this opportunity to define their place in the new order. Historians have tended to neglect Napoleon's encounter with the Jews or to relegate it to the status of a curiosity worthy of a line or two. Those who have examined it at any length have tended to reduce their analysis to praise or blame for the emperor and/or the Jews.[6] More interesting for an understanding of the political culture in which the meetings took place, however, are the questions of why Napoleon made a public issue out of the Jews and why he resolved the perceived problems associated with them in the manner in which he did. Moreover, a close examination of the Jews' strategies of self-representation reveals more than a minority capitulating to or resisting a more powerful force but rather shows the susceptibility of official discourses to revision and re-definition. Finally, contemporary communications between Jews, car-ried out in Hebrew, show how the very attempt at assimilating the Jews ultimately served to reinforce their identity as a distinctive group.

THE FABRICATION OF A LIBERATOR

Napoleon was by any measure a very busy man. Why did he take time out of his full schedule, which included the conquest of much of Europe, to stage the regeneration of a tiny minority whose legal status had pre-sumably been fixed by the Constituent Assembly in 1791? There is a general consensus among historians who have dealt with the matter that Napoleon's convocation of the Assembly of Notables in 1806 and, by implication, his calling of the Sanhedrin shortly thereafter were pro-voked by complaints about usury that Alsatian Gentiles had lodged ear-lier that year. In this respect they have taken the decree of May 30, 1806, in which Napoleon explained his measures as responses to usury, at face value.[7] But one is justified in asking whether the reputed effect followed naturally from the supposed cause. There is little doubt that Napoleon considered usury a real problem in Alsace and that he held the Jews collectively responsible for its effects on the peasantry. The decree of May 30 makes this belief clear. Nevertheless, Napoleon had a number of options at his disposal. He could have left it to the courts to punish usurers, as some members of his Council of State advised. Toward this end, he could have ordered his legislature to enact a law on usury, which was still undefined in 1806. In fact, this is precisely what he did in Sep-tember of the following year. Thus if he created the Assembly of Not-ables and the Sanhedrin to solve the problem of usury, he made that so-lution redundant within months by passing a law that dealt far more directly and efficiently with the very same problem. Insofar as Napoleon lacked qualms about discriminating against the Jews as a group, he was capable of enacting laws of exception regulating and restricting their business practices. That he was capable of the latter is proved by the fact that he did, in fact, issue a number of discriminatory decrees, beginning on March 30, 1806, with the suspension of judgments on Jewish loans and culminating in the decrees of March 17, 1808, which further re-stricted the economic activities of Jews and Jews alone.[8]

One wonders why, given these options, Napoleon chose, in addition to the measures just enumerated, to summon rabbis and Jewish laymen from the farthest reaches of his empire, to "revive" an institution that had died with the Roman destruction of the Second Temple, and to have it convene publicly, in pomp and solemnity, in the Hôtel de Ville. Although he was not physically present at any of the meetings of the Assembly of Notables or the Grand Sanhedrin, he met numerous times with his Council of State to outline a solution to the perceived problem of the Jews in the empire, drafted decrees to this effect, and played a decisive role in the creation of the Jewish assemblies. Considering the emperor's famous appetite for power, one must ask what was in it for him. Chateaubriand believed that Napoleon had financial motivations, but Napoleon knew better than to see in the Jews a significant source of wealth.[9] Rather, he saw in them a wealth of *symbolic* opportunities. Napoleon had famously paid scrupulous attention to symbols in his own self-representation, a habit indicating his belief that the signs of power and legitimacy were inseparable from power and legitimacy themselves. He accordingly used the ceremonial surrounding his Jewish policy to suggest his possession of these coveted attributes.

To understand the symbolic use Napoleon made of the Assembly of Notables and the Sanhedrin in 1806 and 1807, it is helpful to examine his prior relationship to the Jews. In February 1797, in the midst of the Italian campaign, Napoleon and his troops entered the papal city of Ancona and promptly liberated the ghetto. A Jewish chronicler, writing in Hebrew, recounted the dramatic events surrounding the liberation. He began by introducing a certain Frenchman, who "among all the captains of the army is the greatest." The leader's name was Chelek Tov, meaning literally "Good Lot" or, in Italian, "Buona Parte." Relating this extraordinary man immediately to the fate or "lot" of the Jews, the chronicler continued, "He is good . . . to the Jews and he loves them greatly," adding that "the glory of his name is known within the gates and his fame goes throughout the land." He reported that the first French soldiers to reach the ghetto were Jews themselves. They addressed their brethren in front of the synagogue, "'Oh children of Israel, our brothers, you will never again see among Christians evil ones who seek to do you harm.'" At this "great salvation" the Jews "answered with heroic cries . . . to God." They entered the synagogue and recited the Song of the Sea, the passage from Exodus in which the Israelites thank God for having saved them from the Egyptians, "for this was the chapter of the redemption from Pharaoh." That evening every house in the ghetto displayed a candle in its window "for the glory of the French army." The next morning, "the head of the great army, Chelek Tov, may God preserve him," and the magistrates of the city "opened the gates of the ghetto which had been closed" and led the Jews outside. They removed the humiliating cloth patches that Jews had been required to wear on their hats and replaced them with revolutionary tricolor cockades. The following Sabbath, two days later, the Jews held a thanksgiving service in which they recited special prayers, including the Song of the Sea and a prayer celebrating "the entry of the redeemer of Italy . . . the head of the great army, Chelek Tov, may God preserve him."[10]

Napoleon would go on to open ghettos elsewhere in Italy, and one can see from the Ancona case how such dramatically staged liberations worked to his advantage. Just as the enclosed space of the Bastille had symbolized the oppression of the French, the locked ghetto confining the Jews unmistakably symbolized their oppression. The simple act of opening the gates therefore publicized Napoleon's role as liberator. This image was of great value to the young general. By 1797 the appearance of the revolutionary wars as wars of liberation had long since faded, and for many people, especially on the side of the "liberated," the French invasions were little more than cynical plundering raids. The opening of a ghetto provided a perfect opportunity to revive the sense of idealism that had initially served to justify France's clashes with its neighbors. That the Ancona ghetto was a papal creation was all the more useful to the general, who in the spirit of republican anticlericalism was inclined to associate the papacy with despotism. At the same time, Bonaparte sought not to supplant traditional religious imagery but to appropriate it for his own ends. To the Jews he appeared as a new Moses, whose arrival prompted them to sing the Song of the Sea, and by implication the pope appeared as a wicked Pharaoh. Moreover, by stripping the Jews of the humiliating marks that had designated their inferior status and replacing them with tricolor cockades indicating liberty, Napoleon and his troops appeared to have performed a kind of resurrection. The Ancona chronicler wrote that when the French entered Ancona, "our spirits were alive and our souls, which had been dead to us, returned within us."[11] This was precisely the impression that Napoleon must have hoped to make. It was one he would make repeatedly during his reign as emperor, and it afforded the opportunity to be portrayed as a messianic, even godlike personage. This image, moreover, supported his claims to rightful rule not only over the Jews but over all his resuscitated and redeemed subjects.

It is in the context of the liberation of Italian Jews that one can make sense of some otherwise curious claims made in 1799 about the Jews' relationship to Napoleon. In February of that year a departmental commissioner claimed in a letter to Philippe-Antoine Merlin, a member of the Directory government, that he had met a Jew in Douai who told him that Napoleon was the Messiah and that he was going to restore the Temple of Jerusalem. When the commissioner dryly remarked that Bonaparte ate lard and blood sausage, the Jew purportedly insisted, "There are 1,500,000 Jews in Europe who, if necessary, will sacrifice their fortunes and their lives for this glorious enterprise [of restoring the Temple]." The commissioner recalled the "emotion" with which the "child of Abraham" spoke "again and again of the 1,500,000 Hebrew soldiers" and of his conviction that Napoleon was the Messiah.[12] It would be naïve to take these claims at face value and to conclude that a substantial number of Jews literally saw Napoleon as the Messiah. Nevertheless, it is important not to dismiss the commissioner's letter out of hand because it helps to assess the extent of the *rumor,* evident from other sources as well, that Napoleon planned to conquer the Holy Land with the help of Jewish troops. No less a source than the *Moniteur Universel,* which after Napoleon's accession to power would become the government's official newspaper, propagated this rumor. On May 22, 1799, in the midst of the Egyptian and Syrian campaigns, the newspaper reported, "Bonaparte has published a proclamation in which he invites the Jews of Asia and Africa to come and gather under his banners to reestablish the ancient kingdom of Jerusalem[.] He has already armed a great number and his battalions threaten Aleppo."[13]

While there is no evidence that Bonaparte published any "proclamation" inviting Jews to restore Jerusalem, and while no Jewish "battalions" ever threatened cities in the Near East or elsewhere, it is historically significant that such beliefs were possible.[14] These rumors reflected the self-image that Napoleon had already projected as a liberator of oppressed peoples, who in turn were epitomized by the prophetically long-suffering Jews. This symbolic configuration turned out to be serviceable again in 1806 and 1807 when Napoleon once again cast himself as a figure who combined the attributes of Moses, the Messiah, and indeed God himself. Napoleon's rivals certainly saw his treatment of the Jewish question as indicative of an attempt to be seen as a kind of Messiah. In a September 1806 report to the Austrian emperor on the Assembly of Notables and the proposed Sanhedrin, Metternich wrote, "The Israelites of all the lands have their eyes turned to the Messiah who seems to free them from the yoke under which they find themselves." The Holy Synod of Russia made the same connection, claiming that Napoleon was bent on having himself proclaimed the Messiah.[15] If this language seems exaggerated, the figurative association between Napoleon and the Messiah only conformed to the imagery that the Napoleonic state itself used to describe the liberation of the Jews under imperial auspices. Thus Louis-Mathieu Molé, the commissioner responsible for the Assembly of Notables, asked the deputies rhetorically, "If any personage from past centuries returned to life and such a spectacle came to his eyes, would he not believe himself transported to within the walls of the Holy City . . . would he not believe that a terrible revolution had renewed human things all the way down to their foundation?" [16] The restoration of Jerusalem, as Christians and Jews alike knew, could only be accomplished with the coming of the Messiah.

Did Napoleon have his rivals, Austria and Russia, in mind when he ostentatiously adopted the role of savior of the Jews? One can only guess. The primary audience for this performance, in any event, was not the Jews, a minuscule and weak minority, but the non-Jews within Napoleon's quickly expanding empire. For these observers, Napoleon's messianic imagery alluded not merely to the liberation of the Jews but to the salvation of the French from the purported anarchy of revolution and of other people from the alleged despotism of their previous rulers. Yet if the image of the Son (in Christian terms) yielded symbolic advantages, Napoleon stood to gain even more by likening himself to the Father. This was because God, more so than the Messiah, traditionally bore precisely the *political* attributes that Napoleon wished to have recognized in his own person. If the Messiah was known as a king (of the Jews or Jerusalem), God combined the functions (or, to use a Trinitarian corporeal metaphor, the bodies) that opponents of absolutism had long hoped to separate: executive, judicial, and legislative. Thus Napoleon could legitimize his neo-absolutist rule by having himself portrayed as godlike.

In some cases this fusion was achieved, as under Bourbon absolutism, through paternal language. Molé accordingly assured the deputies in the Assembly of Notables that they "deserve . . . such paternal treatment" as the emperor was according them. He produced an even more telling likeness when he warned them to tell the truth about their religion, apprising them that Napoleon "is as firm as he is just . . . is equally capable of *knowing anything*, rewarding anything and punishing anything." This claim of omniscience, an attribute otherwise reserved for the Almighty, was not without its purpose. It supported the more politically relevant claim according to which the emperor was the embodiment of *justice*. Indeed, the language of justice recurred throughout the proceedings of the Jewish assemblies. Sometimes justice was understood in its broadest sense of right over wrong. Thus Napoleon himself declared in the decree of May 30 that the "unjust greed" of Jewish usurers was ruining the peasants of Alsace. Molé assured the notables, "For the first time you are going to be judged justly," which combined the word's general meaning of righteousness with the more specific notion of justice as judicial activity, the work of a judge, which the emperor was now to perform.[17]

By implication, Napoleon's divine character served to justify his executive as well as his judicial functions, that is, his capacity to "reward" and "punish" in accordance with the laws. Yet the emperor had less invested in this part of the constitutional triad than in the legislative branch. Like Rousseau, who had significantly pronounced "the Legislator" to be godlike, regarded the *making* of the laws as the true task of the sovereign, and relegated their execution to the category of onerous if necessary service, Napoleon celebrated legislation as the noblest of state activities. (Of course, he conveniently omitted Rousseau's requirement that the Legislator retreat from all public activity after making the fundamental laws, and suggested that precisely his godlike character justified the concentration of all functions of state in his own person.) He deliberately cultivated the persona of the Legislator, repeatedly authoring constitutions, codifying laws, and issuing decrees that carried the force of law. In this context one can understand the pronouncements of Diogène Tama, whose *Collection des actes de l'assemblée des Israélites de France et du royaume d'Italie* clearly conformed to the official view of the proceedings. Tama explicitly connected the Napoleonic activity of issuing decrees with the work of God, writing of the decree that established the Assembly of Notables, "This is the work of . . . a type of grandeur unknown on earth; it has all the features of the decrees of Providence. It will carry with all generations the sweet conviction that already saw, in our august Emperor, the living image of the Divinity."[18]

Elsewhere, as will be shown, Napoleon was likened to Moses, whom Rousseau and other political thinkers had praised as a model legislator.[19] Like the comparison to God, the representation of Napoleon as a Mosaic figure therefore served in the articulation of a discourse of the law. Such a discourse was all the more crucial to a regime whose very origins in a coup d'état smacked of illegitimacy, even illegality. Napoleon's accession to a hereditary imperial throne of his own creation—to say nothing of the royal throne of "Italy"—only called renewed attention to the question of legitimacy, and the emperor therefore lost no opportunity to have himself cast in the cleansing light of the Law. The Assembly of Notables and the Sanhedrin provided just such opportunities. Together they constituted a veritable Simchat Torah, or Festival of the Law, but with this difference. The point of the traditional Jewish festival had been the celebration of God's Law or Torah. The Napoleonic Simchat Torah was to be a celebration of Napoleonic law. References to Napoleon's laws necessarily abounded in the two assemblies, the latter of which was open to the public and both of which Tama described in publications that included the principal speeches and written reports.[20] The very composition of the assemblies, which resembled law courts, if not legislatures, continually highlighted the law as the ultimate object of concern. The assemblies' task was to interpret, codify, canonize, and decree, and although these mandates were overlapping and potentially contradictory, the important thing was that their object was always the Law. Most important, the conclusion that the designated Jews were expected to reach, and which they did in fact reach, was that obedience to the law of Napoleon and obedience to the law of God were equally obligatory, and violation of either was equally sinful.

Implicit in this discourse of law was a definition of citizenship that served Napoleon's needs. The Rousseauian ideal of the citizen as a participant in sovereignty, or the making of laws that conform to the general will, was clearly now anathema. It was unclear, however, what was to take its place, and what it meant to be a citizen of the French Empire or the Kingdom of Italy. The Jewish assemblies provided an opportunity for the Napoleonic state to publicize its conception of citizenship. Frequently this conception was presented negatively, and both Napoleon and Molé repeatedly implied that, whatever a citizen was, the Jews were not yet in possession of the requisite qualities. Revealingly, the emperor was careful to convoke not an assembly of Jewish "citizens" but "an assembly of individuals professing the Jewish religion and inhabiting French territory."[21] His questionnaire suggested that Jewish citizens in fact existed, as it asked, "Do Jews who were born in France and are treated by the law as French citizens see France as their Fatherland?" Molé, however, negated any assurances potentially furnished by this query when he told the deputies, "His Majesty wants you to be French," adding, "It is up to you to accept this title, and to remember that to make yourselves unworthy of it would be to renounce it."[22] Here citizenship, or being "French," was a privilege, a "title" that had to be earned and could similarly be revoked. The previous chapter demonstrated that the revolutionaries themselves did not have a conception of citizenship based purely on human rights but also saw it as a *titre* indicative of virtuous behavior; with Napoleon the tendency to see citizenship as a set of duties rather than rights only increased. In his concluding speech to the Assembly of Notables, Molé again emphasized the conditional nature of citizenship, and though he used the language of rights, he quickly divested this mantra of any recognizable content. He proclaimed, "His Majesty wanted there to remain no excuse for those who would not become citizens," and added, "He accords you the free exercise of your religion and the full enjoyment of your political rights." It was unclear what "political rights" were under the Napoleonic empire, but it hardly mattered, since Molé went on to say, "But in exchange for the august protection that he accords you, he demands a religious guarantee [promising] the complete observation of the principles enunciated in your responses [to the twelve questions]."[23] Thus "rights" were eminently alienable, and in any event were no more than "august protection."

Yet explicit reference to the word *citoyen* was rare in the state's official pronouncements regarding the Jews. Far more frequent was the use of the word *subject (sujet)*, as in Molé's exhortation, "Our most ardent wish is to be able to tell the Emperor that he counts among his *subjects* of the Jewish religion only faithful *subjects,* who are determined to conform to all the laws and to the morality that all the French *[tous les Français]* must follow and practice."[24] Here the message was clear: "the French" might be called citizens, potentially counting Jews among them, but they were really subjects defined by their obligations, foremost among which was obedience.

In addition to furnishing the opportunity to exalt, sacralize, and even fetishize the law while drawing attention away from its dubious origins and to define citizenship/subjecthood in terms of pure obedience, the public "emancipation" of the Jews entailed other benefits for Napoleon. Specifically, the unusual, perhaps unique, configuration of temporal and spatial features of the Jews as they were popularly imagined enabled the ceremonies signaling their "regeneration" to attest dramatically to the emperor's sacred (hence legitimate) power. Concerning their place in time, the Jews were both "antique" and contemporary, relics of the very old and, especially insofar as one associated them with commerce and moneylending, harbingers of (a fearfully decadent) modernity. They were at once aboriginal, almost coeval with creation itself, and "eternal," guaranteed by the divine plan to remain in existence. Their spatial aspects were similarly paradoxical. As descendants of the people of

Judea, they were distinctly of the "orient," yet their prophetically guaranteed presence as wanderers among the nations made them ubiquitous. Even those who had never met a Jew could therefore imagine the Jews to be forever in their midst. Thus the Jews were simultaneously strange and familiar, and if they were "long ago and far away," they were also inevitably "here and now." This combination made them an especially popular object of discussion. As exotic and mysterious, they were susceptible to imagined depictions. Yet as evidently familiar and known, they provided authors, readers, speakers, and listeners with a shared confidence in the ability to describe them accurately and "scientifically." Moreover, because science was known to have practical applications, it was apparently possible to change, correct, or "regenerate" the Jews by reversing the causes that had led to their universally acknowledged decline. They therefore appealed at once to the imagination, the intellect, and the utopian impulses of their contemporaries, and when Napoleon called them to Paris, he could count on the attention of "subjects" and foreign observers alike.

Furthermore, the "antique" yet "eternal" character of the Jews rendered them an especially vivid marker of Napoleon's power. Edward Said has shown how European representations of "orientals" as eternal, timeless, static, and devoid of history suggested a passivity in the latter that made them the seemingly rightful objects not only of description, but also of possession and ultimately colonization. By implication, the fabled passivity and stasis of the oriental only underscored the vibrant activity and change (read: progress) of Europeans, and hence their (evidently legitimate) power.[25] In this context one can understand why Napoleon, himself an imperialist in more than one respect, directed his attention to the Jews, whom tradition had long marked as eternal, even "obstinate." Yet the passive Jews did not merely indicate Napoleon's power by contrast to his activity. Unlike many orientalists, who were content to leave the objects of their description in their eternal passivity, Napoleon sought to do the impossible: *to change* the Jews, the proverbially changeless people. By transforming the conditions and moral character of the Jews, who were believed to have remained the same for centuries, he would perform a kind of miracle.

Napoleon and his supporters therefore had a vested interest in emphasizing the Jews' antiquity, for the older the Jews, the more spectacular their regeneration, and the more powerful their regenerator. It is not a coincidence, then, that in his decree of May 30 the emperor pointed to "the state of degradation in which [the Jews] have *long* languished" and opined that usury had been a practice "to which many among them have resorted from father to son *for many centuries.*" Similarly, Molé addressed the Jewish notables as "descendants of the most ancient people on earth," an expression that served both to flatter the Jews by referring to their venerable longevity and to recall the might of the ruler who could change their long-standing character. Tama made this connection explicit when he wrote, in connection with the calling of the Sanhedrin, of "the great man who wished for an assembly, unprecedented in the records of modern history, *antique* and famous in the religious annals of the Israelites, to be recalled for an instant to existence, in order to hasten [the Jews'] complete moral and civil regeneration."[26]

Similarly, the spatial features associated with the Jews made them an ideal object of imperial attention. Their connection with Palestine, an exotic, "oriental" land, drew attention to the vastness of Napoleon's influence, its dramatic extension in space. Indeed, it is not far-fetched to see his efforts to bring the Jews firmly and publicly under his control as a way of symbolically acquiring those regions of the Near East that he had failed to conquer in 1799. In any event, the fact that the Jews whom Napoleon convoked were famously *dispersed* seemingly attested both to the extent of the empire and to its powerfully centralized character. This interpretation at least helps to explain Napoleon's otherwise bizarre decision to resolve an obviously local problem, a conflict between Alsatian Jews and Alsatian peasants, by calling Jews from as far away as Venice to an assembly in Paris. It is, moreover, borne out in the sources. Thus Molé addressed the notables, "*Summoned from the ends of this vast Empire,* none of you is ignorant of the issue over which His Majesty has reunited you." Napoleon's jurisdiction appeared even larger when the deputies were informed that the Sanhedrin's decisions should carry with "all the Jews of *all countries* and for all centuries, the greatest possible authority."[27]

An engraving by François-Louis Couché, *Napoléon le Grand rétablit le culte des Israélites, le 30 mai 1806,* and its accompanying inscription vividly epitomize all of the representational strategies discussed thus far (see frontispiece). Centrally placed is Napoleon himself, crowned with laurels, clothed in his imperial robes, and standing in front of his throne. With his right hand he holds a tablet bearing the inscription "Loi donnée à Moïse." Farther to his right the chief rabbi, in his ceremonial dress, gazes admiringly at him. In the left foreground two robed men with long hair and beards kneel before the emperor and extend their arms to a seated female allegory of Judaism, toward which the viewer's attention is otherwise guided by Napoleon's outstretched arm. In a gesture that alludes unmistakably to Michelangelo's God giving life to Adam, Napoleon reaches out to the limp hand of the visibly weak woman, who can barely support the original Tablets of the Law with her other arm. She is leaning against a statue of a lion, evidently the Lion of Judah, which alludes to the ancient yet lost glory of the Jewish people, as do the adjacent oil lamp and large seven-stemmed candelabra. Visible in what appears to be a crypt is another female allegory of Judaism, the medieval Synagoga, her head bowed and arms folded across her shoulder, as she was typically depicted in the sculpture that adorned cathedrals. In the background on the far right is a mountain, no doubt an allusion to Mount Sinai.[28]

The symbolism of Couché's engraving was abundantly clear. As in previously discussed representations, Napoleon was a messianic figure who restored the Jews to their ancient glory. The inscription accompanying the engraving indicated that the emperor was "a new Cyrus," alluding to the Persian king who had authorized the rebuilding of the Temple in Jerusalem after its first destruction by the Babylonians. But the trope of the restoration of the Temple, from which Napoleon had profited in the past, conjured images of the more famous and long-awaited Restorer: the Messiah. At the same time, Napoleon stood even more obviously for Moses, the prototypical Lawgiver, who in turn embodied the legislative qualities of God himself. Napoleon's godlike nature was apparent by virtue of the prostrate Hebrews, who could only rightfully kneel before the Almighty. An even clearer sign of divinity was his life-giving gesture, an act that in turn indicated the equally divine quality of justice.

The personage to whom Napoleon was giving life was, not coincidentally, a woman. Although allegories were typically female, here the feminization of Judaism entailed a specific set of meanings. The figure of Synagoga was frequently represented with a broken sword, hence powerless, suggesting the emasculated status of the Jews. Although no broken sword is visible in the engraving by Couché, it is not unlikely that viewers mentally added this iconographic detail to the picture. Furthermore, as a proverbially "perfidious" figure, Synagoga alluded to the faithlessness of that other prototypical female, Eve. The virtuous doppelgänger of Synagoga/Eve, like the virtuous Mary of the familiar virgin/whore dichotomy, nevertheless suggested the passivity, hence femininity, of the Jewish people, and it was this very submissiveness that defined their virtue in the Napoleonic state.

Finally, Couché reinforced the impression of the Jews as an exotic and timeless people with roots in the distant past; he therefore made their "regeneration" under Napoleon's auspices a kind of miracle that, like the ability to impart life more generally, again alluded to the power of God. The setting, personages, and objects populating the image all pointed to a distant place over which Napoleon nevertheless seemed to extend his rule. The inscription reinforced this message, adding a facet of temporal distance to that of spatial extension: "An antique nation, once the unique depository of the will of the Most High, and governed by the divine legislation of Moses, is dispersed for more than seventeen centuries over the face of the globe. In relation to all the Peoples, it mixes with none of them, and it seems to exist only to see passing before it the torrent of the centuries that carries them."[29] The antiquity, dispersal, and passivity of the Jewish subjects, combined with yet another reference to legislation, all combined in a single message: Napoleon was powerful and legitimately so.

SIMCHAT TORAH

Despite his legendary grip on political power, Napoleon did not have a monopoly on representations of Jews. As soon as he ordered Jewish spokesman to explain themselves and their religion, he implicitly relinquished at least some control over the discourse that otherwise defined them. This was by no means an equal exchange. The state, if not Napoleon himself, formulated the twelve leading questions to which both assemblies were required to respond and maintained the power to punish the Jews collectively should their spokesmen write anything even hinting at reluctance to follow the law as the emperor laid it down. Still, the Jews managed to use the Napoleonic Simchat Torah to tell their side of the story: to demonstrate not only that their religion prohibited violations of what Napoleon called "civil morality" but also that it invented civil morality; to prove that their proverbial obstinacy was merely fidelity in another guise and thus evidence of a special aptitude for patriotic devotion; to show that their famed legalism was precisely what made them valuable in a state whose crowning achievement was the codification of the law. Indeed, even before Napoleon formally called upon the Jews to speak for themselves, they took repeated opportunities to do so.

To a greater extent than during the Revolution, the period of Napoleonic rule furnished the Jews with occasions to speak for and on behalf of themselves. Although the revolutionary ideal of a citizen as morally superior and hence distinct prevented the contrary disdain for "particularism" from gaining absolute control over republican discourse, as the previous chapter has shown, under Napoleon a revival of Old Regime corporatism made particularism even less of a problem. Instrumental though they were, Napoleon's concordat with the pope, followed by an official recognition of Calvinism and Lutheranism, showed a consideration for religion as a social and political force, and the Jews had reason to hope that they would receive a comparable, if not equal, recognition. Moreover, the principle of national indivisibility had to be modified under an empire, which by definition was a multinational state, and though Napoleon himself would repeat the accusation that the Jews were a "nation within the nation," his very conquest of foreign "nations" rendered that charge considerably less damning. Finally, certain cultural features of the period facilitated Jewish self-representation. The popularity of exoticism in general and "orientalism" in particular, which Napoleon himself cultivated largely as a means of foregrounding his imperial power and justifying his transnational authority, left a cultural space in which the Jews could celebrate and even exaggerate their alterity.

Thus the genre of patriotic liturgy, which had flourished under the Old Regime and declined during the Revolution, returned with a vengeance. Jews wrote songs, poems, sermons, and other religious texts to celebrate Napoleon's repeated escapes from assassination, the victories of his armies, the Peace of Amiens, the imperial coronation, Napoleon's birthday, his marriage to Marie-Louise, her pregnancy, and the birth of the king of Rome, among other occasions.[30] Between these events and the two celebrated assemblies, Jewish spokesman had abundant opportunities to define themselves and their relationship to the Napoleonic polity.

The most urgent task was to show that the Jews were loyal to the state. The simplest and most direct way of creating this impression had been learned under the Old Regime: proclaiming the sacredness of the temporal leader. Clearly Napoleon wished to be regarded as chosen by God, hence the presence of the pope at his elaborate coronation ceremony, and Jews accordingly supported the emperor's self-image. The rabbi of Haguenau did not even wait for the coronation to proclaim Bonaparte's chosenness. Already under the Consulate he took the occasion of a sermon following Napoleon's escape from assassination to call the First Consul *"der ausgewählte Gottes,"* or "God's Chosen." Similarly, Rabbi David Sintzheim of Strasbourg celebrated the 1805 victory at Austerlitz with a sermon in which he called Napoleon "the Elect of the Lord."[31]

The ultimate sign of the sovereign's divine sanction to rule was the unction he received at his coronation ceremony. Under the Old Regime, Jews had frequently referred to the monarch's anointing, which happily alluded to the inaugural rites of Israel's biblical kings. Similar use of this image was made under Napoleon. Like the concept of chosenness, it predated the imperial coronation. The French translation of a Hebrew thanksgiving ode sung by the Jews of Metz on the occasion of Bonaparte's escape from a second assassination attempt referred to the First Consul as "the first" of "the three sacred anointed ones." After Napoleon rid himself of the other two anointed ones and became emperor, Rabbi Sintzheim, now presiding over the Assembly of Notables, reinforced the impression of the Jews' reverence for their consecrated leader by paraphrasing the Psalm of David, "You have loved justice and hated iniquity; that is why your God has anointed you with oil of joy over all those who will participate in your glory."[32]

Consequently, Napoleon's Davidic status was typically invoked. The rabbi of Mantua, Abraham de Cologna, thanked God for thwarting Napoleon's enemies "as the enemies of David . . . of old" on the "terrible day" of the Battle of Lützen. Similarly, Rabbi Sègre portrayed the "pious emperor," kneeling in prayer following his victory over the Russians, as "the Prophet King himself" had done after his conquests. Celebrating Napoleon's birthday in 1806, the same rabbi called the emperor "the Solomon of our century." On the occasion of the imperial coronation another Jewish leader epitomized Napoleon as an amalgam of the two kings of Israel, a ruler in whom God combined "the strength of the victor over Goliath and the Philistines and the wisdom of Solomon."[33] These images of Davidic monarchy were advantageous in multiple ways. They corresponded to the familiar ideals of kingship, classifying the ruler as fierce, pious, wise, and just. In addition, they served to portray the Jews themselves as unquestionably obedient to a monarch whose practices merely mirrored God's will and hostile to foreign and domestic enemies who, according to the logic of the Jewish representations, were not just adversaries but sinners meriting destruction. Accordingly, they suggested that Jews and Gentiles belonged to the same human community and were deserving of equal consideration.

There were other means as well of creating this impression of belonging. In particular, certain narrative conventions served to blend the history of France and other countries in Napoleon's empire with the history of the Jews. This was easy to do, since Jews as well as Christians had long employed a single metanarrative—a template narrative of redemption—to describe their history as a descent from primitive innocence and happiness into a long dark age of barbarism, followed by a return to virtue and bliss. We have seen how important this master plot was to late eighteenth-century reformers and revolutionaries, and how it made the prospect of the regeneration of the Jews both recognizable and (at least to most Gentiles) appealing. This story of Paradise, Fall, and Salvation was no less significant to the Napoleonic era. The only difference was that in the Napoleonic version of the story the misery that for revolutionaries stopped in 1789 continued until 1799. Thus Jewish spokesmen repeatedly sought the sympathy of their Gentile audiences by telling the story of the Jews' fall from ancient greatness, miserable dispersion among hostile nations, then regeneration under Napoleon's auspices.

In an example that epitomizes the lachrymose narrative, Berr Isaac Berr recalled before the Assembly of Notables the "memorable epoch when the Jewish people was subjugated, . . . rendered slaves, and dispersed by the hurricane of misfortune to all the corners of the inhabited world." Praising the Jews for "remaining faithful to the belief of their ancestors, despite executions and tortures," he deplored the fact that "the more they wanted to remain Jews, the more they ceased to be men." Persecution had instilled separatism, animosity, and trickery in the Jews, and Berr could only regret the lost opportunities: "Mingling in the midst of civilized peoples, what useful citizens they would have become had a barbaric policy not made that impossible!" Happily, however, this situation was about to change. Napoleon was the first ruler who deigned "to convoke before his throne those who would be able to help him ease their misfortune and cure the plagues of Israel."[34]

The resemblance between this story and those Napoleon and his supporters repeatedly told about the salvation of France and its similarly unhappy neighbors is so close that in certain versions it is difficult to tell who, precisely, is being saved. For example, Jacob Mayer's ode on "the elevation of His Majesty Napoleon to the imperial dignity" describes in general terms the phenomena of unjust suffering followed by divine justice. The French translation relates the situation of "unhappy people" who "languish under oppression" until God "pours onto the heads of the guilty a torrent of misery." The next stanza describes "the people whom you [God] chose in your mercy." Its "glory was . . . tarnished, and the power of its name was about to disappear forever." But then "the elect of the people" appeared, and, Mayer exulted, "upon the enemies of God he pours his anger, and through him the impious lose themselves in the abyss." Who are the "people" in these passages? The language of chosenness and election, the dramatic development from greatness to weakness and back to greatness, and the division of the world into pious and impious all suggest a story about the Jews. Yet in the following stanza Mayer revealed the subject of his ode, "Oh France, oh my fatherland [patrie]! You once drank from the bitter cup," and further, "Upon the bloody debris of the throne, vile and perfidious men had established their frightful domination; blood flowed from all sides; a funereal veil covered the altars." The conclusion is not difficult to predict. Napoleon appears on the scene, dispenses justice, and reestablishes domestic peace.[35] But the remarkable effect of Mayer's description is that it thoroughly blends the stories of Jewish regeneration and the regeneration of France.

In a sermon honoring Napoleon's birthday in 1809, the rabbi of Nancy similarly blended the history of the Jews with that of the French. Significantly alluding to Isaiah's description of the world shortly before the appearance of the Messiah, he invoked "that time of misfortune and those internal divisions, when fury and violence crashed down upon us." He went on to describe a miraculous transformation, when "a beam of light shone upon us in the dark regions of death," and "he appeared, the one whose arm sustains the weight of empire," the "great hero of marvelous wisdom" who "became the arbiter of peace and the father of the peoples." Upon the appearance of this Savior, "the enemy armies dispersed," and "peace was reborn in our hearths."[36]

In addition to likening Napoleon to biblical kings, if not the Messiah himself, and adopting a single grand narrative of regeneration, another way of indicating membership in the Napoleonic polity was to employ familial imagery. Family metaphors had long been used to conceive of, justify, and celebrate the grouping of human beings under various systems of law, government, and administration, and, as we have seen, Jews had already suggested their membership in an imagined French family under the Old Regime and during the Revolution. Clearly, family language was central to the discourse of Napoleon's regimes as well, especially the empire, though it was transformed to make room for a "father" that the Revolution had symbolically eliminated. Molé had assured the Jews that they "deserve . . . such paternal treatment" as they were receiving. Jewish leaders eagerly appropriated this paternal language. Likewise, in the proceedings of the Assembly of Notables and the

Sanhedrin, the adjective *paternal* appeared frequently, modifying Napoleon's "wishes," "instructions," "views," "sentiments," "solicitude," and "goodness."[37] Napoleon himself appeared frequently as a father. One deputy declared, "The Government calls us to it as a father calls his children," and another asserted that the emperor "act[s] with us less as a sovereign than as a father."[38] On numerous occasions, moreover, Jewish leaders described themselves as the emperor's "children."[39]

Whether the Napoleonic father was scolding or protective was often an open question. Yet the image suggested that the Jews were equal to other imperial "children." One deputy at the Assembly of Notables made this clear by claiming, "Catholics and Lutherans, Jews and Calvinists, His Majesty . . . only sees in them children of the same father."[40] That phrase suggested a relationship not only to the emperor but also to the Heavenly Father. It also mirrored the conclusion to Grégoire's *Essai sur la régénération physique, morale et politique des Juifs,* no doubt familiar to much of the audience, in which the abbé addressed his readers as "children of the same father," by which he meant God, and urged them to "remove all pretexts to the aversion of your brothers, who one day will all be reunited in the same cradle."[41] Elsewhere the line between the imperial father and God was blurred, as Napoleon seems to have intended, and Sintzheim even designated the emperor "the father of all the peoples."[42] If this comment deified Napoleon, it also suggested that the Jews were equal to the emperor-God's other children.

A common paternity, whether in Napoleon or God, therefore implied the fraternity of all "children." The theme of fraternity was ineluctable at the Jewish assemblies convoked by imperial decree, as the participants were required to rule on whether Jews who were "treated by the law as citizens" viewed "the French" as their "brothers." Buttressed by numerous citations from the sacred texts, the assemblies unequivocally declared the fraternity between Jews and non-Jews in the French empire. One deputy assured his coreligionists that if God sent them "a second Moses," that legislator "would say to us: love the Christians; cherish them as your brothers, unite yourselves with them, envisage yourselves as children of the same family."[43]

Elsewhere the spokesmen reinforced the impression that Jews were part of the French and imperial family. The Sanhedrin's ruling on "civil and political relations" between Jews and non-Jews included the claim that "everything obliges [the Jew] not to isolate his interest from the public interest, nor his destiny, any more than that of his family, from the destiny of the grand family of the state"; and in the preamble to its decisions it reiterated the necessity of Jews to "belong to the grand family of the state." In response to the prevalent mistrust of Jewish statements as insincere, qualified, or obscure, the deputies made ingenious use of the family metaphor to guarantee their honesty, and also to show their support for "freedom of opinion," by declaring, "We have explained ourselves . . . before the very eyes of His Majesty, with the same frankness, the same freedom of opinion that we would have used in the bosom of our domestic hearths." As if to assure even further the sincerity of their words, they expressed family feelings in poetry and song. In an ode in honor of Napoleon's birthday, one deputy proclaimed his joy at becoming "part of the grand and magnanimous family of Frenchmen." At the same ceremony, the assembly sang the familiar aria by Grétry, "Où peut-on être mieux qu'au sein de sa famille?"[44]

Symbolic statements such as those listed here may have conveyed the impression that the Jews were prepared to relinquish their identity as Jews and metaphorically marry into the family that Napoleonic rule appeared to furnish. This impression was no doubt reinforced by one Jewish deputy who happily reported that Napoleon "wants to melt us more intimately into the general mass of the greatest people on earth." Elsewhere, however, the Jews sent a very different message about their willingness to erase the mental borders between themselves and their Gentile neighbors. Most obviously, the majority of deputies at the Assembly of Notables opposed intermarriage, and the Sanhedrin concurred that "marriages between Israelites and Christians" could not "be invested with religious forms."[45]

In other ways as well, Jewish leaders emphasized the value they placed upon their specificity as a discrete community. The use of Hebrew in public acclamation of the Napoleonic regimes was in itself an eloquent statement of Jewish difference. The Hebrew language had faced a mixed reception during the eighteenth century. Diderot had seen it as a means of the sort of obscurantism he abhorred in Christians as well as Jews.[46] Hebrew characters, employed in the Yiddish of eastern Jews, as well as in the sacred biblical language, were often feared as a tool of another kind of concealment, namely, that of the terms of an agreement, or as a method of engaging in some other form of conspiracy. In Alsace during the Revolution their use was therefore outlawed in the keeping of business records and in communication between Jews and non-Jews.[47] Another current of thinking, however, valorized the Hebrew language. Johann Gottfried Herder had written admiringly of the "spirit of the Hebrew language," and by the time Napoleon came to power, it had become validated through a professorial chair at the Institut de France.[48] As an "oriental" language, Hebrew attracted the attention of the same savants who were interested in Arabic, though the latter was more thoroughly studied. This attention coincided happily with a revival of Hebrew (at the expense of an increasingly derided Yiddish) among Jewish scholars, especially those proponents of the *Haskalah*: Moses Mendelssohn and his followers in France and Germany, who believed that proper religious practice depended on a more precise understanding of the language in which the sacred texts were written. Yet the prestige offered by Gentile scholars contributed undoubtedly to the prevalence of Hebrew texts.

Additional evidence of this prestige comes from the praise that French orientalists accorded Jews who expressed themselves in the biblical language. When, for example, an Alsatian savant translated into German a Hebrew poem on the occasion of Napoleon's escape from assassination, he praised the author, Lippmann Moses Büschenthal, as "a young man full of talent and knowledge, to whom the eternal MENDELSSOHN himself, were he still alive, would confer well-merited applause." He went on to praise the poem for "express[ing] beautifully and often with the fire of Asaph, the Israelites' feelings of thanks for BONAPARTE's rescue." Professing sensitivity to the specificities of the Hebrew language, the translator assured his readers that he had remained as faithful as possible to the original, "even in its figures and turns of phrase," and that he had made a concerted effort "to retain unadulterated, insofar as the genius of the German language is capable of this, the particularities of oriental poetry."[49] Another Jewish poet, Elie Lévy, earned even greater praise for his Hebrew hymn on the occasion of the Peace of Amiens. The father of French orientalism himself, Sylvestre de Sacy, praised Lévy for "the grandeur and noble simplicity" of his work, "drawn from the true sources of [Hebrew] poetry."[50] The editors of the *Magasin Encyclopédique* cited Sacy's verdict as evidence of "the richness and elevation of [Lévy's] poetic verve" and the "strength and sentiment" of the language, and the *Courrier des Spectacles* similarly praised the poem.[51] Meanwhile, an admirer from Strasbourg, the Protestant scholar Théophile-Frédéric Winckler, complained to a friend of Lévy that the poem, which he found "superb," was "not for sale anywhere." He requested copies for himself and his colleagues and suggested that Herder himself would be interested in reading the poem.[52]

As a result of praise such as this, the Jewish translator of two odes composed for Napoleon's birthday could confidently write a lengthy introduction describing the revival of patriotic Hebrew poetry, to whose history he saw the odes as belonging. Michel Berr lamented that Hebrew had been "neglected in France," but he noted that it was "cultivated in Germany by a large number of distinguished savants as one of the most beautiful classical languages of antiquity." He referred explicitly to Herder's enthusiasm for the language and proudly pointed to role of "the famous Jew Mendelssohn" in reviving it among the Jews. Distinguishing between the "scholastic" Hebrew of the Middle Ages and the "pure Hebrew" written by his contemporaries, Berr gave numerous examples of the latter in patriotic celebrations: the "first Hebrew hymn" of modern times, composed by "M. Enesheim [sic], savant geometer and philologist, currently in Paris"; the "generally admired" ode by Lévy, which "seemed to betoken . . . the enthusiasm of David and the sensibility of Asaph"; and the work of Büschenthal, a poet "inspired as though on the banks of the Jordan."[53]

One sees in these descriptions of the Hebrew language, by Jews as well as Gentiles, that it served to indicate the Jews' otherness, their imagined distance from Gentiles in both space (hence the image of the Jordan River) and time (hence the allusions to David and Asaph). Jewish leaders clearly valued this metaphoric distance. Their imagined spatial distance associated them with the glory of Napoleon's territorial conquest—the failure of his easternmost ventures notwithstanding. They also conjured images of "oriental" mystery and the fabled wisdom of the East. Insofar as it had traditionally been ascribed to Jews, mystery was largely a negative quality, the inscrutability of an adversary who was deliberately concealing desirable knowledge (often about something so prosaic as the value of an object or a loan). In the context of a burgeoning orientalism, both academic and popular, it was possible to reverse the negative connotations of Jewish mystery and to represent it as a virtue, all the more positive as it was about to be revealed in the form of wisdom. Unlike the inscrutable hieroglyphs to which Napoleon's Egyptian campaign had called renewed attention, the Jews appeared prepared to yield their mysteries.

Even more rhetorically valuable than the imagined spatial distance of the Jews was their perceived relation to temporal distance. The metanarrative of Jewish regeneration always referred, implicitly or explicitly, to an idealized origin in the distant past, a golden age that preceded exile, persecution, and moral corruption. Napoleon and his supporters had taken advantage of the Jews' "antiquity" in order to emphasize the power of a ruler whose prodigious abilities included the capacity to correct centuries-old defects. When combined with a sense of the Jews' "eternal" or static nature, this exoticist configuration suggested their passivity and, hence, the activity and power of the one who would change them. Yet the Jews were able to turn these clichés to their representational advantage. They referred repeatedly and proudly to their antiquity. Berr Isaac Berr dated "the origin of this people" to "the cradle of the human race." Abraham Furtado exalted the Jews as "one of the most ancient peoples in the world" and boasted of "the antiquity of our origins." The words *antique* and *antiquity* recurred continuously during the sessions of the Assembly of Notables and the Sanhedrin. Sintzheim called the Jews "the descendants of antique Jacob," and a member of the Assembly of Notables referred to the Torah as "the revered monument of our antique splendor." Furtado marveled at the Sanhedrin, "this antique body whose origins are lost in the night of time," and declared, "Contemplating this assembly of men who are commendable for their piety, knowledge and virtues, we believe ourselves transported to that venerable antiquity so well described in our sacred books." When Cologna exhorted the Sanhedrin to encourage "useful professions" and military service, his stated goal was to "revive the glory of an antique people."[54]

If antiquity was paired with "glory" or "splendor," however, it more frequently accompanied the more modest virtues of simplicity and equality. When asked whether "the law of the Jews prohibits them from usury toward their brothers," the Assembly of Notables took the opportunity to construct an elaborate counterimage to the prevalent figure of the Jewish usurer. Drawing on an exegetical tradition that both Jews and Gentiles had repeatedly invoked in the eighteenth century, the notables argued that interest on loans between Jews was forbidden not because Jews regarded foreign peoples as the appropriate target for money-lending—they also denied that Jewish law permitted usury against non-Jews—but because interest was foreign to their rustic society. They claimed that the intent of this prohibition, like that of the sabbatical and Jubilee years in which debts were forgiven, was to "tighten again among [the Jews] the bonds of fraternity, to prescribe reciprocal benevolence and to induce them to help each other disinterestedly." Furthermore, the "legislator" had wished to "establish among them an equality of goods and a mediocrity of private fortunes." The notables insisted that the sage laws had worked and that "primitive equality" reigned in ancient Israel.[55]

The Sanhedrin confirmed this view, and in a speech to that body Sintzheim offered a veritable pastorale:

> All the monuments of history attest to the simplicity of our ancestors. The pastoral and agricultural life was their occupation, rustic games their sole pleasures. They had neither manufacture nor navigation; all the commerce with their neighbors had naturally to be limited to a few exchanges at a time when money was so rare and its various uses so limited. They lived in a happy ignorance of all that sumptuousness which is only known to the great and opulent nations. They enjoyed a happiness without pomp and knew how to practice virtues without renown.

In order to understand the laws such as the one prohibiting interest on loans to "brothers," Sintzheim added, it was necessary to recall "that primitive purity of morality of antique Israel" and "that spirit of charity and humanity that was admired in our ancestors." [56]

The trope of primitive or antique virtue enabled the Jews simultaneously to represent themselves as capable of regeneration and to critique European civilization as corrupt and corrupting. Such a critique was evident in Sintzheim's praise of the ancient Jews' "happy ignorance" of luxury, and the Sanhedrin as a body made this stance even clearer. In its doctrinal condemnation of usury, it asserted that the misunderstanding of the Mosaic legislation on moneylending came from an anachronistic attribution of "the morals and habits of modern nations to the highest antiquity," adding, "One falsely accords to the birth of societies what only belongs to their mature age, and often to their decrepitude." [57]

Finally, the Jews celebrated yet another quality that had long made them extraordinary in the eyes of non-Jews, namely, their reputed legalism. The continuity of this prejudice from Christian theologians to Enlightenment writers has already been examined. [58] With Napoleon's accession to power, however, the law acquired a new prestige. In an attempt to reduce citizenship to obedience, Bonaparte had raised the law to a sacred status. Not only did the self-proclaimed Legislator attempt to secure obedience by issuing grand fundamental laws or constitutions based ostensibly on universal and "natural" principles. He even deigned to concern himself with the particularities of civil law, including both the tangled mess of "custom" and the relics of Justinian's digests, hence the celebrated *Code civil*. Indeed, recognizing that control over civil law tightened his grip on civil society, he treated the former as an instrument of his own power over the latter. The totemic status of the law, to which the festivities surrounding the Assembly of Notables and Sanhedrin were dedicated, provided an unprecedented opportunity for the people whose religion had long been derided for its legalism to proclaim proudly that they were in fact people of the law. Napoleon had given them a Simchat Torah, and they were more than ready to celebrate the Law in all its grandness and minutiae.

A striking indication of the Jews' readiness to associate themselves with legal interpretation is the extent to which the term *docteur* appears in the published records of their proceedings. Although Sintzheim addressed the Sanhedrin in Hebrew, the official French translation has the rabbi addressing his colleagues as *"docteurs."*[59] Even more significant is the fact that the Sanhedrin's President Furtado, the rich Bordelais merchant who, according to the more scrupulous Alsatian rabbis, "had only learned the Bible from Voltaire," used similar language in his French speeches.[60] He called the rabbis *"docteurs"* or, more frequently, *"docteurs de la loi."*[61] This was especially telling because the very term *docteur,* when used by the philosophes to describe a theologian, Christian or Jewish, had connoted hairsplitting casuistry, Jesuitical or pharisaic reasoning. Even the great advocate of equality for the Jews, Abbé Grégoire, had used the epithet as a term of abuse.[62] That a partisan of the Enlightenment could use it as an honorific was an eloquent sign that the study of the law, religious as well as civil, was now in favor. The Jewish representatives adopted other proud titles to indicate their expertise in legal matters. Cologna, speaking in Italian, called the members of the Sanhedrin "most enlightened senators" *(chiarissimi senatori),* and Furtado called the body "this august areopagus." In his French translation of Sintzheim's closing speech to the Sanhedrin, Furtado had the rabbi refer to its delegates as "legislators," and a member of the Assembly of Notables proclaimed, "Our descendants . . . will cover with benedictions these wise and venerable interpreters of the law."[63]

Their credentials as "interpreters of the law" thus established, the Jewish representatives could confidently and authoritatively proceed with the business of interpreting the law. In particular, they emphasized its divine origin. Sintzheim called it "the miraculous bush of our divine legislator," which is "never consumed," and members of the Assembly of Notables referred to "our divine Legislator," "our holy Legislator," "our holy law," and "the divine law." Holy or divine laws were by definition perfect, thus Sintzheim uttered the tautology, "The law of the Lord is perfect," and another Jewish representative reasoned similarly, "The law of God ordains all that is just and good."[64]

Moreover, the representatives made it clear that by "law of God" or "law of the Lord," they did not mean only the Pentateuch and the books of the prophets but also the much maligned Talmud, the "oral law" that included the postbiblical code known as the Mishna and its later commentary, the Gemara. As indicated in previous chapters, the Talmud had long been an object of abuse not only among Christian theologians but also among philosophes and their followers. Yet the members of the Jewish assemblies took the Napoleonic veneration of law in general and codified law in particular as an occasion to rehabilitate the Talmud in the public eye. Accordingly, they cited it repeatedly to support the civic doctrine that they were charged with affirming. In response to the question of whether the Jewish religion forbids any occupations, the deputies cited, in addition to biblical sources praising work, the Mishnaic aphorism "Love work and flee from idleness" and declared, referring to the Gemara tractate Kiddushin, "the Talmud . . . positively declares that the family father who does not teach a profession to his son raises him to a life of brigandage." On the question of fraternal relations between Jews and non-Jews, the Assembly of Notables asserted, "This doctrine is professed by the Talmud." Specifically, it invoked the Noahide laws, the abbreviated code of moral conduct given, according to the Talmudic tractate Sanhedrin (!), to Noah and his family—who lived prior to the covenants between God and Abraham and Moses, respectively—and to all the "nations" apart from Israel. Because Christianity complied with these basic rules, the deputies argued, the Jews considered Christians to be their "brothers." The Sanhedrin likewise cited the Noahides, along with other Talmudic dogma and more familiar biblical passages, in its doctrinal statement on fraternity; and in his speech to the modern Sanhedrin, Rabbi Cologna cited the ruling of its ancient predecessor, in the language of learned Christendom: *Pii cujuscumque nationis aeternae vitae participes sunt.*[65]

Finally, the spokesmen invoked the Talmud when commenting on the conditions under which the Jewish religion authorized lending at interest. The Assembly of Notables declared that, "according to the Talmud," interest could be collected only on commercial loans, though it did not cite a specific tractate. The Sanhedrin similarly had recourse to the Oral Law in its decisions on moneylending, insisting that distinguishing between Jews and non-Jews in such loans was contrary to the opinions of the *"docteurs talmudistes."* David Sintzheim argued that insofar as there were Jewish usurers, they practiced their trade despite "the

terrible menaces of the God of Israel" and "the censure of the most esteemed doctors." As to those who falsely believed that the Talmudists
authorized usury, Sintzheim insisted, "This is to misunderstand the wisdom and the virtues of so many venerable doctors who, uniquely occupied with the study of the law, have transmitted to us decisions that are
as wise as they conform to the principles of social order." [66]

This last declaration clearly defended the integrity of the falsely accused "venerable doctors," a professional group that of course included
Sintzheim himself. It also contained an implicit criticism of those who
would "misunderstand" their "wisdom and virtues." Other statements
at the two assemblies were even more critical of non-Jews who failed to
see the perfection of Jewish law. Cologna complained that "our faith"
had been "up to now misunderstood by some and calumniated by others." Furtado went further still, claiming that "the majority" of non-
Jews, "enchained by popular prejudices . . . imbued with the false idea
that it was impossible to operate our regeneration, attributed to our
dogmas effects that were only due to their laws, and reproached us for
habits that they forced us to contract." The claim that bad laws had
produced Jewish "vice" was not new, and even Napoleon's decree of
May 30 itself had blamed usury on a long history of persecution. Yet
Furtado's dichotomy between "us" and "them," which significantly undermined the repeated professions of fraternity elsewhere in the proceedings, reveals the vehemence of his belief that the Jews had been li-
beled and that non-Jews must take collective responsibility for the
damage. Nevertheless, Furtado's tongue-lashing paled in comparison to
jeremiads by Sintzheim himself. The Alsatian rabbi solemnly addressed
his coreligionists as they were about to rule on the question of usury,
"You are going to exculpate, by your judicious decisions, the law of
Moses of a vice that only issues from the corruption of the human heart,
but which the hatred, ignorance and intolerance of fanatical centuries
have regarded as inherent to the law of Israel." Elsewhere he denounced
"the ignoramus and the prevaricator who would dare advance that our
law teaches us to cheat foreign nations! He profanes the name of Israel,
he does not know the way of the Lord." [67]

These were serious accusations: hatred, ignorance, fanaticism, pre-
varication, blasphemy. Among the accused, implicitly, was Abbé Grégoire, who had called for a renunciation of antisocial doctrines purportedly advanced by Talmudic "doctors." [68] More serious still, and most
ironically, the emperor himself and his commissioner Molé were impli-
cated in the wide-reaching denunciation of all who questioned the mo-

rality of the Talmud. Sintzheim and the other Jewish spokesmen could not have known that Napoleon had told Molé only two months before the opening of the Assembly of Notables that "the evil" of usury "comes above all from that undigested compilation called the Talmud, in which, next to [the Jews'] veritable biblical traditions, one finds the most corrupt morality wherever relations with Christians are concerned." Nor could he have known that Molé responded that among the authors of the Talmud were "a large number . . . inspired by the hatred of Christianity," and whose commentary included "the most contemptible refinements on the art of extorting money."[69] Still, they might well have suspected that Napoleon, like so many other non-Jews, harbored prejudices about the content of the Talmud, which in any event he could not have been thought capable of reading.

Officially, of course, Napoleon had called the Jewish representatives to Paris only to clear them of charges that were themselves baseless. Thus Cologna congratulated Napoleon for deigning "to denounce . . . the calumny" of those who saw Jewish law as anti-social.[70] Here one is reminded of those remonstrances of the *parlements* in which frustrated magistrates could not accuse the king himself of despotism and instead blamed unnamed officials acting in his name. It was impossible to indict the emperor for calumny, still less for fanaticism or blasphemy. Yet it was assertive enough under the circumstances to foreground the severity of these crimes and to hint that their perpetrators would be accountable to God. Even if the repeated attacks on Israel's slanderers were not aimed directly at Napoleon, they still constituted an extraordinarily powerful attack on any non-Jews who harbored doubts about the divinity and perfection of "Mosaic law."

Thus Jewish representatives undermined any impression they might have conveyed about a willingness to "melt" into the Napoleonic state by simultaneously representing themselves as unapologetically different from, if not superior to, their Gentile neighbors and rulers. Even in their likening of the emperor to a consecrated Jewish king in the line of David and Solomon, they suggested a refusal to change their own specific identity and instead symbolically transformed Napoleon's identity from that of Christian ruler to that of Jewish king. Furthermore, by declaring Napoleon's law to be in conformity with God's law, they nevertheless drew a palpable distinction between the two kinds of Torah. "The law of the Lord is perfect," Sintzheim assured his audience, and later, at the close of the Sanhedrin, he suggested the Jews' title to or possession of that object, claiming, "the law *of Israel* is perfect." By contrast, none of the representatives characterized Napoleon's laws as perfect. Elsewhere Sintzheim glorified the divine law, remembering the martyrs who had suffered "because we remained faithful to our laws, to those laws that the Lord himself gave us by his revelation in the midst of lightning bolts and thunder." Napoleon was an admirable legislator, but his laws came without thunder and lightning. Nowhere was the difference between divine and Napoleonic law clearer than when Sintzheim congratulated the Sanhedrin for having "succeeded in reconciling" God's "holy law, his pure law, with the institutions of this wise monarch who puts all his trust in the God whom we adore." There was clearly no competition between the "holy" and "pure" laws of God and the "institutions" of a "wise monarch."[71]

Similarly, the Jewish representatives expressed their approval for what Napoleon called civil morality. Again, however, they made it apparent that these values were "Hebrew" or "Israelite" in origin and implicitly congratulated their non-Jewish compatriots for having discovered belatedly what the Jews had long known. When Napoleon asked them about fraternity, they suggested that they had invented it or, more precisely, that their ancestors had practiced this virtue before any laws promoting it had to be codified. Furtado claimed that the fraternity Napoleon hoped to see encouraged between Jews and their non-Jewish neighbors only conformed to "an eternal law of sociability contemporary to the origin of the species" and "a universal law that preceded all apparatus of religious and political institutions."[72] In other words, it was long familiar to the Jews, who, as the representatives repeatedly assured, were coeval with human origins and as "eternal" as the natural laws that "institutions" such as Napoleon's were now said to be following. Finally, as has been shown, the deputies repeatedly implied that equality was not an invention of the French Enlightenment, Revolution, and Napoleonic successor states but of those Jews who had practiced the "primitive equality" so elusive to modern people.

Paradoxically, by approving of Napoleon's legal codes and official morality, Jewish representatives implicitly proclaimed the superiority, priority, and universality of Judaism and the imperfection, youth, and specificity of Napoleonic law and morality. Just as a bishop's or pope's consecration of a temporal ruler implied the approval, hence the superior moral position, of the Catholic Church, the rabbinical confirmation of the Napoleonic state amounted to a reversal of the hierarchical relations initially envisaged by the emperor. Now it was Judaism that was deigning to confirm Napoleon's rights. Finally, the practice of consecration took on a nearly literal form in numerous benedictions by the *docteurs de la loi d'Israël*. Repeatedly the Jewish representatives stated that God had "chosen" or "elected" Napoleon, and in the process likened him to the anointed kings of Israel. Referring to God's project of restoring Israel to its ancient dignity, Berr Isaac Berr asked, "To whom could the accomplishment of such designs be confided? Is it not to him alone, to the mortal whom heaven has chosen as the elect of its heart, to whom it has confided the fate of nations, because he is the only one capable of governing with wisdom?" Sintzheim made the connection between Napoleon and the biblical kings even clearer. In a sermon to the Assembly of Notables, he began by citing the following passage from the Book of Isaiah:

> This is my servant whose defense I shall take; this is my elect *[élu]* in whom my heart has placed all of its affection. I shall spread out my spirit upon him, and he shall render justice unto the nations; he shall not be at all sad or precipitous when he exercises his judgment on earth, and the islands shall await his law. I am the Lord who has preserved you, who has established you to be the reconciler of the people and the light of the nations.

To remove any doubt as to the identity of this ruler, Sintzheim proclaimed of God, "He has chosen Napoleon to place him on the throne of France and Italy"[73]

On the surface declarations such as these might appear obsequious, and indeed it is as a result of this impression that historians have dismissed Jewish leaders under Napoleon as insincere. But what the Jews proffered with one hand they took away with the other. By making him a "servant" of the Lord, who in turn fought his battles, Sintzheim deprived the emperor of his autonomy and his famed "genius." By praising him as the only "mortal" capable of "governing with wisdom," Berr both emphasized the mortality of the man who no doubt preferred to be described as immortal and indicated that his "wisdom" was defined in terms of its conformity with the law of God, in other words, *their* law.

In his concluding address before the Sanhedrin, Sintzheim put the following words into God's mouth:

> Who is the one who shall come to the aid of my people? . . . I have named him my elect one; my will has chosen him to be the dominator of the nations and to distribute benefits to men. The hero . . . shall be the liberator of Israel; the hero who shall overturn the throne of the mighty and raise up that of the humble is the hero whom I destine to raise from the dust the

descendants of antique Jacob. . . . I have called him, I have sanctified him, and all the nations shall recognize by his deeds that I have not at all reproved my people and that I have not at all removed my affections from the midst of Israel.[74]

This imagined speech epitomizes the multivalency of the rhetoric employed by the Jewish representatives. There is a superficially slavish quality to the image of Jews languishing in the "dust" prior to their liberation at the hands of Napoleon and a corresponding sense of Napoleon's unsurpassed, even messianic, greatness, and in this respect Sintzheim's words correspond to the Couché engraving of the emperor preparing to raise the figure of Judaism from the ground. Yet here Napoleon's grandeur is limited by God's "will," which has chosen him as a mere instrument of the Jews' salvation, while their subservience is mitigated by the fact that God has retained his favor for "Israel." By implication, this fidelity, mirroring the quintessentially divine quality of immutability, is contrasted to the incontinence of "the nations" that have persecuted the Jews. It is the positive face of obstinacy, and Sintzheim eagerly appropriates this quality, which is moreover implicit in the term *antique,* on behalf of his coreligionists. Thus the identity of the Jews remains distinct, and this distinction is positively valued. Not only does God refer to the Jews as "my people," suggesting a celebration of their persistent difference. God's sanctification of Napoleon alludes to the perfection of the Jewish religion and, by implication, the virtue of its practitioners. If Napoleon "raised" the Jews from the dust, then, they symbolically raised him to the status of consecrated Jewish king.

WHOSE IDEOLOGICAL TRIUMPH?

If the Jewish communications directed at Gentiles during the Napoleonic period give us an impression of the rhetorical strategies by which a marginal group valorized itself and its beliefs before a suspicious, demanding, and more powerful audience, the communications between the Jews themselves provide an opportunity to view the impact of the encounter with Napoleon and his regimes on the identity of those Jews who by election or self-selection played the role of cultural translators. Scores of Hebrew sources—poems, songs, sermons, and other compositions—attest to the message that Jews were sending to other Jews about the meaning of the historical situation in which they found themselves. In most, though not all, cases the Hebrew texts accompanied vernacular translations and were published in bilingual editions. At least some of the impetus for such publications probably came, as I have suggested, from the rage for everything "oriental" that marked Napoleonic France from the time of the Egyptian campaign. Moreover, as indicated earlier, a few Gentile scholars had varying degrees of proficiency in the language of the Old Testament. Still, Hebrew texts were primarily directed toward learned Jews, not to mention God, who was invariably invoked and no doubt—considering the piety of the composers in question—not in vain. And if questions about the sincerity of vernacular acclamations miss the point of the value of such documents to historians, they are entirely irrelevant to any reading of the Hebrew texts. What these sources do provide are a means of judging the effect, or lack thereof, of the demands that Napoleonic political culture placed on the Jews. By implication, moreover, they speak volumes about the relative power or weakness of the Napoleonic regimes' legitimizing discourses.

Despite the geographic and cultural distances between the various Jewish communities from Paris to Warsaw, Hebrew depictions of Napoleon were remarkably similar. For the Jews of Ancona Napoleon was a Mosaic liberator who prompted them to sing the Song of the Sea. In a Hebrew chronicle from around 1800, another Italian Jew, Issachar Chaim Carpi of Revere, similarly likened Napoleon to Moses. Alluding at once to the biblical Exodus and Napoleon's recent Egyptian campaign, Carpi wrote that Napoleon "stretched out his hand over the sea" to quell the waves and "flew [like an] eagle" to Egypt, where he performed "wonders." Elsewhere in Carpi's account Napoleon took on the appearance of David, whose enemies, as the Psalm proclaimed, "have fallen, as the chaff dispersed before the wind."[75]

In faraway Alsace, Büschenthal's 150-line ode, published initially in Hebrew only, also represented Napoleon as a composite of Moses and David. The poet wrote of the Egyptian campaign, "Like an eagle [Napoleon] crossed the paths of the seas and spread his wings over the land of Egypt. He proclaimed liberty to her inhabitants, set the oppressed free and broke the slaves' bonds." Like David, Büschenthal's Napoleon showed pious clemency. After the enemy has "bowed, fallen and lain" before him, he "still speaks words of grace and pity, stretches out his hand and gives him his covenant of peace." Furthermore, he enjoyed God's special protection against his foes. In his depiction of Napoleon's delivery from assassination, the poet imagined how God saw the conspirators' plot and "despised the evildoers with his anger." " 'Behold,' God said, 'My chosen one is alone, and among the peoples no man is with him . . . there is no one to help him . . . and no one to sustain him.' "

God therefore declared, "'Truly I shall aid him with my hand! Let my wrath strike [the assassin] down! I shall bring the proud and the haughty low. . . . I shall give strength to my Anointed One.'" God delivered the First Consul. "And it came to pass that, just as a strong east wind breaks clouds of darkness, his enemies were dispersed before him."[76]

Elsewhere in the Hebrew literature Napoleon is likened to another anointed king: the Messiah. In a poem that Rabbi Jacob Mayer wrote for a Parisian congregation on the occasion of the Senate's proclamation of empire, the composer exulted, "They shall place a crown of imperial dominion upon his head, and they shall call him father," alluding to Isaiah's well-known prophecy of the Messiah, "And his name shall be called . . . Everlasting Father." In an ode on the emperor's coronation, the same author proclaimed of Napoleon, "Dominion is upon his shoulder" *(ha-misra al shichmo)*, just as Isaiah prophesied of the Messiah, "Dominion shall be upon his shoulder" *(va-tehi ha-misra al shichmo)*. He continued by alluding to the same prophecy, "The sycamores have been cut down, but cedars will sprout forth. / The earth is at rest and quiet, and its people shout for joy."[77] A Polish Jew similarly made use of messianic symbolism, and in a hymn on the occasion of Napoleon's arrival in Warsaw depicted the emperor as a "son of man" appearing "with the clouds of heaven." This was an unmistakable allusion to Daniel's dream of the Messiah descending from the clouds: "I saw in the night visions, / And, behold, there came with the clouds of heaven / One like unto a son of man . . . / And there was given him dominion, / And glory, and a kingdom."[78]

Finally, Jewish composers went so far as to liken Napoleon to God. Büschenthal asked, "Who is this [man] who, though marked out with the style of a man, like a god *[ke-eloah]* rages from his heaven against his enemy?" Lévy referred to Napoleon as a *goel,* a term that literally means "redeemer" but is used repeatedly in the Bible to indicate God, who bears this name, for example, when he rescues the Jews from Egypt and delivers them from Babylonian captivity. In his ode on the declaration of empire, Mayer compared Napoleon to the sun, using the Hebrew word *shemesh,* which is also one of God's names in the Bible. In an ode in honor of Napoleon's birthday, Mayer spelled out the comparison:

> The Seraphim on high say to the Creator,
> "Yours is dominion, for you have called everything forth from
>   nothingness."
> O Napoleon! You too shall reign. You have founded the kingdom

In peace and truth, which you have erected.
Like the sun that gives its light to the planets,
So your light shines on kings and exalted ones.[79]

Still another example of Mayer's use of solar symbolism can be seen in his song in honor of the imperial coronation. Here the composer depicted the emperor as a flame of the sun, whose heat resuscitated the earth after a deathlike winter:

As long as the sun was behind the clouds,
The earth mourned. The fields were laden with ice.
Suddenly the sun sent us a flame of its fire. He governs today.
Mandrakes give forth fragrance. The most precious fruits are over
    our gates.
When Napoleon hid his face, we perished.
When his light shone upon us, we found redemption.

A more obvious allusion to God would have been difficult to find. Though not all readers would necessarily have connected "the most precious fruits" *(peri megadim)* to the Song of Solomon, in which the worshiper describes the paradise inhabited by the object of worship (i.e., God), the similarity between this stanza and Psalm 104, a staple of regular devotions, would have been impossible to miss: "Thou [God] hidest Thy face, they [living creatures] vanish; / Thou withdrawest their breath, they perish, / And return to their dust. / Thou sendest forth Thy spirit, they are created; / And Thou renewest the face of the earth."[80]

The association of Napoleon with life-giving light can be seen elsewhere in contemporary Hebrew compositions. Lévy described the period prior to Napoleon's accession to power as a time when "a thick darkness almost covered the face of our land" and when "violence and strife . . . destruction and war . . . darkened, as clouds over the sun, all the lights of our well-being." Yet suddenly "in the middle of the night a star arrived from Corsica, and there was light." Practically every Jew knew the meaning of the phrase, *va-yehi or:* "and there was light." Any pupil who had read as far as three verses into the Bible would have encountered this expression, along with its antecedent, "Let there be light!" which together epitomized God's creative power.[81] In a hymn that Mendel Kargeau composed on the occasion of Napoleon's coronation, the famous line from Genesis appeared again. Here a clear distinction was made between God, the author of the miraculous transformation from darkness to light, and Napoleon, the manifestation of the miracle, but the sense of the miraculous is nevertheless unmistakable. Like Lévy, Kargeau contrasted the darkness of a time prior to Napoleon's accession to power with the light of his reign:

Yes, a fog covered the gloomy land as among tombstones.
The leaders within resembled grave-dwellers
Until God let his voice be heard, "I have healed the wound.
I have chosen Bonaparte to rule the nation." And there was light
      [va-yehi or].[82]

It would be a mistake to conclude that the Jews literally saw Napoleon as God, or a god, or the Messiah. The *likening* of Napoleon to such figures was different from *identifying* him as any of them. The production of such likenesses is nevertheless highly significant. It shows how Jews conceived of their historical situation as a kind of redemption. The figurative contrasts between the darkness of the past and the light of the present enabled Hebrew composers to articulate the sense that for the first time since the destruction of Jerusalem the Jews might achieve the kind of happiness that the prophets promised only for the End of Days. The many contrasts between death and life, barrenness and fertility, clouds and sun, ice and warmth, similarly underscored the radical difference between the miserable existence of the past and the imminent promise of earthly happiness. Furthermore, this binary splitting of the past and the present was typically articulated by a primal pairing of low and high. Thus Lévy wrote of Napoleon as "a precious gift from God in Heaven, / Who sent him earthward from the heights during the days of war / To be his land's redeemer." Employing a similar opposition of heights and depths, Moïse Milliaud of Carpentras celebrated Napoleon's birthday in 1806 with a hymn depicting the emperor as "raising" the Jews "up from ruin," and Jacob Mayer had the emperor "lift[ing] a dejected people up from the dust."[83] This sort of imagery vividly suggested a sudden intervention in the course of history, as though "from above," and it accounts for the frequency with which Hebrew poets depicted Napoleon as a winged creature: an eagle (even before the imperial coronation), an angel, or "a cherub with extended wings."[84] A more literal account of the unprecedented character of Napoleon's reign can be seen in the letter written in Hebrew by the Assembly of Notables inviting "the children of their religion" to choose suitable representatives for the Grand Sanhedrin. The deputies described this convocation by declaring, "God has shown us a great deed, the likes of which our fathers did not see since the day of Judah's dispersion."[85]

By blending Jewish history with the history of their neighbors in the Diaspora, the Hebrew authors suggested a common fate. This sense was augmented by frequent depictions of Jews and Gentiles as members of a single family. When Mayer proclaimed, "They shall place a crown of imperial dominion upon his head, and they shall call him father," and when Cologna wrote, "Behold! He shall be forever called father of the multitude of nations," they were not just using apocalyptic imagery to indicate the miraculous improvement in their situation. They were also suggesting a fraternal relationship with Napoleon's other children. More explicit references to this relationship come from Mayer, who urged his coreligionists to thank God, "For in the midst of a great and mighty nation you have found brothers," and Rabbi Samuel Wittersheim of Metz, who celebrated the emperor's birthday with a hymn that referred to his non-Jewish compatriots as "blood relations."[86]

Finally, through a creative process of naming, Jewish composers articulated a sense of belonging to the nation that liberated them. Lévy called France "Erets Frankraykh," a mixture of Hebrew (*erets,* land) and Yiddish via German (*Frankraykh,* France), which conjured the name of Erets Yisrael, or the Land of Israel, and conveyed the comparable idea of sacred soil. Elsewhere he designated France "this good land, like Eden the Garden of God," and invoked "my people and my land," thus using the possessive form of both nouns to indicate his belonging. He referred to his compatriots as "sons of France," and alternatively feminized the synecdoche by calling France "daughter of France" and "daughter of my people." Milliaud sacralized the land, and especially the city of Paris, when he called it "[God's] holy city" and compared it to biblical Tyre, "Bestower of Crowns, about which glorious things are spoken." Mayer made France familiar and evoked a sense of belonging by addressing an imagined Jewish compatriot as "Yehuda Tsarfati," meaning simply "French Jew."[87]

The name Yehuda Tsarfati epitomizes the sense of Jewish identity as it was constructed by Hebrew poets during the Napoleonic period. The quality of Frenchness was adopted, while the discrete identity of "Jew" remained intact. And one sees throughout the texts of Jewish self-representation during the Napoleonic period, the formative period in which the paradigmatic version of postrevolutionary Franco-Judaism was being established, a persistent sense of Jewish distinctness. In the very prayer with which Sintzheim inaugurated the Sanhedrin, the sense of Jewish distinction is acute. The rabbi addressed God, "who chose Abraham, Isaac and Jacob, your servants, and their descendants after

them to be your chosen people *[am segula]* from among all the peoples"
and thanked him for having revealed the Torah "to your people" *(le-am-cha)*. Nor was this distinction between Israel and other peoples abolished in the present day, as Sintzheim praised God for having sent a ruler
whose "eye is open to the goodness of your people Israel *[amcha yisrael]*
inhabiting France and Italy," and who convoked the Sanhedrin "to teach
our brothers *[achenu]*, the children of Israel *[bene yisrael]* residing in all
the places of his realm, the right path."[88] This last appellation was a reminder that if Napoleon's Gentile subject-citizens were, like the Jews, his
children and hence their brothers, a special fraternity obtained among
the "children of Israel."

Even as the Jews embraced Napoleon as their father, France as their fatherland, Gentile compatriots as their brothers; even as they exalted
their emperor as chosen by God, his realm as a Holy Land, and recounted the history of France as a sacred history in which God inter-
vened to end an age of tribulation and begin a millennium of peace and
justice, they nevertheless distinguished themselves as a separate people.
Indeed, it was paradoxically *through* these processes of embracing that
Jews maintained a separate identity. By familiarizing the French and
their leader, by saying, in effect, they are *like* the Jews in one way or another, Jewish observers did not change their own core beliefs, values,
or character any more than the traveler who repeatedly remarks that
foreign customs and institutions are *like* their presumed counterparts
back home. The process of sacralizing Napoleon, his state, and the values by which it reputedly functioned only augmented the process of familiarization, since it entailed the invocation of personages and concepts
with which Judaism had made its practitioners eminently familiar.

The paradoxical process by which the familiarization of a foreign
culture solidified a group's identity as a discrete people affords an invaluable opportunity to reflect on the meaning of that famous sociological concept: assimilation. In the introduction to *Marvelous Possessions*,
Stephen Greenblatt describes the surprise he felt on a visit to Bali when
he saw a group of locals who had gathered to watch a religious ceremony on a VCR. This activity involved "the assimilation of the other"
insofar as the video machine "suggested the astonishing pervasiveness
of capitalist markets and technology" and "their extension into the furthest corners of the earth." On the other hand, "the Balinese adaptation
of the latest Western and Japanese modes of representation seemed so

culturally idiosyncratic and resilient that it was unclear who was assimilating whom." If the VCR, "a sophisticated version of international capitalism's representational machinery," was able "to diminish difference" by familiarizing the Balinese with images and values otherwise foreign to them, it also permitted "a surprising amount of local autonomy." Greenblatt "witnessed . . . the pleasure of self-representation," prompting him to wonder, "Whose ideological triumph is being registered here?"[89]

A similar dynamic can be seen in the expressions of Jews at the time of Napoleon. In this case the "representational machinery" in question was a moral-political discourse featuring a vocabulary of law and justice, which the Napoleonic regime continually employed toward the twin goals of securing legitimacy and obedience, but which the Jews were able to appropriate for ends that neither the emperor nor his supporters could have anticipated. Moreover, self-representation was the principal activity, though in the case of Napoleon and the Jews this involved both the "pleasure" of a triumphant story that Jews related to one another and the arguably less pleasurable activity of representing a collective Jewish "self" to a suspicious and skeptical audience headed by a ruler who claimed the godlike capacity simultaneously to legislate, prosecute, judge, and punish. With respect to both kinds of self-representation, however, we are permitted to wonder à la Greenblatt who was assimilating whom. Was the dominant culture of the Napoleonic state making the Jews more like itself, or were the Jews making that culture more like their own? The evidence considered here suggests that the Jews were assimilating *la grande nation* far more than they were being assimilated to it.

To take the example of Napoleon's legal code, the Jewish representatives assimilated it in both senses of the word. First, they *incorporated* it, took it on as their own and made it a part of their corporate-religious constitution, apparently without changing the nature of that constitution, just as an organism ingests or consumes without altering its own nature. Second, they *likened* it to something, namely, the sacred code or Torah that they claimed to have received from God. But there is a difference between likeness or resemblance on the one hand and identity on the other, between likening and identifying as the same. The assimilation of divine law to Napoleonic law rested upon an unequivocal sense that the former was both prior and superior to the latter. Accordingly, the official circular letter announcing the Sanhedrin wrote of Napoleon:

His observant eye has looked and discerned in the holy ways of the Torah
of Moses lasting and strong principles, upon which it stood upright in the
face of the misfortunes of the ages. These are principles to which our holy
fathers in their rightful well-being adhered from generation to generation,
and which are from the most ancient times. For it [the Torah] contains the
innocence of its righteousness, and to this day the peoples have seen it and
benefited from it; the nations have praised it. How greatly valued is this ornament by their measures, this ornament which is a book for the ages![90]

The phrases "from generation to generation" *(le-dor va-dor)*, "from the
most ancient times" *(me-olam)*, and "for the ages" *(ha-itim)* emphasize
the antiquity and durability of the Torah. They implicitly place its adherents above "the nations" who "praised" and "benefited from it" but
were not, after all, its original recipients. That Napoleon should have
"discerned" the "lasting and strong principles" long recognized by
other Gentiles only after exercising his "observant eye" suggests, perhaps inadvertently, a certain obtuseness on his part. In any event it once
again distinguished the Jews as the age-old repositories of precisely the
"civil morality" that Napoleon and his supporters appeared to have discovered belatedly. It consequently placed the adherents to Mosaic law in
a position to judge and approve of the Napoleonic regime. In this context one might return to Greenblatt's question, "Whose ideological triumph is being registered here?"

Was there something about the political culture of Napoleonic rule
that facilitated the Jews' self-representation (to themselves as well as to
Gentiles) as simultaneously prepared for a revolutionary transformation
and proverbially obstinate in their attachment to an ancient tradition?
Were there characteristic weaknesses in the legitimizing discourses that
enabled the Jews to express the humblest gratitude for being lifted out
of the dust while simultaneously distinguishing themselves as quintessentially qualified to designate Napoleon, as it were, kosher? To both
questions the answer is undoubtedly yes. If the Jews sent conflicting signals, these corresponded to the conflicting signals sent by Napoleon and
his supporters. As a self-proclaimed reconciler of factions, religious and
political, and as a mythical Lawgiver, Napoleon called for the assimilation (in the sense typically ascribed to the term) of all groups in the society over which he claimed the right to rule. Yet as an empire-builder
he had all reason to emphasize the national diversity that marks, by definition, any empire. To demonstrate his miraculous power at liberating
the oppressed and inducing the "civil morality" that the revolutionaries
had conspicuously failed to produce, he had good reason to stage both

the emancipation and the moral regeneration of the Jews, whom popular wisdom had long designated the most miserable and the most incorrigible of peoples. At the same time, however, he needed the Jews to remain recognizably Jewish, to underscore the extent and diversity of his empire and to pay homage to his position as a Mosaic legislator, messianic redeemer, and godlike governor. Under these cultural circumstances, it is not surprising that the Jews not only refused to relinquish their famed otherness but also positively delighted in the distinction that Napoleon permitted and in a certain sense even invited them to display. Of course, Jews had taken advantage of discursive ambiguities and contradictions in the past. But the fact that they were able to do so under a ruler who arguably invented modern propaganda and whose control of an ideological apparatus inspired generations of dictatorial epigones should raise the question of when, if ever, political discourses have the monolithic power that is so often attributed to them.

Conclusion

Jews and Other "Others"

What can one conclude from the evidence put forth in this book about representations of Jews in France between 1715 and 1815? It is possible to see these findings as merely confirming the failure, willful or otherwise, of European writers and political actors truly to perceive the Other. The story of such failures has of course been told countless times. Tamise Van Pelt has traced the problem of the Other to Plato's *Sophist,* "in which the Stranger participates in a dialogue on the ontological problems of being and non-being, of the One and the Other."[1] If reflection on alterity has not been a continuous preoccupation since Plato's time, it has certainly been popular during the past two centuries, and more popular still in recent decades. Although there are as many perspectives on the problem(s) of alterity as there are commentators on it, it is possible to detect something like a consensus among many scholars, especially over the past few decades, that the Enlightenment and the "modernity" it reputedly engendered failed in its project of universal liberation to appreciate, tolerate, or in many cases even to perceive the multiplicity, particularism, difference, or otherness that characterized and characterizes the human world.

Among the most lucid theorists of this failure on the part of the Enlightenment were Max Horkheimer and Theodor Adorno. In *Dialectic of Enlightenment,* their seminal critique of "Enlightenment" and the "instrumental reason" that they attributed to it, Horkheimer and Adorno argued that with the "disenchantment of the world" which the Enlightenment victoriously opposed to the mythic cosmology of animism came a reduction of all particularities to instances of universal concepts. For the scientist this meant that every object had to be fit into universal schemas of species and genera. For the moralist it meant that nothing was valuable—neither actions nor individuals—except insofar as it was valuable for something else, preferably a universal principle such as happiness or utility. Thus, "for the Enlightenment, whatever does not conform to the rule of computation and utility is suspect." The increase in the activity of commodity exchange, whose dominant principle was fungibility, fed the habit of regularization, until "equivalence itself [had] become a fetish." As a result the Enlightenment "excise[d] the incommensurable. Not only [were] qualities dissolved in thought, but men [were] brought to actual conformity." Social distinctions were deemed absurd, but "under the leveling domination of abstraction" individuals formed what Hegel had called a "herd."[2]

Much of this critique of "enlightened" hostility toward the incommensurable has reappeared more recently under the rubric of postmodernism. Although this term can never be defined to the satisfaction of all who are associated with it, Lyotard has revealingly associated "postmodern knowledge" with "refin[ing] our sensitivity to differences and reinforc[ing] our ability to tolerate the incommensurable." Similarly, Zygmunt Bauman argues that postmodern ethics require a respect of others "precisely in their otherness." Examples of similar statements could be multiplied, and indeed the story of modernity's failure to respect alterity might ironically be included alongside the story of redemption and other metanarratives that Lyotard has urged his contemporaries to regard with postmodern suspicion.[3] Yet have I not simply repeated this postmodern metanarrative, which was arguably original when Horkheimer and Adorno were writing—however indebted they were to Hegel's dialectical critique of the Enlightenment—but which is now something of a truism? On the contrary, I hope to use the story told in the preceding chapters to question and to complicate inherited "common knowledge" about the construction and uses of alterity.

The impression one is likely to get from reading the many works devoted to the subject of the Other is that one "Other" is as good as the next. Indeed, the tendency to capitalize "Other," a convention that I have at times followed myself, suggests the unvarying or eternal nature of a formal, Platonic category of Otherness to which all particular examples ultimately refer. Paradoxically, however, this operation of universalization risks repeating precisely the error of abstraction—and consequent failure to recognize incommensurability—with which the Enlightenment has been reproached. Yet apart from any (evidently moral) failure to appreciate the specificity of discrete individuals or groups, the assumption that all "others" have been perceived (or not perceived), represented, and constructed in the same manner is, I believe, historically inaccurate. This contention cannot be proved without the help of a method dear to the Enlightenment itself, namely, that of comparison. A truly exhaustive comparison between representations of Jews and representations of other "others"—including self-representations—is impossible in the remaining space of this study. Here I can do little more than issue a reasoned plea for what I would like to call comparative heterography as a field of investigation.[4] Still, even an impressionistic comparison of the ways in which different "others" were represented can begin to reveal the specificities involved in the construction of alterity.

A comparison between Jews and Native Americans in the early modern European imaginary is especially instructive. After all, both Jews and the "savages" of the Americas were popular subjects for depiction. Michel de Certeau has famously observed that "theorizing always needs a Savage," by which he seems to have meant something like the Other that has become so paradoxically familiar.[5] One might ask whether the Jews, who provided the subject matter for so many thought experiments—about citizenship, human perfectibility, the possibility of pluralism, and so on—were equally necessary to theorizing. To say that they fulfilled the same role that de Certeau attributes to the Savage, however, would stretch the meaning of "Savage" well beyond what contemporaries would have recognized. If anything, the Jews were more likely to represent civilization and all its attendant ills—capitalism, luxury, degeneration, and so on—than they were to signify savagery or wildness. Of course, there was never a single image of the Native American "savage." Tzvetan Todorov has shown that Columbus oscillated between representations of the people he encountered in the New World as morally flawless and unspeakably wicked. It was easy for him to move from one extreme to another because he knew nothing about them. They were "a blank page awaiting the Spanish and Christian inscription"; thus Columbus could project his fantasies about innocence and guilt onto them, an act that was nothing like true perception. The extent to which Americans were truly a *tabula rasa* is debatable, as written "knowledge" from the Bible and classical sources was readily invoked in European descriptions of them. But the Jews were certainly anything but a *tabula rasa* susceptible to the random attribution of traits, either in Columbus's time or in later centuries. On the contrary, they were a *tabula scripta,* a tablet upon which the received wisdom of generations had been written. The very invocation of the Jews when speaking of the Native Americans suggested a desperate need to ground description in tradition, preferably written, that is, *scriptura.* Thus Columbus wrote to his royal patrons of the paired accomplishments of 1492: his conquest of "regions of India" and the expulsion of the Moors and the Jews from Spain. Later generations of writers would assimilate the inhabitants of the New World to the Jews of the Old World. When the seventeenth-century Dutch Jew Menasseh ben Israel postulated that the Native Americans were descendants of the Lost Tribes of Israel, he may have been attempting to improve the image of the Jew by associating it with that of the noble savage. Yet he was only repeating what Christians had written before him, and the postulated filiation of the American "savages" to Israel continued into the nineteenth century.[6]

The representation of Native Americans as descendants of Jews served the practice, no doubt comforting for visitors to the New World and armchair tourists alike, of familiarization. Anthony Pagden has called this process of likening the "principle of attachment" and shown how Europeans repeatedly understood America in terms furnished by classical and Christian texts.[7] Stephen Greenblatt has detected a similar operation of familiarization in Columbus's descriptions, and Todorov himself has indicated the extent to which biblical and classical texts obstructed Columbus's view of American difference.[8] Yet if the construction of Jewish parentage for Indians was a typical move for Europeans seeking to reconcile themselves to the foreignness of the New World inhabitants, in the eighteenth century there was little question of the similarity between *contemporary* Jews and Indians. To be sure, the biblical Jews described in a number of Enlightenment texts were paragons of primitive innocence, as I have shown in previous chapters, and in this respect were quite similar to the noble savages who frequently appeared as remnants of an age prior to the corruption of civilization. The Jew of modern times, however, if occasionally described as capable of regaining the lost innocence of antiquity, was more likely to epitomize corruption, a quality that ill-suited representations of American "*sauvages.*" Voltaire's *Candide* provides an ideal view of this binary thinking as it represents Jews and Native Americans in a single text. In that novel the isolated inhabitants of fabled El Dorado in South America embody the natural virtues of primitive humanity. They practice a natural religion, adoring their Creator without asking for favors, and they despise the gold and jewels that make people rich in Europe. The Jews, by contrast, practice the formulaic yet meaningless rites bequeathed by history while displaying the greatest moral failures, including the dishonest pursuit of precisely what was disdained in El Dorado. Nor was this an unorthodox pair of representations. The figure of the Indian who disdains what passes for wealth in Europe could be positively spun as epitomizing generosity or negatively spun as indicating gullibility. Thus Columbus could marvel at the largesse of the Americans and even boast of having cheated them by trading worthless items for valuable goods, and later generations of Euro-Americans would similarly recount with ironic pleasure the myth that Indians sold Manhattan Island for twenty-four dollars in beads.[9] Nevertheless, anyone portraying Jews as similarly naïve about or indifferent to relative value in capitalist modernity would be running counter to a more powerful image of Jewish guile and greed. When Lessing invented generous Jews for his plays *Die Juden* and *Nathan der Weise,* he was deliberately undermining his readers' expectations of how a Jew should behave, yet when writers invoked the generous savage, they made no such demands upon their readers, who would have immediately recognized the cliché.[10]

The specific contours of Jewish alterity as constructed by Enlightenment writers come into sharper relief still when compared with representations of blacks. William Cohen has shown that, in contrast to Native Americans (as well as other "exotic" people), Africans attracted relatively little interest from eighteenth-century writers. This difference in degree of interest is itself worth noting because it underscores the question I have posed at various points in this book about the reasons for disproportionate interest in Jews while other "others" failed to constitute a "question." What eighteenth-century writers did say about blacks—and how these representations differed from those of Indians as well as Jews—is nevertheless revealing. There are no doubt similarities between contemporary depictions of blacks and Jews, and the discursive proximity between these two imagined groups is certainly greater than that between Indians and Jews. In particular, blacks in the eighteenth-century French imaginary shared with Jews the reputation for moral deficiency. As Cohen has observed, the moral "meaning of blackness" had long been negative in the Christian as well as classical traditions, and French commentators therefore frequently "saw the blackness of Africans as symbolic of some inner depravity." More specifically, blacks and Jews were repeatedly accused of lying and stealing, and the same proverbial cunning in business matters attributed to Jews (and foreign to typical representations of Native Americans) was associated with black Africans.[11]

Although the ability to cheat suggested intellectual, if not moral, competency, Europeans repeatedly questioned the intellectual capacity of blacks; so great was the assumption of black inferiority in cognitive ability that Abbé Grégoire was compelled to refute it with *An Enquiry Concerning the Intellectual and Moral Faculties and Literature of Negroes.*[12] Jews were also charged with intellectual shortcomings, even "stupidity," yet more often they were accused, as has been shown, of being overly or inappropriately cerebral, either wasting their rationality on Talmudic hairsplitting or employing their *esprit calculateur* to deceive gullible yet virtuous citizens. Another significant contrast in depictions of blacks and Jews is that the former were typically seen as licentious. If later Judeophobes would characterize Jewish men as lustful (especially for Gentile women), such portrayals were rare in the eighteenth and early nineteenth centuries.[13] Jews were associated with unsanctioned sexual activity, but in an indirect way. As purveyors of money, they reputedly encouraged *luxe,* which in turn connoted lechery to many moralists. They were believed fabulously capable of "seducing" young Gentile men especially into borrowing from them at ruinous rates, but it was the Gentile, not the Jew, who seemed to lack control over his sexual appetites.[14]

There were also positive depictions of blacks, even if, as Cohen maintains, these were greatly outnumbered by negative representations. Blacks were sometimes described as faithful or steadfast, attributes that contrasted with the notion of the "perfidious" Jew but accorded with the quite prevalent image of Jews as faithful to their religion. The slaves in Bernardin de Saint-Pierre's *Paul et Virginie* are faithful even to the point of dying of grief when their masters die. The philosophe Helvétius glorified the Africans who committed suicide rather than submitting to slavery and in a sense valorized a very different sort of person, yet the fiercely independent African was also a figure of fidelity, that is, to liberty. The blacks in the imaginary of both authors resembled the martyred Jews who bravely chose death over a renunciation of their religion. These images of fidelity, reputedly a "natural" virtue of the unschooled and uncivilized, were in turn associated with the image of the noble savage. A conflation of American and African "savages" enabled French writers to project the qualities of noble savagery onto Africans, thereby praising the black as a paragon of natural morality uncorrupted by civilization.[15] To the degree to which blacks were thus "ennobled," however, they looked less like the Jews who were thought to be removed from nature.

Finally, it is instructive to compare French representations of Jews with those of women in the age of enlightenment and revolution. For much modern scholarship, women have been the paradigmatic "other," and a great deal of what we know about how and why others are posited, how such positing forms identities and power relations, and the implications for understanding politics and history comes from women's studies and gender studies. How representations of women resembled and differed from those of Jews (as well as other "others") is therefore crucial to any understanding of the specific place of Jews in the imaginary of eighteenth-century and early nineteenth-century French writers and political actors.

Commenting on Michel de Certeau's claim that "theorizing always needs a Savage," Josette Féral writes, "The Savage in the West has always been the Woman. . . . She is needed so that her difference can act as a confirmation of man's 'natural superiority' and of his 'birthright' to be the best."[16] This is undoubtedly true if one sees difference as identical with savagery, if the "Savage" is simply the "Other," but the ambivalence of many men toward civilization during the Enlightenment and afterward suggests that the place of women in (male) theorizing might not have been so simple. Moreover, contemporary texts confirm this suspicion. Certainly women, like "savages," were often accorded a special proximity to nature. If seventeenth-century Cartesian feminists such as Poulain de la Barre could argue that "the mind has no sex," eighteenth-century theorists (and many of their descendants) tended to reduce women to their bodily existence.[17] According to one French doctor, because of the internal position of female genital organs "the internal influence continually recalls women to their sex." Following Rousseau's reasoning in *Émile,* he argued that men, whose genitalia were external, were less influenced by their biological maleness, thus "the male is male only at certain moments, but the female is female throughout her life."[18] This distinction implicitly established as an exclusively male prerogative all independence from biological determinism. It suggested that Nature dictated to women, as it did to savages, whereas men could hope to escape this lower form of existence. Of course, men did not always decry the reputedly natural character of women, since this could also be associated with such virtues as natural affection and the desire to nurture. The Rousseauian praise of breast-feeding mothers, a metonymic reduction of women to characteristic body parts that in turn epitomized natural virtue, is only the most obvious example of this trend.[19]

Both the negative and positive associations of women and nature are discursively far removed from typical depictions of Jews, especially modern Jews, who were far more likely to epitomize civilization than nature. Women, however, were not exclusively equated with nature. Indeed, there was a very strong tendency to link them with civilization. Unlike the association with nature, which could be positive or negative, the connection between women and civilization appears to have been almost wholly negative. Already in the seventeenth century, as Joan Landes has shown, men who wished to critique the unnatural character of civilization gendered it feminine. In contrast to the transparent world of nature, according to this new optic, feminine civilization was opaque, disfigured. Thus in *La critique de l'école des femmes* and *Les précieuses*, Molière criticized as unnatural the speech of fashionable women. In the eighteenth century Diderot, Rousseau, and other commentators similarly worried about the distorting influence of women on language. Landes writes, "Women, especially salonnières, were accused repeatedly of artifice and authorship of stylized discursive practices in conflict with nature."[20] The political implications for an emerging republicanism were clear. Feminine opacity and artifice were associated with private cabals, themselves linked to "oriental" tyranny and its aristocratic supporters. By contrast, the transparent, public, universal, and therefore masculine language of republican men with nothing to hide was the prerequisite to liberty. Moreover, the propensity of civilized women to stylized forms of expression ostensibly encouraged attachment to *luxe*, an unnatural vice of civilization that threatened sexual deregulation (another sign of the reign of women) and social dissolution.

French writers, it will be recalled, similarly associated Jews with opacity, dissimulation, conspiracy, and luxury, all features of civilization that good republicans deplored. The opacity of Jews, which Grégoire and others linked to their use of foreign languages, was augmented by their perceived skill in lying. Worse than the immediate effects of duplicity (i.e., the impoverishment of the duped Gentile) were the moral effects of such striking examples of dishonesty. François Hell claimed that the "Christian" forger of receipts in the infamous Affair of the False Receipts had only learned his craft from the Jews to whom he had been exposed. Similarly, Rousseau condemned women for allegedly teaching

men how to dissimulate.[21] When combined with selfish concerns, dissimulation in the republican imagination led inevitably to the subordination of the commonweal to the desires of invisible private interests. It
is not a coincidence, in this respect, that Montesquieu's Rica deplored
the alleged reign of powerful women at court and in Paris as "like *a new
state within the state*," a phrase mirroring the language repeatedly used
to denounce the fabled particularism of the Jews. Given that Sieyes deployed similar imagery to denounce the nobility—calling them *imperium in imperio*—one can see why the political status of women and Jews
was in doubt from the very beginning of the Revolution.[22] Finally, in yet
another discursive linkage between Jews and women, contemporaries
attributed to both a tendency toward excesses or false use of the imagination. Philosophes described women as particularly susceptible to
bouts of delirium, hallucinations, and the failure to distinguish between
reality and dreams, failings that Diderot explained in terms of the "terrible spasms" of the uterus.[23] Similarly, as has been shown, eighteenth-
century thinkers accused the Jews of an *imagination déreglée,* epitomized in the "dreams" of the Talmudists, rabbis, and their followers and
explained as the consequence of persecution.[24] Since this malfunction-
ing of the intellect was frequently contrasted to the natural reasoning of
the primitive Israelites, civilization itself implicitly shared the blame for
the degeneration of a faculty that God (in the natural theology of the
deists) had created perfect. Whether the same could be said of civilization's role in the imagination of women was unclear, since the biological determinism of the century would seem to have absolved civilization
of any guilt in the flaws of the uterus. Yet it is significant that Rousseau
could write, "The imagination, which causes such ravages among us,
never speaks to the heart of savages."[25] Thus neither women nor Jews
were posited as savages. In fact, they constituted problems precisely insofar as they departed from notions of primitive virtue and embodied
the moral and intellectual defects of civilization.

One of the most striking similarities between representations of
women and those of Jews is that both groups evoked a paradoxical sense
of simultaneous strangeness and familiarity. Greenblatt has remarked
on the coexistence of marvel and recognition in perceptions of others
from the time of Herodotus to our own day.[26] Yet surely some "others"
are more recognizable than others. If visitors to the New World and Africa were able to familiarize the inhabitants they encountered by likening them to figures available from written texts and folklore, and if later
writers could avail themselves of a quickly growing body of recognizable

images for describing "savages" and blacks, describers of women and Jews certainly had more sources still. There are arguably few "others" whom men have described more often than women and Jews. If women were familiar partially because of their proximity as mothers, wives, sisters, and half the inhabitants of the globe, the many discourses about them, inherited and adapted from classical and biblical texts as well as proverbial "common sense," surely facilitated the creation of recognizable features, even if the types created ranged from saintly to wicked, from the Virgin to the Whore. The confidence with which men could claim to know women was far greater than any corresponding confidence in their ability to describe Native Americans, blacks, or many other "exotic" people. What the Jews lacked in numbers and proximity they made up for in their presence in written and oral traditions. Just as men "knew" women largely on the basis of things written and said about them in the past and present, Gentiles had a corresponding body of "knowledge" about Jews. In both cases the Bible was crucial in establishing mythical stereotypes, but more recent accretions of written knowledge and folklore provided additional sources for description. Therefore, women and Jews, though quintessentially "other," were among the most complete *tabulae scriptae*. The work of description was therefore all the easier, since the objects of description themselves came with their own scripts, and this helps to account at least partially for the extent to which they were written about. At the same time, Jews and women were depicted as strange, inscrutable, indecipherable. Indeed, it was precisely the opacity of both groups, moralized as dissimulation, that most distinctively marked them as familiar. What was apparently best known about both "others" was that they were unknowable. Finally, the location of women and Jews at the crossroads of familiarity and strangeness, their unstable association with the known and the unknown, helps to account for the obsessive repetitiveness with which they were problematized and theorized.

Despite the striking discursive similarities between Jews and women, it would be wrong to claim that Jews simply equaled women in the minds of Gentile men, that one "other" was the same as the next. Important differences were present in the representational strategies and attitudes of non-Jewish men toward both. In particular, if women were thought to be ruled by their bodies and, more specifically, their wombs, Jewish men were not similarly essentialized along biological lines. Jews did play a significant role in the construction of masculinity. Sander Gilman and George Mosse have shown how masculinity in modernity

has been defined in opposition to Jewishness. Susan Kassouf has similarly demonstrated how the construction of specifically "scholarly" diseases, including hemorrhoids (which were likened to menstruation),
feminized the Jews who were thought to suffer disproportionately from
them.[27] Though Grégoire dismissed the myth that Jewish men menstru-
ated as "foolishness," his need to refute this belief suggests that some
people held it. Grégoire himself maintained that Jews had distinctive
physical characteristics, which he moreover regarded as repulsive. Yet
if the reign of the uterus over women was typically thought to be ines-
capable, the physical deficiencies of Jews were deemed remediable. Like
the blackness of Africans that a combination of Galenic humor theory
and Buffonian notions of degeneration explained as the product of pro-
longed exposure to the sun, Jewish deformations were widely seen as the
consequence of reversible factors. Thus Grégoire explained the physical
features he saw in the Jews in terms of unsanitary conditions in the *quar-
tiers juifs,* a propensity to early marriage and childbearing, and the over-
consumption of fish.[28]

Furthermore, just as the perceived physical difference of Jews was
viewed as reversible, such a reversal was deemed desirable. Grégoire and
others sought precisely the physical along with the "moral and political" *régénération* of the Jews. By contrast, no one conceived of the possibility or the desirability of altering, reducing, or eliminating the physical difference of women. No one proposed their physical regeneration.
Rather, men proclaimed their attraction to that which was physically
specific to women and added moral meaning to this difference by associating it with nurture and domesticity, qualities whose political ramifications are well known. Instead of envisaging the assimilation of
women into a world of universal citizenship, as was the case with the
Jews, men relegated them to the private domain that Nature had reputedly assigned them. Insofar as they harbored a Rousseauian fear of the
"public" women of civilization, they tended to see the latter as deviat-
ing from their natural place, to which they could presumably return simply through an act of the will. The physical difference of women was not
perceived as a problem in need of a solution. On the contrary, it was the
subject of paeans. Ironically, a physical repulsion of Jews could serve as
the point of departure for arguments in favor of their integration into the
political community, whereas the physical difference that men claimed
to value in women justified their exclusion from the body politic.

This admittedly cursory comparison of Native Americans, blacks,
women, and Jews as constructed by Frenchmen in the period in question

suggests the need of "theorizing" not for an Other but for various others; not only for a savage but for figures embodying civilization; not only for blank screens onto which arbitrary fantasies could be projected but for scripts that facilitated description and explanation. Recognizing the specificity of Jewish alterity is the first step in explaining both why Jews were the subject of such intense scrutiny and how they operated symbolically in the thinking of those who wrote or spoke about them. All "others" were conceivably "good to think," to return to Lévi-Strauss's turn of phrase, and there was often considerable overlap in what they were good to think about. All the groups examined here facilitated thinking about the advantages and disadvantages of civilization and "savagery," though in different ways. Native Americans, blacks, and Jews operated in theories of perfectibility, degeneration and regeneration, and indeed human malleability *tout court;* women were less convenient for this purpose insofar as men had a vested interest in seeing them as biologically determined.

Yet in contrast to Native Americans and blacks, whose religious difference had long appeared the result of ignorance and whose conversion was consequently believed inevitable, the Jews were marked as a people who possessed knowledge of Christianity but "obstinately" refused to accept it. Their conversion was consequently a miracle prefiguring, as Jansenist theologians put it, the Second Coming. Most commentators on the Jewish question were not premillennial Christians, and insofar as they emphasized the importance of attachment to the *nation* over adherence to Christianity, their attempts to transform the Jews fit with prevalent notions of secular modernity. Still the conversionist impulse survived intact, and the Jews remained the object of this ancient urge. The importance of this survival cannot be overstressed. It indicates the durability of religious habits well into the period famous for its secularization and dechristianization.

Other factors played a role in the prominence of the Jewish question in France before, during, and after the Revolution. Among the most important of these were negative factors, conditions that prevented other likely candidates for "theorizing" from coming to the forefront. Any speculation about the equality, regeneration, or assimilation of blacks compromised the lucrative slave economy and invited the secession of white planters in the Caribbean. Any serious discussion of the place of women in the postabsolutist state risked the conclusion that men ought to share power equally with them rather than holding a monopoly on sovereignty. One could conduct thought experiments with the Jews at little risk to the economic or political dominance of white, male Gentiles. Indeed, as suggested in chapter 5, the ostentatious conferral of equality on Jews could serve as a way of drawing attention away from the persistence of more glaring inequalities, including slavery itself. Nevertheless, the cultural fact of prior Jewish inscription provided a positive impetus for the interest in the Jews. Tradition provided the keys to the allegorical use of the Jews; it made their symbolic significance readily comprehensible, even if contemporaries adapted and transformed prior meanings to fit new circumstances. Recourse to tradition might raise some eyebrows among historians who have learned that this principle, once taken for granted, is often an "invention."[29] But the fact that tradition is sometimes invented does not mean that it is always invented; and just because memory is sometimes fabricated for presentist purposes does not mean that it is never inherited from the past. In the context of the subject treated in this book, tradition is that which induced people who had never before seen a Jew to believe that the Jews were duplicitous, greedy, and obstinate; that they were the ultimate obstacle to the dream of a selfless, indivisible polity; and that, consequently, their assimilation would constitute a modern miracle. Positing a name does not verify the existence of its referent, and one might suspect that invoking tradition, or prejudice for that matter, comes perilously close to a reifying tautology. I am aware of these dangers, but the undeniable differences in the composition of the many defining others of the period in question suggest that something other than random projection was at work. They suggest that some images adhered more readily to some groups than others. To call the source of this difference tradition does not deny its complexity, fluidity, and often self-contradictory character. It simply calls attention to the strength and continuity of representations that modernity is typically assumed to have supplanted.

ASSIMILATION, POWER, AND IDENTITY

If the story of non-Jewish representations of Jews cautions against the simplifying tendency to regard others as abstract manifestations of an eternal Other and suggests the need to track the specific uses of specific others as symbolically constituted (at least in part) by tradition, the story of Jewish self-representation is also instructive. Here one can see an example of a marginal or peripheral group contesting, negotiating, and otherwise adjusting familiar descriptions of itself and in the process coauthoring, as it were, its own cultural text. It is difficult to compare the self-representational acts of the Jews with those in similar circumstances, that is, posited as different. After all, historians have paid very little attention to the phenomenon in question. Insofar as they have considered self-representation, they have concentrated on that of political rulers and elite social strata. But what about "the weak"?[30] We know very little about how groups typically posited as different participated in their own description. In some cases it may be impossible to know. For instance, the Native Americans "discovered" by Columbus and other Europeans did not have access to the language and print, the "mimetic capital," to use Greenblatt's terminology, necessary to describe themselves in unmediated fashion, and any efforts to explain themselves were necessarily (mis-)translated by people who could only perceive them through the prism of their own prejudices and agendas. With respect to women, Joan Scott has shown how Olympe de Gouges fashioned an identity for herself and the women she claimed to represent out of discursive materials otherwise managed by men.[31] Nevertheless, whereas Scott's work explores the possibilities for self-representation in the context of postrevolutionary feminism, there is no systematic investigation, to my knowledge, of women's self-representation in the age of Rousseau, Diderot, and the many men whose very understanding of the natural order, the public and the private, sentiment and rationality was based largely on binary oppositions of male and female.

The relative lack of a comparative context entails the risk that the story of Jewish self-representation will simply confirm, quite paradoxically, the stereotypical picture of Jews as a clever people who shrewdly manipulated language in order to persuade their Gentile neighbors of their loyalty, virtue, and general fitness for citizenship. The provisional comparison to female strategies à la Gouges does not necessarily reduce this risk, as it might inadvertently perpetuate the mythic essentialization of both Jews and women as manipulative and sly. My hypothesis is that Jews, women, and other "others" have all had the potential to turn the tables on their describers in one way or another, that they have all been equally clever in this respect, but that differing historical circumstances—such as level of literacy, access to print culture, and the differing symbolic meanings that made various groups more or less interesting to contemporaries—have limited the extent to which they actualized that potential. This hypothesis is based on the no longer startling assumption that cultural meanings are fluid, that texts, written or otherwise, are not given but subject to revision by their "readers," though the possibilities for revision are limited by tradition. By extension, there is no reason to believe that marginal, oppressed, or "weak" people have been less capable of such revision than those who wield greater power. Only future research, however, can show precisely when and how marginal groups took the initiative in representing themselves.

Still, the case of Jewish self-representation by itself has important ramifications because it enables us to problematize some of the key concepts and models that the social sciences as well as the humanities have long employed to explain what happens when cultures with varying degrees of power meet. One such concept is that of assimilation. Although the verb *assimilate* derives from the Latin *assimilis* (similar to, like) and has for centuries denoted both likening and a process of literal incorporation or ingestion, its familiar social-scientific meaning dates from the last quarter of the nineteenth century. There is no *Begriffsgeschichte*, to my knowledge, of this fundamental concept, and the following remarks are a poor substitute for such a desperately needed study, yet at least two texts suggest that this word was invented in the context of the Jewish question as it appeared in its racialized form in the 1870s and 1880s. The first modern usage of *assimilation* in French that I have been able to find, using the ARTFL database of French literature, is in the *Journal* of Edmond and Jules de Goncourt, who in 1878 recorded a conversation in which the political philosopher and biblical critic Ernest Renan allegedly delivered a "wordy dissertation . . . on the faculties of assimilation of the Judaic races."[32] One can see how this concept, born of the organic language of nascent sociology and embellished by the image of digestion, appealed to those who wished to ask how the Jews could relate to the Gentile inhabitants and values of the nation, itself an old concept undergoing redefinition as a living body. The racialized conception of Jews, moreover, must have made the problem of assimilation all the more compelling, since it suggested the interaction between essentially foreign living substances. Whereas previously the Jews were obstinate by choice, now they could be imagined as biologically incommensurable.

Despite its origins in a racist episteme, and at the risk of anachronism, it is indeed possible to apply the concept of assimilation to the encounter of non-Jews and Jews in eighteenth-century and early nineteenth-century France. From the perspective of many Gentiles the task at hand was the assimilation of the Jews, that is, their incorporation into a larger social body through a substantive transformation of their character, values, and beliefs to match those of a non-Jewish population. The proverbial obstinacy of the Jews made them a test case for the possibility of an indivisible, universal community, whether conceived as a nation or an empire or some larger collectivity of enlightened, virtuous beings. French Gentiles had a discursive interest in the persistence of Jewish "particularism," even during the Revolution, when this trait was most vehemently denounced, since it was the Jews' alleged embodiment of civic vice that helped to define the ideal citizen. Yet if this contradiction is visible with hindsight, there is no reason to believe that contemporaries experienced it. At the same time, nothing even approaching the sort of assimilation envisaged by French Gentiles actually took place. Whether and to what extent the Jews assimilated in this manner after 1815 is debatable, and in recent years historians have emphasized the persistence of old practices and beliefs among French Jews well into the nineteenth century, but it is certain that in the century prior to Waterloo there was no desire among Jews to be digested by the French body politic or by French society.

This refusal to assimilate in the prescribed manner, even among those hailed by philosophes and reformers as more men than Jews, does not in itself damage the concept of assimilation as typically understood since the late nineteenth century. The explanatory poverty of this notion of assimilation becomes clearer when one examines it together with its defining opposite: resistance. The choice for marginal or peripheral groups as typically presented by scholars of intercultural contact is between assimilation and resistance, that is, if the more powerful culture of the "center" is not presumed sufficiently hegemonic to make all attempts at resistance futile. This binary model sees identity as a fixed sum of quantities that can only be altered through exchange of one's "own" features for those of a different (and dominant) culture. The case of the Jews, however, belies the dichotomous model of assimilation versus resistance. The Jews' repeated apologies for their Jewish religion and indeed the repeated insistence that their reputed obstinacy was in fact the virtue of fidelity hardly suggest the abandonment of particularism that assimilation would seem to mandate. Nevertheless, their repeated insistence on the excellence of the moral values to which the French proclaimed allegiance was hardly resistance. Clearly, other concepts are needed to describe what was taking place.

Not all theorists of intercultural contact are locked into the either-or model of assimilation and resistance. In recent years a number of scholars have attempted to transcend this antinomy by positing the notion of hybridity. Drawing upon the Russian literary critic Mikhail Bakhtin, postcolonial theorist Homi Bhabha has "developed the concept of hy-

bridity to describe the construction of cultural authority within conditions of political antagonism or inequity." He writes:

> At the point at which the precept attempts to objectify itself as a general-
> ized knowledge or a normalizing, hegemonic practice, the hybrid strategy
> or discourse opens up a space of negotiation where power is unequal but its
> articulation may be equivocal. Such negotiation is neither assimilation nor
> collaboration. It makes possible the emergence of an "interstitial" agency
> that refuses the binary representation of social antagonism. Hybrid agen-
> cies find their voice in a dialectic that does not seek cultural supremacy or
> sovereignty. They deploy the partial culture from which they emerge to
> construct visions of community, and versions of historic memory, that give
> narrative form to the minority positions they occupy.[33]

Of all the models discussed so far, Bhabha's comes the closest to describing the dynamic of Jewish self-representation in France between 1715
and 1815. In the face of "generalized knowledge" about the nature of
the Jews, spokesmen for this minority group took advantage of a situation in which "power [was] unequal but its articulation [was] equivo-
cal"—as, for example, when Gentiles demanded of the Jews that they
transform themselves radically while remaining faithful to a tradition
that preserved the mythic values of primitive innocence. Their "negoti-
ation" was "neither assimilation nor collaboration" as these terms are
normally defined, and Jews almost always "refuse[d] the binary representation of social antagonism."

The notion of hybridity, however, does not appear to correspond to
the consciousness of the Jews themselves. Insofar as the latter can be re-
constructed, one finds in it a refusal of the sort of compromise that is
implicit to the hybridity model. If Olympe de Gouges could boast of
her "amphibious" nature, question the discrete "administration of the
sexes in nature," and title a pamphlet, "Le cri du sage; par une femme,"
her contemporary Zalkind Hourwitz vehemently protested against the
treatment of Jews as "a type of amphibian."[34] Hourwitz wanted it all:
to retain his identity as a Jew *and* to be recognized as a member of the
universal community of men. And these desiderata, despite the idiosyn-
crasies that alienated him from other Jewish spokesmen, were characteristic of his coreligionists. How they resolved this paradox has been
demonstrated in earlier chapters. They assimilated, but in the opposite
manner to the process as it is normally described. Rather than being
assimilated into France, they assimilated France into themselves. They
achieved this mental objective, moreover, by the triple technique of familiarization, sacralization, and appropriation. Like tourists in a foreign

land, they constructed affinities[35] between the customs and values of their hosts and their own, though they were careful to suggest the function of their own culture as the font of what they were praising. In addition, they sacralized France by likening French rulers to the anointed and divinely elected kings of Israel, enemies of France to Amalekites and Sons of Belial, the laws of the land to the Law of God, and French principles of civic virtue to the divine morality of Judaism. No less than simple familiarization, sacralization enabled Jews to appropriate French values without sacrificing their identity. On the contrary, their identity was dramatically strengthened as a result of this triple process, since it consisted of an image of Judaism as a gift, not a scourge, to the world.

These practices of representation, finally, suggest a rethinking of the relationship between sacralization and appropriation on the one hand and power on the other. Typically understood since Durkheim as a means of social solidification through consensus, sacralization can also be seen as a strategy of self-assertion and empowerment by outsiders. Furthermore, appropriation is usually employed to describe the process by which the powerful invoke the values or habits of ordinary people in the creation of self-serving ideologies or discourses. Yet the case of the Jews shows that appropriation, which sacralization entails, can serve the goals of the margins. Thus the type of assimilation in which the Jews actually engaged implies the existence of power where one is least likely to expect it: among "the weak."

This paradox should not be surprising to postmodern thinkers who subscribe to Foucault's understanding of power as located in unlikely places, though it runs against the grain of his notion of omnipotent discourse. The notion that anyone can assert power through assimilation is perhaps best expressed by Nietzsche, from whom Foucault derived much of his thinking about power.[36] Describing "that commanding something which the people call 'the spirit,'" Nietzsche wrote, "Its needs and capacities are so far the same as those which physiologists posit for everything that lives, grows, and multiplies." He emphasized its "power to appropriate foreign strands" and "its inclination to assimilate the new to the old, to simplify the manifold, and to overlook or repulse whatever is totally contradictory." And further: "Its intent in all this is to incorporate new 'experiences,' to file new things in old files— growth, in a word—or, more precisely, the *feeling* of growth, the feeling of power." Refining his physiological imagery, Nietzsche concluded that "'the spirit' is relatively most similar to a stomach."[37]

Even if the figurative language of this digestive metaphysics is over-

drawn, it corresponds strikingly to the situation of the Jews, who appropriated, incorporated, and assimilated, who filed "new things" such
as the Enlightenment and revolutionary principles in the "old files" of
Jewish tradition. It might be objected that the feeling of power experienced by those who assimilated the surrounding foreign culture was
quite a different thing from real power, which can coerce other people
and things according to the dictates of one's will. Furthermore, it might
be objected that the sort of strategy that Jews employed to recast the
novelties of the Enlightenment and the Revolution as Jewish tradition
was simply assimilation (according to the typical sociological model) in
disguise, that they merely invented palliatives to ease the pain of a traumatic assault on their identity. I do not wish to render judgment on the
extent to which the Jews gained or lost power as "objectively" conceived, or whether the undeniable challenges to their identity resulted in
a loss or a gain. These questions would merely reintroduce the *questions
mal posées* of whether the Enlightenment, the Revolution, and "emancipation" were good or bad for the Jews. What I have sought to do in
this book is to reconstruct the subjective perceptions of the historical
figures themselves, their complex techniques of understanding, their elusive feelings, as imperfectly recorded by their words. And the words
of the Jews suggest that the sort of assimilation in which they engaged
buttressed their sense of self-respect while simultaneously reducing the
shock of contact with a suspicious, powerful, and at times antagonistic
society.

At this point I might be accused of a self-contradiction. In the first
half of this conclusion I stressed the specificity of the Jews in the mental
landscape of France from 1715 to 1815. In the second half I hypothe-
sized a commonality between Jews and other marginal groups and indeed, insofar as I have endorsed Nietzsche's universal theory of human
nature, between Jews and the rest of the human race. Yet both claims, it
seems to me, are plausible. It is possible that the Jews were specific in
their symbolic meaning(s), in the qualities that Gentiles attributed to
them, though they shared their defensive modes of self-representation
with other historical outsiders and shared their habits of mental assimilation (as reformulated previously) with the rest of humanity. Both the
emphasis on specificity and the hypothesis of commonality, in any event,
are based on my conviction that the Jews, as well as other "others," are
separated from the universal only by mistake, and that their responses
to this mental ghettoization are likely to reveal their commonality with
the rest of humanity. In this conviction I risk transgressing against the

postmodern ethics that require me to respect the "otherness in the other," since I cannot be sure just how other she is by nature and how other I (with the help of others) have made her. I risk committing the postmodern sin of refusing to recognize the incommensurable and as such bear the mark of the very century that failed in so many instances to respect that which, for whatever reason, appeared to be different.

It is possible to respond that the failures of the Enlightenment and the revolutions it inspired are due not to their universalism but to the limits of their universalism, that they praised the ideal of common humanity while not fully believing it. This sort of wavering would help to explain why the Jews, so readily associated with the themes of universalism and particularism, returned again and again to the agenda of those whose favorite topic was "man" in general. As symbols of eternal, obstinate incommensurability, they could be employed in thought experiments about the possibility of a generalized understanding of the human world. Still, I cannot justify my emphasis on human commonality by resorting to ethical arguments. Only further research into the symbolic use and self-representation of outsiders, comparative heterography, can test my assumption. Such work might show that the specificity of the Jews as constructs of their Gentile observers was less marked than I have suggested. Further research into the strategies of self-representation deployed by marginal groups might show that the techniques of the Jews were less widespread than I have supposed, and that Nietzsche's stomach, though offering a vivid correspondence to the activities of the Jews in the century that I have studied, is not common to all people. Whatever the results, the questions are worth pursuing. Interest in questions of sameness and difference has never been so pronounced, nor, perhaps, has it ever been so justified, yet our understanding of them is still in its infancy. I hope that this book will prompt new approaches to an old problem.

Epilogue

At the beginning of this book I asked my readers to "forget" what they knew about the Jews from the late nineteenth century to the present day. I made this request in order to restore the sense of strangeness to an eighteenth-century and early nineteenth-century "Jewish question" that subsequently appeared the inevitable prologue to an equally inevitable future. By problematizing that question, I believe, I have revealed aspects of eighteenth-century and early nineteenth-century French history that a teleological approach to the subject would have obscured. Having engaged the historical subject in this manner, I would now like to venture some observations about the situation of French Jewry in recent decades and accordingly allow readers to return from their state of self-imposed oblivion. The story just told about representations of Jews in France between 1715 and 1815 is highly relevant to an understanding of recent French history—not because the prior history somehow prefigured, foreshadowed, or otherwise determined the subsequent history but because of the striking similarities between the two ages. For once again the Jews are a "question" in France. They are a matter of public discussion. They are "good to think" about some of the most urgent issues of the day. And if they are heavy in symbolic significance, they are also people, who as people would naturally like to have some say in the meanings that they convey.

The memory that I would like to recall is not that of Vichy, the Occupation, and the Holocaust but rather a screen memory of that catastrophe, the image of events that a subsequent generation constructed, since it is the memory of the Shoah, rather than the Shoah itself, that has been the decisive factor in the return of the Jews to public consciousness. For a quarter century after the Liberation the French had very little to say about the Jews. This silence conformed to the official Gaullist myth of the Resistance, according to which the French had collectively fought the Germans in one way or another despite the military defeat of May 1940. In this context any attention to the Jews risked raising the painful question of French complicity in the unspeakable crimes of their reputed enemies.

By 1968, however, the Jews had begun to come out of obscurity, and ever since they have increasingly attracted public attention. The Six-Day War, during which a significant contingent of French Jews defied the government's pro-Arab stance and supported Israel, thereby incurring the wrath of General de Gaulle, appears in retrospect to have been a turning point in the transition from silence to speech, invisibility to visibility. Nevertheless, as Henry Rousso has shown, the events of May 1968 were themselves decisive insofar as they provoked renewed attention to the Vichy period. During that fateful month, when demonstrators assaulted a host of national myths, the heroic story of the *Résistance* was one of the most conspicuous casualties. Indeed, fully toppling the Gaullist vision of France as the nation of resisters, protesters denounced the police, the servants and symbols of the Republic, as SS agents. Simultaneously and, I would like to suggest, not coincidentally, the women and men of May 1968 rallied around the German-Jewish radical Daniel Cohn-Bendit, and when he was deported for his subversive activities, demonstrators displayed their solidarity by shouting, "We are all German Jews!" This proclamation represented a dramatic display of empathy with the Jews, not only those of German nationality but implicitly others, including French Jews, who had been victimized by the Nazis. At the same time, this identification with the victim constituted an attack on the French state, which the demonstrators implicitly but unmistakably likened to the Third Reich.[1]

Soon thereafter, a regionalist movement in the provinces and increased immigration from the Third World—as well as the racist backlash that quickly followed—fueled a movement for *le droit à la différence*. Moreover, the 1970s and 1980s saw a dramatic decline in support for communism, which in France had allied itself with the most doctrinaire Jacobinism and, by extension, a proclaimed hostility to any "particularist" loyalties. By the time the Republic celebrated the bicentennial of the French Revolution in 1989, then, there were many groups, including Jews but also including Vendéen royalists, who found support for their opposition to the old revolutionary ideal of the indivisible nation. It would be pointless to speculate on the impact of discussions relating specifically to the Jews on the cases of other "others" and vice versa. No doubt the various proclamations of the right to be different fed off each other. As in the eighteenth and early nineteenth centuries, however, the Jews meant something that other markers of difference did not.

In particular, since 1968 the Jews have come to serve as living reminders of the *années noires* and, more specifically still, of French guilt during the war years. In much the same manner as the philosophes emphasized the persecution that Jews suffered at the hands of fanatical Christians by summoning the image of an auto-da-fé, French intellectuals and politicians have returned repeatedly to the Jews to indict the culture that made their extermination possible. Though this tendency began on the margins, with a younger generation accusing its more powerful elders, it has by now become the official policy of a state that seeks once and for all to atone for past crimes. Beginning in 1993, every July 16—just two days after Bastille Day—the French have observed an official holiday on the anniversary of the infamous 1942 roundup by French police of thousands of Jews for deportation to the death camps: the "National Day for commemorating racist and anti-Semitic persecutions committed under the de facto authority of the so-called 'government of the French State.'" This holiday exists despite a previously instituted "National Day" commemorating the wartime deportations in general, which is still observed on the last Sunday in May.[2]

In the July 16 commemoration one detects elements of a tradition that arguably goes back to the eighteenth century. In addition to the emphasis on the sufferings that Jews have endured, this holiday recalls certain revolutionary festivals denouncing the Old Regime and affirming a new commitment not so much to equality as to generosity. Specifically, there are echoes of the Night of August 4, when the nobles conspicuously denounced their privileged heritage. And more precisely, July 16 resembles the initial "emancipation" of the Jews between 1789 and 1791, when revolutionary lawmakers atoned for the fanaticism of prior generations and displayed their superior largesse by welcoming the Jews into the newly constituted French nation. Accordingly, if the movement to enfranchise propertied Jewish men in 1789 diverted attention from the larger groups—women, the poor, and people of color, enslaved or otherwise—who remained excluded from full citizenship, the national remorse at crimes against the Jews could easily obscure the fact that xenophobia and racist violence still mar the French landscape. Most important, the collective repudiation of anti-Semitism every July 16 is crucial to the formation of a French self-image as a tolerant people, a refuge for the oppressed and guardian of human rights, in much the same way as the Jewish "emancipation" over two centuries earlier enabled revolutionaries to articulate, celebrate, and sacralize their self-image as an indivisible and morally excellent nation.

There are without a doubt significant differences in how the Jews were depicted two centuries ago and how they are now viewed. Today, with the exception of the extreme Right, the French no longer express worries about whether Jews can be good citizens or whether they constitute a "nation within a nation." On the contrary, something like the opposite is now taking place. As Pierre Birnbaum has shown, French politicians have increasingly adopted the habit of referring to the Jews as a "community," a practice unthinkable a generation ago, when the Jacobin revulsion against particularism retained the status of ideological orthodoxy. Rather than ask the Jews to lose their presumed special fellow feeling for their coreligionists and embrace the indivisible French nation, they go out of their way to show that they cherish this "community."[3] A cynical explanation of this trend would suggest that politicians simply pander to whatever group they can reasonably expect to recruit for support, but such a strategy takes for granted the general acceptance of a pluralistic nation composed of "communities," and no one dared employ it until quite recently. It would appear that the right to be different has finally triumphed.

Yet this "right" can easily become an unwelcome duty, particularly if someone else is defining the difference in question. Already in 1980 the philosopher and public intellectual Alain Finkelkraut wrote that the allure of being "other" induced many Jews, including himself, to reverse the well-known maxim "A Jew within, a man without" to an ethos according to which "we're Jews without, for our friends, for the public, for the outside world, while within, in the intimacy of our daily lives, we're just like everybody else . . . without any cultural specificity all our own."[4] Finkelkraut laments the "emptiness" of this kind of Jewishness, but one does not have to long for some rich or "authentic" Jewish identity to worry about the imposed communitarianization of the Jews, which today is a far more widespread phenomenon than it was two decades ago.

This communitarianization is all the more troubling, it seems to me, insofar as it is based on the remorse of a self-proclaimed French nation in search of a validating self-image. To be sure, remorse is preferable to the denial of past crimes, and there is no question that the Gaullist silence regarding French complicity in the Holocaust was wrong. Now, however, the danger lies not in forgetting but in obsessive repetition. Whether and to what extent this talking cure might ease French consciences is debatable. What is more certain is that the process risks ghettoizing the Jews and, worse still, defining them principally as victims. And this victim status could easily become self-perpetuating. As Hannah Arendt observed, pity "has just as much vested interest in the existence of the unhappy as thirst for power has a vested interest in the existence of the weak," and even if the Jews are only *imagined* to be "unhappy," as collective victims of past crimes, their imagined separation from the rest of French society will remain pronounced.[5]

Despite the differences between the age of enlightenment and revolution on the one hand and the present day on the other, then, the similarities are noteworthy. Once again the Jews help non-Jews in France think about matters of fundamental importance to them. Above all, they assist in the articulation of what the French nation is: whether it is a tolerant and generous people, respectful of "the Rights of Man" and remorseful for past violations of them, and whether it can accommodate diversity. Furthermore the Jews again risk being defined by others and face the challenge of reclaiming control of the discourse that labels them. In this endeavor the strategies employed by the Jews of the past are instructive. In the past Jews denied the binary opposition between French (or enlightened) and Jewish values, insisting that what worthy Gentiles believed and practiced was little more than the recently discovered ethics that the Jews had long known. Today Jews might remind their Gentile compatriots that the pluralism and multiculturalism which seem poised to define Frenchness in the new millennium were familiar to the Jews of antiquity, and that the penchant for atonement which has come to characterize French political culture, however problematic it may be, is a feature of the culture that long ago invented Yom Kippur. Yet it is not sufficient simply to claim possession of values that otherwise appear to be new and French. Rather, it is necessary to insist in other ways as well that the dichotomy between the French and the Jews, now articulated as a distinction between the "nation" and the "community," is as specious today as it was in the eighteenth century. Indeed, even in 1789 the French nation was more of an ideal, a principle about which people could and did disagree—to the point of civil war—than a discrete entity. Revolutionary ideology, moreover, held in contradictory fashion that citizenship derived from universal human rights yet belonged only to those who proved exceptionally worthy of the "title." Nor were "the Jews" the solid and cohesive nation that Gentiles imagined them to be. Today they are even less so, for if the divisions between Sephardic and Ashkenazi, between rich and poor, existed two hundred years ago as they do today, the choices among varieties of Judaism, not to mention the options of agnosticism and atheism, were largely unavailable to the Jews of the eighteenth and early nineteenth centuries. As for the French nation today, the content of this idea is as volatile and contested as it ever was. Consequently, defining "others" will continue to be sought, and Jews, along with other fictitious "communities," will be impressed into the service of constructing Frenchness. They will also continue to be human beings, not merely abstract symbols whose meanings can be manipulated in a sort of identity mathematics, and in this respect they are quite different from the totems that in Lévi-Strauss's analysis are "good to think" but suffer no damage from being fetishized.

At the same time, there is reason to be optimistic. It is possible that the current trend toward pluralism and multiculturalism will continue to be a defining feature of political culture in France, and that consequently the habit of reifying the French people on the one hand and the Jews on the other will diminish, together with the tendency to oppose Frenchness to the qualities of other "others." At the moment this trend requires imagined others, and Jews in particular, to whom French citizens can show their generosity, atonement, and pity. Yet if it becomes normal rather than exceptional, traditional rather than revolutionary, then the tendency toward pluralism and multiculturalism itself will diminish the habit of reifying the distinctions: French/Jewish and French/ Other. As long as these distinctions are made, however, one must continue to protest that people are human beings first and something else insofar as they wish to be, and to insist on their being neither feared nor pitied but respected as equals.

Notes

INTRODUCTION

1. Yosef Hayim Yerushalmi, *Zakhor: Jewish History and Jewish Memory* (Seattle: University of Washington Press, 1982).

2. Maurice Halbwachs, *On Collective Memory,* edited, translated, and with an introduction by Lewis A. Coser (Chicago: University of Chicago Press, 1992), 60.

3. See, for example, Léon Kahn, *Les Juifs de Paris pendant la Révolution* (Paris, 1898).

4. I borrow this expression, which has come to indicate any history that seeks to validate a political tradition, from Sir Herbert Butterfield, *The Whig Interpretation of History* (London: G. Bell and Sons, 1931).

5. Robert Anchel, *Napoléon et les Juifs* (Paris: Presses Universitaires de France, 1928).

6. Arthur Hertzberg, *The French Enlightenment and the Jews* (New York: Columbia University Press, 1968), 10 and passim; and Simon Schwarzfuchs, *Napoleon, the Jews and the Sanhedrin* (London: Routledge and Kegan Paul, 1979).

7. The term *emancipation,* which came to describe the elimination of all legal distinctions between Jews and non-Jews only in the late 1820s, was borrowed from the movement for "Catholic Emancipation" in Great Britain. Jacob Katz, "The Term 'Jewish Emancipation': Its Origin and Historical Impact," in *Studies in Nineteenth-Century Jewish Intellectual History,* ed. Alexander Altman (Cambridge: Harvard University Press, 1964), 1–25. When I use *emancipa-*

tion, I am simply following convention rather than implying that the condition of Jews prior to the French Revolution was one of enslavement.

8. The seminal work in the historiographical reassessment of the French Revolution is François Furet, *Interpreting the French Revolution,* trans. Elborg Forster (Cambridge and Paris: Cambridge University Press and Maison des Sciences de l'Homme, 1981); Henry Rousso, *The Vichy Syndrome: History and Memory in France since 1944,* trans. Arthur Goldhammer (Cambridge: Harvard University Press, 1991); and Judith Friedlander, *Vilna on the Seine: Jewish Intellectuals in France since 1968* (New Haven, Conn.: Yale University Press, 1990), 38–64.

9. Shmuel Trigano, *La République et les Juifs après Copernic* (Paris: Presses D'Aujourd'hui, 1981), 36–83.

10. Patrick Girard, *La Révolution française et les Juifs* (Paris: Robert Laffont, 1989).

11. Robert Badinter, *Libres et égaux... l'émancipation des Juifs 1789–1791* (Paris: Fayard, 1989). The official voice of French Jewry is decidedly more in favor of "particularism" today than it was at the time of the bicentenary. On this change, see Michael Robert Shurkin, "Decolonization and the Renewal of French Judaism: Reflections on the Contemporary French Jewish Scene," *Jewish Social Studies* 6 (spring 2000): 156–76.

12. Furet, *Interpreting the French Revolution,* 17.

13. Roger Chartier, *The Cultural Origins of the French Revolution,* trans. Lydia G. Cochrane (Durham, N.C.: Duke University Press, 1991), 7.

14. On this historiographical subfield, see Lynn Hunt, ed., *The New Cultural History* (Berkeley and Los Angeles: University of California Press, 1989).

15. Michael André Bernstein, "Victims-in-Waiting: Backshadowing and the Representation of European Jewry," *New Literary History* 29 (fall 1998): 625–51.

16. Eugen Weber, "Reflections on the Jews in France," in *The Jews in Modern France,* ed. Frances Malino and Bernard Wasserstein (Hanover, N.H.: University Press of New England, 1985), 8, 16.

17. Stephen Greenblatt, *Marvelous Possessions: The Wonder of the New World* (Chicago: University of Chicago Press, 1991), 6–8.

18. The Project for American and French Research on the Treasury of the French Language (ARTFL) is a digitized library administered jointly by the Institut National de la Langue Française of the Centre National de la Recherche Scientifique and the Divisions of the Humanities and Social Sciences at the University of Chicago. It includes novels, plays, correspondence, memoirs, pamphlets, travel narratives, speeches, and poetry. Subjects include philosophy, history, economics, literary criticism, and the natural sciences.

19. Claude Lévi-Strauss, *Totemism,* trans. Rodney Needham (Boston: Beacon Press, 1963), 89.

20. On the debates over dechristianization, see Chartier, *The Cultural Origins of the French Revolution,* 92–110, 121–22.

21. Mona Ozouf, *Festivals and the French Revolution,* trans. Alan Sheridan (Cambridge: Harvard University Press, 1988), esp. 262–82.

22. Abbé Henri Grégoire, *Essai sur la régénération physique, morale et poli-*

tique des Juifs (Paris, 1789) [reprinted in *La Révolution française et l'émancipation des Juifs* (Paris: EdHis, 1968), vol. 3], 132. Cf. Paul Grunebaum-Ballin, "Grégoire convertisseur? ou la croyance au 'Retour d'Israël,' " *Revue des études juives* 121 (1962): 383–98.

23. Alexis de Tocqueville, *The Old Regime and the French Revolution,* trans. Stuart Gilbert (New York: Anchor Books, 1955), 10–13.

24. Zosa Szajkowski, "Judaica-Napoleonica: A Bibliography of Books, Pamphlets and Printed Documents, 1801–1815," in *Jews and the French Revolutions of 1789, 1830 and 1848* (New York: Ktav Publishing House, 1970), 972.

25. See chapter 4.

26. Jean-Étienne-Marie Portalis (minister of religion) to the Central Consistory of French Israelites, undated [1808 or 1809]. Archives Nationales, F 19 11031. The minutes of the Central Consistory first mention a specific request for a patriotic service on May 9, 1809. Archives of the Consistoire Central des Israélites Français, Paris, 1 B 1.

27. Robert Darnton, *The Great Cat Massacre and Other Episodes in French Cultural History* (New York: Vintage, 1984), 122.

28. Numerous letters between Jewish officials and both the grand master of ceremonies and the minister of religion between 1811 and 1815 indicate the failure of the Jews to secure the right of participation in imperial festivities. Archives Nationales, F 19 11031, and Archives of the Consistoire Central, 1 C 2.

29. Clifford Geertz, *The Interpretation of Cultures* (New York: Basic Books, 1973), 448.

30. Grégoire, *Essai,* 45.

CHAPTER 1

1. Elie Scheid, *Histoire des Juifs d'Alsace* (Paris, 1882), 148; Georges Weill, "L'Alsace," in *Histoire des Juifs en France,* ed. Bernhard Blumenkranz (Toulouse: Privat, 1972), 149–51, 163; and Arthur Hertzberg, *The French Enlightenment and the Jews* (New York: Columbia University Press, 1968), 115.

2. Jacqueline Rochette, *Histoire des Juifs d'Alsace des origines à la Révolution* (Paris: Librairie Lipschutz, 1938), 79–80; and Scheid, *Juifs d'Alsace,* 180, 188–98.

3. Weill, "L'Alsace," 150, 161, 174–78; Hertzberg, *French Enlightenment,* 113, 117–19; and Roland Marx, "La régénération économique des Juifs d'Alsace à l'époque révolutionnaire et napoléonienne," in *Lés Juifs et la Révolution Française,* ed. Bernhard Blumenkranz and Albert Soboul (Paris: Commission Française des Archives Juives, 1989),106–7.

4. Weill, "L'Alsace," 178.

5. Zosa Szajkowski, *Jews and the French Revolutions of 1789, 1830 and 1848* (New York: Ktav Publishing House, 1970) , 315–21; and Simon Schwarzfuchs, *Du Juif à l'Israélite: Histoire d'une mutation 1770–1870* (Paris: Fayard, 1989), 67–73.

6. Weill, "L'Alsace," 150, 168–72.

7. Scheid, *Juifs d'Alsace,* 152, 172, 199, 226.

8. [François Hell], *Observations d'un Alsacien sur l'affaire présente des Juifs*

d'Alsace (Frankfurt, 1779). On the "affair of the false receipts" see Szajkowski, *Jews and the French Revolutions,* 202–19; and Hertzberg, *French Enlightenment,* 120, 227, 287–88, 292, 314.

9. Scheid, *Juifs d'Alsace,* 152; and Rochette, *Juifs d'Alsace,* 70.

10. Françoise Job, *Les Juifs de Nancy* (Nancy: Presses Universitaires de Nancy, 1991), 21–25.

11. Ibid., 27–34, 40–43.

12. Ibid., 45–50.

13. Ibid., 63, 69.

14. Roger Clément, *La condition des Juifs de Metz dans l'Ancien Régime* (Paris: Imprimerie Henri Joure, 1903), 21–37, 107–12, 232–37, 239–43, 249–50, 254–57, 260–62, 268–70.

15. Ibid., 241, 260, 268.

16. Ibid., 38–40.

17. Ibid., 25–26, 28, 30, 32, 34, 49–51, 243–46, 262–68.

18. Ibid., 37, 60–64.

19. Robert Anchel, *Les Juifs de France: La roue de fortune* (Paris: Janin, 1946), 153–212.

20. Abraham Cahen, *Le rabbinat de Metz pendant la période française* (Paris, 1886).

21. Clément, *Condition des Juifs,* 67–76.

22. Frances Malino, "Competition and Confrontation: The Jews and the Parlement of Metz," in *Les Juifs au regard de l'Histoire: Mélanges en l'honneur de Bernhard Blumenkranz,* ed. Gilbert Dahan (Paris: Picard, 1985), 327–41.

23. Hertzberg, *French Enlightenment,* 164.

24. Jonathan I. Helfand, "The Symbiotic Relationship between French and German Jewry in the Age of Emancipation," *Leo Baeck Institute Year Book* 29 (1984): 331–50.

25. Clément, *Condition des Juifs,* 132 n; and Anchel, *Juifs de France,* 207.

26. Théophile Malvezin, *Histoire des Juifs à Bordeaux* (Bordeaux, 1875), 113–14.

27. Gérard Nahon, ed., *Les "nations" juives portugaises du sud-ouest de la France (1684–1791): Documents* (Paris: Centro Cultural Português, 1981), 32–35.

28. "Lettres Patentes du Roy, pour les Portugais des généralitez de Bordeaux et d'Auch," in Nahon, *"Nations" juives,* no. xii.

29. Frances Malino asserts that by the time of the Revolution "the Jews of Bordeaux had integrated themselves into the French community." They "had assimilated the French standards for acceptability (derived from the increasingly more secularized bourgeois world in which they were living)." Their religious practice was a "Judaism which was compatible with 18th century rationalism," and "one looks in vain . . . for indications of a profound religiosity and spirituality in the life of the [Portuguese] *nation.*" By contrast, "the Ashkenazic Jews of France . . . chose to remain culturally estranged from their environment, to dress and live in accordance with traditional Jewish practice." *The Sephardic Jews of Bordeaux: Assimilation and Emancipation in Revolutionary and Napoleonic France* (University: University of Alabama Press, 1978), 26, 25, 20.

30. Isaac de Pinto, *Apologie pour la nation juive, ou réflexions critiques sur le premier chapitre du VIIe tome des oeuvres de M. de Voltaire au sujet des Juifs. Par l'auteur de "l'Essai sur le luxe"* (Amsterdam, 1762).

31. *Adresse à l'Assemblée Nationale* (Paris, 1789) [reprinted in *La Révolution française et l'émancipation des juifs* (Paris: EdHis, 1968), vol. 5].

32. Hertzberg, *French Enlightenment*, 90, 112, 115–17, 130.

33. Malino, *Sephardic Jews*, 15, 8.

34. Malvézin, *Juifs à Bordeaux*, 173–74.

35. Szajkowski, *Jews and the French Revolutions*, 256.

36. "Lettres de naturalité et dispense pour les portugais appelez nouveaulx chrétiens," and "Arrêt du Conseil qui expulse quatrevingt-treize familles de Juifs de Guienne," in Nahon, *"Nations" juives*, nos. viii, i.

37. Francia de Beaufleury, *L'établissement des Juifs à Bordeaux et à Bayonne* (Paris: Year VIII; reprint, Bayonne: Les éditions Harriet, 1985), 46–51, 83.

38. "Privilès octroiés par le roy aulx Espaignolz et Portugais de la ville de Bourdeaux," and "Sauvegarde octorée par le roy aux Espaignols et Portugais de la ville de Bourdeaux," in Nahon, *"Nations" juives*, nos. ix, x.

39. Malvézin, *Juifs à Bordeaux*, 116.

40. Beaufleury, *L'établissement*, 22–23.

41. "Appendice II: Rapport sur les Juifs de Bordeaux (1733)," in *Le Registre des délibérations de la nation juive portugaise de Bordeaux (1711–1787)*, ed. Simon Schwarzfuchs (Paris: Centro Cultural Português, 1981), 599–605.

42. *Archives parlementaires de 1787 à 1860, recueil complet des débats législatifs et politiques des chambres françaises. Première série (1787–1799)*, ed. Jérôme Mavidal (Paris: 1867–1913), vol. 11, 520.

43. Schwarzfuchs, *Registre des délibérations*, nos. 74, 206, 234, 235, 241, 238, 285, 332, 339, 349, 350, 367, 417, 461, 462, 481, 494, 514.

44. Ibid., no. 279.

45. Henry Léon, *Histoire des Juifs de Bayonne* (Paris, 1893), 141–49.

46. For a cause célèbre involving the divorce of a Sephardic couple see "CLXXIe cause. Question d'état sur les mariages des Juifs. Le divorce est-il admis parmi eux?" *Causes célèbres, curieuses et intéressantes, de toutes les cours souveraines du royaume, avec les jugemens qui les ont décidées*, vol. 65 (Paris, 1780), 3–240.

47. Malvézin, *Histoire des Juifs*, 150; Beaufleury, *L'établissement*, 24; Malino, *Sephardic Jews*, 19.

48. Beaufleury, *L'établissement*, 32–33.

49. Malino, *Sephardic Jews*, 24.

50. Schwarzfuchs, *Registre des délibérations*, nos. 166, 533.

51. "Appendice II: Rapport sur les Juifs de Bordeaux (1733)," in Schwarzfuchs, *Registre des délibérations*, 599–605.

52. Armand Lunel, *Juifs du Languedoc, de la Provence et des États français du Pape* (Paris: Albin Michel, 1975), 46–48.

53. Pierre Charpenne, *Histoire des réunions temporaires d'Avignon et du comtat Venaissin à la France* (Paris, 1886), vol. 2, 69–220.

54. Malvézin, *Histoire des Juifs*, 184–92, 198–200, 207–12; and Beaufleury, *L'établissement*, 46–51, 83.

55. Léon Kahn, *Les Juifs de Paris au dix-huitième siècle d'après les archives de la Lieutenance générale de police à la Bastille* (Paris, 1894), 5–38, 72–73.

56. Abbé Emmanuel Joseph Sieyes, *Qu'est-ce que le tiers-état?* (1789; reprint, Paris: Société de l'histoire de la Révolution française, 1888), 31.

57. Gary Kates, "Jews into Frenchmen: Nationality and Representation in Revolutionary France," in *The French Revolution and the Birth of Modernity*, ed. Ferenc Fehér (Berkeley and Los Angeles: University of California Press, 1990), 109. Cf. Salo Baron, "Ghetto and Emancipation: Shall We Revise the Traditional View?" *Menorah Journal* 14 (June 1928): 515–26.

58. See, for example, "LVIIIe cause. Question d'état sur les Juifs de Metz," in *Causes célèbres*, vol. 23 (1776), 64–98. See also the discussion of this case in chapter 4.

59. Nahon, *"Nations" juives*, 32–35.

60. See, for example, Berr Isaac Berr, *Lettre du Sr. Berr-Isaac-Berr, négociant à Nancy, Juif, naturalisé en vertu des lettres-patentes du roi, enregistrées au parlement de Nancy, député des Juifs de la Lorraine; à Monseigneur l'évêque de Nancy, député à l'Assemblée nationale* (1790; reprint, Paris: EdHis, 1968) [EdHis, vol. 5].

61. "LVIIIe cause."

62. Baron, "Ghetto and Emancipation."

CHAPTER 2

1. For the argument that the Enlightenment was good for the Jews, see, for example, Heinrich Graetz, *Geschichte der Juden von den ältesten Zeiten bis auf die Gegenwart*, vol. 10, *Geschichte der Juden vom Beginn der Mendelssohn'schen Zeit (1750) bis auf die Gegenwart* (1870; reprint, Leipzig: Oskar Leiner, 1900), esp. 1–94, 119–250. For the claim that the Enlightenment was bad for the Jews, see Simon Dubnow, *Weltgeschichte des jüdischen Volkes von seinen Uranfängen bis zur Gegenwart*, vol. 7, *Die Geschichte des jüdischen Volkes in der Neuzeit: Die zweite Hälfte des XVII. und das XVIII. Jahrhundert* (Berlin: Jüdischer Verlag, 1928), esp. 404–11; and, more recently, Arthur Hertzberg, *The French Enlightenment and the Jews* (New York: Columbia University Press, 1968).

2. *Voltaire électronique* (Chadwyck-Healey, 1999), CD-ROM.

3. The ARTFL database suggests that eighteenth-century French authors were nearly seventy times more likely to mention Jews (2,352 hits) than Basques (32 hits).

4. Claude Lévi-Strauss, *Totemism*, trans. Rodney Needham (Boston: Beacon Press, 1963), 89.

5. Charles-Louis de Secondat, baron de Montesquieu, *Lettres persanes* (Amsterdam, 1721; reprint, Paris: F. Roches, 1929), letter 30, p. 69.

6. Ibid., letter 143, p. 163; letter 60, p. 128.

7. Ibid., letter 60, p. 127; letter 67, pp. 151–52.

8. Montesquieu, *De l'esprit des lois* (1755; reprint, Paris: Les Belles Lettres, 1958), bk. 26, chap. 7, p. 302.

9. Blaise Pascal, *Pensées sur la Religion* (1661; reprint, Paris: Luxembourg,

1952), §297, 317, pp. 190, 198; Jacques-Bénigne Bossuet, *Méditations sur l'Evangile* (1704; reprint, Paris: Vrin, 1966), 111; François de Salignac de la Mothe-Fénélon, *Sermons et entretiens,* in *Oeuvres,* vol. 17 (1706; reprint, Paris: Imprimerie de J.-A. Lebel, 1823), 298; and *Lettre à Louis XIV* (1694; reprint, Neuchatel: Ides et Calendes, 1961), 69.

10. Bossuet, *Méditations,* 267; and *Discours sur l'histoire universelle* (Paris: S. Mabre-Cramoisy, 1681), 294.

11. Montesquieu, *Lettres persanes,* letter 60, p. 127; and *Esprit des lois,* bk. 24, chap. 2, p. 267.

12. Montesquieu, *Lettres persanes,* letter 60, p. 128.

13. Montesquieu, *Esprit des lois,* bk. 25, chap. 13, pp. 279–82.

14. See, for example, Montesquieu, *Lettres persanes,* letter 78, p. 19; *Esprit des lois,* bk. 12, chap. 4, p. 113; bk. 21, chap. 20, p. 122; bk. 28, chap. 1, p. 34; bk. 28, chap. 7, p. 44.

15. Montesquieu, *Esprit des lois,* bk. 21, chap. 6, p. 83; chap. 20, pp. 121–22.

16. Ibid., bk. 25, chap. 13, p. 282.

17. Steve Larkin, *Correspondance entre Prosper marchand et le marquis d'Argens* (Oxford: Voltaire Foundation, 1984), 202–26, 230–34, 246–54; and Newell Richard Bush, *The Marquis d'Argens and His Philosophical Correspondence: A Critical Study of d'Argens' Lettres juives, Lettres cabalistiques and Lettres chinoises* (Ann Arbor, Mich.: Edwards Brothers, 1953), 234–35. The version analyzed in this chapter is *Lettres juives, ou Correspondance philosophique, historique & critique, Entre un Juif Voyageur à Paris, & ses Correspondans en divers endroits. Nouvelle édition augmentée de XX Nouvelles Lettres, de Quantité de Remarques, & de plusieurs Figures* (La Haye: Pierre Paupie, 1738).

18. Prosper Marchand to Jean-Baptiste de Boyer, marquis d'Argens, undated [March 1737], and Marchand to d'Argens, undated [March 1737], in Larkin, *Correspondance,* nos. 34, 37.

19. D'Argens to Marchand, undated [February 1737], in Larkin, *Correspondance,* no. 27.

20. D'Argens to Marchand, undated [November/December 1736], in Larkin, *Correspondance,* no. 20; and François-Marie Arouet de Voltaire to d'Argens, 20 January [1737], 28 January [1737], 2 February [1737], 22 June [1737], 2 October [1740], [c. 26 August 1751], [c. 28 August 1751], [?August 1752], [c. 20 August 1752], [?August/September 1752] [November/December 1752], in *Correspondence and Related Documents,* ed. Theodore Besterman (Toronto: University of Toronto Press, 1969), D1263, D1271, D1277, D1342, D2322, D4555, D4559, D4979, D4986, D5000, D5088.

21. *Le pour et contre,* vol. 3, tome 12, no. 176, pp. 313–14.

22. Dieudonné Thiébault, *Souvenirs de vingt ans de séjour à Berlin* (Paris, 1805; reprint, Paris: Firmin-Didot, 1891), vol. 2, 377. Cited in Bush, *Marquis d'Argens,* 16.

23. *Mémoires pour l'histoire des sciences & des beaux arts* (July 1736): 1349–62; and Aubert de La Chesnaye, *Correspondance historique, philosophique et critique entre Ariste, Lisandre et quelques autres amis. Pour servir de*

réponse aux Lettres juives (The Hague, 1737–38). I have seen only volumes 1 and 3 of this work.

24. Tzvetan Todorov, *On Human Diversity: Nationalism, Racism, and Exoticism in French Thought,* trans. Catherine Porter (Cambridge: Harvard University Press, 1993), 354.

25. D'Argens, *Lettres juives,* vol. 2, letter 45, p. 43; vol. 3, letter 110, pp. 268–73; vol. 5, letter 167, p. 107; vol. 5, letter 181, p. 369.

26. Ibid., vol. 1, letter 9, p. 79.

27. Ibid., vol. 1, letter 2, pp. 14–16. Emphasis added.

28. Ibid., vol. 4, letter 127, pp. 61–62.

29. Ibid., vol. 2, letter 44, pp. 29–36.

30. See, for example, Heinrich Graetz, "Voltaire und die Juden," *Monatsschrift für Geschichte und Wissenschaft des Judentums* 17 (1868): 161–74, 201–23; Hannah Emmrich, *Das Judentum bei Voltaire* (Breslau, 1930); Pierre Aubery, "Voltaire et les Juifs: Ironie et démystification," *Studies on Voltaire and the Eighteenth Century* 24 (1963): 67–79; Peter Gay, *Voltaire's Politics: The Poet as Realist* (Princeton, N.J., 1959; reprint, New Haven, Conn.: Yale University Press, 1988), 351–54; Gay, *The Party of Humanity: Essays in the French Enlightenment* (New York: Knopf, 1964), 103–8; Léon Poliakov, *Histoire de l'antisémitisme,* vol. 2, *L'âge de la science* (Paris: Calmann-Lévy, 1981), 31–40; and Hertzberg, *French Enlightenment,* passim.

31. Voltaire, *Essay sur l'histoire générale* (Geneva, 1756), 46, 286, 292–93, 343; "Le philosophe ignorant" (1766), in *Mélanges,* ed. J. Van Den Heuvel (Paris: Gallimard, 1961), 929; and Voltaire, "Traité sur la tolérance" (1763), in *Mélanges,* 635–36.

32. Voltaire, *Candide, ou l'optimisme* (1759; reprint, Paris: Hachette, 1913), 48. Cf. "L'histoire de Jenni" (1775), in H. Bénac, ed., *Romans et Contes* (Paris: Garnier, 1963), 497; *Histoire générale,* 178, 226; and *Précis du Siècle de Louis XV* (Geneva, 1770), 102.

33. Voltaire, "Sermon du rabbin Akib prononcé à Smyrne le 20 novembre 1761 (traduit de l'hébreu)" (1761), in *Oeuvres,* vol. 24, pp. 277–84.

34. Voltaire, *Dictionnaire philosophique* (1764; reprint, Paris: Garnier, 1954), 26, 179, 402.

35. Gay, *Voltaire's Politics,* 351–54; and *The Party of Humanity,* 103–8.

36. Voltaire, *Histoire générale,* 294; and *Dictionnaire philosophique,* 306–7.

37. Voltaire, "Sermon des cinquante" (1762), in *Oeuvres,* vol. 24, p. 438.

38. Theodore Besterman, ed., *Voltaire's Notebooks* (Geneva: Institut et Musée Voltaire, 1952), 31. Cited in Gay, *Voltaire's Politics,* 353; "Sermon du rabbin Akib," 282, 281; and *La bible enfin expliquée* (Geneva, 1756), 462. Cf. *Dîner du comte de Boulainvilliers,* in which one character refers ironically to "the holy Jewish church, our mother, whom we detest yet whom we always cite." In Van Den Heuvel, ed., *Mélanges,* 1232.

39. Voltaire, "Traité sur la tolérance," 635.

40. Voltaire, "Un chrétien contre six juifs ou réfutation d'un livre intitulé lettres de quelques juifs portugais, allemans, et polonais" (1776), in *Oeuvres,* vol. 29, p. 582. Voltaire was responding to Abbé Antoine Guénée, *Lettres de quel-*

ques Juifs portugais et allemands à M. de Voltaire, avec des réflexions critiques, &c., et un petit commentaire extrait d'un plus grand (Paris, 1769).

41. Voltaire, "Sermon du rabbin Akib," 284.

42. Voltaire, *La Henriade* (1714), in *Oeuvres,* vol. 8, 136.

43. Voltaire, "Lettres . . . sur Rabelais," 519; "Questions de Zapata traduites par le sieur Tamponet, docteur de Sorbonne" (1767), in *Oeuvres,* vol. 26, 173; and *Dictionnaire philosophique,* 305.

44. Voltaire, "La Religion Naturelle," in *Poëmes sur la religion naturelle et sur la destruction de Lisbonne* (Paris, 1756), 16; and "Sermon du rabbin Akib," 281.

45. Hertzberg, *French Enlightenment,* 306, 307.

46. Voltaire, *Candide,* 144–45.

47. Ibid., 208, 216.

48. Voltaire, *Dictionnaire philosophique,* in *Oeuvres,* vol. 19, pp. 524–25. Cf. Montesquieu, *Esprit des lois,* vol. 3, bk. 21, chap. 20.

49. Voltaire, *Histoire générale,* 292–93, 9.

50. Voltaire, "Un chrétien," 579.

51. Voltaire, "Lettres . . . sur Rabelais," 516–22.

52. Isaac Pinto, *Réflexions critiques sur le Ier chapitre du tome VIIe des Oeuvres de M. de Voltaire* (Amsterdam, 1762). This work is discussed in chapter 4.

53. Voltaire to Isaac Pinto, July 21, 1762, in *Correspondence and Related Documents,* D10600.

54. Rousseau, *Rousseau juge de Jean-Jacques* (1776; reprint, Paris: A. Colin, 1962), 186; *Émile, ou, de l'éducation* (1762), in *Oeuvres complètes,* vol. 4 (Paris: Gallimard, 1969), 621; *Lettres à M. d'Alembert* (1758; reprint: Geneva: Droz, 1948), 28; *Du contrat social* (1762; reprint, Geneva: C. Bourguin, 1947), 358.

55. Rousseau, *Lettre à C. de Beaumont* (Amsterdam, 1763), 79, 89–90; *Contrat social,* 359; and *Lettres écrites de la montagne* (1764), in *Oeuvres,* vol. 3 (Paris: Gallimard, 1964), 732–34, 799.

56. Rousseau, *Collection complète des oeuvres de J.-J. Rousseau* (Geneva, 1782–89), vol. 1, 422–23. I am grateful to David Bell for this reference.

57. Rousseau, *Contrat social,* 208–10.

58. Frank A. Kafker, in collaboration with Serena L. Kafker, *The Encyclopedists as Individuals: A Biographical Dictionary of the Authors of the Encyclopédie* (Oxford: Voltaire Foundation, 1988); and *The Encyclopedists as a Group: A Collective Biography of the Authors of the Encyclopédie* (Oxford: Voltaire Foundation, 1996), xv–xxv, 3–16.

59. *Encyclopédie, ou Dictionnaire raisonné des sciences, des arts et des métiers* (Paris, 1751–72), s.v., "Chaussure," 3:260.

60. *Encyclopédie,* s.v., "Cymbale," 4:594.

61. *Encyclopédie,* s.v., "Juif," 9:24, 25. The passage beginning, "Reduced to running . . ." is practically identical to one in Voltaire's "L'Opinion en alphabet" (1752), written fourteen years before the appearance of the *Encyclopédie* volume containing the article "Juif." Voltaire, *Oeuvres,* vol. 19, pp. 524–26.

62. *Encyclopédie,* s.v., "Croisades," 4:503; "Inquisition," 8:773; "Lois," 9:647; "Mets," 10:472; "Egra," 5:432. Jaucourt's treatment of Visigothic law appears to have been taken from Montesquieu, *Esprit des lois,* bk. 28, chap. 1, p. 34.

63. *Encyclopédie,* s.v., "Talmud," 15:869; "Orale, loi," 11:552; "Targum," 15:913; and "Pharisien," 12:491.

64. *Encyclopédie,* s.v., "Gemare," 7:544; "Enfer," 5:666; "Faune," 6:436; "Rabbin," 13:735–36; "Bibliothèque," 2:229; "Messie," 10:404; "Phylactère," 12:535; "Juifs, Philosophie des," 9:33; "Guéonim, ou Géhonim," 7:982; and "Cozri," 4:424.

65. *Encyclopédie,* s.v., "Juifs, Philosophie des," 9:25; "Judaïsme," 9:3; "Juif," 9:24; and "Nature," 11:42.

66. *Encyclopédie,* s.v., "Juifs, Philosophie des," 9:31–33.

67. *Encyclopédie,* s.v., "Caraites," 2:669–71.

68. *Encyclopédie,* s.v., "Usure," 17:542–45.

69. *Encyclopédie,* s.v., "Juif," 9:25.

70. *Encyclopédie,* s.v., "Londres," 9:683; "Livourne," 9:600; "Frankfort," 7:283; "Salonicki ou Salonichi," 14:577; "Pologne," 12:930; and "Mets," 10:472.

71. On the moral significance of transparency in Rousseau, see Jean Starobinski, *Jean-Jacques Rousseau: La transparence et l'obstacle, suivi de sept essais sur Rousseau* (Paris: Gallimard, 1970), 13–316. On the political implications of transparency, see Lynn Hunt, *Politics, Culture, and Class in the French Revolution* (Berkeley and Los Angeles: University of California Press, 1984), 44.

72. "Diderot, *The Definition of an Encyclopedia,*" in *The Old Regime and the French Revolution,* ed. Keith Michael Baker (Chicago: University of Chicago Press, 1987), 71, 88–89.

73. *Encyclopédie,* s.v., "Hébraique," 8:80.

CHAPTER 3

1. Zosa Szajkowski, *Jews and the French Revolutions of 1789, 1830 and 1848* (New York: Ktav Publishing House, 1970), 202–19.

2. Sarah Maza, *Private Lives and Public Affairs: The Causes Célèbres of Prerevolutionary France* (Berkeley and Los Angeles: University of California Press, 1993).

3. Arthur Hertzberg, *The French Enlightenment and the Jews* (New York: Columbia University Press, 1969), 287, 288.

4. [François-Joseph-Antoine Hell], *Observations d'un Alsacien sur l'affaire présente des Juifs d'Alsace* (Frankfurt, 1779), 14; Saint Augustine, *The City of God against the Pagans,* trans. William Chase Greene (Cambridge: Harvard University Press, 1960), vol. 6, bk. 18, chap. 46, pp. 46–51; Blaise Pascal, *Pensées sur la religion* (1662; reprint, Paris: Éditions du Luxembourg, 1952), § 311, p. 196; Voltaire, *Lettres philosophiques* (1734; reprint, Paris: Hachette, 1915–17), letter 25, pp. 184–226.

5. Hell, *Observations,* 16, 21–28, 38. On Voltaire's attitude toward persecution of the Jews and accusations of ritual crimes, see chapter 2.

6. Ibid., 33–38.

7. Ibid., 6, 7.

8. Ibid., 12.

9. On Rousseau's preoccupation with "unmasking" and "unveiling," see Jean Starobinski, *Jean-Jacques Rousseau: La transparence et l'obstacle, suivi de sept essais sur Rousseau* (Paris: Gallimard, 1970), 13–316.

10. *Observations, 13.*

11. Jean-Jacques Rousseau, *Du contrat social* (1762; reprint, Geneva: C. Bourquin, 1947), bk. 4, chaps. 1, 4.

12. Malesherbes, remonstrating on behalf of the *Cour des aides* in 1775, paired the two abuses of secrecy and despotism, writing, "This despotism of the administrators and, above all, this system of secrecy is what we must denounce to Your Majesty." "Remonstrance of the *Cour des aides* (6 May 1775)," in *The Old Regime and the French Revolution*, ed. Keith Michael Baker (Chicago: University of Chicago Press, 1987), 57–58.

13. Hell, *Observations,* 41–49.

14. Ibid., 61–64.

15. Patrice Higonnet, *Goodness beyond Virtue: Jacobins during the French Revolution* (Cambridge: Harvard University Press, 1998), 135–36.

16. On the republican meaning of transparency during the Revolution, see Lynn Hunt, *Politics, Culture, and Class in the French Revolution* (Berkeley and Los Angeles: University of California Press, 1984), 44.

17. Hell, *Observations,* 100–101. Cf. Abbé Emmanuel Joseph Sieyes, *Qu'est-ce que le tiers-état?* (1789; reprint, Paris: Société de l'histoire de la Révolution française, 1888), 31.

18. Sieyes, *Essai sur les privilèges* ([Paris], 1789). I am grateful to Sarah Maza for alerting me to the importance of this essay.

19. Hell, *Observations,* 100–101. Emphasis added.

20. Ibid., 38–39. Emphasis added.

21. Ibid., 123.

22. Jean Chrétien Ferdinand Hoefer, *Nouvelle biographie universelle depuis les temps les plus reculés jusqu'à nos jours, avec les renseignements bibliographiques et l'indication des sources à consulter* (Paris, 1852–66), vol. 29, pp. 846–47.

23. [Philippe-François de Latour-Foissac], *Le cri du citoyen contre les Juifs de Metz. Par un capitaine d'infanterie* (Lausanne [Metz], 1786), 3.

24. Ibid., 2, 3, 5, 6, 15, 19 n, 21. Cf. Deut. 7:6, 14:11, 23:19; Ps. 137:9.

25. Latour-Foissac, *Cri du citoyen,* 1, 2.

26. See chapter 2.

27. Latour-Foissac, *Cri du citoyen,* 2. Emphasis in the original.

28. Ibid., 1. Emphasis added.

29. Ibid., 8, 10, 11, 13. Emphasis added.

30. Ibid., 2, 4, 6, 13, 15, 19, 21, 24, 25, 26.

31. Ibid., 11.

32. Ibid., 7, 13.

33. Ibid., 24–26.

34. [Pierre-Louis Lacretelle], "LVIIIe cause. Question d'état sur les Juifs de

Metz," *Causes célèbres, curieuses et intéressantes, de toutes les cours souveraines du royaume, avec les jugemens qui les ont décidées*, vol. 23 (Paris, 1776),
64–98. On Lacretelle, see David A. Bell, *Lawyers and Citizens: The Making of
a Political Elite in Old Regime France* (New York: Oxford University Press,
1994), 164–67, 175–80.

35. Lacretelle, "Question d'état," 67, 70, 73.

36. Ibid., 74–75.

37. Ibid., 75–77, 81–82.

38. Ibid., 80, 87, 94, 95.

39. Ibid., 88–89.

40. Ibid., 96, 97. Emphasis added.

41. *Prix proposés, en 1788, par la Société royale des sciences et des arts de
Metz, pour les concours de 1789 et 1790* (Metz, 1788).

42. Thiéry, *Dissertation sur cette question: Est-il des moyens de rendre les
Juifs plus heureux et plus utiles en France? Ouvrage couronné par la Société
royale des sciences et des arts de Metz. Par M. Thiéry, Avocat au Parlement de
Nancy* (Paris, 1788) [reprinted in *La Révolution française et l'émancipation des
Juifs* (Paris: EdHis, 1968), vol. 2], 1–2, 23.

43. Sara Maza, "Luxury, Morality, and Social Change: Why There Was No
Middle-Class Consciousness in Prerevolutionary France," *Journal of Modern
History* 69 (June 1997): 216–21.

44. Thiéry, *Dissertation*, 22. Emphasis added.

45. Ibid., 2, 25–27.

46. Ibid., 29.

47. Ibid., 4–8, 13–14.

48. Ibid., 58–62.

49. Ibid., 20, 58–62, 90–94.

50. Ibid., 85–90.

51. Ibid., 84–85.

52. See chapter 5.

53. Thiéry, *Dissertation*, 80, 83.

54. Ibid., 71–76.

55. Abbé Henri Grégoire, *Essai sur la régénération physique, morale et politique des Juifs* (Paris, 1789) [reprinted in *La Révolution française et l'émancipation des Juifs* (Paris: EdHis, 1968), vol. 3], 16, 35–37, 75, 79, 84, 97, 150.

56. Ibid., 72–78. Emphasis added.

57. Ibid., 78–79. Grégoire wrote of Hell's pamphlet, "The author has been
contested on the truth of his inculpations, and I do not wish to reproach the Hebrews of today, as he does, for the death of the Savior. But has it been proved
that everything he wrote is false?" Ibid., 219 n.

58. Ibid., 73.

59. Ibid., 28, 65, 99, 100, 205 n–206 n.

60. Grégoire cited the epistolary novel in his endnotes. Ibid., 207 n.

61. Ibid., 16, 43–44, 71. Emphasis added.

62. Ibid., 1, 26, 85, 115.

63. Ibid., 1–13, 17–24, 43, 81–85, 124.

64. Ibid., 32–33, 101, 106, 113, 116.

65. Ibid., 110–12.

66. Ibid., 94, 97–98, 108, 168–69, 184–85.

67. Ibid., 95–96, 99. Emphasis added.

68. Ibid., 83, 111, 145–46, 168–70.

69. Ibid., 114–15.

70. Ibid., 117, 118.

71. Ibid., 120–23, 145–46, 163–64.

72. Ibid., 108, 160, 164–67, 186.

73. Ibid., 152, 153, 167–79.

74. Ibid., 147–50.

75. Ibid., 89, 111, 114, 122, 123, 150, 153, 160, 170, 171, 186.

76. Ibid., 108.

77. Ibid., 25–27.

78. Ibid., 69.

79. Ibid., 29–30.

80. Ibid., 29–30, 69, 98, 186, 189, 190.

81. Honore Gabriel Riquetti, comte de Mirabeau, *Sur Moses Mendelssohn, sur la réforme politique des Juifs: Et en particulier sur la révolution tentée en leur faveur en 1753 dans la grande Bretagne* (London, 1787) [reprinted in *La Révolution française et l'émancipation des Juifs* (Paris: EdHis, 1968), vol. 1], 19–23.

82. Ibid., 56.

83. Ibid., 55. Emphasis added.

84. Ibid., 31, 37, 39, 40, 55.

85. Ibid., 2, 57.

86. Ibid., 1.

87. Ibid., 59–61.

88. Ibid., 62, 63, 63 n.

89. Ibid., 62–64, 66.

90. Ibid., 68–69.

91. Ibid., 77.

92. Ibid., 81.

93. Ibid., 88–89.

94. Ibid., 65, 66, 88–89.

95. Dale Van Kley, "Church, State, and the Ideological Origins of the French Revolution: The Debate over the General Assembly of the Clergy in 1765," *Journal of Modern History* 51 (December 1979): 629–66.

96. Although Mirabeau and others lauded the *juif philosophe* Moses Mendelssohn, they were more impressed by his virtue than his rationality and argued for the creation of French Mendelssohns largely on patriotic grounds.

97. Montesquieu, *Lettres persanes,* letter 60, p. 127; and *Esprit des lois,* bk. 21, chaps. 6, 20, pp. 83, 121–22.

98. Voltaire, "Sermon des cinquante" (1762), in *Oeuvres,* vol. 24, p. 438.

99. Maza, "Luxury," esp. 216–23; and Colin Jones, "The Great Chain of Buying: Medical Advertisement, the Bourgeois Public Sphere, and the Origins of the French Revolution," *American Historical Review* 101 (February 1996): 13–40.

100. "Question d'état," 65; Mirabeau, *Sur Moses Mendelssohn,* 66; Grégoire reported that the Jews "are men like us . . . before they are Jews." *Essai,* 108.

101. Max Horkheimer and Theodor W. Adorno, *Dialectic of Enlightenment,* trans. John Cumming (New York: Continuum, 1972); Ronald Schechter, "Rationalizing the Enlightenment: Postmodernism and Theories of Anti-Semitism," *Historical Reflections/Réflexions historiques* 25 (summer 1999): 281–306.

102. Julia Douthwaite, "*Homo ferus:* Between Monster and Model," *Eighteenth-Century Life* 21 (May 1997): 176–202.

103. Mona Ozouf, *Festivals and the French Revolution,* trans. Alan Sheridan (Cambridge: Harvard University Press, 1988), 9.

104. Ozouf, *Festivals,* 9 and passim; cf. Ozouf, "La Révolution française et la formation de l'homme nouveau," in *L'homme régénéré: Essais sur la Révolution française* (Paris: Gallimard, 1989), 116–45.

105. Jean-François Lyotard, *The Postmodern Condition: A Report on Knowledge,* trans. Geoff Bennington and Brian Massumi (Minneapolis: University of Minnesota Press, 1984), xxiv.

106. Rita Hermon-Belot, "Préface" to Grégoire, *Essai sur la régénération physique, morale et politique des Juifs* (Paris: Flammarion, 1988), 27–30.

CHAPTER 4

1. I have adapted this term from Edward Said, who has profitably read postcolonial literature in "contrapuntal" relation to European writing on non-Europeans. *Culture and Imperialism* (New York: Knopf, 1994).

2. [Isaac Pinto], *Apologie pour la nation juive, où réflexions critiques sur le premier chapitre du VIIe tome des oeuvres de M. de Voltaire au sujet des Juifs. Par l'auteur de "l'Essai sur le luxe"* (Amsterdam, 1762); *Monthly Review* 28 (1763): 570; Pinto, *Réponse de l'auteur de l'Apologie de la Nation Juive à deux critiques, qui ont été faites de ce petit Ecrit, dans le Monthly Review, & dans la Bibliothèque des sciences & des arts; avec des lettres du même auteur tant à Mgr. le Maréchal Duc de Richelieu, qu'à Mr. de Voltaire, et leurs réponses* (The Hague, 1766).

3. Pinto, *Apologie,* 12–13.

4. Ibid., 15–16. Emphasis added.

5. Ibid., 19–20.

6. Ibid., 22–23, 27–29.

7. Ibid., 22–23, 45.

8. Ibid., 45–46. Emphasis, indicating Voltaire's formulation, in the original.

9. Arthur Hertzberg, *The French Enlightenment and the Jews* (New York: Columbia University Press, 1968), 55–56.

10. [Israel Bernard de Valabrègue], *Lettre ou réflexions d'un milord à son correspondant à Paris, au sujet de la requête des marchands des six-corps, contre l'admission des Juifs aux brevets* (London, 1767), 7–8.

11. Ibid., 8, 50–51, 70–71.

12. Ibid., 8–9, 20–21, 51.

13. Ibid., 41, 61–62.

14. Ibid., 69–70. Emphasis added.

15. Isaïah Berr Bing, *Lettre du Sr I. B. B. Juif de Metz, à l'auteur anonyme d'un écrit intitulé: Le cri du citoyen contre les Juifs* (Metz, 1787), 2.

16. Ibid., 3, 9.

17. Ibid., 7–11, 13, 18–19, 20–23.

18. Ibid., 49–50.

19. Ibid., 22–23.

20. Ibid., 22–25.

21. Ibid., 33–38.

22. Ibid., 33, 35 n–37 n, 40–44.

23. Ibid., 45–49, 52–53.

24. Ibid., 45, 53–54

25. Ibid., 29–30.

26. Zalkind Hourwitz, *Apologie des Juifs en réponse à la question: Est-il des moyens de rendre les Juifs plus heureux et plus utiles en France? Ouvrage couronné par la Société royale des arts et des sciences de Metz. Par Zalkind-Hourwitz, Juif polonois* (Paris, 1789). Facsimile reproduction in *La Révolution française et l'émancipation des Juifs* (Paris: EdHis, 1968), vol. 4.

27. Ibid., 6–8, 12, 13.

28. Ibid., 3 n, 10, 18 n, 26–27, 33–34, 42, 66.

29. Ibid., 54–56.

30. Ibid., 27, 27 n–28 n, 38, 61, 61 n, 62, 64 n–65 n, 66, 85, 85 n.

31. Ibid., 27 n–28 n, 62, 82. Emphasis in the original.

32. Ibid., 3 n, 12, 15.

33. Ibid., 15, 19–21, 26–27.

34. Ibid., 34 n, 35–36, 65, 70–71, 71 n, 73.

35. Ibid., 1–4.

36. Ibid., 36–41.

37. "Avis de Camus sur la demande de permis d'imprimer pour *L'Apologie des Juifs* de M. Zalkind Hourwitz, Juif polonais.—26 janvier 1789." Archives Nationales 0143 M 771, no. 15. Cited in Bernhard Blumenkranz, ed., *Documents modernes sur les Juifs: XVIe–XXe siècles*, vol. 1, *Dépôts parisiens* (Paris: Commission française des Archives juives, 1979), 239; Jacques Godard, *Discours prononcé, le 28 janvier 1790, par M. Godard, avocat au Parlement, l'un des représentans de la Commune, en présentant à l'assemblée générale de la Commune, une députation des Juifs de Paris. Imprimé par ordre de l'assemblée* ([Paris], 1790) [reprinted in *La Révolution française et l'émancipation des Juifs* (Paris: EdHis, 1968), vol. 5], 7–8; Zalkind Hourwitz to Malesherbes, no date. "Chartrier de Tocqueville. Papiers de Lamoignon. Correspondance reçue par Malesherbes." Dossier 136, no. 1–23. AN 1204 154 AP II (m), cited in Blumenkranz, *Documents modernes*, vol. 1, p. 368. For a thorough account of Hourwitz's career, see Frances Malino, *A Jew in the French Revolution: The Life of Zalkind Hourwitz* (Oxford: Blackwell, 1996).

38. See, for example, Edward Muir, *Civic Ritual in Renaissance Venice* (Princeton, N.J.: Princeton University Press, 1981); Robert Darnton, *The Great Cat Massacre and Other Episodes in French Cultural History* (New York: Vin-

tage, 1984), 107–43; and Mary Ryan, "The American Parade: Representations of the Nineteenth-Century Social Order," in *The New Cultural History,* ed. Lynn Hunt (Berkeley and Los Angeles: University of California Press, 1989), 131–53.

39. Zosa Szajkowski, *Franco-Judaica: An Analytical Bibliography of Books, Pamphlets, Decrees, Briefs and Other Printed Documents Pertaining to the Jews in France 1500–1788* (New York: American Academy for Jewish Research, 1962), 137; and Szajkowski, "Judaica-Napoleonica: A Bibliography of Books, Pamphlets and Printed Documents, 1801–1815," in *Jews and the French Revolutions of 1789, 1830 and 1848* (New York: Ktav Publishing House, 1970), 972.

40. Michèle Fogel, *Les Cérémonies de l'information dans la France du XVIe au milieu du XVIIIe siècle* (Paris: Fayard, 1989), 133–245.

41. Darnton, *Great Cat Massacre,* 122.

42. Jer. 29:7; Avot 3:2; Berakhot 58a; Baba Batra, chaps. 4–6. For examples of the weekly Sabbath prayer for the king of France, see Mardochée Venture, *Prières journalières à l'usage des Juifs portugais ou espagnols* (Nice, 1772), 321–22; and *Seder selichot mi-kol ha-shanah ke-minhag elzoz* [A book of penitential prayers for the whole year, according to the custom of Alsace] (Karlsruhe, 1769).

43. In an untranslated Hebrew manuscript discovered among the rabbi's papers, Lunel described Damiens as "an oppressor," an "insolent, errant enemy" who "walked on the path of darkness," thought "poisonous thoughts," and "with a two-edged sword in his hand" attacked the king. He expressed his outrage at the "haughtiness of heart," which moved Damiens "to strike at the pure body of the king as he was sitting with all the anointed princes in the palace of the king of France, the greatest of kings," and praised God for having given the assassin "weak hands," thus saving the monarch. He concluded by bidding his congregation, "Sing the praises and the glory of the one who saved the life of the king of France and overturned the haughtiness of the Belial [i.e., wicked man] who aimed to lift his hand against the well-beloved king Louis XV!" This full text of the prayer is reproduced in the Hebrew original in M. Lipschutz, "Notes et mélanges: Un poème hébraïque sur l'attentat de Damiens," *Revue des études juives* 84 (1927): 94–95.

44. [Jacob Athias], *Prière faite par les Juif[s] de Bordeaux, pour demander à Dieu le rétablissement de la santé du roy* [Bordeaux, 1744]; David Athias, *Priere faite par les Juifs portugais de Bordeaux, à l'occasion de l'attentat commis sur la personne sacrée du roi* (n.p., [1757]); Jacob Sarhy, *Prière faite par les Juifs avignonois de Bordeaux … à l'occasion de l'attentat affreux commis sur la personne sacrée de Sa Majesté* [Bordeaux, 1757]; [Samuel Hellmann], "Prière composée par le rabin de la communauté des Juifs de Metz, à l'occasion de l'exécrable attentat … sur la personne de Sa Majesté Loüis quinze," manuscript, C 57, Archives Départementales de la Moselle; Israel Bernard de Valabrègue, *Précis de la prière que les Juifs avignonois établis à Bordeaux, et ceux d'Avignon, actuellement à Paris, ont faite … pour obtenir de Dieu le rétablissement de la santé de Monseigneur le dauphin* (n.p., [1765]); [Néhémie Reicher], *Plaintes et lamentations sur la mort du Roi Louis XV, de glorieuse mémoire, ordonnées par les syndics de la communauté des Juifs de Lorraine* (Nancy, [1774]);

[Lion Asser], *Traduction d'une prière hébraïque, composée par le rabin des Juifs de Metz . . . pour le repos de l'âme de Louis XV* (Metz, [1774]); and Mardochée Venture, *Prière prononcée le premier mai 1774. Par les Juifs avignonois, et avignonois de Bordeaux, demeurant à Paris, à l'occasion de la maladie de Sa Majesté Louis XV le Bien-Aimé* (Paris, 1774).

45. [Jonathan Eibeschütz], *Compliment au roy fait par le rabin des Juifs de Metz* (Metz, 1744); [Lion Asser], *Traduction de la prière hébraïque, composée par le rabin des Juifs de Metz . . . pour obtenir de Dieu le rétablissement de la santé du Roi* (Metz, 1774); Juda David Crémieu and Moïse de Roque-Martine, *Prière faite par les Juifs du Comté-Venaissin, pour demander à Dieu, la guérison de Monseigneur le dauphin* (n.p., [1765]); and [Valabrègue], *Prière que les Juifs d'Avignon et de Bordeaux résidens à Paris, ont mise et chantée en hébreu, le jour du sacre de Louis XVI* [Paris, 1775].

46. [Jacques Baltus], *Journal de ce qui s'est fait à Metz, au passage de la reine. Avec un recueil de plusieurs pièces sur le même sujet* (Metz, 1725); Michel Goudchaux, Mayer Isaac Berr, and Mayer Max, *Prière publique ordonnée à l'occasion de la grossesse de la Reine, par les . . . sindics de la communauté des Juifs établis en Lorraine* (Nancy, 1778); and *Traduction des actions de grâces qui seront chantées cejourd'hui . . . , à l'occasion de l'heureuse délivrance de la reine . . . dans toutes les villes, villages de la province de Lorraine, où synagogue est établie* (Nancy, 1781).

47. Bernard de Valabrègue, *Odes prononcées par les Juifs d'Avignon et de Bordeaux résidants à Paris, dans leur assemblée, à l'occasion du sacre de Louis XVI, le 11 juin 1775* (Paris, 1775).

48. Francia de Beaufleury, *L'Etablissement des Juifs à Bordeaux et à Bayonne* (Year VIII; reprint, Bayonne: Éditions Harriet, 1985), 33; and [Eibeschütz], *Compliment au roy.*

49. *Traduction de la prière hébraïque, ajoutée par les Juifs de la synagogue de Metz aux Psaumes et prières particulières qu'ils font journellement pour l'heureux accouchement de la reine* [Metz, 1778]. Emphasis in the original. Cf. Ps. 2:1 and 48:7; [Isaïah Berr Bing], *Traduction de l'hymne ou cantique hébraïque, que les Juifs de Metz ont récité, et fait exécuter en musique dans leur synagogue, le 18 novembre 1781, jour des réjouissances faites pour la naissance de Monseigneur le dauphin* (Metz, [1781]); *Traduction des actions de grâces.* Cf. Exod. 14:21, "And Moses stretched out his hand over the sea; and the Lord caused the sea to go back by a strong east wind all the night, and made the sea dry land, and the waters were divided"; Juda-David Crémieu, *Lettre de félicitation de Crémieu, Juif de Carpentras au duc de Crillon au sujet de la prise de l'île et fort de Minorque* (n.p., [1782]).

50. [Hellmann], "Prière composée . . . à l'occasion de l'exécrable attentat"; Athias, *Priere . . . à l'occasion de l'attentat;* David Athias, *Actions de grâce rendues à Dieu, par les Juifs portugais de Bordeaux, le 20. janvier 1757. Pour le rétablissement de la santé du roy* (Bordeaux, 1757); Sarhy, *Prière . . . à l'occasion de l'attentat affreux;* and Sarhy, *Actions de graces que les Juifs avignonois de Bordeaux ont chantées le 23 janvier 1757, pour remercier l'Eternel d'avoir conservé la vie de Louis XV le Bien-Aimé* [Bordeaux, 1757].

51. [Jonathan Eibeschütz], *Délibération concluë dans l'assemblée générale*

*des syndics et communauté des Juifs de Metz, pour les prières publiques . . . ,
aux fins d'obtenir de Dieu le recouvrement de la santé de Sa Majesté* [Metz,
1744]; *Ode tirée de la prière faite par les Juifs portugais de Bordeaux, pour demander à Dieu le rétablissement de la santé du roy* (Paris, 1744); [Néhémie Reicher], *Prières ordonnées par les syndics de la communauté des Juifs de Lorraine . . . pour demander à Dieu le rétablissement de la santé du Roi* (Nancy, 1774); [Reicher], *Plaintes et lamentations;* [Asser], *Repos de l'âme de Louis XV;* and Juda-David Crémieu, *Discours composé en hébreu et traduit en français, par le Rabin Juda-David Crémieu l'aîné, de Carpentras, prononcé devant l'assemblée générale des Juifs, convoqués dans la synagogue de la même ville* (N.p., [1774]).

52. Jacob Athias, *Prière faite par les Juifs portugais de Bordeaux, pour obtenir de Dieu le rétablissement de la santé de Monseigneur le dauphin* (n.p., [1752]); Valabrègue, *Précis;* Crémieu and Roque-Martine, *Prière;* David Athias, "Priere que les Juifs portugais de Bordeaux ont faite, pour demander à Dieu le rétablissement de la santé de Monseigneur le dauphin," *Mercure de France,* January 1766, 82–87; and Athias, "Prière que les Juifs portugais ont faite à Bordeaux pour demander à Dieu le rétablissement de la santé de la reine," *Mercure de France,* May 1768, 41–4.

53. *Lettre circulaire des preposés généraux des Juifs d'Alsace aux rabbins de cette province, à l'occasion de la maladie du roi. Du 4 mai 1774* (n.p., [1774]); *Traduction de la prière hébraïque . . . pour l'heureux accouchement;* and *Traduction des actions de grâces.*

54. Athias, "La santé de Monseigneur le dauphin"; *Lettre circulaire;* Athias, *Prière pour l'heureuse délivrance;* and [Asser], *La santé du Roi.*

55. Athias, *Prière pour l'heureuse délivrance;* Goudchaux, Berr, and Max, *La grossesse de la Reine;* Athias, "La santé de Monseigneur le dauphin"; and [Asser], *La santé du Roi.*

56. [Eibeschütz], *Compliment au Roy; Traduction de la prière hébraïque . . . pour l'heureux accouchement;* Athias, "La santé de Monseigneur le dauphin"; "La santé de la Reine," and *Prière pour l'heureuse délivrance.*

57. The 1729 festivities were recorded in Hebrew by Salomon Libschütz, the *hazan* or cantor of the Jewish community, and subsequently translated into French in Abraham Cohen, "Une Fête nationale à Metz," *La vérité israélite* 8 (1862): 372–77. Contemporary accounts of festivities include [Baltus], *Passage de la reine;* and [Baltus], *Journal de ce qui s'est fait pour la réception du roy dans sa ville de Metz le 4. août 1744* (Metz, 1744); [Baltus], *Annales de Metz, depuis l'an 1724 inclusivement* (Metz, 1789); *Supplément aux affiches pour les Trois-Évêchés et la Lorraine (no. 48) du jeudi 30 novembre 1775;* Hourwitz, *Apologie,* 18 n; *Traduction du cantique hébraïque, exécuté en musique dans la synagogue des Juifs de Metz, pour l'arrivée de Monsieur frère du roi* (Metz, [1783]); *Détail des cérémonies qui ont été observées par les Juifs de la province d'Alsace, à l'occasion de la naissance de Monseigneur le dauphin* (Strasbourg, n.d.); Simon Schwarzfuchs, ed., *Le Régistre des délibérations de la nation juive portugaise de Bordeaux (1711–1787)* (Paris: Centro Cultural Portugês, 1981), nos. 495, 532.

58. Cohen, "Fête nationale"; Baltus, *La réception du roy; Annales de Metz;* and *Détail des cérémonies.*

59. Cohen, "Fête nationale"; Baltus, *La réception du roy; Annales de Metz; Détail des cérémonies;* and *Régistre des délibérations,* nos. 495, 532.

60. Cohen, "Fête nationale." On Abraham Lévy, see Archives Nationales, MC CX, 342. Cited in Blumenkranz, *Documents modernes,* vol. 1, 374–75.

61. Cohen, "Fête nationale"; Baltus, *La réception du roy; Annales de Metz; Détail des cérémonies;* and *Régistre des délibérations,* nos. 495, 532.

62. *Passage de la reine;* Cohen, "Fête nationale"; Baltus, *La réception du roy; Annales de Metz; Détail des cérémonies;* and *Régistre des délibérations,* nos. 495, 532.

63. Louis Urbain Aubert, Marquis de Tourny to Comte de Saint-Florentin, 10 September 1744; De Tourny to Saint-Florentin and D'Argenson, 19 August 1752; Saint-Florentin to de Tourny, 25 August 1752; D'Argenson to de Tourny, 12 September 1752; and de Tourny to D'Argenson, 23 September 1752. Archives Départementales de la Gironde, Bordeaux, C 18: nos. 99, 100, 101, 104 and C 1090 (folder, "Juifs. Culte et Religion 1735–1768"): nos. 117, 118, 124, 125.

64. André Bernheim, "Prière pour le Roi Louis XV," *Revue des études juives* 90 (1949–50): 95–96; E.Q.B., *Bibliothèque de la Reine Marie-Antoinette au chateau des Tuileries: Catalogue authentique publié d'après le manuscrit de la Bibliothèque Nationale* (Paris, 1884), 171; Athias, "La santé de Monseigneur le dauphin"; and "La santé de la Reine"

65. Cohen, "Fête nationale"; Szajkowski, *Franco-Judaica,* 139; and Hourwitz, *Apologie,* 18 n.

CHAPTER 5

1. For a positive assessment of the "emancipation," see, for example, Théodore Reinach, *Histoire des Israélites depuis l'époque de leur dispersion jusqu'à nos jours* (Paris: Librairie Hachette et Cie, 1884), 286–339; David Feuerwerker, *L'émancipation des Juifs en France, 1789–1860: De l'Ancien régime à la fin du Second Empire* (Paris: Albin Michel, 1976); and Robert Badinter, *Libres et égaux . . . l'émancipation de Juifs 1789–1791* (Paris: Fayard, 1989). For a negative assessment, see Shmuel Trigano, "From Individual to Collectivity: The Rebirth of the 'Jewish Nation' in France," in *The Jews in Modern France,* ed. Frances Malino and Bernard Wasserstein (Hanover, N.H.: University Press of New England, 1985), 245–81; Trigano, "The French Revolution and the Jews," *Modern Judaism* 10 (May 1990): 171–90; and Patrick Girard, *La Révolution française et les Juifs* (Paris: Robert Laffont, 1989). A full bibliography on the Jews and the French Revolution would take up many pages, but a useful list of some of the most prominent contributions is in Dominique Schnapper, "Les Juifs et la nation," in *Histoire politique des Juifs de France: Entre universalisme et particularisme,* ed. Pierre Birnbaum (Paris: Presses de la Fondation nationale des sciences politiques, 1990), 296–310.

2. *Archives parlementaires de 1787 à 1860, recueil complet des débats lég-*

islatifs et politiques des chambres françaises. Première série (1787–1799), ed. Jérôme Mavidal (Paris: 1867–1913), vol. 31, 372–73.

3. Ibid., vol. 10, 781–82; vol. 11, 364; and Feuerwerker, *Émancipation,* 380.

4. *Les Juifs d'Alsace doivent-ils être admis au droit de citoyens actifs? Lisez et Jugez* (n.p., 1790); and Charles Louis Victor, Prince de Broglie, *Opinion de M. le Prince de Broglie, député de Colmar, sur l'admission des Juifs à l'état civil* (n.p., n.d.).

5. *Archives parlementaires,* vol. 9, 203.

6. Feuerwerker, *Émancipation,* 431.

7. *Lisez et Jugez,* 143–44.

8. *Archives parlementaires,* vol. 31, 441–42.

9. On Jewish debts, see Zosa Szajkowski, *Jews and the French Revolutions of 1789, 1830 and 1848* (New York: Ktav Publishing House, 1970), 592–763. On the term *emancipation,* which was imported from the movement for "Catholic Emancipation" in Great Britain in the late 1820s, see Jacob Katz, "The Term 'Jewish Emancipation': Its Origin and Historical Impact," in *Studies in Nineteenth-Century Jewish Intellectual History,* ed. Alexander Altman (Cambridge: Harvard University Press, 1964), 1–25.

10. At least seventy polemical pamphlets from 1789 to 1791, not including broadsides, translations, duplicate editions, and foreign works, are listed in Szajkowski, *Jews and the French Revolutions,* 849–918. Fifty of the most important pamphlets are reproduced in volumes 5 through 8 of *La Révolution française et l'émancipation des Juifs* (Paris: EdHis 1968). Among the journals that followed the debates closely were the *Moniteur, Courrier de Versailles, Mercure de France, Gazette de Paris, Courier français, Annales patriotiques, Courrier de Provence, Point du Jour,* and *Révolutions de Paris.* Even Marat, who claimed that the discussion on Jewish rights was a waste of time, reported it nonetheless in *L'ami du peuple,* no. 76, December 24, 1789, 5–8, and no. 77, December 25, 1789, 2–3, 6–7.

11. *Archives parlementaires,* vol. 11, 710.

12. Gary Kates, "Jews into Frenchmen: Nationality and Representation in Revolutionary France," in *The French Revolution and the Birth of Modernity,* ed. Ferenc Fehér (Berkeley and Los Angeles: University of California Press, 1990), 109.

13. *Archives parlementaires,* vol. 9, 479, 600; vol. 10, 754–56. On the political alignments of La Rochefoucault, Liancourt, Clermont-Tonnerre, and Malouet, see Timothy Tackett, *Becoming a Revolutionary: The Deputies of the French National Assembly and the Emergence of a Revolutionary Culture (1789–1790)* (Princeton, N.J.: Princeton University Press, 1996), 247, 252.

14. Badinter, *Libres et égaux,* 202–3.

15. *Archives parlementaires,* vol. 10, 758.

16. *Nouvelle biographie universelle* (Paris, 1862–70), vol. 23, 839–40; and Gerlof D. Homan, *Jean François Rewbell: French Revolutionary, Patriot, and Director (1747–1807)* (The Hague: Martinus Nijhoff, 1971), 43.

17. [François-Joseph-Antoine Hell], *Observations d'un Alsacien sur l'affaire*

présente des Juifs d'Alsace (Frankfurt, 1779), 16, 119–120, 123; and *Archives parlementaires*, vol. 10, 777–78. Emphasis added.

18. *Motion en faveur des Juifs, par M. Grégoire, curé d'Embermenil, député de Nancy; précédée d'une notice historique, sur les persécutions qu'ils viennent d'essuyer en divers lieux, notamment en Alsace, et sur l'admission de leurs députés à la barre de l'Assemblée nationale* (Paris, 1789).

19. *Archives parlementaires*, vol. 10, 779.

20. Elena Russo has shown the striking similarity between Montesquieu's valorization of noble magnanimity, which she sees as indicative of a republican critique of "bourgeois economy," and the fascination of early twentieth-century anthropologists and literary critics with the potlatch ceremonies of "archaic societies." "Virtuous Economies: Modernity and Noble Expenditure from Montesquieu to Caillois," *Historical Reflections/Réflexions historiques* 25 (summer 1999): 251–78.

21. Frances Malino, *A Jew in the French Revolution: The Life of Zalkind Hourwitz* (Oxford: Blackwell, 1996), 239.

22. *Archives parlementaires*, vol. 10, 754–58; vol. 11, 364.

23. Jean Starobinski, *Jean-Jacques Rousseau: La transparence et l'obstacle, suivi de sept essais sur Rousseau* (Paris: Gallimard, 1970), 13–316. On the political significance of transparency during the Revolution, see Lynn Hunt, *Politics, Culture, and Class in the French Revolution* (Berkeley and Los Angeles: University of California Press, 1984), 44.

24. Kates, "Jews into Frenchmen," 109.

25. Sarah Maza, "Luxury, Morality and Social Change: Why There Was No Middle-Class Consciousness in Prerevolutionary France," *Journal of Modern History* 69 (June 1997): 199–229.

26. Mona Ozouf, *Festivals and the French Revolution*, trans. Alan Sheridan (Cambridge: Harvard University Press, 1988), esp. 262–82.

27. On the concept of *"l'homme nouveau"* see Mona Ozouf, "La Révolution française et la formation de l'homme nouveau," in *L'homme régénéré: Essais sur la Révolution française* (Paris: Gallimard, 1989), 116–45.

28. *Adresse présentée à l'Assemblée Nationale, le 26 Août 1789, par les Juifs résidans à Paris* [Paris, 1789], 2–4 [reprinted in *La Révolution Française et l'émancipation des Juifs* (Paris: EdHis 1968), vol. 5]. Future references to this collection will be indicated as EdHis.

29. Jean-Jacques Rousseau, *Du Contrat Social* (1762; reprint, Geneva: C. Bourquin, 1947), bk. 2, chap. 2, pp. 208–10; and Abbé Emmanuel Joseph Sieyes, *Qu'est-ce que le tiers-état?* (1789; reprint, Paris: Société de l'histoire de la Révolution française, 1888), 31.

30. *Adresse présentée à l'Assemblée Nationale, le 31 Août 1789, par les députés réunis des Juifs, établis à Metz, dans les Trois Evêchés, en Alsace & en Lorraine* (n.p., n.d.) [EdHis vol. 5]; Isaïah Berr Bing, *Mémoire particulier pour la communauté des Juifs établis à Metz, rédigé par Isaac Ber-Bing, l'un des membres de cette communauté* (1790) [EdHis vol. 5]; and *Pétition des Juifs établis en France, adressée à l'Assemblée Nationale, le 28 janvier 1790, sur l'ajournement du 24 décembre 1789* (Paris, 1790) [EdHis vol. 5].

31. *Lettre adressée à M. Grégoire, curé d'Emberménil, député de Nancy, par les députés de la Nation juive portugaise, de Bordeaux* (Paris, [1789]) [EdHis vol. 8]; and *Adresse à l'Assemblée Nationale* (Paris, 1789) [EdHis vol. 5], 1–2.

32. *Adresse présentée . . . le 31 Août 1789*, 13–14; and *Mémoire pour les Juifs de Lunéville et de Sarguemines* (n.p., [1789]) [EdHis vol. 5], 8, 5. In February 1790 the dissenting Jews of Lorraine omitted the request for corporate independence and asked to be included in the Assembly's deliberations on the Ashkenazi Jews of Paris. *Nouveau mémoire pour les Juifs de Lunéville & de Sarguemines; Présenté à l'Assemblée Nationale, le 26 février 1790* (Paris, 1790) [EdHis vol. 5].

33. *Adresse présentée . . . le 31 Août 1789*, 2, 9; *Lettre adressée à M. Grégoire*, 2–3; *Adresse à l'Assemblée Nationale*; and *Adresse présentée à l'Assemblée Nationale*, 6, 5.

34. "What is a nation? A body of associates living under a *common* law and represented by the same legislature." Sieyes, *Qu'est-ce que le tiers-état?* 31.

35. Joan Scott, "French Feminists and the Rights of 'Man': Olympe de Gouge's Declarations," *History Workshop Journal* 28 (autumn 1989): 1–21; and Scott, *Only Paradoxes to Offer: French Feminists and the Rights of Man* (Cambridge: Harvard University Press, 1996), 19–56.

36. *Adresse présentée . . . le 26 Août 1789*, 4, 6; *Adresse présentée . . . le 31 Août 1789*, 13–15; *Nouveau mémoire pour les Juifs de Lunéville & de Sarguemines*, 3, 5, 7; *Adresse à l'Assemblée Nationale*, 4; *Pétition des Juifs établis en France*, 11, 14; *Adresse des Juifs alsaciens au peuple d'Alsace* (n.p., n.d.) [EdHis vol. 5], 3; and *Pétition des Juifs établis en France*, 92–93.

37. *Reponse des Juifs de la province de Lorraine à l'adresse présentée à l'Assemblée Nationale, par la Commune toute entière de la ville de Strasbourg, 24 juillet 1789* (n.p., [1789]), 5; *Adresse des Juifs alsaciens*, 3; and *Adresse présentée . . . le 31 Août 1789*, 8.

38. Isaïah Berr Bing, *Lettre du Sr I. B. B. Juif de Metz, à l'auteur anonyme d'un écrit intitulé: Le cri du citoyen contre les Juifs* (Metz, 1787) [EdHis vol. 8], 20–23; Bing, *Mémoire particulier*, 14–15 and 15 n; and *Pétition des Juifs établis en France*, 52–55.

39. *Pétition des Juifs établis en France*, 73–74, 75–76.

40. Bing, *Mémoire particulier*, 9–10.

41. *Adresse présentée . . . le 31 Août 1789*, 11; *Réponse des Juifs . . . de Lorraine*, 20; and *Pétition des Juifs établis en France*, 57. Emphasis in the original.

42. *Lettre adressée à M. Grégoire*, 3; *Adresse à l'Assemblée Nationale*, 3, 7–8; *Adresse présentée à l'Assemblée nationale, par les Juifs domiciliés à Paris* (Paris, 1791), 1; *Nouvelle Adresse des Juifs à l'Assemblée Nationale, 31 Décembre 1789* (Paris, 1789), 1–2; *Lettre d'un citoyen, aux Gardes-citoyens de la ville de Nancy, en réponse de cette question: Les Juifs doivent-ils être admis dans la Milice Nationale?* [Nancy, 1790]; and [Jacob Berr], *Réflexions sur Lettre d'un citoyen, aux Gardes-citoyens de la ville de Nancy, en réponse de cette question: Les Juifs doivent-ils être admis dans la Milice Nationale?* [Nancy, 1790].

43. Feuerwerker, *Émancipation des Juifs*, 302 n; *Nouveau mémoire pour les Juifs de Lunéville & de Sarguemines*, 5–6; *Adresse à l'Assemblée Nationale*, 8.

On the "epidemic of silver-buckle removal," see Simon Schama, *Citizens: A Chronicle of the French Revolution* (New York: Knopf, 1989), 441.

44. Schama, *Citizens*, 439–41.

45. *Archives parlementaires*, vol. 17, 218–19.

46. Bing, *Mémoire particulier*, 17, 25–26. Cf. Abbé Henri Grégoire, *Essai sur la régénération physique, morale et politique des Juifs* (Paris, 1789) [EdHis vol. 3], 82.

47. *Pétition des Juifs établis en France*, 23–24.

48. See chapter 2.

49. *Pétition des Juifs établis en France*, 23.

50. Ibid., 27–30. Cf. Grégoire, *Essai sur la régénération*, 54–64.

51. Hannah Arendt, *The Origins of Totalitarianism* (New York: Harcourt Brace Jovanovich, 1973), 17–18.

52. François Furet, *Interpreting the French Revolution* (Cambridge and Paris: Cambridge University Press and Maison des sciences de l'homme, 1981).

53. Joan Scott's work is an exception to this rule. "French Feminists," and *Only Paradoxes to Offer*.

54. Clifford Geertz, *The Interpretation of Cultures* (New York: Basic Books, 1973), 448.

55. The full title is *Beschreibung von der Veränderung, oder Aufruhr in Frankreich, was man nennt Revolution von Paris die Kapital, auch die Versammlung die [sic] Deputierte aus dem ganzen Königreich. Diese Versammlung nennt man Etats-Généraux* [Description of the Change, or Uprising in France, which is called Revolution of Paris the Capital, also the Assembly of Deputies from the whole Kingdom. This Assembly is called Etats-Généraux] (Metz, 1789). In transliteration I have used standard German and French spelling. The following remarks are based on the original text reproduced in *Le journal révolutionnaire d'Abraham Spire*, ed. and trans. Simon Schwarzfuchs (Paris: Verdier, 1989). For historical background on the text and its author, see the introduction by Schwarzfuchs, pp. 7–17. The *Zeitung* is also reproduced in *Le journal révolutionnaire* and translated by Schwarzfuchs. As with the *Beschreibung*, I have relied on the original text, though I have followed the editor's helpful dating of the issues according to the Gregorian calendar.

56. Benedict Anderson, *Imagined Communities: Reflections on the Origin and Spread of Nationalism* (London: Verso, 1983).

57. *Beschreibung*, 2 n, 11 n, 21 n, 19 n, 48 n, 52 n.

58. Ibid., 4, 5, 12.

59. Ibid., 30.

60. Ibid., 16 n, 51, 56, 61, 63, 72.

61. Ibid., 67, 85.

62. Ibid., 96, 108–9; *Zeitung*, November 22–27, 1789; December 13–18, 1789; December 27, 1789–January 1, 1790; January 24–29, 1790.

63. *Beschreibung*, 95, 100, 107–8.

64. *Zeitung*, January 31–February 5, 1790.

65. *Zeitung*, January 31-February 5, 1790.

66. *Archives parlementaires*, vol. 11, 364.

67. *Zeitung*, January 31–February 5, 1790.

68. *Zeitung*, February 7–12; February 14–19, 1790.

69. Heinrich Graetz, *Geschichte der Juden von den ältesten Zeiten bis auf die Gegenwart*, vol. 11, *Geschichte der Juden vom Beginn der Mendelssohn'-schen Zeit (1750) bis in die neueste Zeit (1848)* (1876; Leipzig: Oskar Leiner, 1900), 135–36, 198, 225; and Joseph Klausner, *Historiah shel ha-sifrut ha-ivrit ha-chadashah* [History of Modern Hebrew Literature], vol. 1 (Jerusalem, 1952), 321.

70. Jonathan I. Helfand, "The Symbiotic Relationship between French and German Jewry in the Age of Emancipation," *Leo Baeck Institute Year Book* 29 (1984): 331–50.

71. Isa 5:1–7. Cf. Prov. 29:4, "By justice a king gives stability to the land"; and Prov. 20:28, "His throne is supported by righteousness."

72. Cf. Ps. 85:11, "In our land shall righteousness and truth meet."

73. Voltaire, "Lettres à s. a. mgr le prince de ***** sur Rabelais et sur d'autres auteurs accusés d'avoir mal parlé de la religion chrétienne" (1767), in *Oeuvres*, vol. 26, p. 515.

74. Judg. 6:28.

75. Isa. 63:4; Job 28:25–26.

76. Ps. 89:38; Deut. 11:21.

77. [Moïse Ensheim], *La-Menatseach shir le-Moshe Ensheim hushar be-yom gavra yad yoshve erets moledetenu al kol oyevenu mesaviv* [A song to the precentor by Moïse Ensheim, sung on the day when the hand of the inhabitants of our fatherland prevailed over all the surrounding enemies] (Metz, 1792).

78. *Procès-Verbal dressé par les Représentans de la Commune, de la fête célébrée à Metz, en réjouissance du succès des Armées de la République en Savoie. Du 21 octobre 1792, l'an premier de la République* (Metz, 1792). "This canticle . . . sung on 21 October [1792] in the synagogue of Metz, to the tune of the 'Marseillaise,' manifests, with regard to the content, the political exaltation of the time." *Archives israélites* 1 (1840): 35. I have discussed the text and the festival at which it was sung at greater length in my "Translating the 'Marseillaise': Biblical Republicanism and the Emancipation of Jews in Revolutionary France," *Past and Present* 143 (May 1994): 108–35.

79. Isa. 21:9.

80. Isa. 14:4.

81. Judg. 5:9; Zech. 13:4; Prov. 26:28.

82. *Cantique composée par le Citoyen Moyse Ensheim, à l'occasion de la fête civique célébrée à Metz, le 21 octobre, l'an 1er de la République, dans le temple des citoyens israélites*, trans. Isaïah Berr Bing (Metz, 1792).

83. Cf. Horace, "Exegi monumentum aere perennius," *Odes*, III, 30. I am grateful to Juliet Vale for pointing out this allusion.

84. Arendt, *Origins of Totalitarianism*, 8, 23.

CHAPTER 6

1. Robert Anchel, *Napoléon et les Juifs* (Paris: Presses Universitaires de France, 1928), 42–61.

2. Diogène Tama, *Collection des actes de l'assemblée des Israélites de France et du royaume d'Italie, convoquée à Paris par décret de Sa Majesté impériale et royale, du 30 mai 1806* (Paris and Strasbourg, 1807), 107–9.

3. *Detail officiel de tout ce qui s'est passé à la première et deuxieme séances de l'Assemblée des Juifs* (Paris, 1806); and Tama, *Collection des actes*, 132–33.

4. *Discours de MM. Les Commissaires de S.M. Impériale et Royale, prononcé à l'Assemblée des Français professant le culte de Moïse, dans la séance du 18 septembre* [Paris, 1806]; and Tama, *Collection des actes*, 237–40.

5. Tama, *Collection des procès-verbaux et décisions du Grand Sanhédrin, convoqué à Paris, par ordre de Sa Majesté L'Empereur et Roi, dans les mois de février et mars 1807: Publiée par M. Diogène Tama* (Paris, 1807; reprint, Paris: Commission française des Archives juives, 1979), 96.

6. Robert Anchel criticized Napoleon's "regime of oppression" over the Jews in his *Napoléon et les Juifs*. Simon Schwarzfuchs similarly condemned Napoleon's Jewish policy in his *Napoleon, the Jews and the Sanhedrin* (London: Routledge and Kegan Paul, 1979). Simon Dubnow criticized both the emperor and the Jews, whom he considered obsequious. *Weltgeschichte des jüdischen Volkes, von seinen Uranfängen bis zur Gegenwart*, trans. from the Russian by Dr. A. Steinberg, vol. 8, *Die neueste Geschichte des jüdischen Volkes: Das Zeitalter der ersten Emanzipation (1789–1815)* (Berlin: Jüdischer Verlag, 1928), 141–57. Ironically, Dubnow's assessment mirrored that of the anti-Semite Albert Lemoine in his *Napoléon Ier et les Juifs* (Paris, 1900). For an apologetic assessment of Napoleon's Jewish policy, see François Pietri, *Napoléon et les Israélites* (Paris: Berger-Levrault, 1965).

7. See, for example, Anchel, *Napoléon*, 75–86; Schwarzfuchs, *Napoleon*, 45; and Jacob Katz, *Out of the Ghetto: The Social Background of Jewish Emancipation, 1770–1870* (Cambridge: Harvard University Press, 1973), 140.

8. Anchel, *Napoléon*, 87, 252–352; Schwarzfuchs, *Napoleon*, 45, 48, 123–27.

9. François de Chateaubriand, *Mémoires d'Outre-Tombe*, vol. 2 (Paris: Flammarion, 1948), 381.

10. Baruch Mevorach, ed., *Napoleon u-tekufato* [Napoleon and his age] (Jerusalem: Sifriat Dorot, 1968), 17–36.

11. Ibid., 17.

12. François (Commissioner of the Department of the Nord) to Merlin (Member of the Directory), 10 Ventôse Year VII (February 28, 1799), AF III 21 bis, folder 70, Archives Nationales, Paris.

13. *Moniteur Universel*, 3 Prairial Year VII (May 22, 1799).

14. Franz Kobler has argued that the "proclamation" was authentic and that Napoleon indeed intended to reestablish Jerusalem for the Jews. *Napoleon and the Jews* (New York: Masada Press, 1975). Simon Schwarzfuchs has persuasively shown that the document to which Kobler refers was a forgery, yet he maintains that a "legend" was "created, and accepted in Europe, that many North African Jewish soldiers had joined Bonaparte's army." *Napoleon*, 25–27.

15. Anchel, *Napoléon*, 221–22; Schwarzfuchs, *Napoleon*, 166, 174–75.

16. *Discours de MM. Les Commissaires*; and Tama, *Collection des actes*, 237.

17. *Détail officiel;* and Tama, *Collection des actes,* 107–8, 131.

18. Tama, *Collection des actes,* 107. Cf. Jean-Jacques Rousseau, *Du contrat social* (1762; reprint, Geneva: C. Bourquin, 1947), bk. 2, chap. 7: "Il faudroit des dieux pour donner des loix aux hommes."

19. On Rousseau see chapter 2. Cf. Claude Emmanuel Joseph Pierre, marquis de Pastoret, *Moyse, consideré comme législateur et comme moraliste* (Paris, 1788).

20. Tama's *Collection des actes* originally appeared in twelve issues available to subscribers under the title *Collection des écrits et des actes relatifs au dernier état des individus professant la religion hébraïque.* Tama refers to the wishes of his *"souscripteurs"* in *Collection des actes,* 153.

21. Tama, *Collection des actes,* 109.

22. *Détail officiel;* and Tama, *Collection des actes,* 133, 131.

23. *Discours de MM. Les Commissaires;* and Tama, *Collection des actes,* 238.

24. *Détail officiel;* and Tama, *Collection des actes,* 132. Emphasis added.

25. Edward Said, *Orientalism* (New York: Vintage, 1978), esp. 229–30.

26. Tama, *Collection des actes,* 108, 237; and Tama, *Collection des procès-verbaux,* 37. Emphasis added.

27. *Détail officiel; Discours de MM. Les Commissaires;* and Tama, *Collection des actes,* 130, 239. Emphasis added.

28. François-Louis Couché, *Napoléon le Grand rétablit le culte des Israélites, le 30 mai 1806* (Paris, [1806]).

29. Ibid.

30. Zosa Szajkowski, "Judaica-Napoleonica: A Bibliography of Books, Pamphlets and Printed Documents, 1801–1815," in *Jews and the French Revolutions of 1789, 1830 and 1848* (New York: Ktav Publishing House, 1970), 971–1016.

31. Lazar Hirsch, *Rede des Bürgers Lazar Hirsch, Rabbiners in Hagenau, gehalten den verflossenen 18. Ventose 12, bey Gelegenheit des Dankfestes, welches die jüdische Gemeinde, für die Erhaltung des theuren Lebens des Ersten Konsuls Bonaparte, in der dasigen Synagoge beging* (Strasbourg, [1804]); and David Sintzheim, *Sermon prononcé dans la grande synagogue à Strasbourg, le 2 brumaire an 14 pour célébrer les glorieuses victoires de S.M., l'Empereur des Français* (Strasbourg, [1805]).

32. *Ode en actions de grâces sur la découverte d'une conspiration contre le gouvernement français, et la vie du Premier Consul; pour être chantée dans la synagogue des Juifs de Metz, vendredi 18 ventôse, à cinq heures du soir* (Metz, 1804); and Tama, *Collection des actes,* 217. Cf. Ps. 45:8.

33. Abraham de Cologna, *Discours prononcé le 23 mai 1813, à l'occasion des actions de grâces rendues à l'Eternel, pour la grande victoire remportée par l'armée française au camp de Lützen* (Paris, 1813); S. Sègre, *Discours prononcé dans le temple de la rue Ste-Avoye, le dimanche 25 décembre 1808, lors de la célébration de la fête de la réddition de la ville de Madrid* (Paris, 1808); Tama, *Collection des actes,* 207; and Lazare Chailly, "Ouverture de la fête religieuse célébrée par les français du culte judaïque, à l'occasion du couronnement de Napoléon," in *Fête religieuse célébrée à Paris, le 10 pluviôse an XIII, par les*

français du culte judaïque, à l'occasion du couronnement de Napoléon (Paris, Year XIII [1805]).

34. Tama, *Collection des actes,* 160–61.

35. Jacob Mayer, *Ode pour célébrer le jour immortel de l'élévation de Sa Majesté Napoléon à la dignité impériale* (Paris, Year XII [1804]).

36. *Discours prononcé par le rabin du consistoire de Nancy, le 15 août 1809, jour de l'anniversaire de la fête de Sa Majesté l'Empereur et Roi* (n.p., n.d). Cf. Isa. 9:4, "For every boot stamped with fierceness, / And every cloak rolled in blood, / Shall be for burning, for fuel of fire"; Isa 9:1, "The people that walked in darkness / Have seen a great light; / They that dwelt in the land of the shadow of death, / Upon them hath the light shined"; and Isa. 9:6, "And dominion shall be upon his shoulder, and his name shall be called . . . Everlasting Father."

37. *Détail officiel;* Tama, *Collection des actes,* 131, 135, 147, 277, 266; Tama, *Collection des procès-verbaux,* 19, 11.

38. Lipman Cerfberr, *Discours pour l'ouverture de l'Assemblée générale des Juifs, prononcé le 26 juillet 1806* (Paris, 1806); Abraham de Cologna, *Discorso pronunziato nella grande sinagoga di Parigi, all'occasione dell'apertura del Gran Sanedrin* (Paris, 1807).

39. David Sintzheim, *Discours prononcé par M. le Grand Rabbin D. Sintzheim, président du Consistoire central des Israélites, à Paris; dans le temple de la rue Ste.-Avoye, aujourd'hui 4 décembre 1808, anniversaire du jour du couronnement de S. M. I. et R.* (Paris, 1808); Abraham de Cologna, *Discours prononcé par Mr. Abraham Cologna, membre du collège électoral des savans du royaume d'Italie, Grand-Rabbin du Consistoire central des Israélites, le 13 mai 1809, dans le temple de la rue Ste.-Avoie, à l'occasion des victoires remportées par l'armée française aux champs de Tann, Eckmühl, Ratisbonne, etc.* (Paris, [1809]); and Bernard Zay, *Hymne pour célébrer solennellement le jour immortel du couronnement de Sa Majesté Napoléon* (Metz, 1805).

40. Tama, *Collection des actes,* 154. Furtado similarly described Napoleon as the "common father of all his subjects" and claimed, "Whatever religion they profess, he only sees in them all the members of a single family." Tama, *Collection des actes,* 136.

41. Abbé Henri Grégoire, *Essai sur la régénération physique, morale et politique des Juifs* (Paris, 1789) [reprinted in *La Révolution française et l'émancipation des Juifs* (Paris: EdHis, 1968), vol. 3], 194.

42. [David Sintzheim], *Discours prononcé par le chef du Grand Sanhédrin à la clôture des séances* (Paris, [1807]); and Tama, *Collection des procès-verbaux,* 130.

43. Tama, *Collection des actes,* 143–44.

44. Tama, *Collection des procès-verbaux,* 78, 95; and Tama, *Collection des actes,* 183, 234, 245.

45. Tama, *Collection des actes,* 152, 155; and Tama, *Collection des procès-verbaux,* 54.

46. See chapter 2.

47. *Délibération du conseil général du département du Bas-Rhin, du 11 juin 1793, l'an deuxième de la République françoise* [Strasbourg, 1793].

48. Johann Gottfried Herder, *Vom Geist der ebräischen Poesie* (Dessau, 1782–83).

49. Schaller, "Vorrede des Uebersezers [*sic*]," in Lippmann Moses Büschenthal, *Ein Psalm an Bonaparte, nachdem ihn Jehova von seinen Feinden und Meuchelmördern errettet hatte. Aus dem Hebraeischen des B[üschenthal] Lippmann Moses übersetzt von Gottfried Jakob Schaller.* Strasbourg, Year IX [1801].

50. Silvestre de Sacy to Elie Lévy, 20 Brumaire Year X (November 11, 1801), reprinted in *Hymne à l'occasion de la paix, chantée en hébreu et lue en français, dans la grand synagogue, à Paris, le 17 brumaire an X* (Paris, Year X [1801]). On Sacy, see Said, *Orientalism*, 18, 83, 122–30, 147–50.

51. "Poésie. Ha-Shalom. Hymne à l'occasion de la Paix . . . ," *Magasin Encyclopédique*, 7th ser., 5 (1801): 364–69; *Courrier des spectacles*, 23 Brumaire Year X (October 14, 1801) and 18 Nivose Year X.

52. Théophile-Frédéric Winckler to August Lamey, undated, MC CXVII, folder 1058, Archives Nationales, Paris.

53. Michel Berr, "Avertissement du Traducteur," in Jacob Mayer and Abraham de Cologna, *Odes hébraïques pour la célébration de l'anniversaire de la naissance de S.M. L'Empereur des Français et Roi d'Italie* (Paris, 1806), 1–9.

54. [Sintzheim], *Discours prononcé par le chef;* Abraham Furtado, *Rapport de M. Furtado au Grand Sanhédrin, en lui proposant les trois premières décisions doctrinales* [Paris, 1807]; Cologna, *Discorso;* Tama, *Collection des procès-verbaux,* 12, 27, 128; and Tama, *Collection des actes,* 210.

55. Tama, *Collection des actes,* 189–91.

56. Tama, *Collection des procès-verbaux,* 87.

57. Ibid., 67.

58. See chapter 2.

59. [Sintzheim], *Discours prononcé par le chef;* and Tama, *Collection des procès-verbaux,* 88, 89, 123, 124, 131.

60. Etienne-Denis, duc Pasquier, *Histoire de mon temps: Mémoires du Chancelier Pasquier, publiés par M. le Duc d'Audiffret-Pasquier de l'Académie française* (Paris, 1893), vol. 1, 276.

61. Furtado, *Rapport;* and Tama, *Collection des procès-verbaux,* 29, 63, 77, 98, 111.

62. Grégoire, *Essai sur la régénération,* 67, 105, 177.

63. Cologna, *Discorso;* Furtado, *Rapport;* [Sintzheim], *Discours prononcé par le chef;* Tama, *Collection des actes,* 156; and Tama, *Collection des procès-verbaux,* 6, 27, 123.

64. [Sintzheim], *Discours prononcé par le chef;* Tama, *Collection des actes,* 197–99; and Tama, *Collection des procès-verbaux,* 52, 62, 91, 96, 125.

65. Tama, *Collection des actes,* 171, 181; Tama, *Collection des procès-verbaux,* 8–9, 76, 81; Cologna, *Discorso.* The biblical citations mentioned earlier were to Prov. 24, 27, 28–29; Lev 19:34; and Mich 6:8. The Talmudic citations were to Avot 1 and 6; Kidushin 1; and Hirubin 7.

66. Tama, *Collection des actes,* 190; and Tama, *Collection des procès-verbaux,* 84, 94.

67. Cologna, *Discorso;* Furtado, *Rapport;* and Tama, *Collection des procès-verbaux,* 7–8, 29–30, 58, 84.

68. See chapter 3.

69. Anchel, *Napoleon,* 93.

70. Cologna, *Discorso;* and Tama, *Collection des actes,* 10.

71. [Sintzheim], *Discours prononcé par le chef;* Tama, *Collection des actes,* 212; and Tama, *Collection des procès-verbaux,* 58, 127. Emphasis added.

72. Tama, *Collection des procès-verbaux,* 101.

73. Tama, *Collection des actes,* 162, 211, 215–16. Sintzheim's paraphrase comes from Isa. 42:1–6.

74. [Sintzheim], *Discours prononcé par la chef;* and Tama, *Collection des procès-verbaux,* 128–29.

75. Memoirs of Issachar Chaim Carpi, in Mevorach, *Napoleon u-tekufato,* 42. Cf. Exod. 14:21, "And Moses stretched out his hand over the sea; and the Lord caused the sea to go back by a strong east wind all the night, and made the sea dry land, and the waters were divided." Cf. also Ps.35:5.

76. Lippmann Moses Büschenthal, *Mizmor le-Ponaparte ba-yom hitsil Adonai oto mi-kaf oyevav u-miyad zerim ha-mevakshim et nafsho* [A psalm to Ponaparte on the day when the Lord delivered him from the palm of his foes and from the hand of the enemies who sought (to take) his life] (Strasbourg, 1801). Cf. the "strong east wind" with which God rescued the Israelites from the Egyptians. Exod. 14:21.

77. Mayer, *Mizmor shir al yom meshichat adonenu Napoleon ha-adir kaiser Franze* [A psalm on the day of the anointing of Napoleon the Magnificent, Emperor of France]. Published with French translation: *Ode pour célébrer le jour immortel de l'élévation de Sa Majesté Napoléon à la dignité impériale; composée en hébreu par J. Mayer* (Paris, Year XII [1804]); and "Mizmor le-todah al yom meshichat u-nishva keter malchut adonenu Napoleon ha-adir kaiser France [A psalm of thanksgiving on the day of the anointing and the royal coronation of our lord Napoleon the magnificent, Emperor of France]." Published with French translation: "Cantique pour célébrer le jour du sacre et du couronnement de S.M. Napoléon, Empereur des Français," in *Fête religieuse.* For the sources of Mayer's imagery, see Isa 9:6, 9:9, and 14:7.

78. *Shir hod le-chavod adonenu ha-kaiser* [A song of splendor in honor of our lord the emperor] (Warsaw, 1807; reprinted in *Kwartalnik* 2 [1913]: 121–27). Cf. Dan. 7:13, 14.

79. Mayer, *Mizmor shir al yom meshichat;* and *Mizmor shir al yom huledet adonenu Napoleon ha-adir kaiser tsarfatim u-melech italia yarom hodo* [A hymn on the birthday of our lord Napoleon the Magnificent, Emperor of the French and King of Italy, may his splendor grow]. Published with French translation: *Ode pour célébrer le jour de l'anniversaire de la naissance de Napoléon, Empereur des françois et Roi d'Italie* (Paris, 1806).

80. Mayer, "Mizmor le-todah al yom meshichat." Cf. Song of Sol. 4:13; and Ps. 104:29–30.

81. Elie Lévy, *Ha-Shalom. Ha-Shirah ha-zot sharu ha-yehudim ba-vet tefilatam poh Paris ba-yom hushav ha-cherev la-nada* [The peace. The Jews sang this song in their house of prayer here in Paris on the day when the sword was returned to the sheath]. Published with French translation: *Hymne à l'occasion de la paix* (Paris, Year X [1801]). Cf. Gen. 1:3.

82. Mendel Kargeau, "Zot ha-shirah asher sharu kahal yeshurun ba-vet tefilatam la-adah al semichat levavam u-lepaer hod melacham [This is the song that the congregation of Israel sang with joyous hearts at their assembly in their house of prayer to glorify the splendor of their king]," in *Fête religieuse*.

83. Lévy, *Ha-Shalom;* Moïse Milliaud, *Mizmor shir le-Napoleon ha-gadol ha-kaiser ve-ha-melech* [A hymn to Napoleon the Great, the emperor and king]. Published with French translation: *Cantique adressé à Napoléon le Grand, Empereur des François et Roi d'Italie* (Paris, 1806); and Mayer, *Mizmor shir al yom huledet.*

84. Carpi wrote that Napoleon "flew [like an] eagle" to Egypt, thus alluding to the passage in Exodus (19:4) in which God carries the Children of Israel out of Egypt "on the wings of eagles." Mevorach, *Napoleon u-tekufato.* Not surprisingly, this image appeared in Hebrew texts more frequently after the declaration of empire. See, for example, Bernard Zay, *Hymne à l'occasion de l'avènement de Sa Majesté Impériale Napoléon au trône de l'empire des français. Pour être chanté dans la grande synagogue de Metz, vendredi, 3 messidor an 12, à six heures du soir; Traduite de l'hébreu* ([Metz, 1804]); Mayer, *Mizmor shir al yom meshichat;* and Samuel Wittersheim, *Mizmor shir yom halidat ha-kaiser u-melech Napoleon yarom hodo* [A hymn on the birthday of the Emperor and King Napoleon, may his splendor grow]. Published with French translation: *Hymne chanté par les députés françois professant le culte de Moïse, dans leur temple à Paris, le 15 août 1806, jour de la naissance de notre auguste empereur et roi* (Paris, 1806). Mayer depicted Napoleon as an "angel" sent "to protect and deliver." "Mizmor le-todah al yom meshichat." The description of Napoleon as "a cherub with extended wings" comes from *Shir hod le-chavod.* It is an allusion to the apocalyptic creature described by Ezekiel as combining the features of an eagle, a man, a lion, and an ox. Ezek.28:13–16.

85. *Me-asefat pekidi bene yisrael yoshve tsarfat ve-italia ha-nikhelet ba-ir paris li-vene emunatam u-le-shomre toratam eteret shalom ve-emet* [From the assembly of officers, the children of Israel, residents of France and Italy, gathered together in the city of Paris, to the children of their religion and guardians of their law of abundance, peace and truth]. Published with French translation: *L'assemblée des députés des Israélites de France et du royaume d'Italie, à leurs coreligionnaires* (Paris, 1806).

86. Mayer, *Mizmor shir al yom meshichat;* and Cologna, "Ba-yom hitka-desh chag huledet ha-adir Napoleoni Kaiser ha-tsarfatim u-melech italia [On the day of the festival celebrating the birthday of the magnificent Napoleon, Emperor of the French and King of Italy]." Published with French translation: "Ode pour the Jour de la Naissance de Napoléon de Grand, Empereur des françois et Roi d'Italie," in Mayer and Cologna, *Odes hébraïques;* Mayer, *Mizmor shir al yom huledet;* and Wittersheim, *Mizmor shir yom halidat.* Wittersheim used the word *"se'er,"* or "flesh," a synecdoche for "relations by blood."

87. Lévy, *Ha-Shalom;* Milliaud, *Mizmor shir le-Napoleon;* and Mayer, *Mizmor shir al yom huledet.*

88. David Sintzheim, *Tefilat yesharim karii anshe ha-edah shem sanhedrin behitasef yechdav ba-ir ve-em Paris ha-mehulelah mi-taam adonenu ha-adir*

Napoleon ha-rishon kaiser ha-tsarfatim u-melech italia yarom hodo [Prayer of the Israelites, called among the people of the community by the name Sanhedrin, as they gathered together in the city of Paris, the celebrated metropolis, by decree of our magnificent lord Napoleon the First, Emperor of the French and King of Italy, may his splendor grow]. Published with French translation: *Prière des membres du Sanhédrin, récitée dans leur assemblée convoquée à Paris le 1er jour d'Adar de l'année 5567* (Paris, 1807).

89. Stephen Greenblatt, *Marvelous Possessions: The Wonder of the New World* (Chicago: University of Chicago Press, 1991), 3–4.

90. *Me-asefat pekidi bene yisrael.*

CONCLUSION

1. Tamise Van Pelt, "Otherness," *Postmodern Culture* 10 (January 2000): 1.

2. Max Horkheimer and Theodor W. Adorno, *Dialectic of Enlightenment,* trans. John Cumming (New York: Continuum, 1972), 6, 17, 12–13. For an analysis of Horkheimer and Adorno in the context of theories of anti-Semitism, see my "Rationalizing the Enlightenment: Postmodernism and Theories of Anti-Semitism," *Historical Reflections/Réflexions historiques* 25 (summer 1999): 281–306.

3. Jean-François Lyotard, "Excerpts from *The Postmodern Condition: A Report on Knowledge,*" in *A Postmodern Reader,* ed. Joseph Natoli and Linda Hutcheon (Albany: State University of New York Press, 1993), 73; Zygmunt Bauman, "Postmodernity, or Living with Ambivalence," in Natoli and Hutcheon, *Postmodern Reader,* 14; and Lyotard, *The Postmodern Condition: A Report on Knowledge,* trans. Geoff Bennington and Brian Massumi (Minneapolis: University of Minnesota Press, 1984), xxiv.

4. Readers familiar with Michel de Certeau may recognize an apparent similarity between heterography and the heterologies to which de Certeau refers in his *Heterologies: Discourse on the Other,* trans. Brian Massumi (Minneapolis: University of Minnesota Press, 1986). Yet if heterologies are the methods by which others are examined, heterography is the description itself, and comparative heterography involves a comparison of other-descriptions.

5. Cited in Joan Landes, *Women and the Public Sphere in the Age of the French Revolution* (Ithaca, N.Y.: Cornell University Press, 1988), 66; and Josette Féral, "The Powers of Difference," in *The Future of Difference,* ed. Hester Eisenstein and Alice Jardine (Boston: G. K. Hall, 1980), 88.

6. Tzvetan Todorov, *The Conquest of America: The Question of the Other,* trans. Richard Howard (New York: Harper and Row, 1984), 36–38, 50; Menasseh ben Israel, *The Hope of Israel,* trans. Moses Wall, ed. Henry Méchoulan and Gérard Nahon (1652; reprint, Oxford: Oxford University Press, 1986); and Gordon M. Sayre, *Les Sauvages Américains: Representations of Native Americans in French and English Colonial Literature* (Chapel Hill: University of North Carolina Press, 1997), 81, 131.

7. Anthony Pagden, *European Encounters with the New World: From Renaissance to Romanticism* (New Haven, Conn.: Yale University Press, 1993),

17–49. For a discussion of European explanations of the New World in terms furnished from classical authors, see Pagden, *The Fall of Natural Man: The American Indian and the Origins of Comparative Ethnology* (Cambridge: Cambridge University Press, 1982), esp. 10–26.

8. Stephen Greenblatt, *Marvelous Possessions: The Wonder of the New World* (Chicago: University of Chicago Press, 1991), 8, 15, 86–87, 112; and Todorov, *Conquest,* 14–24.

9. Todorov, *Conquest,* 38–39. Cf. Peter Francis, "The Beads That Did *Not* Buy Manhattan Island," *New York History* 67 (January 1986): 4–22.

10. Gotthold Ephraim Lessing, *Die Juden: Ein Lustspiel in Einem Aufzuge verfertiget im Jahr 1749* (1749; reprint, Stuttgart: Reclam, 1981); and Lessing, *Nathan der Weise; Ein Dramatisches Gedicht, in fünf Aufzügen* (1779; reprint, Stuttgart: Reclam, 1990).

11. William B. Cohen, *The French Encounter with Africans: White Response to Blacks, 1530–1880* (Bloomington: Indiana University Press, 1980), 6–7, 13–15, 21.

12. Henri Grégoire, *An Enquiry Concerning the Intellectual and Moral Faculties and Literature of Negroes: Followed with an Account of the Life and Works of Fifteen Negroes & Mulattoes Distinguished in Science, Literature and the Arts,* trans. D. B. Warden (Brooklyn, 1810).

13. Cohen, *French Encounter,* 16–20, 66, 89. Those familiar with Voltaire's *Candide* will be able to point to Don Issachar, the lecherous Jew who shares Cunégonde with the (equally lecherous) Inquisitor, yet this depiction of Jewish incontinence was unusual, even in Voltaire's work. Far more widespread was Grégoire's claim that the Jews were good spouses. Indeed, it was precisely their perceived solidarity, as families and as larger Jewish communities, that non-Jews appear to have feared. Grégoire, *Essai sur la régénération physique, morale et politique des Juifs* (Paris, 1789) [reprinted in *La Révolution française et l'émancipation des Juifs* (Paris: EdHis, 1968), vol. 3], 35–36.

14. See chapter 3.

15. Jacques Henri Bernardin de Saint-Pierre, *Paul et Virginie* (1787; reprint, Paris: Gallimard, 1965); Claude-Adrien Helvetius, *De l'homme* (London, 1773), 373; and Cohen, *French Encounter,* 70–73.

16. Féral, "The Powers of Difference," 88.

17. Londa L. Schiebinger, *The Mind Has No Sex? Women in the Origins of Modern Science* (Cambridge: Harvard University Press, 1989); Elisabeth Badinter, ed., *Qu'est-ce qu'une femme? Un débat* (Paris: P.O.L., 1989); and Thomas Laqueur, "Orgasm, Generation, and the Politics of Reproductive Biology," *Representations* 14 (spring 1986): 3.

18. Joan Scott, *Only Paradoxes to Offer: French Feminists and the Rights of Man* (Cambridge: Harvard University Press, 1996), 49. Cf. Jean-Jacques Rousseau, *Emile ou de l'éducation,* vol. 4 of *Oeuvres complètes* (Paris: Gallimard, 1969), 697.

19. Mary Jacobus, "Incorruptible Milk: Breast-feeding and the French Revolution," in *Rebel Daughters: Women and the French Revolution,* ed. Sara E. Melzer and Leslie W. Rabine (New York: Oxford University Press, 1992), 54–75.

20. Landes, *Women and the Public Sphere,* 30, 45, 28.

21. [François-Joseph-Antoine Hell], *Observations d'un Alsacien sur l'affaire présente des Juifs d'Alsace* (Frankfurt, 1779), 135; and Landes, *Women and the Public Sphere,* 87–88.

22. Montesquieu, *Lettres persanes* (Amsterdam, 1721; reprint, Paris: F. Roches, 1929), letter 107, p. 76; and Abbé Emmanuel Joseph Sieyes, *Qu'est-ce que le tiers-état?* (1789; reprint, Paris: Société de l'histoire de la Révolution française, 1888), 31.

23. Scott, *Only Paradoxes,* 27.

24. See chapter 2.

25. Scott, *Only Paradoxes,* 28.

26. Greenblatt, *Marvelous Possessions,* esp. 119–51.

27. Sander Gilman, *The Jew's Body* (New York: Routledge, 1991), 63–64, 76, 99, 127, 133–34, 137, 196, 207; George L. Mosse, *The Image of Man: The Creation of Modern Masculinity* (New York: Oxford University Press, 1996); Susan Kassouf, "The Shared Pain of the Golden Vein: The Discursive Proximity of Jewish and Scholarly Diseases in the Late Eighteenth Century," *Eighteenth-Century Studies* 32 (fall 1998): 101–10.

28. Cohen, *French Encounter,* 80–83; and Grégoire, *Essai sur la régénération,* 48–52.

29. Eric Hobsbawm and Terence Ranger, eds., *The Invention of Tradition* (Cambridge: Cambridge University Press, 1983).

30. I have placed the word "weak" in quotation marks because, though it is commonly used—for example, in James C. Scott's *Weapons of the Weak: Everyday Forms of Peasant Resistance* (New Haven, Conn.: Yale University Press, 1985)—it emphasizes lack of power, whereas I am arguing that even marginal groups can wield a certain kind of power, that is, that of self-definition, however different this sort of power is from the power of the state.

31. Scott, *Only Paradoxes,* 19–56.

32. Edmond de Goncourt and Jules de Goncourt, *Journal,* vol. 2, entry of Tuesday, March 21, 1878 (Paris: Flammarion, 1959), 750.

33. Homi K. Bhabha, "Culture's In-Between," in *Questions of Cultural Identity,* ed. Stuart Hall and Paul du Gay, (London: Sage, 1996), 58.

34. Scott, *Only Paradoxes,* 23, 33; and Frances Malino, *A Jew in the French Revolution: The Life of Zalkind Hourwitz* (Oxford: Blackwell, 1996), 103.

35. I am adapting the phrase "construction of affinities" from Harry Liebersohn, "Discovering Indigenous Nobility: Tocqueville, Chamisso, and Romantic Travel Writing," *American Historical Review* 99 (June 1994): 749.

36. Louis Miller has argued that Foucault misunderstood Nietzsche, but more important to my argument is the fact that, as Miller acknowledges, Foucault's work on the German philosopher is "a classic postmodern appropriation of Nietzsche." "Foucault, Nietzsche, Enlightenment: Some Historical Considerations," *Historical Reflections/Réflexions historiques* 25 (summer 1999): 354.

37. Friedrich Nietzsche, *Beyond Good and Evil: Prelude to a Philosophy of the Future,* trans. Walter Kaufmann (New York: Vintage, 1966), 160.

EPILOGUE

1. Henry Rousso, *The Vichy Syndrome: History and Memory in France since 1944,* trans. Arthur Goldhammer (Cambridge: Harvard University Press, 1991), 98–99.

2. Éric Conan and Henry Rousso, *Vichy: An Ever-Present Past,* trans. Nathan Bracher, foreword by Robert O. Paxton (Hanover, N.H.: University Press of New England, 1998).

3. Pierre Birnbaum, *Jewish Destinies: Citizenship, State, and Community in Modern France,* trans. Arthur Goldhammer (New York: Hill and Wang, 2000).

4. Alain Finkelkraut, *The Imaginary Jew,* trans. Kevin O'Neill and David Suchoff (Lincoln: University of Nebraska Press, 1994), 96.

5. Hannah Arendt, *On Revolution* (New York: Viking, 1963), 84.

Bibliography

UNPUBLISHED PRIMARY SOURCES

Archives Nationales, Paris

AF III 21 bis
F 19 1786
F 19 1841
F 19 1849b
F 19 11031
MC CXVII

Departmental Archives

Bouches-du-Rhône (Marseille) C 3443
Gironde (Bordeaux) C 18, C 1090, C 3662
Moselle (Metz) C 57, 17 J 66
Vaucluse (Avignon) I J 338

Other Manuscript Deposits

Alliance Israélite Universelle, Paris: Ms. 738
Bibliothèque Inguimbertine, Carpentras: Ms. 894
Bibliothèque municipale d'Avignon: Ms. 2564
Bibliothèque Nationale, Paris: Nouv. acq. fr. 22706
Consistoire Central, Paris: 1 B 1, 1 C 2, B3

PUBLISHED PRIMARY SOURCES

Journals and Newspapers

Affiches pour les Trois-Évêchés et la Lorraine
L'ami du peuple
Annales patriotiques
Chronique de Paris
Le Courrier de Provence
Le Courrier de Versailles
Le Courrier français
Gazette de Paris
Le Journal de Paris
Mémoires pour l'histoire des sciences & des beaux arts
Mercure de France
Le Moniteur
Le Patriote françois
Le Point du Jour
Le pour et contre
Révolutions de Paris

Other Published Primary Sources

Abbadie, Jacques. *Traité de la verité de la religion chrétienne*. Rotterdam, 1684.
Action de grâces à l'occasion de l'heureuse délivrance de la reine et de la naissance du dauphin, récitée pour la première fois, par les syndics de la nation juive avignonoise résidans à Paris, dans leur assemblée et réiterée à Bordeaux par les Juifs avignonois dans leur synagogue, le 20 novembre 1781, à la réquisition de MM. Joseph Petit, syndic, et Isaac Lange, adjoint. Traduite de l'hébreu. Bourdeaux, 1781.
Adresse à l'Assemblée Nationale. Paris, 1789. Reprint, Paris: EdHis, 1968.
Adresse de l'Assemblée des Représentans de la Commune de Paris, à l'Assemblée Nationale, sur l'admission des Juifs à l'Etat Civil. Suivie d'un arrêté des représentans de la Commune sur le même objet. Et de la réponse de M. le Président de l'Assemblée Nationale à la députation de la Commune. [Paris, 1790]. Reprint, Paris: EdHis, 1968.
Adresse des Juifs alsaciens au peuple d'Alsace. N.p., n.d. Reprint, Paris: EdHis, 1968.
Adresse présentée à l'Assemblée Nationale, le 26 Août 1789, par les Juifs résidans à Paris. [Paris, 1789]. Reprint, Paris: EdHis, 1968.
Adresse présentée à l'Assemblée Nationale, le 31 Août 1789, par les députés réunis des Juifs, établis à Metz, dans les Trois Evêchés, en Alsace & en Lorraine. N.p., n.d. Reprint, Paris: EdHis, 1968.
Adresse présentée à l'Assemblée Nationale, par le député des Juifs espagnols et portugais, établis au Bourg Saint-Esprit les-Bayonne. 1790. Reprint, Paris: EdHis, 1968.

Adresse presentée à l'Assemblée Nationale, par les Juifs domiciliés a [sic] *Paris.* [Paris, 1791]. Reprint, Paris: EdHis, 1968.

Archives parlementaires de 1787 à 1860, recueil complet des débats législatifs et politiques des chambres françaises. Première série (1787–1799). Edited by Jérôme Mavidal. Paris: 1867–1913.

Argens, Jean-Baptiste de Boyer, marquis d'. *Lettres juives, ou Correspondance philosophique, historique & critique, Entre un Juif Voyageur à Paris, & ses Correspondans en divers endroits. Nouvelle édition augmentée de XX Nouvelles Lettres, de Quantité de Remarques, & de plusieurs Figures.* The Hague: Pierre Paupie, 1738.

Arrêté de l'Assemblée Générale des représentans de la Commune [Paris, 1790]. Reprint, Paris: EdHis, 1968.

[Asser, Lion]. *Traduction de la prière hébraïque, composée par le rabin des Juifs de Metz, pour être récitée soir et matin, et même pendant la nuit dans la synagogue, après les dix-huit Pseaumes de David, et autres prières publiques et extraordinaires, qui ont été enjointes par délibération expresse de la communauté, pour obtenir de Dieu le rétablissement de la santé du Roi.* Metz, 1774.

———. *Traduction d'une prière hébraïque, composée par le rabin des Juifs de Metz, et par eux récitée dans leur grande synagogue jusqu'au neuf du mois de juin inclusivement, pour le repos de l'âme de Louis XV, Roi de France, de glorieuse mémoire.* Metz, [1774].

Athias, David. *Actions de grâce rendues à Dieu, par les Juifs portugais de Bordeaux, le 20. janvier 1757. Pour le rétablissement de la santé du roy. Composé en hébreu par le Rabin Athias, et traduit en français.* Bordeaux, 1757.

———. *Prière faite par les Juif[s] de Bordeaux, pour demander à Dieu le rétablissement de la santé du roy. Traduite de l'hébreu le 20 août 1744.* [Bordeaux, 1744].

———. *Priere faite par les Juifs portugais de Bordeaux, à l'occasion de l'attentat commis sur la personne sacrée du roi; et actions de grâces pour son heureuse convalescence.* N.p., [1757].

———. *Prière faite par les Juifs portugais de Bordeaux, pour obtenir de Dieu le rétablissement de la santé de Monseigneur le dauphin, le 9 août 1752, jour auquel ils ont observé, pour cet effet, un jeûne général, et fait des aumônes publiques. Composée en hébreu par leur rabin HH. Athias, et traduite par M.***.* N.p., [1752].

———. *Prière pour l'heureuse délivrance de la reine, que les Juifs portugais de Bordeaux ont récitée en cette ville le premier décembre 1778, et jours suivans, devant le Pentateuque; et les Juifs portugais de Paris le 19 du même mois, au matin, dans leur assemblée de la rue Saint André-des-Arcs; composée en hébreu et en espagnol, à Bordeaux, par leur Rabin, le Sieur David Athias, et traduite en françois par leur agent, à Paris.* [Paris], 1779.

———. "Prière que les Juifs portugais de Bordeaux ont faite, pour demander à Dieu le rétablissement de la santé de Monseigneur le dauphin, le 21 novembre 1765, jour auquel ils se sont abstenus de toutes sortes d'affaires, ont fait des aumônes publiques, et ont observé un jeûne général de vingt quatre heures. Composée en hébreu par leur rabin, le Haham David Athias, et tra-

duite en françois par le sieur P . . . . . ., leur agent à Paris, pensionnaire et in-
terprête du roi." *Mercure de France,* January 1766, 82–87.

————. "Prière que les Juifs portugais ont faite à Bordeaux pour demander à
Dieu le rétablissement de la santé de la reine, le 10 mars 1768, jour par eux
arrêté pour observer, à cet effet, un jeûne général, et faire des aumônes publiques. Composée en hébreu et en espagnol par leur rabin, le sieur David
Athias, et traduite en françois par le sieur Péreire, pensionnaire et interprète
du roi, membre de la Société royale de Londres, agent des Juifs portugais à
Paris." *Mercure de France,* May 1768, 41–44.

Augustine, Saint. *The City of God against the Pagans.* Translated by William
Chase Greene. Cambridge: Harvard University Press, 1960.

[Avigdor, J. S.]. *Discours prononcé à l'Assemblée des Israélites de l'Empire
Français et du Royaume d'Italie; par J. S. Avigdor (de Nice), secrétaire de
l'Assemblée, Membre du Comité de Neuf et du Grand Sanhédrin.* Paris,
1807.

Bachaumont, Louis Petit de. *Mémoires secrets pour servir à l'histoire de la république des lettres en France, depuis 1762 jusqu'à nos jours.* London, 1780.
Reprint, Franborough: Gregg International, 1970.

Baker, Keith Michael, ed. *The Old Regime and the French Revolution.* Chicago:
University of Chicago Press, 1987.

[Baltus, Jacques]. *Annales de Metz, depuis l'an 1724 inclusivement, par feu
Monsieur Baltus, notaire, ancien conseiller-échevin de l'hotel de ville, pour
servir de supplément aux preuves de l'histoire de Metz.* Metz, 1789.

————. *Journal de ce qui s'est fait à Metz, au passage de la reine. Avec un recueil de plusieurs pièces sur le même sujet.* Metz, 1725.

————. *Journal de ce qui s'est fait pour la réception du roy dans sa ville de Metz
le 4. août 1744. Avec un recüeil de plusieurs pièces sur le même sujet, et sur
les accidens survenus pendant son séjour.* Metz, 1744.

Beaufleury, Francia de. *L'Etablissement des Juifs à Bordeaux et à Bayonne.* Year
VIII. Reprint, Bayonne: Éditions Harriet, 1985.

[Berr, Berr Isaac]. *Discours des députés des Juifs des provinces des Evêchés,
d'Alsace & de Lorraine, prononcé à la Barre de l'Assemblée Nationale, par
le sieur Berr-Isaac-Berr, l'un des députés de la Lorraine, & l'extrait du
procès-verbal de l'Assemblée Nationale y relatif.* Paris, 1789. Reprint, Paris:
EdHis, 1968.

————. *Lettre du Sr. Berr-Isaac-Berr, négociant à Nancy, Juif, naturalisé en
vertu des lettres-patentes du roi, enregistrées au parlement de Nancy, député
des Juifs de la Lorraine; à Monseigneur l'évêque de Nancy, député à l'Assemblée nationale.* 1790. Reprint, Paris: EdHis, 1968.

[Berr, Jacob]. *Réflexions sur Lettre d'un citoyen, aux Gardes-citoyens de la ville
de Nancy, en réponse de cette question: Les Juifs doivent-ils être admis dans
la Milice Nationale?* [Nancy, 1790].

Bing, Isaïah Berr. *Lettre du Sr. I. B. B. Juif de Metz, à l'auteur anonyme d'un
écrit intitulé: Le cri du citoyen contre les Juifs.* Metz, 1787. Reprint, Paris:
EdHis, 1968.

————. *Mémoire particulier pour la communauté des Juifs établis à Metz, ré-*

digé par Isaac Ber-Bing, l'un des membres de cette communauté. 1790. Reprint, Paris: EdHis, 1968.

——. *Traduction de l'hymne ou cantique hébraïque, que les Juifs de Metz ont récité, et fait exécuter en musique dans leur synagogue, le 18 novembre 1781, jour des réjouissances faites pour la naissance de Monseigneur le dauphin.* Metz, [1781].

Bossuet, Jacques-Bénigne. *Discours sur l'histoire universelle.* Paris: S. Mabre-Cramoisy, 1681.

——. *Méditations sur l'Evangile.* 1704. Reprint, Paris: Vrin, 1966.

Bouche, Charles François. *De la restitution du Comté Venaissin, des ville et état d'Avignon; motion imprimée sous l'autorisation de l'Assemblée Nationale, par son décret du 21 novembre 1789.* Paris, 1789.

Broglie, Louis Victor, Prince de. *Opinion de M. le Prince de Broglie, député de Colmar, sur l'admission des Juifs à l'état civil.* N.p., n.d.

Büschenthal, Lippmann Moses. *Mizmor le-Ponaparte ba-yom hitsil Adonai oto mi-kaf oyevav u-miyad zerim ha-mevakshim et nafsho* [A psalm to Ponaparte on the day when the Lord delivered him from the palm of his foes and from the hand of the enemies who sought (to take) his life]. Strasbourg, 1801.

——. *Ein Psalm an Bonaparte, nachdem ihn Jehova von seinen Feinden und Meuchelmördern errettet hatte. Aus dem Hebraeischen des B[üschenthal] Lippmann Moses übersetzt von Gottfried Jakob Schaller.* Strasbourg, Year IX [1801].

——. *Pseaume à Bonaparte quand Jehova l'eut sauvé des assassins. Traduit en français, sur la traduction allemande.* Strasbourg, Year IX [1801].

Cerfberr, Lipman. *Discours pour l'ouverture de l'Assemblée générale des Juifs, prononcé le 26 juillet 1806.* Paris, 1806.

Chateaubriand, François de. *Mémoires d'Outre-Tombe.* Paris: Flammarion, 1948.

Coeffeteau, Nicolas. *Histoire romaine.* Paris: G. Loyson, 1646.

Cologna, Abraham de. *Discorso pronunziato nella grande sinagoga di Parigi, all'occasione dell'apertura del Gran Sanedrin, dal Signor Abramo Cologna, rabino in Mantova, ex-legislatore e membro attuale del collegio elettorale dei dotti del regno d'Italia, deputato all'assemblea degl' Israeliti, e assessore del gran Sanedrin. Tradotto in francese dal signor Furtado, presidente dell' assemblea.* French title: *Discours prononcé à la grande synagogue de Paris, à l'occasion de l'ouverture du Grand Sanhédrin . . . .* Paris, 1807.

——. *Discours prononcé le 23 mai 1813, à l'occasion des actions de grâces rendues à l'Eternel, pour la grande victoire remportée par l'armée française au camp de Lützen.* Paris, 1813.

——. *Discours prononcé par Mr. Abraham Cologna, membre du collège électoral des savans du royaume d'Italie, Grand-Rabbin du Consistoire central des Israélites, le 13 mai 1809, dans le temple de la rue Ste.-Avoie, à l'occasion des victoires remportées par l'armée française aux champs de Tann, Eckmühl, Ratisbonne, etc., etc.; suivi d'une prière composée en hébreu par D. Sintzheim, traduite par M. Elie Halévy.* Paris, [1809].

Couché, François-Louis. *Napoléon le Grand rétablit le culte des Israélites, le 30 mai 1806*. Paris, [1806].

Crémieu, Juda-David. *Discours composé en hébreu et traduit en français, par le Rabin Juda-David Crémieu l'aîné, de Carpentras, prononcé devant l'assemblée générale des Juifs, convoqués dans la synagogue de la même ville*. N.p., [1774].

————. *Lettre de félicitation de Crémieu, Juif de Carpentras au duc de Crillon au sujet de la prise de l'île et fort de Minorque*. N.p., [1782].

Crémieu, Juda David, and Moïse de Roque-Martine. *Prière faite par les Juifs du Comté-Venaissin, pour demander à Dieu, la guérison de Monseigneur le dauphin; composée par les Rabbins Juda David Crémieu, l'aîné, et Moïse de Roque-Martine, de Carpentras; traduite litteralement de l'hébreu*. N.p., [1765].

Décision du Comité de Constitution. Réquise par David D Silveyra, Syndic Agent des Juifs François Patentés. [Paris, 1790]. Reprint, Paris: EdHis, 1968.

Délibération du conseil général du département du Bas-Rhin, du 11 juin 1793, l'an deuxième de la République françoise. Strasbourg, 1793.

Détail des cérémonies qui ont été observées par les Juifs de la province d'Alsace, à l'occasion de la naissance de Monseigneur le dauphin; et traduction faite par le Sr. Simon Hallé, secrétaire-interprète juré de la nation juive d'Alsace, des lettres écrites, pseaumes et cantiques qui ont été chantés dans la synagogue à Bischheim-au-Saum le 20 novembre 1781. Strasbourg, n.d.

Détail officiel de tout ce qui s'est passé à la première et deuxieme séances de l'Assemblé des Juifs. Paris, 1806.

Discours de MM. Les Commissaires de S.M. Impériale et Royale, prononcé à l'Assemblée des Français professant le culte de Moïse, dans la séance du 18 septembre. [Paris, 1806].

Discours prononcé par le rabin du consistoire de Nancy, le 15 août 1809, jour de l'anniversaire de la fête de Sa Majesté l'Empereur et Roi. N.p., n.d.

Dohm, Christian Wilhelm von. *Über die bürgerliche Verbesserung der Juden*. Berlin, 1781.

[Eibeschütz, Jonathan]. *Compliment au roy fait par le rabin des Juifs de Metz*. Metz, 1744.

————. *Délibération concluë dans l'assemblée générale des syndics et communauté des Juifs de Metz, pour les prières publiques . . . , aux fins d'obtenir de Dieu le recouvrement de la santé de Sa Majesté*. [Metz, 1744].

Encyclopédie, ou Dictionnaire raisonné des sciences, des arts et des métiers. Paris, 1751–72.

[Ensheim, Moïse]. *La-Menatseach shir le-Moshe Ensheim hushar be-yom gavra yad yoshve erets moledetenu al kol oyevenu mesaviv* [A song to the precentor by Moïse Ensheim, sung on the day when the hand of the inhabitants of our fatherland prevailed over all the surrounding enemies]. French title: *Cantique composée par le Citoyen Moyse Ensheim, à l'occasion de la fête civique célébrée à Metz, le 21 octobre, l'an 1er de la République, dans le temple des citoyens israëlites*. Translated by Isaïah Berr Bing. Metz, 1792.

[Fare, Anne-Louis-Henri de la]. *Opinion de M. l'évêque de Nancy, député de*

Lorraine, sur l'admissibilité des Juifs à la plénitude de l'état civil, et des droits de Citoyens actifs. Paris, 1790.

Fénélon, François de Salignac de la Mothe-. *Sermons et entretiens.* Vol. 17 of *Oeuvres.* 1706. Reprint, Paris: Imprimerie de J.-A. Lebel, 1823.

Fête religieuse célébrée à Paris, le 10 pluviôse an XIII, par les français du culte judaïque, à l'occasion du couronnement de Napoléon. Paris, Year XIII [1805].

[Furtado, Abraham]. *Rapport de M. Furtado au Grand Sanhédrin, en lui proposant les trois premières décisions doctrinales.* [Paris, 1807].

Godard, Jacques. *Discours prononcé, le 28 janvier 1790, par m. Godard, avocat au Parlement, l'un des représentans de la Commune, en présentant à l'assemblée générale de la Commune, une députation des Juifs de Paris. Imprimé par ordre de l'assemblée.* [Paris], 1790. Reprint, Paris, EdHis, 1968.

Goudchaux, Michel, Mayer Isaac Berr, and Mayer Max. *Prière publique ordonnée à l'occasion de la grossesse de la Reine, par les sieurs Michel Goudchaux, Mayer Isaac Berr l'aîné, et Mayer Max, sindics de la communauté des Juifs établis en Lorraine, pour être récitée en leurs synagogues.* Nancy, 1778.

Grégoire, Abbé Henri. *An Enquiry Concerning the Intellectual and Moral Faculties and Literature of Negroes: Followed with an Account of the Life and Works of Fifteen Negroes & Mulattoes Distinguished in Science, Literature and the Arts.* Translated by D. B. Warden. Brooklyn, 1810.

———. *Essai sur la régénération physique, morale et politique des Juifs.* Paris: 1789. Reprint, Paris: EdHis, 1968.

———. *Motion en faveur des Juifs, par M. Grégoire, curé d'Embermenil, député de Nancy; précédée d'une notice historique, sur les persécutions qu'ils viennent d'essuyer en divers lieux, notamment en Alsace, et sur l'admission de leurs députés à la barre de l'Assemblée nationale.* Paris, 1789. Reprint: Paris: EdHis, 1968.

Guénée, Abbé Antoine. *Lettres de quelques Juifs portugais et allemands à M. de Voltaire, avec des réflexions critiques, &c., et un petit commentaire extrait d'un plus grand.* Paris, 1769.

[Hell, François]. *Observations d'un Alsacien sur l'affaire présente des Juifs d'Alsace.* Frankfurt, 1779.

Herder, Johann Gottfried. *Vom Geist der ebräischen Poesie.* Dessau, 1782–83.

Hirsch, Lazar. *Rede des Bürgers Lazar Hirsch, Rabbiners in Hagenau, gehalten den verflossenen 18. Ventose 12, bey Gelegenheit des Dankfestes, welches die jüdische Gemeinde, für die Erhaltung des theuren Lebens des Ersten Konsuls Bonaparte, in der dasigen Synagoge beging.* Strasbourg, [1804].

Hourwitz, Zalkind. *Apologie des Juifs en réponse à la question: Est-il des moyens de rendre les Juifs plus heureux et plus utiles en France? Ouvrage couronné par la Société royale des arts et des sciences de Metz. Par Zalkind-Hourwitz, Juif polonois.* 1789. Reprint, Paris: EdHis, 1968.

Israel, Menasseh ben. *The Hope of Israel.* Translated by Moses Wall. Edited by Henry Méchoulan and Gérard Nahon. 1652. Reprint, Oxford: Oxford University Press, 1986.

Les Juifs d'Alsace doivent-ils être admis au droit de citoyens actifs? Lisez et Jugez. N.p., 1790.

La Chesnaye, Aubert de. *Correspondance historique, philosophique et critique entre Ariste, Lisandre et quelques autres amis. Pour servir de réponse aux Lettres juives.* Vols. 1 and 3. The Hague, 1737–38.

[Lacretelle, Pierre-Louis]. "LVIIIe cause. Question d'état sur les Juifs de Metz," 64–98. *Causes célèbres, curieuses et intéressantes, de toutes les cours souveraines du royaume, avec les jugemens qui les ont décidées.* Vol. 23. Paris, 1776.

———. *Plaidoyer pour Moyse May, Godechaux et Abraham Lévy, Juifs de Metz. Contre l'hôtel-de-ville de Thionville et le Corps des Marchands de cette ville.* Bruxelles, 1775.

[La Fare, Anne-Louis Henry de]. *Opinion de M. l'évêque de Nancy, député de Lorraine, sur l'admissibilité des Juifs à la plénitude de l'état civil, et des droits de citoyens actifs.* [1789]. Reprint, Paris: EdHis, 1968.

Larkin, Steve. *Correspondance entre Prosper marchand et le marquis d'Argens.* Studies on Voltaire and the Eighteenth Century, 222. Oxford: Voltaire Foundation, 1984.

[Latour-Foissac, Philippe-François de]. *Le cri du citoyen contre les Juifs de Metz. Par un capitaine d'infanterie.* Lausanne [Metz], 1786.

Lessing, Gotthold Ephraim. *Die Juden: Ein Lustspiel in Einem Aufzuge verfertiget im Jahr 1749.* 1749. Reprint, Stuttgart: Reclam, 1981.

———. *Nathan der Weise; Ein Dramatisches Gedicht, in fünf Aufzügen.* 1779. Reprint, Stuttgart: Reclam, 1990.

Lettre adressée à M. Grégoire, curé d'Emberménil, député de Nancy, par les députés de la Nation juive portugaise, de Bordeaux. Paris, [1789]. Reprint, Paris: EdHis, 1968.

Lettre circulaire des préposés généraux des Juifs d'Alsace aux rabbins de cette province, à l'occasion de la maladie du roi. Du 4 mai 1774. N.p., [1774].

Lettre d'un citoyen, aux Gardes-citoyens de la ville de Nancy, en réponse de cette question: Les Juifs doivent-ils être admis dans la Milice Nationale? [Nancy, 1790].

Lettres patentes du Roi, confirmatives de privilèges, dont les Juifs portugais jouissent en France depuis 1550; données à Versailles en moi de juin 1776. Bordeaux, 1781.

Lévy, Elie. *Ha-Shalom. Ha-Shirah ha-zot sharu ha-yehudim ba-vet tefilatam poh Paris ba-yom hushav ha-cherev la-nadan.* . . . [The peace. The Jews sang this song in their house of prayer here in Paris on the day when the sword was returned to the sheath. . . .]. French title: *Hymne à l'occasion de la paix, chantée en hébreu et lue en français, dans la grand synagogue, à Paris, le 17 brumaire an X.* Paris, Year X [1801].

Loi relative aux Juifs. Donnée à Paris, le 13 novembre 1791. 1791. Reprint, Paris: EdHis, 1968.

Mayer, Jacob. *Mizmor shir al yom huledet adonenu Napoleon ha-adir kaiser tsarfatim u-melech italia yarom hodo* [A hymn on the birthday of our lord Napoleon the Magnificent, Emperor of the French and King of Italy, may his splendor grow]. French title: *Ode pour célébrer le jour de l'anniversaire de la naissance de Napoléon, Empereur des françois et Roi d'Italie; Composée en hébreu par J. Mayer, et traduite en françois par Michel Berr, homme de loi, membre de plusieurs académies, député pour le département de la Seine à l'assemblée des citoyens françois professant la religion juive, convoquée par décret du 30 mai 1806.* Paris, 1806.

———. *Mizmor shir al yom meshichat adonenu Napoleon ha-adir kaiser Franze* [A psalm on the day of the anointing of Napoleon the Magnificent, Emperor of France]. French title: *Ode pour célébrer le jour immortel de l'élévation de Sa Majesté Napoléon à la dignité impériale; composée en hébreu par J. Mayer.* Paris, Year XII [1804].

Mayer, Jacob, and Abraham de Cologna. *Odes hébraïques pour la célébration de l'anniversaire de la naissance de S.M. L'Empereur de Français et Roi d'I-talie, par J. Mayer et Abraham de Cologna; traduites en français par Michel Berr . . . avec un avertissement du traducteur.* Paris, 1806.

[Mayer-Marx et al.]. *Pétition des Juifs établis en France, adressée à l'Assemblée Nationale, le 28 janvier 1790, sur l'ajournement du 24 décembre 1789.* 1790. Reprint, Paris: EdHis, 1968.

Me-asefat pekidi bene yisrael yoshve tsarfat ve-italia ha-nikhelet ba-ir paris li-vene emunatam u-le-shomre toratam eteret shalom ve-emet [From the assembly of officers, the children of Israel, residents of France and Italy, gathered together in the city of Paris, to the children of their religion and guardians of their law of abundance, peace and truth]. French title: *L'assemblée des députés des Israélites de France et du royaume d'Italie, à leurs coreligionnaires.* Paris, 1806.

Mémoire pour les Juifs de Lunéville et de Sarguemines. N.p., [1789]. Reprint, Paris: EdHis, 1968.

Mevorach, Baruch, ed. *Napoleon u-tekufato* [Napoleon and his age]. Jerusalem: Sifriat Dorot, 1968.

Milliaud, Moïse. *Mizmor shir le-Napoleon ha-gadol ha-kaiser ve-ha-melech* [A hymn to Napoleon the Great, the emperor and king]. French title: *Cantique adressé à Napoléon le Grand, Empereur des François et Roi d'Italie, par Moïse Milliaud, député du département de Vaucluse à l'assemblée des citoyens françois professant le culte de Moïse.* Paris, 1806.

Mirabeau, Honore Gabriel Riquetti, comte de. *Sur Moses Mendelssohn, sur la réforme politique des juifs: et en particulier sur la révolution tentée en leur faveur en 1753 dans la grande Bretagne.* Vol. 1. London, 1787. Reprint, Paris: EdHis, 1968.

Montesquieu, Charles-Louis de Secondat, baron de. *De l'esprit des lois.* 1755. Reprint, Paris: Les Belles Lettres, 1958.

———. *Lettres persanes.* Amsterdam, 1721. Reprint, Paris: F. Roches, 1929.

Nahon, Gérard, ed. *Les "nations" juives portugaises du sud-ouest de la France (1684–1791): Documents.* Paris: Centro Cultural Português, 1981.

Nouveau mémoire pour les Juifs de Lunéville & de Sarguemines; Présenté à l'Assemblée Nationale, le 26 février 1790. Paris, 1790. Reprint, Paris: EdHis, 1968.

Nouvelle Adresse des Juifs à l'Assemblée Nationale. 24 Décembre 1789. Paris, 1789. Reprint, Paris: EdHis, 1968.

*Ode en actions de grâces sur la découverte d'une conspiration contre le gou-
    vernement français, et la vie du Premier Consul; pour être chantée dans la
    synagogue des Juifs de Metz, vendredi 18 ventôse, à cinq heures du soir.
    Traduite de l'Hébreu.* Metz, 1804.
*Ode tirée de la prière faite par les Juifs portugais de Bordeaux, pour demander
    à Dieu le rétablissement de la santé du roy.* Paris, 1744.
*Opinion de M. le comte Stanislas de Clermont-Tonnerre, député de Paris, le 23
    décembre 1789.* 1789. Reprint, Paris: EdHis, 1968.
Pascal, Blaise. *Lettre à Louis XIV.* 1694. Reprint, Neuchatel: Ides et Calendes,
    1961.
———. *Pensées sur la religion.* 1662. Reprint, Paris: Éditions du Luxembourg,
    1952.
Pasquier, Etienne-Denis, duc. *Histoire de mon temps: Mémoires du Chancelier
    Pasquier, publiés par M. le Duc d'Audiffret-Pasquier de l'Académie française.*
    Paris, 1893.
Pastoret, Claude Emmanuel Joseph Pierre, marquis de. *Moyse, consideré comme
    législateur et comme moraliste.* Paris, 1788.
*Pétition des Juifs établis en France, adressée à l'Assemblée Nationale, le 28 jan-
    vier 1790, sur l'ajournement du 24 décembre 1789.* Paris, 1790. Reprint,
    Paris: EdHis, 1968.
Pinto, Isaac de. *Apologie pour la nation juive, ou réflexions critiques sur le pre-
    mier chapitre du VIIe tome des oeuvres de M. de Voltaire au sujet des Juifs.
    Par l'auteur de "l'Essai sur le luxe."* Amsterdam, 1762.
———. *Recueil de lettres patentes, et autres pièces en faveur des Juifs portugais
    contenant leurs privilèges en France.* Paris, 1765.
———. *Réponse de l'auteur de l'Apologie de la Nation Juive à deux critiques,
    qui ont été faites de ce petit Ecrit, dans le Monthly Review, & dans la Bib-
    liothèque des sciences & des arts; avec des lettres du même auteur tant à Mgr.
    le Maréchal Duc de Richelieu, qu'à Mr. de Voltaire, et leurs réponses.* The
    Hague, 1766.
———. *Seconde lettre circulaire en défense des Juifs Portugais.* Paris, 1767.
*Prix proposés, en 1788, par la Société royale des sciences et des arts de Metz,
    pour les concours de 1789 et 1790.* Metz, 1788.
*Procès-Verbal dressé par les Représentans de la Commune, de la fête célébrée à
    Metz, en réjouissance du succès des Armées de la République en Savoie. Du
    21 octobre 1792, l'an premier de la République.* Metz, 1792.
"Récit de ce que les Juifs résidens à Paris ont fait à l'occasion de la maladie de
    Monseigneur le Dauphin." *Journal de Trévoux ou mémoires pour servir à
    l'histoire des sciences et des arts* 66 (1766): 91–93.
[Reicher, Néhémie]. *Plaintes et lamentations sur la mort du Roi Louis XV, de
    glorieuse mémoire, ordonnées par les syndics de la communauté des Juifs de
    Lorraine, et récitées dans leurs synagogues, après avoir fait distribuer des
    aumônes. Composées par le rabin de Lorraine. Et traduites par le Sr. Berr-
    Isaac Berr, le jeune.* Nancy, [1774].
———. *Prières ordonnées par les syndics de la communauté des Juifs de Lor-
    raine, et récitées soir et matin dans leurs synagogues, après avoir dit dix-huit
    Pseaumes de David, pour demander à Dieu le rétablissement de la santé du*

Roi Louis XV, le Bien-aimé. Composées par le rabin de Lorraine. Et traduites par le Sr. Berr-Isaac Berr, le jeune. Nancy, 1774.

Réponse des Juifs de la province de Lorraine à l'adresse présentée à l'Assemblée Nationale, par la Commune toute entière de la ville de Strasbourg, 24 juillet 1789. N.p., [1789].

Rousseau, Jean-Jacques. *Considérations sur le gouvernement de Pologne* (1771). Vol. 3 of *Oeuvres complètes.* Paris: Gallimard, 1969.

———. *Du contrat social.* 1762. Reprint, Geneva: C. Bourquin, 1947.

———. *Emile, ou de l'éducation* (1762). Vol. 4 of *Oeuvres complètes.* Paris: Gallimard, 1969.

———. *Lettres à M. d'Alembert.* 1758. Reprint, Geneva: Droz, 1948.

———. *Rousseau juge de Jean-Jacques.* 1776. Reprint, Paris: A. Colin, 1962.

Saint-Pierre, Jacques Henri Bernardin de. *Paul et Virginie.* 1787. Reprint, Paris: Gallimard, 1965.

Sarhy, Jacob. *Actions de grâces que les Juifs avignonois de Bordeaux ont chantées le 23 janvier 1757, pour remercier l'Eternel d'avoir conservé la vie de Louis XV le Bien-Aimé. Composées en hébreu par le Rabin Jacob Sarhy, et traduites en François.* [Bordeaux, 1757].

———. *Prière faite par les Juifs avignonois de Bordeaux, le 13 janvier 1757, à l'occasion de l'attentat affreux commis sur la personne sacrée de Sa Majesté Louis XV le Bien-Aimé, et pour demander à Dieu de le garantir de toute mauvaise entreprise. Composée en hébreu par le Rabin Jacob Sarhy, et traduite en françois.* [Bordeaux, 1757].

Schaller, Geoffrey-Jacques [Gottfried Jakob]. *Mizmor shir le-Bonaparte chubar be-lashon latini u-neetak el lashon tsarfat ve-ashkenazi meet ha-meshorer Schaller* [A psalm to Bonaparte, composed in Latin and translated into French and German by the poet Schaller]. French title: *Ode à Bonaparte, Premier Consul, conservé pour la troisième fois à la France. Composée en Latin, et traduite en français et en allemand, par Geofroy-Jacques [Gottfried Jakob] Schaller. Nouvelle édition enrichie d'une traduction en hébreux par Lipmann Moyse [Büschenthal].* Strasbourg, Year IX [1800 or 1801].

Schwarzfuchs, Simon, ed. and trans. *Le journal révolutionnaire d'Abraham Spire.* Includes *Beschreibung von der Veränderung, oder Aufruhr in Frankreich, was man nennt Revolution von Paris die Kapital, auch die Versammlung die [sic] Deputierte aus dem ganzen Königreich. Diese Versammlung nennt man Etats-Généraux.* And *Zeitung.* Metz, 1789–90. Reprint, Paris: Verdier, 1989.

———. *Le Régistre des délibérations de la nation juive portugaise de Bordeaux (1711–1787).* Paris: Centro Cultural Portugês, 1981.

Seder selichot mi-kol ha-shanah ke-minhag elzoz [A book of penitential prayers for the whole year, according to the custom of Alsace]. Karlsruhe, 1769.

Sègre, S., David Sintzheim, and Abraham de Cologna. *Discours prononcé dans le temple de la rue Ste-Avoye, le dimanche 25 décembre 1808, lors de la célébration de la fête de la réddition de la ville de Madrid, par Mr. S. Sègre, grand rabbin du Consistoire central des Israélites, à Paris; Suivi d'une prière composée en hébreu, par Mr. D. Sintzheim, président du Consistoire central, et d'une prière et d'un hymne composés en hébreu par Mr. A. de Cologna, grand rabbin dudit consistoire; Traduit en français par Mr. Elie Halévy, tra-ducteur spécial du Consistoire central.* Paris, 1808.

Shir hod le-chavod adonenu ha-kaiser [A song of splendor in honor of our lord the emperor]. Warsaw, 1807. Reprinted in *Kwartalnik* 2 (1913): 121–27.

Sieyes, Abbé Emmanuel Joseph. *Essai sur les privilèges.* [Paris], 1789.

———. *Qu'est-ce que le tiers-état?* 1789. Reprint, Paris: Société de l'histoire de la Révolution française, 1888.

[Sintzheim, David.] *Discours prononcé par le chef du Grand Sanhédrin à la clô-ture des séances. Traduit par A. Furtado.* Paris, [1807].

———. *Discours prononcé par M. le Grand Rabbin D. Sintzheim, président du Consistoire central des Israélites, à Paris; dans le temple de la rue Ste.-Avoye, aujourd'hui 4 décembre 1808, anniversaire du jour du couronnement de S. M. I. et R. Traduit de l'hébreu par M. Elie Halévy, traducteur spécial du Consistoire central.* Paris, 1808.

———. *Sermon prononcé dans la grande synagogue à Strasbourg, le 2 brumaire an 14 pour célébrer les glorieuses victoires de S.M., l'Empereur des Français. Par David Sinzheim, rabbin. Traduit de l'hébreu.* Strasbourg, [1805].

———. *Tefilat yesharim karii anshe ha-edah shem sanhedrin behitasef yechdav ba-ir ve-em Paris ha-mehulelah mi-taam adonenu ha-adir Napoleon ha-rishon kaiser ha-tsarfatim u-melech italia yarom hodo* [Prayer of the Is-raelites, called among the people of the community by the name Sanhedrin, as they gathered together in the city of Paris, the celebrated metropolis, by decree of our magnificent lord Napoleon the First, Emperor of the French and King of Italy, may his splendor grow]. French title: *Prière des membres du Sanhédrin, récitée dans leur assemblée convoquée à Paris le 1er jour d'Adar de l'année 5567.* Paris, 1807.

Tama, Diogène. *Collection des actes de l'assemblée des Israélites de France et du royaume d'Italie, convoquée à Paris par décret de Sa Majesté impériale et royale, du 30 mai 1806.* Paris and Strasbourg, 1807.

———. *Collection des procès-verbaux et décisions du Grand Sanhédrin, con-voqué à Paris, par ordre de Sa Majesté l'Empereur et Roi, dans les mois de février et mars 1807: Publiée par M. Diogène Tama.* Paris, 1807. Reprint, Paris: Commission française des Archives juives, 1979.

[Target, Guy-Jean-Baptiste]. "CLXXIe cause. Question d'état sur les mariages des Juifs. Le divorce est-il admis parmi eux?" 3–240. *Causes célèbres, curieuses et intéressantes, de toutes les cours souveraines du royaume, avec les jugemens qui les ont décidées.* Vol. 65. Paris, 1780.

Thiéry. *Dissertation sur cette question: Est-il des moyens de rendre les Juifs plus heureux et plus utiles en France? Ouvrage couronné par la Société royale des sciences et des arts de Metz. Par M. Thiéry, Avocat au Parlement de Nancy.* Vol. 2. Paris, 1788. Reprint, Paris: EdHis, 1968.

Traduction de la prière hébraïque, ajoutée par les Juifs de la synagogue de Metz aux Psaumes et prières particulières qu'ils font journellement pour l'heureux accouchement de la reine. [Metz, 1778].

Traduction des actions de grâces qui seront chantées cejourd'hui vingt-un no-vembre mil sept cent quatre-vingt-un, à l'occasion de l'heureuse délivrance de la reine, et de la naissance de Monseigneur le dauphin; dans la synagogue des Juifs, établie à Nancy, ainsi que dans toutes les villes, villages de la province de Lorraine, où synagogue est établie, en conséquence de l'invitation du rabin de la Lorraine, et de la délibération des syndics de ladite communauté. Nancy, 1781.

Traduction du cantique hébraïque, exécuté en musique dans la sinagogue des Juifs de Metz, pour l'arrivée de Monsieur frère du roi. Metz, [1782].

[Valabrègue, Israel Bernard de]. *Lettre ou réflexions d'un milord à son correspondant à Paris, au sujet de la requête des marchands des six-corps, contre l'admission des Juifs aux brevets.* London, 1767.

―――. *Odes prononcées par les Juifs d'Avignon et de Bordeaux résidants à Paris, dans leur assemblée, à l'occasion du sacre de Louis XVI, le 11 juin 1775. Tirées du texte original des Pseaumes 20 et 71 (21–72). Mises en vers hébreux, par M. Bernard de Vallabrège, interprète du roi, etc.* Paris, 1775. Hebrew title: *Kol rinah ve-kol todah u-tehilah nishma baveit tefilatanu poh paris ha-ir ha-gedolah be-k[ehila] k[adosha] sfardim anshei avinion ve-bordeos yom asher nimshach u-nekater adoneinu ha-melech Luis ayin yud yar[om] h[odo] yud alef Sivan shanat heh tav kuf lamed heh hitkalah yatsirah . . . ha-tsair yisrael bernard devalabregia sofer u-targman lemelech tsarfat yar[om] h[odo].]* [A song of joy and a song of thanks and praise heard in our house of prayer here (in) Paris, the great city, in the holy congregation of Sephardim, men of Avignon and Bordeaux, the day of the anointing and coronation of our lord the king Louis 16, may his splendor grow, 11 Sivan year 5535 of creation . . . (by) Israel Bernard of Valabreghia junior, scribe and translator to the king of France, may his splendor grow.]

―――. *Précis de la prière que les Juifs avignonois établis à Bordeaux, et ceux d'Avignon, actuellement à Paris, ont faite pendant trois jours consécutifs, [le 19 novembre 1765] pour obtenir de Dieu le rétablissement de la santé de Monseigneur le dauphin, extraite du rituel hébreux, et prononcée en cette langue, par le Sieur Bernard de Valabrègue, secrétaire-interprète du roi, et traduite par le même.* N.p., [1765].

―――. *Prière que les Juifs d'Avignon et de Bordeaux résidens à Paris, ont mise et chantée en hébreu, le jour du sacre de Louis XVI.* [Paris, 1775].

Venture, Mardochée. *Prière prononcée le premier mai 1774. Par les Juifs avignonois, et avignonois de Bordeaux, demeurant à Paris, à l'occasion de la maladie de Sa Majesté Louis XV le Bien-Aimé.* Paris, 1774.

―――. *Prières journalières à l'usage des Juifs portugais ou espagnols.* Nice, 1772.

Voltaire, François Marie Arouet de. *La bible enfin expliquée.* Geneva, 1776.

―――. *Candide, ou, l'Optimisme.* 1759. Reprint, Paris: Hachette, 1913.

―――. *Correspondence and Related Documents.* Edited by Theodore Besterman. Toronto: University of Toronto Press, 1969.

―――. *Dictionnaire philosophique.* 1764. Reprint, Paris: Garnier, 1954.

―――. *Essay sur l'histoire générale.* Geneva, 1756.

―――. *L'homme aux quarante écus.* Paris, 1768.

―――. *Lettres philosophiques.* 1734. Reprint, Paris: Hachette, 1915–17.

————. *Mélanges.* Edited by J. Van Den Heuvel. Paris: Gallimard, 1961.

————. *Oeuvres complètes de Voltaire.* Edited by Louis Moland. Paris, Garnier, 1877–85.

————. *Poëmes sur la religion naturelle et sur la destruction de Lisbonne.* Paris, 1756.

————. *Précis du Siècle de Louis XV.* Geneva, 1770.

————. *Romans et Contes.* Edited by H. Ménac. Paris: Garnier, 1963.

————. *Voltaire's Notebooks.* Edited by Theodore Besterman. Geneva: Institut et Musée Voltaire, 1952.

Wittersheim, Samuel. *Mizmor shir yom halidat ha-kaiser u-melech Napoleon yarom hodo....* [A hymn on the birthday of the Emperor and King Napoleon, may his splendor grow....]. French title: *Hymne chanté par les députés françois professant le culte de Moïse, dans leur temple à Paris, le 15 août 1806, jour de la naissance de notre auguste empereur et roi; composé en langue hébraïque et traduit par Wittersheim l'aîné, député du Bas-Rhin. Dédié à M. Furtado, Président de l'assemblée des députés.* Paris, 1806.

Zay, Bernard. *Hymne à l'occasion de l'avènement de Sa Majesté Impériale Napoléon au trône de l'empire des français. Pour être chantée dans la grande synagogue de Metz, vendredi, 3 messidor an 12, à six heures du soir; Traduite de l'hébreu.* [Metz, 1804].

————. *Hymne pour célébrer solennellement le jour immortel du couronnement de Sa Majesté Napoléon. Pour être chantée en hébreu, dans la grande synagogue de Metz, le ____ frimaire an 13, 1er du règne de l'empereur Napoléon 1er. Composée en hébreu par Bernard Zay, et traduite par Gerson Lévy.* Metz, 1805.

SECONDARY SOURCES

Albert, Phyllis Cohen. *The Modernization of French Jewry.* Hanover, N.H.: Brandeis University Press, 1977.

Anchel, Robert. *Les Juifs de France: La roue de fortune.* Paris: Janin, 1946.

————. *Napoléon et les Juifs.* Paris: Presses Universitaires de France, 1928.

Anderson, Benedict. *Imagined Communities: Reflections on the Origin and Spread of Nationalism.* London: Verso, 1983.

Arendt, Hannah. *The Origins of Totalitarianism.* New York: Harcourt Brace Jovanovich, 1973.

————. *On Revolution.* New York: Viking, 1963.

Aubery, Pierre. "Voltaire et les Juifs: Ironie et démystification." *Studies on Voltaire and the Eighteenth Century* 24 (1963): 67–79.

Badinter, Elisabeth, ed. *Qu'est-ce qu'une femme? Un débat.* Paris: P.O.L., 1989.

Badinter, Robert. *Libres et égaux... l'émancipation des Juifs 1789–1791.* Paris: Fayard, 1989.

Baron, Salo. "Ghetto and Emancipation: Shall We Revise the Traditional View?" *Menorah Journal* 14 (June 1928): 515–26.

Becker, Carl. *The Heavenly City of the Philosophers.* New Haven, Conn.: Yale University Press, 1932.

Bell, David A. *Lawyers and Citizens: The Making of a Political Elite in Old Regime France.* New York: Oxford University Press, 1994.

Berkovitz, Jay R. "The French Revolution and the Jews: Assessing the Cultural Impact." *American Jewish Studies Review* 20 (1995): 25–86.

———. *The Shaping of Jewish Identity in Nineteenth-Century France.* Detroit: Wayne State University Press, 1989.

Bernstein, Michael André. "Victims-in-Waiting: Backshadowing and the Representation of European Jewry." *New Literary History* 29 (fall 1998): 625–51.

Birnbaum, Pierre. *Jewish Destinies: Citizenship, State, and Community in Modern France.* Translated by Arthur Goldhammer. New York: Hill and Wang, 2000.

Blumenkranz, Bernhard, ed. *Documents modernes sur les Juifs: XVIe–XXe siècles.* Vol. 1, *Dépôts parisiens.* Paris: Commission française des Archives juives, 1979.

———. *Le Grand Sanhédrin de Napoléon.* Paris: Commission française des Archives juives, 1979.

———. *Histoire des Juifs en France.* Toulouse: Privat, 1972.

Blumenkranz, Bernhard, and Albert Soboul, eds. *Les Juifs et la Révolution Française.* Paris: Commission française des Archives juives, 1989.

Bush, Newell Richard. *The Marquis d'Argens and His Philosophical Correspondence: A Critical Study of d'Argens' Lettres juives, Lettres cabalistiques and Lettres chinoises.* Ann Arbor, Mich.: Edwards Brothers, 1953.

Cahen, Abraham. "L'émancipation des Juifs devant la Société royale des sciences et des arts de Metz en 1787 et M. Roederer." *Revue des études juives* 1 (1880): 83–104.

———. "Une Fête nationale à Metz." *La vérité israélite* 8 (1862): 372–77.

———. *Le rabbinat de Metz pendant la période française.* Paris, 1886.

Calmann, Marianne. *The Carrière of Carpentras.* Oxford: Oxford University Press, 1984.

Chartier, Roger. *The Cultural Origins of the French Revolution.* Translated by Lydia G. Cochrane. Durham, N.C.: Duke University Press, 1991.

Cherikover, I. H. *Yidn in Frankraykh* [Jews in France]. 2 vols. New York, 1942.

Clément, Roger. *La condition des Juifs de Metz dans l'Ancien Régime.* Paris: Imprimerie Henri Joure, 1903.

Cohen, William B. *The French Encounter with Africans: White Response to Blacks, 1530–1880.* Bloomington: Indiana University Press, 1980.

Conan, Éric, and Henry Rousso. *Vichy: An Ever-Present Past.* Translated by Nathan Bracher. Foreword by Robert O. Paxton. Hanover, N.H.: University Press of New England, 1998.

Darnton, Robert. *The Great Cat Massacre and Other Episodes in French Cultural History.* New York: Vintage, 1984.

Dubnow, Simon. *Weltgeschichte des jüdischen Volkes, von seinen Uranfängen bis zur Gegenwart.* Translated from the Russian by Dr. A. Steinberg. Vol. 7, *Die Geschichte des jüdischen Volkes in der Neuzeit: Die zweite Hälfte des XVII. und das XVIII. Jahrhundert.* Vol. 8, *Die neueste Geschichte des jüdis-*

chen Volkes: Das Zeitalter der ersten Emanzipation (1789–1815). Berlin: Jüdischer Verlag, 1928.

Eisenstein, Hester, and Alice Jardine. *The Future of Difference.* Boston: G. K. Hall, 1980.

Emmrich, Hannah. *Das Judentum bei Voltaire.* Breslau, 1930.

Feuerwerker, David. *L'émancipation des Juifs en France, 1789–1860: De l'Ancien Régime à la fin du Second Empire.* Paris: Albin Michel, 1976.

Finkelkraut, Alain. *The Imaginary Jew.* Translated by Kevin O'Neill and David Suchoff. Lincoln: University of Nebraska Press, 1994.

Fogel, Michèle. *Les cérémonies de l'information dans la France du XVIe au milieu du XVIIIe siècle.* Paris: Fayard, 1989.

Friedlander, Judith. *Vilna on the Seine: Jewish Intellectuals in France since 1968.* New Haven, Conn.: Yale University Press, 1990.

Furet, François. *Interpreting the French Revolution.* Translated by Elborg Forster. Cambridge and Paris: Cambridge University Press and Maison des Sciences de l'Homme, 1981.

Gay, Peter. *The Enlightenment: An Interpretation.* Vol. 2, *The Science of Freedom.* New York: Norton, 1969.

———. *The Party of Humanity: Essays in the French Enlightenment.* New York: Knopf, 1964.

———. *Voltaire's Politics: The Poet as Realist.* Princeton, N.J.: Princeton University Press, 1959. Reprint, New Haven, Conn.: Yale University Press, 1988.

Geertz, Clifford. *The Interpretation of Cultures.* New York: Basic Books, 1973.

———. *Local Knowledge: Further Essays in Interpretive Anthropology.* New York: Basic Books, 1983.

Gilman, Sander. *The Jew's Body.* New York: Routledge, 1991.

Girard, Patrick. *La Révolution française et les Juifs.* Paris: Robert Laffont, 1989.

Godechot, Jacques. "Les Juifs de Nancy de 1789 à 1795." *Revue des études juives* 86 (1928): 1–35.

Graetz, Heinrich. *Geschichte der Juden von den ältesten Zeiten bis auf die Gegenwart.* Vol. 11, *Geschichte der Juden vom Beginn der Mendelssohn'schen Zeit (1750) bis in die neueste Zeit (1848).* 1876. Reprint, Leipzig: Oskar Leiner, 1900.

———. "Voltaire und die Juden." *Monatsschrift für Geschichte und Wissenschaft des Judentums* 17 (1868): 161–74, 201–23.

Greenblatt, Stephen. *Marvelous Possessions: The Wonder of the New World.* Chicago: University of Chicago Press, 1991.

Grunebaum-Ballin, Paul. "Grégoire convertisseur? ou la croyance au 'Retour d'Israël.'" *Revue des études juives* 121 (1962): 383–98.

Grunwald, Max. "Note sur des Marranes à Rouen et ailleurs." *Revue des études juives* 89 (1930): 383–84.

Halbwachs, Maurice. *On Collective Memory.* Edited, translated, and with an introduction by Lewis A. Coser. Chicago: University of Chicago Press, 1992.

Helfand, Jonathan I. "The Symbiotic Relationship between French and German Jewry in the Age of Emancipation." *Leo Baeck Institute Year Book* 29 (1984): 331–50.

Hertzberg, Arthur. *The French Enlightenment and the Jews.* New York: Columbia University Press, 1968.

Hess, Jonathan M. "Sugar Island Jews? Jewish Colonialism and the Rhetoric of 'Civic Improvement' in Eighteenth-Century Germany." *Eighteenth-Century Studies* 32 (fall 1998): 92–100.

Higonnet, Patrice. *Goodness beyond Virtue: Jacobins during the French Revolution.* Cambridge: Harvard University Press, 1998.

Homan, Gerlof D. *Jean François Rewbell: French Revolutionary, Patriot, and Director (1747–1807).* The Hague: Martinus Nijhoff, 1971.

Horkheimer, Max, and Theodor W. Adorno. *Dialectic of Enlightenment.* Translated by John Cumming. New York: Continuum, 1972.

Hunt, Lynn. *The Family Romance of the French Revolution.* Berkeley and Los Angeles: University of California Press, 1992.

———. *Politics, Culture, and Class in the French Revolution.* Berkeley and Los Angeles: University of California Press, 1984.

———. "The Sacred and the French Revolution." In *Durkheimian Sociology: Cultural Studies,* edited by Jeffrey C. Alexander, 25–43. Cambridge: Cambridge University Press, 1988.

———, ed. *The New Cultural History.* Berkeley and Los Angeles: University of California Press, 1989.

Hyman, Paula. *The Emancipation of the Jews of Alsace: Acculturation and Tradition in the Nineteenth Century.* New Haven, Conn.: Yale University Press, 1991.

———. *The Jews of Modern France.* Berkeley and Los Angeles: University of California Press, 1998.

James, C[yril] L[ionel] R[obert]. *Black Jacobins: Toussaint Louverture and the San Domingo Revolution.* New York: Vintage, 1963.

Job, Françoise. *Les Juifs de Nancy.* Nancy: Presses Universitaires de Nancy, 1991.

Jones, Colin. "The Great Chain of Buying: Medical Advertisement, the Bourgeois Public Sphere, and the Origins of the French Revolution." *American Historical Review* 101 (February 1996): 13–40.

Kafker, Frank A., in collaboration with Serena L. Kafker. *The Encyclopedists as a Group: A Collective Biography of the Authors of the Encyclopédie.* Oxford: Voltaire Foundation, 1996.

———. *The Encyclopedists as Individuals: A Biographical Dictionary of the Authors of the Encyclopédie.* Oxford: Voltaire Foundation, 1988.

Kahn, Léon. *Les Juifs de Paris au dix-huitième siècle d'après les archives de la Lieutenance générale de police à la Bastille.* Paris, 1894.

———. *Les Juifs de Paris pendant la Révolution.* Paris, 1898.

Kassouf, Susan. "The Shared Pain of the Golden Vein: The Discursive Proximity of Jewish and Scholarly Diseases in the Late Eighteenth Century." *Eighteenth-Century Studies* 32 (fall 1998): 101–10.

Kates, Gary. "Jews into Frenchmen: Nationality and Representation in Revolutionary France." In *The French Revolution and the Birth of Modernity,* edited by Ferenc Fehér, 103–16. Berkeley and Los Angeles: University of California Press, 1990.

Katz, Jacob. *Exclusiveness and Tolerance: Studies in Jewish-Gentile Relations in Medieval and Modern Times.* London: Oxford University Press, 1961.

————. *Out of the Ghetto: The Social Background of Jewish Emancipation, 1770–1870.* Cambridge: Harvard University Press, 1973.

————. "The Term 'Jewish Emancipation': Its Origin and Historical Impact." In *Studies in Nineteenth-Century Jewish Intellectual History,* edited by Alexander Altman, 1–25. Cambridge: Harvard University Press, 1964.

Kerner, Samuel. "La Vie quotidienne de la communauté juive de Metz au dix-huitième siècle (à partir du Pinkas [Registre] inédit de cette commune, 1749–1789)." Ph.D. diss., University of Paris VIII, 1979.

Kley, Dale Van. *The Religious Origins of the French Revolution.* New Haven, Conn.: Yale University Press, 1996.

Kobler, Franz. *Napoleon and the Jews.* New York: Masada Press, 1975.

Landes, Joan. *Women and the Public Sphere in the Age of the French Revolution.* Ithaca, N.Y.: Cornell University Press, 1988.

Laqueur, Thomas. "Orgasm, Generation, and the Politics of Reproductive Biology." *Representations* 14 (spring 1986): 1–41.

La Rochelle, Ernest. *Jacob Rodrigues Péreire, premier instituteur des sourd-muets en France; sa vie et ses travaux.* Paris: Paul Dupont, 1882.

Lemoine, Albert. *Napoléon Ier et les Juifs.* Paris, 1900.

Léon, Jacob Henry. *Histoire des Juifs de Bayonne.* Paris, 1893.

Lévi-Strauss, Claude. *Totemism.* Translated by Rodney Needham. Boston: Beacon Press, 1963.

Lipschutz, M. "Notes et mélanges: Un poème hébraïque sur l'attentat de Damiens." *Revue des études juives* 84 (1927): 94–95.

Lunel, Armand. *Juifs du Languedoc, de la Provence et des États français du Pape.* Paris: Albin Michel, 1975.

Lyotard, Jean-François. *The Postmodern Condition: A Report on Knowledge.* Translated by Geoff Bennington and Brian Massumi. Minneapolis: University of Minnesota Press, 1984.

Malino, Frances. "Competition and Confrontation: The Jews and the Parlement of Metz." In *Les Juifs au regard de l'Histoire: Mélanges en l'honneur de Bernhard Blumenkranz,* edited by Gilbert Dahan, 327–41. Paris: Picard, 1985.

————. *A Jew in the French Revolution: The Life of Zalkind Hourwitz.* Oxford: Blackwell, 1996.

————. *The Sephardic Jews of Bordeaux: Assimilation and Emancipation in Revolutionary and Napoleonic France.* University: University of Alabama Press, 1978.

Malino, Frances, and Bernard Wasserstein, eds. *The Jews in Modern France.* Hanover, N.H.: University Press of New England, 1985.

Malvezin, Théophile. *Histoire des Juifs à Bordeaux.* Bordeaux, 1875.

Manuel, Frank E. *The Broken Staff: Judaism through Christian Eyes.* Cambridge: Harvard University Press, 1992.

Maza, Sarah. "Domestic Melodrama as Political Ideology: The Case of the Comte de Sanois." *American Historical Review* 94 (December 1989): 1249–65.

———. "Luxury, Morality, and Social Change: Why There Was No Middle-Class Consciousness in Prerevolutionary France." *Journal of Modern History* 69 (summer 1997): 199–229.

———. *Private Lives and Public Affairs: The Causes Célèbres of Prerevolutionary France.* Berkeley and Los Angeles: University of California Press, 1993.

Melzer, Sara E., and Leslie W. Rabine, eds. *Rebel Daughters: Women and the French Revolution.* New York: Oxford University Press, 1992.

Mossé, Armand. *Histoire des Juifs d'Avignon et du Comtat Venaissin.* 1937. Reprint, Marseille: Laffitte Reprints, 1976.

Mosse, George L. *The Image of Man: The Creation of Modern Masculinity.* New York: Oxford University Press, 1996.

Moulinas, René. *Les Juifs du Pape en France: Les communautés du Comtat Venaissin aux 17e et 18e siècles.* Paris: Commission française des Archives juives, 1981.

Ozouf, Mona. *Festivals and the French Revolution.* Translated by Alan Sheridan. Cambridge: Harvard University Press, 1988.

———. *L'homme régénéré: Essais sur la Révolution française.* Paris: Gallimard, 1989.

Pagden, Anthony. *European Encounters with the New World: From Renaissance to Romanticism.* New Haven, Conn.: Yale University Press, 1993.

———. *The Fall of Natural Man: The American Indian and the Origins of Comparative Ethnology.* Cambridge: Cambridge University Press, 1982.

Pluchon, Pierre. *Nègres et Juifs au XVIIIe siècle: Le racisme au siècle des lumières.* Paris: Tallandier, 1984.

Poliakov, Léon. *Histoire de l'antisémitisme.* Vol. 2, *L'âge de la science.* Paris: Calmann-Lévy, 1981.

Raphaël, Freddy, and Robert Weyl. *Juifs en Alsace.* Toulouse: Privat, 1977.

Rétat, Pierre, ed. *L'attentat de Damiens; discours sur l'événement au XVIIIe siècle.* Lyon: CNRS, 1979.

Rochette, Jacqueline. *Histoire des Juifs d'Alsace des origines à la Révolution.* Paris: Librairie Lipschutz, 1938.

Roth, Cecil. "Some Revolutionary Purims." *Hebrew Union College Annual* 10 (1935): 451–82.

Rousso, Henry. *The Vichy Syndrome: History and Memory in France since 1944.* Translated by Arthur Goldhammer. Cambridge: Harvard University Press, 1991.

Russo, Elena. "Virtuous Economies: Modernity and Noble Expenditure from Montesquieu to Caillois." *Historical Reflections/Réflexions historiques* 25 (summer 1999): 251–78.

Said, Edward. *Culture and Imperialism.* New York: Knopf, 1994.

———. *Orientalism.* New York: Vintage, 1978.

Sartre, Jean-Paul. *Réflexions sur la question juive.* Paris: Morihien, 1946.

Sayre, Gordon M. *Les Sauvages Américains: Representations of Native Americans in French and English Colonial Literature.* Chapel Hill: University of North Carolina Press, 1997.

Schama, Simon. *Citizens: A Chronicle of the French Revolution*. New York: Knopf, 1989.

Scheid, Elie. *Histoire des Juifs d'Alsace*. Paris, 1882.

Schiebinger, Londa L. *The Mind Has No Sex? Women in the Origins of Modern Science*. Cambridge: Harvard University Press, 1989.

Schnapper, Dominique. "Les Juifs et la nation." In *Histoire politique des Juifs de France: Entre universalisme et particularisme,* edited by Pierre Birnbaum, 296–310. Paris: Presses de la Fondation nationale des sciences politiques, 1990.

Schwartz, Leon. *Diderot and the Jews*. East Brunswick, N.J.: Associated University Presses, 1981.

Schwarzfuchs, Simon. *Du Juif à l'Israélite: Histoire d'une mutation 1770–1870*. Paris: Fayard, 1989.

———. *Napoleon, the Jews and the Sanhedrin*. London: Routledge and Kegan Paul, 1979.

———, ed. *Le Régistre des délibérations de la nation juive portugaise de Bordeaux (1711–1787)*. Paris: Centro Cultural Portugês, 1981.

Scott, James C. *Weapons of the Weak: Everyday Forms of Peasant Resistance*. New Haven, Conn.: Yale University Press, 1985.

Scott, Joan. "French Feminists and the Rights of 'Man': Olympe de Gouge's Declarations." *History Workshop Journal* 28 (autumn 1989): 1–21.

———. *Only Paradoxes to Offer: French Feminists and the Rights of Man*. Cambridge: Harvard University Press, 1996.

Shurkin, Michael Robert. "Decolonization and the Renewal of French Judaism: Reflections on the Contemporary French Jewish Scene." *Jewish Social Studies* 6 (spring 2000): 156–76.

Sorkin, David. *Moses Mendelssohn and the Religious Enlightenment*. Berkeley and Los Angeles: University of California Press, 1996.

Starobinski, Jean. *Jean-Jacques Rousseau: La transparence et l'obstacle, suivi de sept essais sur Rousseau*. Paris: Gallimard, 1970.

Szajkowski, Zosa. *Franco-Judaica: An Analytical Bibliography of Books, Pamphlets, Decrees, Briefs and Other Printed Documents Pertaining to the Jews in France 1500–1788*. New York: American Academy for Jewish Research, 1962.

———. *Jews and the French Revolutions of 1789, 1830 and 1848*. New York: Ktav Publishing House, 1970.

Tackett, Timothy. *Becoming a Revolutionary: The Deputies of the French National Assembly and the Emergence of a Revolutionary Culture (1789–1790)*. Princeton, N.J.: Princeton University Press, 1996.

Todorov, Tzvetan. *The Conquest of America: The Question of the Other*. Translated by Richard Howard. New York: Harper and Row, 1984.

———. *On Human Diversity: Nationalism, Racism, and Exoticism in French Thought*. Translated by Catherine Porter. Cambridge: Harvard University Press, 1993.

Trigano, Shmuel. "The French Revolution and the Jews." *Modern Judaism* 10 (May 1990): 171–90.

———. *La République et les Juifs après Copernic.* Paris: Presses D'Aujourd'hui, 1981.

Van Pelt, Tamise. "Otherness." *Postmodern Culture* 10 (January 2000): 1–47.

Wolff, Camille. "Les Juifs à Metz." *L'Univers israélite* 53 (1898): 308–9.

Yerushalmi, Yosef Hayim. *Zakhor: Jewish History and Jewish Memory.* Seattle: University of Washington Press, 1982.

Index

Acosta, Uriel, 52
active citizenship, 151–53. *See also* citizenship
actors as citizens, 161–62
Adorno, Theodor, 106, 236–37
Agada (Talmud), 128
agriculture: of biblical Jews, 41, 60, 89, 121–22, 219; Napoleon's decree on, 195; regeneration through, 76–77, 85, 91–92, 104
Alsatian Jews: Christians' relations with, 21–22; citizenship claims by, 170; communal autonomy of, 21; in false receipts dispute, 67–68; in festivals, 142, 145; Napoleonic representations by, 227–28; National Assembly's decree on, 153; patriotic liturgy of, 139; population of, 19; poverty of, 20, 152; taxes / restrictions on, 19–21; use of Hebrew by, 215
alterity. *See* other, the
Ambrose, Saint, 118
Amiens, Peace of, 216
Anchel, Robert, 2, 287n6
Ancona, 199–200, 227
Anderson, Benedict, 180
anointing imagery, 134–36, 140
apologetic literature: appropriation strategies of, 12–13, 130–31, 148–49; on

Christian fanaticism, 123, 128–29; on civic morality of Jews, 120–22, 127–28, 170–72; of Hourwitz, as unorthodox, 126, 128, 130–31; on mercantilist corruption, 122; on mercantilist utility, 116–17, 118–19; on natural rights, 124–26, 129; self-contradictions of, 111–12, 115, 119, 131; *sensibilité* language of, 120; on Sephardim versus Ashkenazim, 113–14, 129; as source material, 10–11; on treatment of Jews abroad, 117–18; as untrustworthy, 131–32. *See also* Jewish self-representation
Apologie des Juifs (Hourwitz), 126, 130, 131
Apologie pour la nation juive (Pinto), 112–14, 115
appropriation: empowerment through, 253–54; by Jewish apologists, 148–49; by Napoleon, of religious imagery, 200–202; of regeneration concept, 12–13, 170; of revolutionary culture, 179, 192–93; sacralization strategy of, 188, 253. *See also* assimilation
Arendt, Hannah, 176–77, 192, 260
Argens, Jean-Baptiste de Boyer, marquis d', 37, 66, 105; cosmopolitan Jew of, 103; defamiliarization device

STUDIES ON THE HISTORY OF SOCIETY AND CULTURE

Victoria E. Bonnell and Lynn Hunt, Editors

Compositor: G&S Typesetters, Inc.
Text: 10/13 Sabon
Display: Sabon
Printer and Binder: Thomson-Shore, Inc.
Index: Patricia Deminna